VOICES
OF
REVELATION

VOICES
OF
REVELATION

Edited by

NANCY H. DEANE *University of New Hampshire*

 Little, Brown and Company   BOSTON

PREFACE

Voices of Revelation is a collection of varied prose forms concerning contemporary issues. It is designed to encourage a student's writing, reading, and thinking — processes which are difficult to separate. One of the biggest problems for most students in the traditional composition course stems from their conviction that they have nothing to say about the assigned topic or even a freely chosen theme after finishing a part of the *Crito* or a delightful essay by E. B. White or a selection from Emerson. Students complain about the lack of relevance; what they read does not relate directly to their experience. Because they seem unable or unwilling to transfer to themselves ideas implicit in such works, *Voices of Revelation* attempts to intrigue students with subjects, forms, and writing patterns that are closer to their life style without sacrificing desired intellectual depth. Other contemporary readers deal with problems and ideas confronting youth. Most of them, however, are based on too lofty a sense of what is relevant, their content corresponds to the professor's idea of intellectual appropriateness, and many of the essays are still locked in nineteenth-century style. Needless to say, confrontation and argument rather than academic detachment are necessary to involve students today. *Voices of Revelation* assumes that students are really seeking answers to crucial questions, and it attempts to engage them, to get them mad or glad enough to write about those questions.

The essays were deliberately chosen to present a discussion of the crisis situation in our universities and our culture, certainly indicated by the chapter headings. If a student is grabbed during his early college experience by those voices (writers) who are not afraid to reveal crises and opinions, perhaps he will find his own answers to the either/or situations in our world. He must be seized by the passion presented in the disciplined, honest discussion of issues and thence led to acknowledge the need for craft and control in his own writing. In other words, the art of communication, especially writing, is control. The writer consciously selects his materials. As committed as he may be to his subject matter, to his idea, to getting something off his chest, the writer still disciplines his passion; he uses form of some kind in order to communicate such passion. The selections in *Voices of Revelation* attempt to show the reader how control works to convince, how form reinforces meaning.

Because the age of the formal essay has already passed away, this text contains a variety of prose types, some of which are new or renewed forms. The majority of essays, of course, follow the conventional structure and can be used to demonstrate rhetorical patterns: definition, comparison-contrast, analysis, argumentation. However, contemporary writing has brought into focus as an art form the interview, derived from the ancient Socratic dialogues, and the meditation, a twentieth-century version from the Age of Faith. The selections also include a parable, a book review, editorials, and letters to the editor. These are the kinds of prose students are acquainted with or will meet during their school years or in the future as professionals, businessmen, government workers and homemakers. They point out that cogent, vigorous persuasion has always depended on and must ultimately depend upon the mastery of form in all its varieties.

For example, the interview is a form which illustrates conscious selection of materials, depending upon the ability of the interviewer to select questions which make the person being interviewed bear the brunt of the argument. In this way the interviewer can show the absurdity or validity of the other person's point of view. There is a deliberate subordination of the questioner here, yet all the time the reader sees the two in relationship and is manipulated to laugh or to appreciate by the questioner. The good interview should establish a dialectic whereby the thesis of the person being questioned is either undermined or enhanced by the antithetical weight of the interviewer. Because students frequently use the interview in sociology and psychology classes to collect data, becoming aware of how to use this form of prose is extremely important. In addition, whereas the argumentative essay has a definite point in mind and establishes it, the interview can be used by the young writer who wants to explore argument and counter-argument rather than assert them. He could create a dialogue between himself and a fictional character which would allow him to develop a thesis and perhaps evolve greater control over his elusive thoughts.

The parable is another renewed form being used by twentieth-century writers. By definition, the parable should answer a question or point a moral. The most famous in Western culture are those used by Jesus to teach his followers. Implicitly, each detail in the best parable is parallel with the situation which called forth the story in the first place. "The Man Who Was Put in a Cage" is a good example of authentic parable and can be used as a model for students to experiment with gentle communication through analogy.

Traditionally, as a form, the meditation was a highly structured, closely woven series of steps whereby the petitioner for grace accepted the basic order of the universe, the controlling force of God, and the ultimate accessibility of God to man through such established means as the church, prayer, and sacrifice. The twentieth-century choice of this form, traditionally rooted in certainty, communicates as much as the content of the meditation. Allen Wheelis, in using this form, reminds us of the contemporary absence of this certainty but further reminds us that despite the absence of conviction men remain linked through all time by their need to explore man's relationship to some ultimate reality. The young writer can profit from a knowledge of the meditation. Too often his heartfelt, serious reflections turn out to be gushy, sentimental clichés which twenty-four hours later prove to be embarassing to him as well as to the reader. Yet Wheelis is able to handle the intense emotion of man's innermost thoughts about his own finiteness in a massive universe; the form of the meditation makes such intense emotion bearable and the reader can then react with more control himself.

Letters to the editor or essays in reply to another writer's point of view are ways of controlling one's own commitment to an idea. Students should be encouraged to examine letters written by contemporaries concerned enough to commit themselves to paper. When students ask for relevance, one of the best writing challenges for them is to respond to published statements.

Thus, *Voices of Revelation*, unlike other contemporary readers, demonstrates that the passion of the good minds today like that of great minds of the past is best communicated through form and discipline. It provides reading materials directly related to the student on campus yet it also encourages him to enlarge his vision to deal with questions relating to his fellowman, his society, and his world. Most important of all, it shows the young writer that craft and control are necessary when writing in response to topics that arouse his interest and emotion.

I would like to thank friends, colleagues, and the members of my family for helping make *Voices of Revelation* possible.

CONTENTS

ix

chapter three

The University:
   Embattled Citadel or Final Betrayal?

chapter four

The New Music:
   A Return to the Tribal or *Blowing Your Mind*?

chapter five

Quests for Identity:
"You Take the High Road, I'll Take the Low Road!"

chapter six

Alpha and Omega:
Man's Stumble Toward Meaning

chapter one

Neutrality as Norm: Morality as Deviance

introduction

One of the pragmatic aims of this book is to convince the student that he must submit to the discipline of form in his writing if he is to communciate effectively. Beyond this professional concern over craft, however, lies a subtler and far more significant concern with the meaning of form, of some controlling and integrating factor in the lives of young people, which manifests itself in every chapter of this book. In short, in order to communicate, you have to "be"; form is an inescapable prerequisite to both writing and being.

Beginning his essay with personal testimony, John Robertson, a student, argues that he wasted four years learning professional skills before discovering that he lacked an awareness of self, of being. The central question of his essay, "How does one act as a moral person in a situation of changing circumstances and frequently conflicting values?" serves to unify all the essays in Chapter One. Robertson discusses alienation and three different approaches for adjusting to today's world. He lists some guiding principles he finds helpful: caring about life, trying to understand it, and being aware of its complexities; and taking some action even though original objectives may not be achieved. Although a more mature writer might use the listing technique less obtrusively, it serves to order the thoughts of a beginning writer. Roberston intends to show that ultimately the educational experience must cultivate a spirit of inquiry that can produce insight, a necessary ingredient, along with faith, hope, and love, for self-fulfillment.

Like Robertson, Ihab Hassan is concerned with the problem of identity, with the search for freedom and self-definition, in his analysis of the modern European and American novel. The alienation of modern man transposes the traditional hero of fiction into an anti-hero. "To become someone, to know who or what one is, to reach finally another being with love, and to do so in terms that society may censure, this is the passionate, bitter concern of the modern anti-hero." After discussing works by Dostoyevsky, Conrad, Joyce, Kafka, Mann, and Hesse, authors who are becoming more and more popular with today's college students, Hassan suggests that the existentialist approach be added to the religious and humanist solutions to man's plight. In this excerpt man becomes both rebel and victim, embodied in Hassan's fresh image of Prometheus and Sisyphus combined.

Another victim is the man in Rollo May's parable, "The Man Who Was Put in a Cage." In the same way that the form of the parable since the time of Jesus has communicated meaning beyond mere literal content, the psychologist in May's brilliant parable discovers a meaning beyond the literal and the psychoanalytic content of his experience. What May illustrates here in the form of parable is man's continuing need to metamorphose his experience, to accept his interpretation of it, and finally to undertake the will to act on it.

The companion piece, "Freedom and Responsibility Reexamined," recasts the intent of the parable. In this rejection of former solutions to the dilemma man faces in making choices and accepting responsibility, Rollo May sets up an extended definition of freedom. He forces the reader to come to grips with his definition by the use of paradox: freedom defined in terms of its apparent denial, the experience of contemporary man in the Nazi concentration camp. Freedom derives from man's consciousness of freedom; this consciousness can only emanate from a centered self. May ends his discussion with his own idea of a free man, how he acts and reacts to daily life. Although May's thoughts are intended mainly for an audience of psychotherapists, his style, moderately conversational, permits any intelligent reader to have access to his thought. May seems always to be aware of his reader and makes a conscious effort to explain the difficult subject of man's freedom and responsibility for an audience of varying degrees of knowledge.

Directly connected to the freedom discussed by Rollo May is the "hang-loose" theory, a new ethic in American society, defined by J. L. Simmons and Barry Winograd. After establishing the characteristics of the ethic, the authors define the ideal person or happener, similar in some ways and yet very different from May's free man. Simmons and Winograd try very hard to communicate the "hang-loose" attitudes of the various groups following this ethic, and in doing so they use colloquialism, shocking descriptions, comparatively terse statements: in short, a kind of "pop" style. Young readers may find themselves drawn immediately into the Simmons and Winograd essay; however, they need to ask whether or not they are being seduced here by the impact of style and the attractiveness of subject matter. Is it possible that the authors identify too closely with the mind set of happeners to present a good analysis of this new ethic? They have been roundly criticized for using the same reasons to describe the emergence of the "hang-loose" ethic as were used to demonstrate the rise of the organization man of the 1950's. (See John Leggett's review of their book in *Trans-action*, December, 1967.) Although good expository writing begins with commitment either to subject matter or to the purpose of communicating ideas, the responsible writer adheres to a necessary detachment in form and control. Self-justification is so evident in the tone of Simmons and Winograd that any disagreement with their attitude would probably bring forth scorn and laughter from them.

Unlike Simmons and Winograd, Richard Rovere is able to bring his own voice into "Freedom: Who Needs It?" and yet maintain that necessary detachment, that control which allows him to argue forcefully for a preservation of our present society. He raises the question: "Has the desire for freedom ever been only a desire for self-expression or self-fulfillment?" Rovere sees in many of the young radicals a disregard, verging on contempt, for basic individual liberties and warns that unless the exercise of freedom becomes also a "defense of liberty," any social change or "talk about human possibilities" may wither away and disappear.

Gaining insight into the human condition is a way of gaining self-awareness, the point at which this discussion began. To Dennis Wrong, a sense of self or identity must be defined as something more than a favorable self-conception because the word identity "has tended to become a value-charged, almost a charismatic, term, with its secure achievement regarded as equivalent to personal salvation." The author structures his essay, "Identity: Problem and Catchword," around a comparison and contrast between the existentialist's view and the sociologist's view of self. Bringing the search for identity to the student level by beginning his essay with a description of Lionel Trilling's short story, "Of This Time, Of That Place," is a successful technique to involve the reader in his analysis and final wish for creating a society "that does not mythologize its own processes of social control and allows men to choose their own identities without making life appear a senseless routine." It is entirely likely that all the writers in this chapter would agree with such a conclusion.

JOHN ROBERTSON
the function of insight

My college career began on a small campus of fewer than nine hundred students, in a small community of fewer than twenty-five thousand people. Though I remember feeling quite alone and anxious at first, I readily became part of what I would now describe as the typical college experience. I played games, sang songs, engaged in snow fights, and studied in my spare time.

As I look back on my freshman year I think that the greatest mistake I made was to put too great a value on belonging. The social environment in which I found myself was especially conducive to this type of error, being dominated by competitive living groups. For the sake of security I paid the price of knowing few people and having only one close friend. I remember marveling at the fact that out of 150 freshmen boys I should have been assigned to room with the one who turned out to be my best friend. With this convenient arrangement I proceeded to convince myself that any other friendships were not worth cultivating. When summer came and I left school I had many pleasant experiences to remember but I still knew but one person more than casually.

One might say that this is not a very severe criticism to make of myself, since most people have only a few intimate friends and many acquaintances. But the point is that close friends should not be a substitute for meaningful encounters with a wide variety of persons. To be able to open up to other people without first having to be sure of their commitment to oneself, is an ability I have since decided is well worth cultivating. Only with such an undemanding attitude is one free to understand other points of view, and in the broadest sense, those "other points of view" are what I think college is for. At that time of my life, however, I was unprepared to enter relationships that would not help to secure my self-confidence against a somewhat strange and perplexing world. As a result, my personal growth remained rather limited. I do not know what would have happened had I returned to this school in the fall — whether my previous habits would have been reinforced or if I would have become sure enough of myself to venture into broader and more challenging encounters. In any event, the following year found me enrolled at the University of California in Berkeley.

From *To Make a Difference*, edited by Otto Butz. Copyright 1967. Reprinted by permission of Harper and Row, Publishers, Inc.

I had taken a liberal arts curriculum the year before with the thought of going on what was called a three-two plan, a plan whereby I would take three years of liberal arts and two of engineering and end up with a degree in both areas. At Berkeley, however, the situation demanded a decision between liberal arts or the college of engineering. The criterion I invoked, that of tangibility and practicability, pointed to the latter; so engineering was my choice. I remember that my impression of the social sciences and humanities was that the knowledge of the former was always uncertain and conjectural and that the latter required an individual capable of complete dedication and endowed with considerable talent. As it was, engineering suited my purpose quite well. The material in an engineering course follows a logical process of presentation. Most courses were complete in themselves or at most relied on clear-cut prerequisites. It was possible to establish well-defined goals and judge progress accordingly. Answers were either right or wrong, and if they were wrong it was simply a matter of finding out how to get the right one. I by no means want to imply that I regarded engineering as simple; on the contrary, for the average student to do well required considerable effort and commitment.

Toward the end of my junior year my values and general orientation to life began to undergo a significant change. Probably what happened to me was an experience common to many people as they mature a little. Stimulated by my contact with a knowledgeable and understanding friend, I began to broaden my intellectual horizons. Instead of dreading the liberal arts courses I had to take in engineering, I found myself reading philosophy, psychology and theology for pleasure, often at the expense of my engineering. This continued until my graduation from Cal, at which time I was anxious to take more nontechnical courses and hardly enthusiastic about embarking on an engineering career. I therefore decided to enroll at San Francisco State College, and took as diversified a curriculum as possible. Though this is an age when technology requires a high degree of specialization, I have become convinced that everyone needs first of all a good general education.

I now look back on my engineering curriculum at Berkeley with strongly critical feelings. It is now obvious to me that I was not really interested in my studies as I am now; they did not seem relevant in the way they do now. In other words, it *now* seems quite clear that I was never cut out to be an engineer. So I ask myself, whom do I blame for the four years that could have been spent more wisely? (It is a question, I might add, that is also of some interest to the taxpayer.)

In trying to answer this question I must examine both myself and the educational system of which I was a part. As far as I myself am concerned, the question I am most often asked is: Why did I change my mind so late? But this seems to me of only secondary importance. The more basic question I must ask myself is why I failed to make a personally more meaningful decision in the first place. And why was this? Possibly it was because I had never been shocked into confronting my own innate self. Possibly I am by nature a passive person who needs more external stimulation than others. Yet I somehow can't believe that I am alone. There are surely a great many people for whom the present educational system does not provide adequate occasions for a sufficiently searching investigation of their own potentialities.

Opportunities to get to know oneself are, of course, most limited of all in our typical engineering curricula. As has often been said, engineering programs are too exclusively concerned with professional training. I believe that the ideal way to remedy this would be to make engineering available only on a graduate level, after several years of more general educational preparation. The present shortcomings of engineering curricula might at least be mitigated if those who teach these courses made greater efforts to address themselves to their students as whole human beings. Yet here too, I must be critical. It was my repeated experience that engineering instructors were precisely the kind of people whom one would expect the present system to produce. In other words, people educated in the ways of the system are returned as its instructors. It is a closed circle which makes for high technical competence but limited human and cultural perspectives.

While part of my error in majoring in engineering undoubtedly resulted from my own lack of self-awareness, part of the blame must thus be attributed to the existing educational system itself. For isn't a conscious knowledge of alternatives presupposed in the notion of free choice? And how can one expect the average American eighteen-year-old, raised in the limited world of our middle-class culture, to make a wise, lifetime vocational choice?

Having by now somewhat enlarged my conception of education and decided to devote myself to some aspect of it as a career, I have been thinking more and more about three basic questions. What are the areas in which education is relevant to the unique problems faced by modern man? Can education facilitate the making of increasingly complex decisions that today confront the average person? And, can education liberate man from a bureaucratic environment that is ceaselessly trying to objectify him? To discuss these questions I must first examine our present social environment, the various ways of reacting to it, and the kinds of specific roles education might play.

Our rapidly changing, technological society seems to have been developing for the past hundred years and, in a more fundamental sense, for the past two millennia. The most obvious changes have occurred in the nature of our tools and in the new organizational forms we have evolved to utilize them. As a result of these developments, we in the United States have for some decades been moving into what one economic historian has termed an age of "high mass consumption."[1] At least potentially, that is, we possess the scientific and technological know-how to eliminate scarcity in regard to everything the human organism needs to sustain itself. In the process, moreover, increased efficiency through automation has made it possible to feed, clothe and shelter ourselves with only a fraction of the time and effort required formerly. These same advances have, of course, also brought the creation of nuclear weapons and the resultant fear and tension that haunt our lives. And as if to compensate for the increased possibility of death by war, medical science has progressed far toward eradicating the most deadly diseases.

Corresponding important changes have occurred in our attitudes toward life. We seem to be undergoing a time of deep-rooted intellectual and ethical ferment. Our traditional world view appears in many ways to have exhausted its potential for providing us with a viable orientation both to nature and other people. This older philosophy that I believe is today being outgrown I associate with the United States during the period it developed from an agrarian to an industrial society. Without wishing to imply any negative connotation, I would call the predominant outlook of this era materialistic. People were judged in terms of the things they possessed. It was as important for nations to strive after industrial pre-eminence as it was for people to acquire the goods industry produced. Being well thought of by one's fellowman was desirable, but one didn't need to bother about it too much, since it would surely result from a successful business career.

[1] W. W. Rostow, *The Stages of Economic Growth*, London, Cambridge University Press, 1960.

People tended to be what David Riesman has called "inner-directed,"[2] in the sense that most of their values and goals became part of their personalities at an early age and remained relatively unchanged from then on. It also became customary for people to think in terms of depersonalized groups. Laborers and managers, the rich and the poor, foreigners and natives, were common descriptive categories. It was a time when most human relationships were economically and socially competitive, a time of sharp class distinctions. Also characteristic of the period was a certain naïveté regarding international relations, afforded us by our physical isolation from other countries. We were "morally virtuous" created by "divine destiny," and happy to give advice to whomever we considered less industrious than ourselves. In summary, the pervasive preoccupation of this earlier era in our history was with the mastery of physical things, and people were rated in terms of their visible achievements in regard to that process.

The philosophy and discipline of materialistic development have made possible a measure of control over nature and standards of living unmatched in history. Yet these happy results have not been without a price. For while an industrially based market economy may be efficient from the point of view of the production and distribution of goods and services, it certainly does not acknowledge all our dimensions as human beings. To experience life and judge people chiefly in terms of such a scheme of values is therefore bound to result in what has come to be called alienation, from oneself as well as from others.

As heirs to the historical period of scientific and industrial dynamism, we face several kinds of problems. To some extent we are still afflicted by the fragmentation and alienation that seem endemic to this kind of developmental process. In addition, we are confronted by the ever increasing complexity that results from our technological achievements, high living standards, and geographical and social mobility. And beyond that, we are experiencing the uncertainties of abandoning much of our traditional world view and groping for another that will somehow enable us to live more fully.

How, in this situation of changing circumstances and frequently conflicting values, does one act as a moral person? How does one make coherent sense of it all and relate oneself to it in one's day-to-day living? As I see it, there are three possible ways to cope with this problem. One is to let oneself be guided by whim, so to speak. React the way you feel at the moment, whether it is consistent with past

[2] David Riesman, *The Lonely Crowd*, New Haven, Yale University Press, 1950.

behavior or not. The second is to accept some ethical code and then act according to it whether it fits or not. And the final way is somehow to bridge the gap between one's ideas and realities and to become intellectually and experientially at one with oneself. The person who evolves such a response to life also acts ethically. But his ethical notions are so broadly human and adaptable that they can become part of his very nature and be applied almost intuitively and in a manner appropriate to every occasion. Such a person's actions are then essentially spontaneous. Yet if he is challenged, he is able to reassure himself and explain to others that his actions do in fact express a coherent set of beliefs and ethical commitments.

But do such spontaneous and intuitively ethical people need to reflect on their acts at all? Can't a person live fully and responsibly without having to be able to explain in words why certain actions are good and desirable, and others not? I am afraid that at our present juncture in history totally spontaneous and at the same time wise and moral behavior is impossible. While a flexible ethical commitment and the clues of everyday life can go a long way toward spontaneously orienting behavior, I believe that no one can dispense with thinking about their actions altogether. Even the most emancipated of us is still bound to be caught up in the rigidities of our traditional ethical assumptions in some measure. And the society in which we live is simply too complex and replete with situations involving value choices for a person to be able to get along without any reflective introspection whatever.

I know of two possible sources of sustaining orientation by which one's reflections and choices can be guided. Both require the person to transcend his immediate cultural conditioning and to try to confront life both more individually and universally. The one orientation is that of faith. The other is that of intellectual awareness or, as the philosopher Whitehead calls it, insight.[3] Of the two, faith is by far the more desirable. For while insight tends to lead only to a cerebral and analytical appreciation of life, faith is able to order the experiencing of our existence in its full, intuitive richness. Yet even though it is more limited, intellectual awareness can perform a vital function. It can enable us to make some sense out of our lives and so preserve our individual integrity while we search for a faith that will once again be satisfying and workable.

Since intellectual awareness operates through concepts and theories,

3 Alfred North Whitehead, *Adventures of Ideas*, New York, Mentor Books, 1960.

there is of course always the danger that we may become so engrossed in our intellectualizing that we lose touch with the living realities we are trying to understand. The only defense against this is continuously to return to our direct, undifferentiated experiences, no matter how disruptive of our neat intellectual exercises this may prove. Such a return to firsthand experience as a corrective to our insight is not only necessary to keep our intellectual awareness practically relevant. It is nowadays insisted upon by students who refuse to accept academic analyses unless they find them meaningful in terms of their own personal concerns. The reason for this is that many of today's young people are engaged in what ultimately amounts to a religious quest. They are exploring themselves and the world with a view to developing new personal and social meanings. And this is why so much current unrest centers in our institutions of higher learning. These formally represent the quest for intellectual awareness. And if they are prepared to incorporate occasions that enable students to relate what they are learning to their own immediate experiences, they can also facilitate going beyond insight to the development of a larger and more inclusive faith.

Among my acquaintances I have observed three basic adjustments to today's world. The most unappealing of these is what I shall call the "unquestioning" approach. It would be too much to term this a philosophy, for it is in fact the very antithesis of the kind of understanding through reason and reflection at which philosophy aims. The distinguishing characteristic of the person who follows this formula is his willingness to accept his society as presently constituted without question and to take its human and moral adequacy for granted. People who operate in this manner are by no means lazy; they are often born gamesmen who devote tireless hours to learning the rules of the social game and how to break them with impunity. Their unconscious assumption is simply that whatever "pays off" in terms of existing social values is thereby an unqualified good.

But to justify such a psychologically and morally undiscriminating attitude one would have to take an entirely relativistic position and maintain that one set of values is as good as any other. And I do not believe this is so. Values *can* be judged, both with reference to basic human needs and in regard to particular historical circumstances. Some values facilitate human nature more fully and effectively than others. Some values are more appropriate in one kind of technological, social or political situation than others. In our present ethical ferment, for example, there are a great many philosophies of life we could follow. Take only such famous figures as Marx, Freud and Sartre. Each of these offers his own interpretation of the world and recommends a different course of action. The implications of their ideas and ideals are significantly different. How, then, are we to make a judgment as to whose explanations and values are best, that is, most likely to prove viable and satisfying? We can do so only by subjecting them — and all ideas and ideals generally — to critical investigation.

On college campuses the unquestioning attitude is expressed most typically by the students who are out to beat the system. Their goal is not to think about themselves and their society but merely to acquire an academic degree. They are not interested in what can truly be called education. Their purpose is only to pass the formal requirements that will give them access to the social and material benefits for which the possession of an academic degree has come to be insisted upon. The social life of such students is dominated by considerations of prestige and status, and whatever surplus energy they have is poured into the pursuit of good times. I do not object to these entertainments in themselves. They are unhealthful only when they are not balanced by a serious side of life. That this kind of existence is today not altogether complete and satisfying is somewhat corroborated by the reactions of such students to the Berkeley Free Speech Movement. During this challenge to the morality of the Establishment, these merely career-minded people kept themselves entirely separate from the dialogue. It was not that they could not be heard, since arrangements existed to accommodate speakers representing all sides of the issue. But rather than engaging in discussion, these people threw garbage at those who did. Such actions seem to me to express deep-seated hostilities, not in the first instance toward the Berkeley rebels but against their own unsatisfying way of life which the Free Speech Movement unwittingly put into question.

The second basic attitude I see among my contemporaries is what I would call the "cynical" approach. It succeeds where the unquestioning attitude fails, but is unacceptable to me for other reasons. It has questioned several or all traditional American values and found them in many ways lacking. But it does not go on from there to search for more suitable patterns of living to replace or supplement those which are found wanting. It is above all a reaction against hypocrisy, and as such it can indeed point to many inconsistencies in our preachments and practices. Our alleged adherence to Christian ethics, our vaunted devotion to peace and the self-determination of peoples, our much-paraded enlightenment on the subject of sex — all are in many ways given the lie by the ways we actually live. Being the overstated ideals they are, they understandably evoke disillusionment. Yet whether this disillusionment justifies giving up on our society altogether is another matter. To me, at least, it does not.

Since I concede many of the points which those who take the cynical view make, I have no easy answer with which to oppose them. Probably the differences between their conclusions and my own are in the last analysis a matter of temperament. Certain personality types react to disillusionment more bitterly than others. I suspect that those who do, thereby give indication that they are suffering from psychological problems that may best be solved on an individual basis. In any event, someone who chooses to reject the possibility of positive action colors the way he sees life from then on. He puts himself beyond the reach of arguments to the contrary because his most fundamental premise is negative. To change he must have new experiences, not another argument.

The final pattern of behavior I have observed among my fellow students is one by which I have been strongly tempted myself. I shall refer to it by Eric Hoffer's term as that of the "true believer."[4] For two and a half of the four years I spent at Berkeley, most of my energies were devoted to engineering. Even so, my studies did not fill me with any great enthusiasm. I believe in retrospect that I longed all the while for someone or something to become really excited about. I would like to have had a cause and remember envying those who did — whether it was civil rights, free speech, anti-Communism, anti-capitalism, or any of the numerous others that were available. But here was my greatest problem: since there are at least two sides to every issue, and since each side is equally dedicated and capable of arguing its case, I could never make a choice. Perhaps if belonging to a group had not seemed to demand such total allegiance, the decision to commit myself might have been easier; but on the other hand, it would also have lost some of its attractiveness.

I think that what most basically troubles me about the "true believer" approach is that it attracts certain personality types who are inclined not to do justice to the complexity of the issues involved. To achieve a feeling of certainty worthy of total dedication, such people are often prepared dangerously to oversimplify problems and solutions. While

[4] Eric Hoffer, *The True Believer*, New York, Mentor Books, 1961.

I cannot, therefore, follow their example, I must point out that when guided by strong, responsible and perceptive leaders, people with this type of personality and orientation to life can play an important part in working toward positive social goals.

Being by disposition and outlook prevented from adopting any of the main attitudes that appear to satisfy many of my contemporaries, I find myself in a rather individual and detached position. All I can fall back on are some very general guiding principles: first, that it is essential to care about life, to try to understand it, and to maintain some mindfulness of its complexities; and second, that some form of action is necessary — even at the risk of acting on the basis of incomplete knowledge and thus failing to achieve one's original objectives. Beyond these principles, I believe with the psychologist and philosopher C. G. Jung that modern man needs essentially four things: faith, hope, love and insight.[5] That is why I am concerned with education. For though education is not the whole answer, it can make a vital contribution at least to the development of insight. While the unquestioning, the cynics and the true believers reject insight as either too threatening or too cautious, I myself am convinced that it today provides our most reliable creative instrument.

And how can education best serve the development of insight? Most importantly, it must cultivate a spirit of inquiry. It must do so by encouraging people to build meaningful bridges between their own personal processes and events in the world at large. Once having triggered such personally rooted intellectual curiosity, education must nourish, structure and at the same time free it so that it can penetrate human experiences as deeply as our faculties make possible. To accomplish this task, education must bring to bear every perspective that human observation and imagination have made available. It must utilize the analyses of the various physical and social sciences. It must combine these with a continuous awareness of historical dimensions. It must offer students opportunities to derive stimulation and meaning from the arts. It must permit them to pursue their studies in frank relationship to the practical problems and moral dilemmas they face in their own lives. And above all, it must recognize that effective education and hence the attainment of insight are ultimately very individual matters. While providing common frameworks and materials, it must invite everyone to think through his realities in his own

---

[5] C. G. Jung, *Modern Man in Search of a Soul*, translated by W. S. Dell and C. F. Baynes, New York, Harcourt, Brace (Harvest), 1933.

ways. For only to the extent people achieve such personally meaningful insights will they be secure enough to go on to modern man's
other three needs — faith, hope and love.

IHAB HASSAN
the modern self in recoil

I

"In its essence literature is concerned with the self," Lionel Trilling
writes in *Freud and the Crisis of Our Culture*, "and the particular concern of the literature of the last two centuries has been with the self in
its standing quarrel with culture."[1] The image of the self in its
standing, and recently embittered, quarrel with culture — indeed in
its quarrel with itself, as Mr. Trilling neglects to say — comes to focus
in the figure of the anti-hero.

In fiction, the unnerving rubric "anti-hero" refers to a ragged assem-
bly of victims: the fool, the clown, the hipster, the criminal, the
poor sod, the freak, the outsider, the scapegoat, the scrubby opportunist,
the rebel without a cause, the "hero" in the ashcan and "hero" on
the leash. If the anti-hero seems nowadays to hold us in his spell, it is
because the deep and disquieting insights revealed to us by modern
literature often require that we project ourselves into the predicament
of victims.

The gradual process of atrophy of the hero may have begun with
Don Quixote, or perhaps even Job, Orestes, and Christ. It enters
the critical phase, however, only late in the eighteenth century. Goethe's
Werther introduces the "tragic" Romantic hero who, in his inordinate
conception of himself, severs the traditional bond between the hero
and his society, and points the way to such extreme stances of alienation as were to find expression in the Byronic and Sadist hero, in the

From Ihab Hassan, *Radical Innocence: Studies in the Contemporary American
Novel*, pp. 20–33. Copyright © 1961 by Princeton University Press. Reprinted by
permission of Princeton University Press.
[1] Lionel Trilling, *Freud and the Crisis of Our Culture* (Boston, 1955), pp. 58f.

gothic and demonic protagonist, in werewolf, ghoul, and vampire. But as the new bourgeois order, which the Romantic hero rejected, became a powerful social reality, the strategy of opposition changed. The characters of Stendhal, Balzac, and Flaubert often seem, as Raymond Giraud has recognized, "heroes of ironies" whose "ideals, desires, and feelings are in disharmony" with their "adult conception of reality."[2] Similarly, the subtitle for *Vanity Fair: A Novel Without a Hero*, suggests that Victorian fiction was quietly disposing of the heroic protagonist. The ambivalences of a bourgeois hero in an overwhelmingly middle-class society raise for him problems of estrangement and communion, sincerity and simulation, ambition and acquiescence, which we recognize as the patent themes of the great novels of the last century. The wretched fate of the lower-class hero, caught between malignant Heredity and crushing Environment in the *roman experimental* of Zola, and in the less experimental but more benign novels of the brothers Goncourt, reflects the familiar bias of Naturalism and marks a further stage in the disintegration of heroism. Victim to immitigable "cosmic laws," with little or no control over his fate in the world, man turns inward again. The next development is predictable. "The way was open from the realist to the intimist novel," Mario Praz concludes in *The Hero in Eclipse in Victorian Fiction*. "Disillusioned observation of life as it really was, led to the eclipse of the hero and the disclosure of man's swarming interior world, made up of disparate and contradictory things."[3]

With the retrenchment of the individual, the drama of good and evil which the hero and villain once objectified in society becomes blurred. The traditional forms of moral conflict are so internalized that no victory or defeat, where self is divided against itself, can claim to be more than pyrrhic. Cunningly introspective, the modern novel redefines the identity of its central character and redirects his energies toward the virtues of love or self-discovery, virtues that are a good deal more personal than social. To become someone, to know who or what one is, to reach finally another human being with love, and to do so in terms that society may censure, this is the passionate, bitter concern of the modern anti-hero. But the modern identity proved an elusive thing to capture. "You mustn't look in my novel for the old stable *ego* of the character," D. H. Lawrence wrote to Edward Garnett. "There is

---

[2] Raymond Giraud, *The Unheroic Hero* (New Brunswick, 1957), p. 189. See also Harry Levin, "From Priam to Birotteau," *Yale French Studies*, VI (1950), 76.
[3] Mario Praz, *The Hero in Eclipse in Victorian Fiction* (New York, 1956), p. 383.

another *ego*, according to whose action the individual is unrecognizable, and passes through, as it were, allotropic states. . . ."[4] A new shifty ego, a new concept of man. The sad history of the anti-hero is nothing more than the history of man's changing awareness of himself. It is the record of his recoil.

The encounter between the new ego and the destructive element of experience, we have insisted, lies at the dramatic center of the modern novel in Europe and America. The encounter is further illumined by some striking European images which define the modern idea of the self and clarify its responses. We shall view some concrete instances of the anti-hero — whom in hope and charity we may simply call "hero." These instances are taken from writers of very different age and background, yet they add to a remarkably persistent theme.

To consider Dostoyevsky's *Notes from Underground*, 1864, modern is perhaps to stretch the idea of modernity to its permissible limit. The document so shrill and anxious, so full of spite and spleen, reveals, in any case, what the modern soul likes most to gnaw upon: itself. The dagger is turned inward, the most refined tortures are reserved for the self. Whom else are we really interested in? Listening for forty years from the crack under his floor, Dostoyevsky's hero looks at existence with a cringe and a snarl. He knows the intense pleasure of degradation and of despair, and knows, while gnashing his teeth, that "there is no one even for you to feel vindictive against, that you have not, and perhaps never will have, an object for your spite. . . ."[5] Precisely the condition which Albert Camus calls, in *The Rebel*, metaphysical rebellion, and which our hero understands as a revolt against "the whole legal system of Nature."[6] But no one is to blame; "consequently there is only the same outlet left again — that is, beat the wall as hard as you can."[7] This frenzy is not only meant to be a protest against the whole order of Nature, the terrible fact that "every sort of consciousness . . . is a disease," or merely a protest against the historical enemies of Dostoyevsky — rationalism, meliorism, and science, the coxcomb fact that two plus two equals four.[8] The frenzy, in the form of caprice, is also directed against our individuality. That Dos-

---

[4] Aldous Huxley, ed., *The Letters of D. H. Lawrence* (London, 1956), p. 198.

[5] *The Short Novels of Dostoyevsky*, Introduction by Thomas Mann (New York, 1945), p. 137.

[6] *ibid.*, p. 137.

[7] *ibid.*, p. 140.

[8] *ibid.*, p. 132.

toyevsky's "insect" can establish his identity only by forcing himself to collide ignominiously with an arrogant officer who does not even recognize his existence is of no importance. The important thing is that it is *he* who *forces* the recognition. This is freedom.

The grotesque image of this strange creature haunts modern literature and remains at the center of our dread. Its cracked reflections in some way or other penetrate the works of most European novelists. And its perverse truths, almost insupportable, infiltrate recent American fiction which does not stem only, as Hemingway claimed, from a book by Mark Twain called *Huckleberry Finn* but also from another, it may be argued with equal pertinence, by Dostoyevsky called *Notes from Underground*. The image, taken up, modified, and recreated by later novelists deserves further attention.

Conrad, we know, shared with Dostoyevsky more than the dubious heritage of a Slavic temper. His metaphysical romances of the seven seas subject the idea of heroism to an ironic rhetoric which is peculiarly modern, and his abiding interest in the theme of the double —his *Secret Sharer* and Dostoyevsky's *The Double* come to mind — probes the distempers of the modern self in a way that seems now familiar. While no character of his strictly reminds us of the hero of the *Notes*, the state of immersion, the desperation felt in the heart of darkness or in the underground habitations of consciousness, the surrender to the "destructive element," compel our terrified assent in the novels of both authors. Kurtz, in *Heart of Darkness*, had perhaps immersed himself too deeply, there where victim and victimizer become one, till he could distinguish only the horror. But Kurtz creeping on all fours in the night-time jungle and Lord Jim erect and dazzling in spotless white are still two sides of the same image, two sides separated really by the enormous distance between action and heroic intention. Conrad does not repudiate human striving. In a celebrated passage from *Lord Jim* he simply points to the way of fulfillment. "A man that is born falls into a dream like a man who falls into the sea," Conrad writes. "If he tries to climb out into the air as inexperienced people endeavor to do, he drowns. . . . The way is to the destructive element submit yourself. . . ."[9] The unintelligent brutality of existence leaves man no other choice.

It is, of course, the unintelligent brutality of existence that dominates the Dublin of Joyce's *Ulysses;* the city becomes a focus, in Eliot's

[9] Joseph Conrad, *Lord Jim* (New York, 1931), p. 214.

famous words, to "the immense panorama of futility and anarchy which is contemporary history."[10] The proportions of the hero are further shrunken, his self pushed further underground in the world of memory and fantasy. The element to which Bloom submits himself, in humor and humility, is the ignominious element. Insult and pathos, loneliness and failure, are his familiars. Leopold Bloom, wandering Jew, mock Odysseus, and lowly Christ, finally appears to us, above all, as "Everyman or Noman."[11] He stands between Stephen Dedalus and Molly Bloom, between intelligence and nature, as a bathetic monument to the generosity of suffering. For intelligence, in the person of Stephen — he is Lucifer and Hamlet and Dedalus — can only cry: *Non serviam!* And Nature, in the person of Molly — Ceres, Hera, eternal Mother Earth — must endlessly murmur: Yes I will Yes. Man, meanwhile, goes clowning his sentimental way into eternity, unable to reconcile himself completely to one or the other.

The two heroes of Joyce and of Dostoyevsky show that humility lies on the other side of spite. But the clown in man has many disguises. He is Bloom, "one lonely last sardine of summer."[12] He is also, as we shall see, an insect, a sentient tubercle, at best a shaggy wolf. The self in recoil cannot afford to be choosy.

Dostoyevsky's metaphor of man as an insect inevitably calls to mind Kafka's story, "Metamorphosis," in which the narrator is transformed into a huge, hideous, and pathetic vermin. This, too, is self-degradation, a form of the self in recoil. This, too, is protest. The theme is everywhere in Kafka, in *The Castle,* in *The Trial,* in "The Penal Colony" or "The Judgment." Man is always judged, and found invariably guilty. He is the victim of an unappeasable power, a horrible and recurrent outrage, and even in his most serene moments he can only exclaim, like the Hunter Gracchus: "I am here, more than that I do not know, further than that I cannot go. My ship has no rudder, and it is driven by the wind that blows in the undermost regions of death."[13] The vision of man is as grotesque as that of Dostoyevsky; but it goes farther, denying man freedom, the sheer horror of choice, and denying him grace. Indeed, of man Kafka can only say, "He found the Archimedean point,

[10] T. S. Eliot, "Ulysses, Order and Myth," in John W. Aldridge, ed., *Critiques and Essays on Modern Fiction* (New York, 1952), p. 426.

[11] James Joyce, *Ulysses* (New York, 1946), p. 712.

[12] *ibid.,* p. 284.

[13] *Selected Stories of Franz Kafka,* Introduction by Philip Rahv (New York, 1952), p. 187.

but he used it against himself; it seems that he was permitted to find it only under this condition."[14] The lever which gives man mastery over his universe, moving worlds at the touch of a finger tip, is still the inbred dagger of the soul. In Kafka as in Dostoyevsky, the sense of compounded guilt and absurdity defines the point at which victimization and rebellion meet.[15]

This view of the human predicament will no doubt seem to many both exigent and extreme. It borders, people argue, on disease. Exactly. In the panoramic view of Thomas Mann, whose sane vision did not prevent him from cultivating a life-long interest in Kafka and Dostoyevsky, disease and even death become an ultimate response to life. The idea informs at least two of his masterpieces, *The Magic Mountain* and *Death in Venice*, and it hovers about his latest work, *The Confessions of Felix Krull*. Hans Castorp reflects, as if prompted by the hero of Dostoyevsky's *Notes*, "Disease was a perverse, a dissolute form of life. And life? Life itself? Was it perhaps only an infection, a sickening of matter? . . . The first step toward evil, toward desire and death, was taken precisely then, when there took place that first increase in the density of the spiritual, that pathologically luxuriant morbid growth . . . ."[16] But the radical disease of consciousness, which the hero of Dostoyevsky resented to the end of his spite, and to which the Kafka hero finally submits in a lucid nightmare, is transmuted by Thomas Mann into a condition of spiritual refulgence. It is thus that Mann is able to claim, with Nietzsche and Dostoyevsky in mind, that "certain attainments of the soul and the intellect are impossible *without disease, without insanity, without spiritual crime*, and the *great invalids* are *crucified victims*, sacrificed to humanity and its advancement, to the broadening of its feeling and knowledge — in short, to its more *sublime health* [italics mine]."[17] Man, we see, pitches himself at the terrible limit of experience, as Lucifer did.

Mann's statement reminds us that grace, if it is to be found at all, lies deep in the soft core of violence. The saint and the criminal stand back to back on either side of the demonic. Both are protestants, both victims. But pure violence, like the demonic, has no reality in the public realm, the domain of action. Pure violence, as we shall repeatedly observe in

---

[14] Franz Kafka, *Dearest Father* (New York, 1954), p. 378.
[15] Parallels between the two novelists are well elaborated by Renato Poggioli, "Kafka and Dostoyevsky," in Angel Flores, ed., *The Kafka Problem* (New York, 1946), pp. 97–107.
[16] Thomas Mann, *The Magic Mountain* (New York, 1955), pp. 285f.
[17] "Introduction," *The Short Novels of Dostoyevsky*, p. xv.

modern fiction, seems almost the ultimate form of introspection. That the saint and the criminal, the suppliant and psychopath — they are conjoined in the recent literature of hipsterism and in such enduring figures as Greene's Pinkie and Faulkner's Christmas — partake of violence compulsively is no surprise. For untrammelled violence is not an act, it is merely a state; it is the experience of world negation. As Miss Arendt saw, the saint and the criminal are both lonely figures: "... the one being for, the other against, all men; they, therefore, remain outside the pale of human intercourse and are, politically, marginal figures who usually enter the historical scene in times of corruption, disintegration, and political bankruptcy. Because of its inherent tendency to disclose the agent together with the act, action needs for its full appearance the shining brightness we once called glory, and which is possible only in the public realm."[18]

It is perhaps unnecessary to recover for our age the Corneillian idea of glory, but when the focus of moral energy moves so far from the center of human effort in the world, losing itself in the domain of holy science or demonic violence, then it is time to give vent to our anxiety. The dissociation of action from intelligence, we remember, is manifest in Dostoyevsky's *Notes* whose hero openly contemns the active life. The consequences of this attitude are not limited to the cult of inactivity, living in a hole, like the man from underground, or in a jar like the hero of Beckett's *The Unnamable*, living, if you will, in the "packing-box shanty on the city dump" thoughtfully reserved by the editors of *Life* for our most promising novelists. The consequences also involve the alienation of the moral and artistic imagination from things of this world, often leading to a criminal state of autonomy.

The rebel-victim, we see, is also the outsider in search of truth.[19] Harry Haller, in Hermann Hesse's *Steppenwolf*, is still an isolate genius of suffering "whose fate it is to live the whole riddle of human destiny heightened to the pitch of a personal torture, a personal hell."[20] He is still grappling with the radical multiplicities of the human ego, oscillating not merely between the wolf and the man, not merely between two poles, such as the body and the spirit, the saint and the sinner, but between "thousands and thousands."[21] In the "Treatise on the Steppen-

[18] *The Human Condition*, p. 180.
[19] See Colin Wilson, *The Outsider* (Boston, 1956), for an extended documentary more valuable for its recognition of the general problem and for its range of significant reference than for its particular insights into the crucial documents it uses.
[20] Hermann Hesse, *Steppenwolf* (New York, 1929), p. 28.
[21] *ibid.*, p. 77.

wolf," however, the outsider is finally made to reckon with the fact that
man may be nothing more than a temporary agreement between warring
opposites, nothing more, in fact, than "a bourgeois compromise" —
such as Bloom!

The idea of man as a transient compromise in the universe entails
the acceptance of permanent outrage. Harry Haller could find some
redemption of that condition in love or art, or even in humor which
reconciles all opposites, and in whose "imaginary realm the intricate
and many-faceted ideal of all Steppenwolves finds its realization."[22]
Other writers — Mauriac, Bernanos, Graham Greene — sought for their
characters a solution more commensurate with their religious faith; for,
as Colin Wilson has loudly noted, the problems of modern man, rebel,
victim, or outsider, lend themselves to an intense religious apprehension
which need not be specifically Christian.[23] Yet even the Christian
novelists, so Jansenist they seem in their insistence on human depravity,
manage to convey only the terrible intricacies of damnation. Thus, for
instance, is the pursuit of damnation conceived in *Brighton Rock* as an
appalling manifestation of the mercy of God. The modern Christian
martyr, it seems, can aspire only to perdition.

To the religious and the humanist solutions of man's plight in the
universe must be added the Existentialist. The basic question here is
still one of freedom, the search for identity under the aspects of violence
or alienation. Freedom, we recall, is known to the hero of the *Notes*
only as caprice; he understands that men, himself included, must seek
freedom and must be repelled and horrified by it. The same ambivalence
haunts the quest of Kafka's characters. Beginning with Gide, however,
the ambivalence is seemingly resolved in favor of positive action. Man
asserts his liberty in a gratuitous act of murder, as in Lafcadio's case,
in acts of social repudiation, or ruthless heroism, as in the case of
Michel and Theseus. Freedom consists of revolt, against morality,
against the social order, against history. But the blood-curdling price is
one that only heroes and supermen can afford. In this direction, the
Existentialist novelists go farther than Gide was willing to go, and their
view is correspondingly more special. Victory, in their novels, depends
on the certainty of defeat, *is* the process of defeat. But unlike the heroes
of classical tragedy, their protagonists act in full foreknowledge of their

[22] *ibid.*, p. 73.
[23] *The Outsider*, p. 261. Also Colin Wilson, *Religion and the Rebel* (Boston,
1957).

fatality, act *only* in *despite* of that fatality. And there is never any reconciliation.

It is thus that Sartre understands man — a creature *condemned* to be free. Antoine Roquentin, in *The Nausea*, suffers from metaphysical disgust. His consciousness is like a decayed trap door through which the sordid impressions of his world endlessly sift. Nothing happens in his life, nothing begins or ends; Phenomena merely change, and Things, grotesque, obdurate, and unnamable, simply exist. Roquentin thinks: "I have only my body: a man entirely alone, with his lonely body, cannot indulge in memories; they pass through him. I shouldn't complain: all I wanted was to be free." [24] Thinking is his game, the famous Cartesian proof of existence his plaything. In Kafka's work, as Erich Heller perceived, a cursed Intelligence asserts its omnipresence; the Cartesian formula becomes, "I think, and therefore I am not." [25] Such negation of being is inadmissible to Sartre; the proper formula should read: "My thought is *me*. . . . At this very moment — it's frightful — if I exist, it is because I am horrified at existing." [26] The change is less of an improvement than it may seem. For as Roquentin comes to believe, existence is nothing if not superfluous. Everything is *de trop*, everything is rooted in the Absurd, the irreducible condition of all reality. Man, we see, is not only a clown or a transient compromise, he is a contingency of existence. The way to true being, seldom realized, lies through Nausea.

Sartre's doctrine that existence precedes essence, carried to its atheistic conclusion, defines no limit to the idea of freedom and gives no value to the concept of being. Camus, a far more accomplished artist if not a more systematic thinker, starts with his "absurdist" philosophy of man and reaches, in *The Rebel* and *The Fall*, a more complex awareness of freedom. In his early novel, *The Stranger*, Meursault surrenders to the absurd, the destructive element, and loses his life, it seems, without ever finding it. In the following novel, *The Plague*, a small light of hope, even of redemption, flickers through the night of human victimization. Doctor Rieux says: "All I maintain is that on this earth there are pestilences and there are victims, and it's up to us, as far as possible, not to join forces with the pestilences. . . . I decided to take, in every predicament, the victim's side, so as to reduce the damage done. Among them, I can at least try to understand how one attains to the third

---

[24] Jean-Paul Sartre, *Nausea* (Norfolk, Conn., n.d.), p. 91.
[25] Erich Heller, *The Disinherited Mind* (New York, 1957), p. 202.
[26] *Nausea*, pp. 135f.

category: in other words, to peace."[27] To join the victims is an act of rebellion against and alienation from the prevalent norm. But such an act is never purely nugatory. "Rebellion," Camus wrote, "though apparently negative, since it creates nothing, is profoundly positive in that it reveals the part of man which must always be defended."[28] Rebellion is therefore an aspiration to order, a means of lifting pain and evil from personal to collective experience. For the rebel-victim, the Cartesian argument par excellence is: "I rebel — therefore *we* exist [italics mine]."[29]

II

The problem of the anti-hero is essentially one of identity. His search is for existential fulfillment, that is, for freedom and self-definition. What he hopes to find is a position he can take within himself. Society may modulate his awareness of his situation, but only existence determines his stand. The recoil of the modern self is its way of taking a stand. The retreat weakens its involvement in the living world. It leads it in the ways of violence and alienation, augments its sense of guilt and absurdity, and affords it no objective standard for evaluating the worth of human action. But living in the world exclusively, living in what Ortega Y Gasset has called the Other, is also brutish and deadening. Complete immersion in the otherness of things is a ghastlier form of alienation: it is alienation from the self. "Without a strategic retreat into the self," Ortega rightly notes, "without vigilant thought, human life is impossible."[30] It is precisely in fear of the Other — total loss of selfhood — that the modern conscience has fallen back on its internal resources. The schizophrenic goes too far in that direction, the rebel-victim remains in the field of our vision.

Camus' statement, "I rebel — therefore we exist," brings to surface a dialectic that has been implicit in all the works we have viewed. In its naked form, the dialectic can be seen as an interplay between the essential Yes and the radical No, two piercing utterances beyond which the human voice cannot rise. Such utterances may sometimes blend. It is only silence they equally abhor. In the modern novel, man seems to overcome the contradictions of his experience, its destructive or demonic

27 Albert Camus, *The Plague* (Paris, 1948), p. 229.
28 *The Rebel*, p. 19.
29 *ibid.*, p. 22.
30 Ortega Y Gasset, *The Dehumanization of Art* (New York, 1956), p. 185.

element, by assuming the role of the anti-hero, the rebel-victim. The rebel denies without saying No to life, the victim succumbs without saying Yes to oppression. Both acts are, in a sense, identical: they affirm the human against the nonhuman. The figure of modern man, when he chooses to assert his full manhood, always bears the brave indissoluble aspects of Prometheus and Sisyphus — the eternal rebel and the eternal victim. The paradox is resolved when man cries, in the ringing words of Jaspers, "Although I am an anvil, as a hammer I can consummate what I must suffer." [31] Sparks from the same anvil were struck when Christ said to his disciples, "For whosoever will save his life shall lose it; and whosoever will lose his life for my sake shall find it." [32]

The condition of modern life may not be more desperate, as relativists sapiently remind us, than those which prevailed in any earlier age. Men, as usual, like to exaggerate their predicament to convince themselves, if nothing else, that they are still alive. All this is beside the point. It is certainly not the wretchedness of modern existence that we have sought to illustrate in this chapter, but rather man's peculiar awareness of his own situation. This awareness is both critical and adverse. The spirit of recoil in modern literature continues to affirm itself despite all our bounties.

The figure of the rebel-victim, however, represents but a single incarnation of the eternal dialectic between the primary Yes and primary No. He is man's answer to the invitation that he abolish himself. But the world has traditionally extended another invitation to the self: the invitation to become an honorable part of it, to become *initiated*. The initiate is the second major incarnation of the dialectic between affirmation and denial. His response is the other major response to experience. And his chosen home is the land which was once full of promises: America.

It may have been possible to distinguish clearly between Europe and America in the time of Whitman and Emerson. Today we lack the confidence such clarity requires. Uncle Sam, never young, is hoary as ever. Europe, we think, has been in America from the beginning; and is not Europe being taken over by America in our days? (Mark Twain noted, more than half a century ago, how Europe was already beginning to emulate American social habits.) Offhand, it may seem right to consider the idea of victimization in the context of European experience,

---

[31] Karl Jaspers, *Man in the Modern Age* (New York, 1957), p. 205.
[32] *Matthew* 16:25.

and natural to look for the idea of initiation in America. Such a view has more elegance than truth to recommend it.

America is not Europe and it is not the self-begotten country it once conceived itself to be. The contemporary American novel is part of the contemporary world, which is perhaps more uniform than any period since the Middle Ages. It is also the fruit of a flourishing native tradition. America has known *both* innocence and guilt, has evolved the patterns both of initiation and defeat in a unique ratio. The American novel comes to contemporary experience from a road Europe did not take, and its vision of the self in recoil is enriched by a vision Europe did not share. What we have observed in this chapter is a dominant image of the modern self. What remains to be seen is the American form of that image, personified by the *converging figures of the initiate and the victim.*

ROLLO MAY
the man who was put in a cage

What a piece of work is man! how noble in reason! how infinite in faculty! in form and moving how express and admirable! ... The paragon of animals!
—SHAKESPEARE, Hamlet

We have quite a few discrete pieces of information these days about what happens to a person when he is deprived of this or that element of freedom. We have our studies of sensory deprivation and of how a person reacts when put in different kinds of authoritarian atmosphere, and so on. But recently I have been wondering what pattern would emerge if we put these various pieces of knowledge together. In short, what would happen to a living, whole person if his total freedom — or as nearly total as we can imagine — were taken away? In the course of these reflections, a parable took form in my mind.

The story begins with a king who, while standing in reverie at the window of his palace one evening, happened to notice a man in the town square below. He was apparently an average man, walking home at night, who had taken the same route five nights a week for many years. The king followed this man in his imagination — pictured him arriving home, perfunctorily kissing his wife, eating his late meal, inquiring whether everything was all right with the children, reading the paper, going to bed, perhaps engaging in the sex relation with his wife or perhaps not, sleeping, and getting up and going off to work again the next day.

And a sudden curiosity seized the king, which for a moment banished his fatigue: "I wonder what would happen if a man were kept in a cage, like the animals at the zoo?" His curiosity was perhaps in some ways not unlike that of the first surgeons who wondered what it would be like to perform a lobotomy on the human brain.

So the next day the king called in a psychologist, told him of his idea, and invited him to observe the experiment. When the psychologist demurred saying, "It's an unthinkable thing to keep a man in a cage," the monarch replied that many rulers had in effect, if not literally, done so, from the time of the Romans through Genghis Khan down to Hitler and the totalitarian leaders; so why not find out scientifically what would happen? Furthermore, added the king, he had made up his mind to do it whether the psychologist took part or not; he had already gotten the Greater Social Research Foundation to give a large sum of money for the experiment, and why let that money go to waste? By this time the psychologist also was feeling within himself a great curiosity about what would happen if a man were kept in a cage.

And so the next day the king caused a cage to be brought from the zoo — a large cage that had been occupied by a lion when it was new, then later by a tiger; just recently it had been the home of a hyena who died the previous week. The cage was put in an inner private court in the palace grounds, and the average man whom the king had seen from the window was brought and placed therein. The psychologist, with his Rorschach and Wechsler-Bellevue tests in his brief case to administer at some appropriate moment, sat down outside the cage.

At first the man was simply bewildered, and he kept saying to the psychologist, "I have to catch the tram, I have to get to work, look what time it is, I'll be late for work!" But later on in the afternoon the man began soberly to realize what was up, and then he protested vehemently, "The king can't do this to me! It is unjust! It's against the law." His voice was strong, and his eyes full of anger. The psychologist liked the man for his anger, and he became vaguely aware that this was a mood he had encountered often in people he worked with in his clinic. "Yes," he realized, "this anger is the attitude of people who — like the healthy adolescents of any era — want to fight what's wrong, who protest directly against it. When people come to the clinic in this mood, it is good — they can be helped."

During the rest of the week the man continued his vehement protests. When the king walked by the cage, as he did every day, the man made his protests directly to the monarch.

But the king answered, "Look here, you are getting plenty of food, you have a good bed, and you don't have to work. We take good care of you; so why are you objecting?"

After some days had passed, the man's protests lessened and then ceased. He was silent in his cage, generally refusing to talk. But the psychologist could see hatred glowing in his eyes. When he did exchange a few words, they were short, definite words uttered in the strong, vibrant, but calm voice of the person who hates and knows whom he hates.

Whenever the king walked into the courtyard, there was a deep fire in the man's eyes. The psychologist thought, "This must be the way people act when they are first conquered." He remembered that he had also seen that expression of the eyes and heard that tone of voice in many patients at his clinic: the adolescent who had been unjustly accused at home or in school and could do nothing about it; the college student who was required by public and campus opinion to be a star on the gridiron, but was required by his professors to pass courses he could not prepare for if he were to be successful in football — and who was then expelled from college for the cheating that resulted. And the psychologist, looking at the active hatred in the man's eyes, thought, "It is still good; a person who has this fight in him can be helped."

Every day the king, as he walked through the courtyard, kept reminding the man in the cage that he was given food and shelter and taken good care of, so why did he not like it? And the psychologist noticed that, whereas at first the man had been entirely impervious to the king's statements, it now seemed more and more that he was pausing for a moment after the king's speech — for a second the hatred was postponed from returning to his eyes — as though he were asking himself if what the king said were possibly true.

And after a few weeks more, the man began to discuss with the psychologist how it was a useful thing that a man is given food and shelter; and how man had to live by his fate in any case, and the part of wisdom was to accept fate. He soon was developing an extensive theory about security and the acceptance of fate, which sounded to the psychologist very much like the philosophical theories that Rosenberg and others worked out for the fascists in Germany. He was very voluble during this period, talking at length, although the talk was mostly a monologue. The psychologist noticed that his voice was flat and hollow as he talked, like the voice of people in TV previews who make an effort to look you in the eye and try hard to sound sincere as they tell you that you should see the program they are advertising, or the announcers on the radio who are paid to persuade you that you should like high-brow music.

And the psychologist also noticed that now the corners of the man's mouth always turned down, as though he were in some gigantic pout. Then the psychologist suddenly remembered: this was like the middle-aged, middle-class people who came to his clinic, the respectable bourgeois people who went to church and lived morally but who were always full of resentment, as though everything they did was conceived, born, and nursed in resentment. It reminded the psychologist of Nietzsche's saying that the middle class was consumed with resentment. He then for the first time began to be seriously worried about the man in the cage, for he knew that once resentment gets a firm start and becomes well rationalized and structuralized, it may become like cancer. When the person no longer knows whom he hates, he is much harder to help.

During this period the Greater Social Research Foundation had a board of trustees meeting, and they decided that since they were expending a fund to keep a man supported in a cage, it would look better if representatives of the Foundation at least visited the experiment. So a group of people, consisting of two professors and a few graduate students, came in one day to look at the man in the cage. One of the professors then proceeded to lecture to the group about the relation of the autonomic nervous system and the secretions of the ductless glands to human existence in a cage. But it occurred to the other professor that the verbal communications of the victim himself might just possibly be interesting, so he asked the man how he felt about living in a cage. The man was friendly toward the professors and students and explained to them that he had chosen this way of life, that there were great values in security and in being taken care of, that they would of course see how sensible this course was, and so on.

"How strange!" thought the psychologist, "and how pathetic; why is it he struggles so hard to get them to approve his way of life?"

In the succeeding days when the king walked through the courtyard, the man fawned upon him from behind the bars in his cage and thanked him for the food and shelter. But when the king was not in the yard and the man was not aware that the psychologist was present, his expression was quite different — sullen and morose. When his food was handed to him through the bars by the keeper, the man would often drop the dishes or dump over the water and then would be embarrassed because of his stupidity and clumsiness. His conversation became increasingly one-tracked; and instead of the involved philosophical theories about the value of being taken care of, he had gotten down to simple sentences such as "It is fate," which he would say over and over again, or he would just mumble to himself, "It is." The psychologist was surprised to find that the man should now be so clumsy as to drop his food, or so stupid as to talk in those barren sentences, for he knew from his tests that the man had originally been of good average intelligence. Then it dawned upon the psychologist that this was the kind of behavior he had observed in some anthropological studies among the Negroes in the South — people who had been forced to kiss the hand that fed and enslaved them, who could no longer either hate or rebel. The man in the cage took more and more to simply sitting all day long in the sun as it came through the bars, his only movement being to shift his position from time to time from morning through the afternoon.

It was hard to say just when the last phase set in. But the psychologist became aware that the man's face now seemed to have no particular expression; his smile was no longer fawning, but simply empty and meaningless, like the grimace a baby makes when there is gas on its stomach. The man ate his food and exchanged a few sentences with the psychologist from time to time; but his eyes were distant and vague, and though he looked at the psychologist, it seemed that he never really *saw* him.

And now the man, in his desultory conversations, never used the word "I" any more. He had accepted the cage. He had no anger, no hate, no rationalizations. But he was now insane.

The night the psychologist realized this, he sat in his apartment trying to write a concluding report. But it was very difficult for him to summon up words, for he felt within himself a great emptiness. He kept trying to reassure himself with the words, "They say that nothing is ever lost, that matter is merely changed to energy and back again." But he could not help feeling that something *had* been lost, that something had gone out of the universe in this experiment.

He finally went to bed with his report unfinished. But he could not sleep; there was a gnawing within him which, in less rational and scientific ages, would have been called a conscience. Why didn't I tell the king that this is the one experiment that no man can do — or at least why didn't I shout that I would have nothing to do with the whole bloody business? Of course, the king would have dismissed me, the foundations would never have granted me any more money, and at the clinic they would have said that I was not a real scientist. But maybe one could farm in the mountains and make a living, and maybe one could paint or write something that would make future men happier and more free. . . .

But he realized that these musings were, at least at the moment, unrealistic, and he tried to pull himself back to reality. All he could get, however, was this feeling of emptiness within himself, and the words, "Something has been taken out of the universe, and there is left only a void."

Finally he dropped off to sleep. Some time later, in the small hours of the morning, he was awakened by a startling dream. A crowd of people had gathered, in the dream, in front of the cage in the courtyard, and the man in the cage — no longer inert and vacuous — was shouting through the bars of the cage in impassioned oratory. "It is not only I whose freedom is taken away!" he was crying. "When the king puts me or any man in a cage, the freedom of each of you is taken away also. The king must go!" The people began to chant, "The king must go!" and they seized and broke out the iron bars of the cage, and wielded them for weapons as they charged the palace.

The psychologist awoke, filled by the dream with a great feeling of hope and joy — an experience of hope and joy probably not unlike that experienced by the free men of England when they forced King John to sign the Magna Charta. But not for nothing had the psychologist had an orthodox analysis in the course of his training, and as he lay surrounded by this aura of happiness, a voice spoke within him: "Aha, you had this dream to make yourself feel better; it's just a wish fulfillment."

"The hell it is!" said the psychologist as he climbed out of bed. "Maybe some dreams are to be acted on."

ROLLO MAY
freedom and responsibility reexamined

Yes! to this thought I hold with firm persistence;
The last result of wisdom stamps it true;
He only earns his freedom and existence
Who daily conquers them anew.
— GOETHE, Faust

The problems of freedom and responsibility are fundamental in a number of ways in counseling and psychotherapy. But we find ourselves in recent years caught in several pressing and critical dilemmas with respect to these issues. The dilemmas are part and parcel of the radical shift and transition of values in the last three or four decades in Western culture, particularly in America. It is, of course, not at all an accident that these are also exactly the decades when counseling, psychotherapy, and psychoanalysis have come to play such important roles in our society. For it is precisely the breakdown and radical transition of values in a society, causing the individuals in that society to founder in storm-shaken seas without solid mooring posts or even buoys and lighthouses which can be depended upon, that makes the professions of helping individuals so necessary.

Several "solutions" have arisen to the dilemmas we face in freedom and responsibility. I wish to cite some of these solutions which I believe to be inadequate, and then turn to what I hope will be a deeper examination of the problems of freedom and responsibility.

One inadequate solution was the assumption, popular a decade or two ago, that our task in counseling and therapy was simply to set the person "free," and, therefore, the values held by the therapist and the society had no part in the process. This assumption was bolstered and rationalized by the then popular definition of mental health as "freedom from anxiety." The therapists most under the influence of this assumption made a dogma out of never making a "moral judgment" and saw guilt as always neurotic and therefore a "feeling" that ought always to be relieved and gotten rid of in counseling and therapy. I recall that in my student days in psychoanalysis in the early 1940's it was argued by

competent and experienced analysts that whether or not the patient was
a gangster or a responsible member of society was no business of theirs
— their task was only to help him become free to do better whatever
he wished.

Probably most therapists had enough common sense and simple
humanity never to follow out such a naive assumption to its full implications. But the subtle effects of the "values-don't-matter" assumption
were in my judgment harmful and are in part responsible for the later
reactions against psychoanalysis and counseling. One harmful effect was
the implication that sexuality was, as Kinsey phrased it, a matter of
"release" on a "sexual object." The accent upon sexual promiscuity —
which developed paradoxically enough into a new dogma that to be
healthy you had to be completely permissive sexually — led to new
anxiety and insecurity in the whole area of sexual behavior among our
contemporaries. The plethora of early marriages we have been witnessing among college students in the past decade seems to me to be,
at least in part, a reaction to the insecurity, anxiety, and loneliness involved in the doctrine of sexual promiscuity. For the "full freedom"
assumption we are describing actually separates and alienates the person from his world, removes whatever structure he had to act within or
against, and leaves him with no guideposts in a lonely, worldless
existence.

The errors in the "full freedom" assumption were not only that it
led to increase of anxiety among counselees and patients, but also that
it was subtly dishonest. For no matter how much the therapist or
counselor might protest that he assumed no values in his practice,
the patient or counselee knew, even if he did not dare to express his
knowledge, that the protestation was not true; and that the therapist
was smuggling in his own values the more perniciously in the very
fact of not admitting them.

Another "solution" offered to our dilemma arose in the last decade
as a reaction to the one mentioned above. This is the *distrust of freedom* present so much in the psychological and psychiatric discussions
around us these days. It is an overemphasis on "responsibility," but
put in the form of moral and social control of the other person. The
contemporary trends toward conformism and the tremendous pressures toward standardization which inevitably accompany television
and mass communication give impetus to this tendency toward control. William H. Whyte in his *Organization Man* is quite accurate

in his pithy cautions to psychologists and psychiatrists at these points. He succinctly states that modern man's enemies may turn out to be "mild looking groups of therapists who . . . would be doing what they did to help you." He refers to the inevitable tendency to use the social ethic of our particular historical period. And thus the very process of helping people may actually make them more conformist and destroy individuality.

Several other social critics have pointed out recently that we are witnessing the birth in psychiatry and psychology of a "new puritanism" and new emphasis on "behavior control." The new puritanism has until recently been most evident in psychiatry, but now emphases on moralism have come from psychologists in the therapeutic field. Whereas a plethora of books came off the psychiatric presses two decades ago adjuring you to "release your sexual tensions" and "express yourself fully," in the last five years the books tell us "Divorce Won't Help" and advise us that "monogamy is the new dogma of science." The new moralism among psychologists is illustrated by the works on therapy of Hobart Mowrer and of Perry London, and by what is termed "reality therapy."[1] As I shall indicate below, I believe that both the exaggerated freedom solution and the identification of therapy and counseling with the moral and social controls of the society are inadequate.

As the new puritanism is represented in psychiatry and psychotherapy, the new emphasis upon "control of the mind and personality," as a denial of the freedom of the person, is perhaps most present in academic psychology. This phase of the dilemma is graphically illustrated by an exchange between Carl Rogers and B. F. Skinner,

[1] See the review by Thomas Szasz of the book *Reality Therapy* by William Glasser, M.D. Dr. Szasz points out that Dr. Glasser relabels everything now called "mental illness" as "irresponsibility." Since, then, the distinction is not made between the moral standards of the patient and those of the therapist, the stage is set for the values of the therapist to be enforced upon the patient at worst, and at best the mores of society to be handed over to the patient under the caption of "adjustment" and "mental health." I understand Dr. Glasser's therapy was worked out originally in his function as psychiatrist in an institution for delinquent girls. This makes sense: the psychopathic personality is the one clinical type which is agreed to be without "conscience" to begin with, and cannot be reached without developing in the patient some social sense. But to extend this type of therapy to every kind of patient is hopelessly to confuse the whole problem of neurosis and mental illness, and to make the therapist society's agent for the destruction of the patient's autonomy, freedom, inner responsibility, and passion.

which I wish to cite. In connection with the most extreme form of this in the operant conditioning of Skinner, Rogers writes:

> Along with the development of technology has gone an underlying philosophy of rigid determinism as illustrated by a brief exchange which I had with Professor B. F. Skinner of Harvard at a recent conference. A paper given by Dr. Skinner led me to direct these remarks to him. "From what I understood Dr. Skinner to say, it is his understanding that though he might have thought he chose to come to this meeting, might have thought he had a purpose in giving his speech, such thoughts are really illusory. He actually made certain marks on paper and emitted certain sounds here simply because his genetic make-up and his past environment had operantly conditioned his behavior in such a way that it was rewarding to make these sounds, and that he as a person doesn't enter into this. In fact if I get his thinking correctly, from his strictly scientific point of view, he, as a person, doesn't exist." In his reply Dr. Skinner said that he would not go into the question of whether he had any choice in the matter (presumably because the whole issue is illusory) but stated, "I do accept your characterization of my own presence here." I do not need to labor the point that for Dr. Skinner the concept of "learning to be free" would be quite meaningless.[2]

We could of course multiply our illustrations many times over to support the point that the issues of freedom and responsibility, choice and determinism, are central and critical in American psychology.

I wish to begin my reexamination of freedom and responsibility by considering this present emphasis upon control. The phrases "control of behavior" and "control of the mind and personality," which I shall use somewhat synonymously in this discussion, raise disquieting questions. Control implies control *by* someone or something. *Who* would control the mind? The person himself? In that case some aspect of his mind or self would be doing the controlling. But this view is not acceptable, for we then find ourselves assuming a fragmented view of the self which is scarcely tenable and only makes our problem more confused. Or do we mean society controls the mind? But society is simply made up of us persons whose "minds" are assumedly to be controlled.

Does the phrase mean that some special group of us — psychiatrists,

[2] Carl Rogers, "Learning to be Free," paper presented at Conference on Evolutionary Theory and Human Progress: Conference C, The Individual and the Design of Culture, Dec. 2-14, 1960. Mimeographed transcription, pp. 15-16, 79.

psychologists, or other scientists — will control the mind, meaning other people's minds? Unfortunately, I think this is the unscrutinized subconscious assumption of many people who use the phrase, namely, that their group will do the controlling, as though *we* knew how the minds of *others* should be controlled. Recently I participated in an emergency conference of psychiatrists and psychologists concerning the pressing problem of war and peace. Several of the papers at the conference proposed that psychiatrists and psychologists be sent to trouble spots in the world, interview diplomats around the globe and report back to their respective state departments their findings so that statesmen with paranoid tendencies and serious maladjustments will be recalled. The trouble with this plan is that such "diagnoses," if they may be called that, always presuppose some criteria and goals as the basis on which you judge. Fortunately, there seems to be no chance whatever that any state department would ever permit any group to arrogate to itself this kind of control. I say fortunately, because there is no reason to believe that the judgments with respect to the goals of life are any better among psychiatrists and psychologists as a group than among philosophers or statesmen themselves, or theologians, writers, or artists.

We note that the word "goals" has now crept into our discussion. It is impossible to keep it out. For control always implies not only control *by* something but *for* something. For what purposes, which means on the basis of which *values,* will the mind be controlled and toward what ends will this control be directed? This disconcerting question has in the past been generally sloughed over in psychological discussions with the rejoinder that as scientists we deal only with means, not goals. But is this not a highly dubious and possibly dangerous attitude? And is not this separation of means and ends even part of the reason for our predicament in twentieth-century civilization, namely, that we possess such powerful means of controlling nature and ourselves — drugs, atomic power, etc. — but we have not kept pace in analyzing what we are controlling for?

Or if we accept the proposal sometimes made in psychological conferences that our computers can set our goals, our technicians determine our policies, we are in my judgment making the most serious error of all. For we are abdicating in the face of our lack of goals and values. The one thing our computers cannot tell us is what our goals ought to be. In this day when we and all sensitive contemporary people are so confused and anxious, it is not surprising we tend to abdicate in favor of the machine. We then tend more and more to ask only the

questions the machine can answer, we teach more and more only the
things the machine can teach, and limit our research to the quantitative
work the machines can do. There then is bound to emerge a real and
inexorable tendency to make our image of man over into the image of
the very machine by which we study and control him.

We must seek, I submit, a new and deeper understanding of freedom which will stand even in a world in which exist such vast and
overwhelming pressures toward control. To do this we must begin,
in my judgment, with the question of what are the distinguishing
characteristics of this being, man, whom we are trying to understand.

A central distinguishing characteristic, we have seen, is man's capacity to be aware of himself as having a world and being interre-
lated with it. Now weighing the long-term future consequences of
his acts — which we have also seen as a capacity of man — is a *social*
act and inevitably implies value-judgments. Hence the concepts of
mind and personality imply the distinctively *social-historical* development which characterizes human beings. Man . . . is not merely pushed
blindly by the march of history, is not *just* the product of history (as
all animals are), but he has the capacity to be self-aware of his history.
He can exercise selectivity toward history, can adapt himself to parts
of it, can change other parts, and within limits mold history in self-
chosen directions. This capacity to transcend the immediate situation
and bring the time determinant into learning gives human behavior
its distinctive flexibility and freedom.

We find, lo and behold, that in defining mind and personality we
have also been talking about *freedom*. For is not man's capacity to
be conscious of himself as the experiencing individual actually also
the psychological basis of human freedom? Hegel puts our point in
one powerful sentence: "The history of the world is none other than
the progress of the consciousness of freedom."

The data we get from our work with patients in psychotherapy seem
to me clearly to support my thesis. When people come for therapy,
they typically describe themselves as "driven," unable to know or
choose what they want, and they experience various degrees of dissatisfaction, unhappiness, conflict, and despair. What we find as we begin
working with them is that they have blocked off large areas of awareness, are unable to feel or be aware of what their feelings mean in
relation to the world. They may think they feel love when actually
they only feel sex; or they think they feel sex when what they actually

wish is to be nursed at mother's breast. They will often say in one way or another: "I don't know what I feel; I don't know who I am." In Freud's terms, they have "repressed" significant experiences and capacities of all sorts. The symptomatic results are the wide gamut of conflicts, anxiety, panic, and depression.

At the beginning of therapy, thus, they present the picture of *lack* of freedom. The progress of therapy can be gauged in terms of the increase of the patient's capacity to experience the fact he is the one who *has* this world and can be aware of it and move in it.[3] One could define mental health, from one side, as the capacity to be aware of the gap between stimulus and response, together with the capacity to use this gap constructively. Thus, mental health, in my judgment, is on the opposite side of the spectrum from "conditioning" and "control." The progress of therapy can be measured in terms of the progress of "consciousness of freedom."

Self implies world, and world, self; each concept — or experience — requires the other. Now, contrary to the usual assumption, these vary upward and downward on the scale together: broadly speaking, the more awareness of self, the more awareness of world, and vice versa. Patients on the verge of psychosis will often reveal overwhelming anxiety as the panic at losing awareness of themselves and their world simultaneously. To lose one's self is to lose one's world, and vice versa.

This inseparable relation of self and world also implies *responsibility*. The term means "responding," "response to." I cannot, in other words, become a self except as I am engaged continuously in *responding* to the world of which I am a part.

What is exceedingly interesting here is that the patient moves *toward* freedom and responsibility in his living as he becomes more conscious of the *deterministic* experiences in his life. That is, as he explores and assimilates how he was rejected or overprotected or hated as a child, how his repressed bodily needs drive him, how his personal history as a member of a minority group, let us say, conditions his development, and even as he becomes more conscious of his being a member of Western culture at a particular traumatic moment in the historical evolution of that society, he finds his margin of freedom likewise enlarged. As he becomes more conscious of the infinite deterministic forces in his life, he becomes more free.

The implications of this point are very significant. *Freedom* is thus

---

[3] Carl Rogers has presented empirical studies which demonstrate this point.

not the opposite to determinism. Freedom is the individual's capacity *to know that he is the determined one*, to pause between stimulus and response and thus to throw his weight, however slight it may be, on the side of one particular response among several possible ones.

Freedom is thus also not anarchy: the beatniks are a symbolic protest against the aridity of our mechanistic society, not an expression of freedom. Freedom can never be separated from responsibility.

Let us now turn to another source of data bearing on our problem. These data are dramatic and vivid but also very important — the experiences of individuals in imprisonment and concentration camps. One might well think that talking about "consciousness of freedom" in such places of terrible travesty on human dignity would be sheer sentimentality. But we find just the opposite may be the case.

Christopher Burney, a young British secret service officer, was dropped behind enemy lines during World War II and captured by the Germans. He was put in solitary confinement, without a book, pencil, or sheet of paper, for eighteen months. In his six-by-six cell, Burney decided that each day he would review in his mind lesson after lesson he had studied in school and college. He worked through theorems in geometry, the thought of Spinoza and other philosophers, outlined in his mind the literature he had read, and so on. In his book *Solitary Confinement* he demonstrates how this "freedom of the mind," as he called it, kept him sane for the eighteen solitary months and made his survival possible.

From the horrors of the Dachau concentration camp, Dr. Bruno Bettleheim reports that he learned a similar lesson. When he first was thrown into this camp, Bettleheim was too weak to swallow food. But an "old prisoner," one who had been there four years, said to him:

> Listen you, make up your mind: do you want to live or do you want to die? If you don't care, don't eat the stuff. But if you want to live, there's only one way: make up your mind to eat whenever and whatever you can, never mind how disgusting. Whenever you have a chance, defecate, so you'll be sure your body works. And whenever you have a minute, don't blabber, read by yourself, or flop down and sleep.

Bettleheim goes on to say, "What was implied was the necessity, for survival, to carve out, against the greatest of odds, some areas of freedom of action and thought, however insignificant." In his book *The Informed Heart* Bettleheim concludes that in the worst of circumstances, the individual must find and hold on to his right to know and act, preserve his "consciousness of freedom," if he is to survive.

I wish now to draw some principles concerning the psychological bases of freedom from this discussion. First, *freedom is a quality of action of the centered self.* We have indicated above that it makes no sense to speak of "part" of the mind or self controlling the rest of the mind. Nor does it make sense to speak, as our Victorian fathers did, of the "will" controlling the mind, or as our Freudian colleagues do, of the "ego" as the seat of freedom and autonomy. David Rapaport has written an essay entitled "The Autonomy of the Ego" as part of the recent developments in Freudianism which seek to include some margin of freedom. Jung has a chapter in one of his books entitled "The Autonomy (or Freedom) of the Unconscious." Or someone might, following Walter B. Cannon's *Wisdom of the Body,* write on "the autonomy of the body." Each has a partial truth; but is not each also fundamentally wrong? For neither the "ego" nor the "unconscious" nor the body can be autonomous or free by itself.

Freedom by its very nature can be located only in the self acting as the totality, the "centered self."[4] Consciousness is the experience of the self acting from its center. The individual's neuromuscular apparatus, his past genetic experience, his dreams, and the infinite host of other more or less deterministic aspects of his experience as a living organism are related in their various ways to this centered act and can only be understood in this relationship.

Certainly one reason for the confusion about freedom in psychology, and a chief reason why psychological studies in the past have confused and covered up rather than revealed the meaning of freedom, is precisely that they have fragmented the person, chopping him up into "stimuli" and "responses" or into "id, ego, superego." We destroy his centeredness by these methods even before we start to study him. If we are to discover anything about psychological freedom in our research, we obviously need some approach like Gordon Allport's "statistics of the single individual," or idiographic method. Or, as I would propose, methods relying on *internal consistency* in the individual and *significant patterning* in contrast to the fragmentation.

The second principle is *freedom always involves social responsibility.* We found in our definition of mind above — the capacity to transcend the immediate situation in time and space and think in long-term consequences — that we could not escape bringing in the social pole

[4] This concept comes from and is developed in the writing of Paul Tillich.

of mind. Subjective "mind" and objective "world" are inseparable correlates.

This principle brings in the *limits* of freedom. Freedom is not license nor ever simply "doing as one pleases." Indeed such living by whim or the state of one's digestion is in a sense the exact opposite to the acting of the centered self we have been talking about. Freedom is limited by the fact that the self always exists in a world (a society, culture) and has a dialectical relation to that world. Abram Kardiner has pointed out in his study of Plainville, U.S.A., that the people in this small mid-western town subscribed "in the main to the American credo of vertical mobility and believe that a man can become anything he wants to. Actually opportunities are very limited for them . . . even if they go away."[5] The error in the Plainville credo, as in most of our popularized ideas of freedom, is that they are externalized — they see the self acting on the world, rather than the self existing in a dialectical relationship *with* the world.

A human being's freedom is limited by his body, by illness, by the fact that he dies, by the limits of his intelligence, by social controls, *ad infinitum*. Bettleheim could not change the inhumanity of the concentration camp, but he could become conscious that he was the one enduring these inhumanities; and then already he has partly transcended them. The capacity consciously to confront limits, normal or barbaric as they may be, is already an act of freedom and liberates one to some extent from self-crippling resentment.

Our third principle is *freedom requires the capacity to accept, bear and live constructively with anxiety*. I refer of course to the *normal* anxiety all of us experience at every step in our psychological growth as well as in this upset contemporary world. For some years I have believed that the popular definition of mental health as "freedom from anxiety" is wrong. It has played into the tendencies of the individual to surrender his originality, take on "protective coloring," and conform in the hope of gaining peace of mind. This emphasis on freedom *from* anxiety has actually tended to undermine freedom.

All of us, to be sure, are in favor of freedom from *neurotic* anxiety — the kind which blocks people's awareness and causes them to panic or in other ways to act blindly and destructively. But neurotic anxiety is simply the long-term result of unfaced normal anxiety. When the

[5] Abram Kardiner, *The Psychological Frontiers of Society*, Columbia University Press, New York, 1945, p. 4.

developing individual, for example, confronts the crisis of weaning, at a later stage the separation from parents in going off to school, then the emergence of sexual problems in the teens, and finds he cannot deal with the anxiety involved but needs to repress it, he has begun the train of events that ultimately results in neurotic anxiety. The same is true with us adults facing the imminence of thermonuclear war: if we repress our normal anxiety in the face of this terrible possibility, we shall develop neurotic anxiety with its various symptoms.

To be free means to face and bear anxiety; to run away from anxiety means automatically to surrender one's freedom. Demagogues throughout history have used the latter strategy — the subjecting of a people to continuous unbearable anxiety — as a method of forcing them to surrender their freedom. The people may then accept virtual slavery in the hope of getting rid of anxiety.

A caution arises here about the use of drugs to reduce anxiety. The use of tranquilizers (except in cases where the patient's anxiety is unbearable, causes destructive regression, or renders him inaccessible to treatment) is highly dubious. We should face the fact that in taking away the person's anxiety, we also take away his opportunity to learn; we take away some of his resources. Anxiety is the sign of inner conflict, and so long as there is conflict, some resolution on a higher level of consciousness is possible. "Anxiety is our best teacher," Kierkegaard said. "He therefore who has learned rightly to be anxious has learned the most important thing."

Freedom is something you grow into. I question the oversimplified statement that we are "born free," except in terms of potentialities. I prefer, rather, to emphasize Goethe's insight in *Faust*, as quoted in the epigraph that heads this chapter.

Let me speak of my own impressionistic picture of the free man. The free man is conscious of his right to have some part in the decisions of his social group or nation which affect him; he actualizes this consciousness by affirming the decisions, or if he disagrees, by registering his protest for the sake of a better decision next time. The free man has respect for rational authority, both that of history and that of his fellowmen who may have beliefs different from his own. The free man is responsible, in that he can think and act for the long-term welfare of the group. He has esteem for himself as an individual of worth and dignity — not the least of the sources of this dignity being his knowing himself to be a free man. He is able, if need be, to stand alone, like Thoreau — willing to be a minority of one when basic principles are at stake. And perhaps most important of all in our day, the free man is able to accept the anxiety which is inevitable in our shaken world and to turn this anxiety to constructive use as motivation toward greater "consciousness of freedom." . . .

J. L. SIMMONS
BARRY WINOGRAD
the hang-loose ethic

The happenings described in the [previous chapter of *It's Happening: A Portrait of the Youth Scene Today*] are the concrete manifestations of an emerging new ethos in American society, which seems most aptly called "the hang-loose ethic." It is cool and irreverent and it reflects a good deal of disaffection toward many of our more traditional roots. For this reason, it is perhaps more worrisome to parents, educators, and officials than the mere wildness or deviant flirtations of youth.

A barefooted man with a beard and a surplus Navy jacket that had "Love IS" written on the back of it was walking down the main street of a small midwestern city, digging the sunlight and thinking that the heat was really pleasant when you got out into it. A group of high school kids rode by him in a car and began shouting to him. "Hey beatnik." "Hey, you're high man." "What color's your dingy?" And, from one of the less imaginative boys, "Why don't you go fly a kite?"

The man looked up musingly, jaywalked across the street to a dime store, bought a kite and some luminous paint and two thousand feet of string. He took them to his battered car and drove around the adjacent suburbs for awhile, rounding up kids to fly the kite with him. Some parents looked him over and scurried their kids away, shaking their heads about the invasion of perverts; others looked into his face and saw nothing evil there, so consented. They drove to the top of a hill overlooking the town, painted the kite with bright psychedelic colors, sent it up and flew it all afternoon. Toward sunset, they cut loose the

From *It's Happening: A Portrait of the Youth Scene Today* by J. L. Simmons and Barry Winograd, McNally and Loftin Publishers. Copyright © 1966 by J. L. Simmons and Barry Winograd. Reprinted by permission.

string and watched their *objet d'art* disappear into the aerial world above them.

The thing about this story is that the young man didn't turn upon his assailants and by opposing them become their likes. Nor did he go into a foetal crouch over a beer, pitying himself as a sensitive and misunderstood soul (which he is) and condemning the society which trains even its children to put down the unusual. He transcended the harassment, rather than succumbing to it by being roused to self-pity or anger.

The emerging ethic is hang-loose in a number of senses, but, its deep-running feature is that things once taken for granted as God-given or American Constitution-given — those basic premises about the world and the way it works — are no longer taken for granted or given automatic allegiance. In other words, many Americans are hanging a bit loose from traditional Americana.

This new ethos is still in the process of forming and emerging; the adherents themselves are mostly unaware of the credo they are participating in making and are already living by. For instance, if you went up to many of the likely young people about town and said, "Say, are you an adherent of the hang-loose ethic?", many of them would look at you oddly and wonder what the hell you were talking about.

Well, if this thing is still so amorphous and you can only speculate about it, and the supposed followers are hardly even aware of it, why bother?

Because we want to see what lies beneath the legion of different concrete happenings. A society can be portrayed in a number of different ways and each gives a different picture of what the society is. It can be done by sketching the material objects, the streets, the buildings, the childhood and adult toys. It can be done by describing the typical behavior, the activities, the rituals, the average life-course of an ordinary member. It can also be done by trying to ferret out the underlying ideology or ethos, which comes forth in a thousand and one different ways and which is the wellspring from which flows the other things, the toys, the scenes, the lives, the typical attitudes and responses. Our attempt to ferret out the ideology behind the happenings is an attempt, then, to dive beneath the trappings and veneers down to the basic world view of the people who are making them happen.

At first glance, it might seem as if the hang-loose ethic is the absence of any morality, that it rejects every ideology, that the followers have no rudder and no star except the swift gratification of all impulses. At a second glance it appears only as a bewildering melange of scenes in various locales. But upon closer examination, one can see that it does embody some values and some guiding principles which, although still ill-formed and vaguely expressed, shape the attitudes and actions of the followers. However, to convey a fuller picture of this ethos, we must sketch the previous American ethics from which it emerged.

Europeans and Americans of the past few centuries have been characterized by most writers as human beings who subscribed to and lived by what is called the Protestant Ethic. This Protestant Ethic was a way of life and a view of life which stressed the more somber virtues, like the quiet good feeling of a hard day's work well done, the idea that the good man always more than earned his pay, and a kind of fierce pragmatism in which the hard and fast, here and now, seeable, touchable, aspects of reality were the only things given the name of reality.

Another thing about the Protestant Ethic was a kind of positive moderatism. Moderation wasn't just a safe course between extremes; moderation was an optimum, positive, good in-and-of-itself thing. Moderation was raised almost to a first principle of ethics. It was a mandate on how to conduct your life.

Anything which veered very far from this somber dignity in oneself and one's accumulations was thought of as bad and suspect. We will see, for example, when we discuss "tripping" that whereas most of the world has regarded exceptional behavior that strays beyond the mundane with an awe combining wonder and terror, in the Western world the wonder has until very recently dropped away and it was suppressed as altogether dangerous. Western man neglected what other times and places made a good deal of, the positive aspects which exceptional experiences might have.

This moderatism carried over into virtually every aspect of the lives of the people. Even in religion and young love, anything smacking too much of mysticism was suspect. The West has relied mostly upon dogma rather than experience in its religious institutions and, despite our hungry romanticism, most of our marriages and other sexual liasons have been made largely by arrangement.

This Protestant Ethic seems to have characterized the majority of our forefathers although there was always a "lunatic" fringe and a subterranean stratum composed of those at the bottom of the social ladder and of outsiders. And, like all people everywhere, the adherents didn't entirely live up to their own ideals. But, the Protestants ran the schools and the courts and the country and the fringe was contained and circumscribed, largely kept at the fringe.

Then, as the decades passed and we moved into the present century, America began to undergo a secularization which involved not only a dwindling of the force of religion but also a dwindling of the force of the work ethic and the rather stiff personal code which surrounded it. Particularly in the mushrooming urban areas after the Second World War, something grew up which William F. Whyte termed "the Social Ethic."

The Social Ethic (or perhaps more aptly, the Sociable Ethic) was a kind of jocular, benign, superficial, "we're all in the same boat," good-will. But it shared many things with the Protestant Ethic from which it evolved under the impact of modern times. It was still taken for granted that getting ahead in the Establishment was the thing to do, and that the accumulation of material wealth was a good thing in and of itself. Whyte used the "organization man" living in the new suburbs as his prototypic example and he made a good argument that this was tending to become the overweening American ethos. Work and play, family and politics, each of these were supposed to be a good thing, a fun thing, a comfortable thing. The Sociable Ethic was a secularization of the Protestant ideology combined with a feeling of comfort and goodwill which is easy to generate in a luxuriant society such as ours.

Risk is minimized in the Sociable Ethic. All parties join in a collusion which reduces the chance of great failure and great success once you've been hooked into the system. Of course, there were some dark counter-themes in this portrait: those thirty percent of the people who were not in any real sense beneficiaries of the luxuriant system. And it certainly was not a comfortable place for them — it was as Baldwin has suggested, another country. This didn't just mean the Negro of the South; it also included most Northern Negroes, the uneducated, the abysmally poor, those who lacked the skills to sell themselves, to make themselves an attractive enough package to get recruited into the system.

But the majority of Americans were in it and were doing fairly well. And the continuities with the earlier ethic remained. There still existed a kind of blandness, a real distrust for the exceptional and the bizarre, and there still remained a real distrust for doing something, let's say, "just for kicks." We had in the fifties almost the Utopian culmination of the principle of moderation. Moderate in politics, moderate in work — not too much because it doesn't really pay, not too little because you might get dropped. Moderate in family which involved a kind of thing where you were moderately attached to your spouse and children and moderately concerned with their welfare and you were moderately unfaithful and moderately blasphemous. But you also gave a moderate allegiance to your family and your company and your country.

This was not a picture window nightmare. Most of those involved were probably moderately comfortable and moderately happy.

Does this mean that these people were apathetic and uninvolved, just going through some motions?

No. They were moderately involved in many things. They cried a little and they cared a little and they strove a little and were proud a little and ashamed a little. You see, these people were veterans of hard times; a world depression which was tough, a world war which was tough, an uncertain time afterwards which was tough. And so at last they arrived in their ranch houses and they could afford cocktails on the way home without much worrying about the price. It was, in a sense, the indulgence of a dream, the dream of building an affluent society. Because in the fifties that's exactly what we had — fantastically affluent compared with anything that had ever existed before.

Certainly, there were a few hot social movements and protests about the thirty percent who weren't "in." But, we must realize that in most times and countries it's been ninety percent or ninety-eight percent. So only thirty percent left out is pretty damn good and something brand new in history. And the first scattered appearance of the beats and the freedom cats must not obscure the fact that the vast majority were (moderately) good Americans in the small sense of not rocking any boats.

Yet even as the sociable ideology was crystallizing and taking hold and Eisenhower was virtually proclaiming moderation the cornerstone of our national policy, a new kind of feeling was beginning to stir across the land — a feeling which had many ties with the past but which was also new.

Although there were precursors in the late fifties when Ginsberg was telling people he'd seen the best minds of his generation driven mad, and hip talk (and an inevitable bit of philosophy behind it) was being picked up by teenagers, the hang-loose ethos really belongs to the sixties because this is the decade in which it is emerging and spreading throughout our society.

When we search for the "philosophy" which is the common denominator running through the variety of happenings — the implicit code of values pushing those involved toward some things and away from other things — some of the characteristics of this yet crystallizing view can be discerned.

One of the fundamental characteristics of the hang-loose ethic is that it is *irreverent*. It repudiates, or at least questions, such cornerstones of conventional society as Christianity, "my country right or wrong," the sanctity of marriage and premarital chastity, civil obedience, the accumulation of wealth, the right and even competence of parents, the schools, and the government to head and make decisions for everyone — in sum, the Establishment. This irreverence is probably what most arouses the ire and condemnation of the populace. Not only are the mainstream institutions and values violated, but their very legitimacy is challenged and this has heaped insult upon moral injury in the eyes of the rank and file.

Sin, as the violation of sacred beliefs and practices, is nothing new and most of us have had at least a few shamefully delightful adventures somewhere along the way. But what is qualitatively new is that the very truth and moral validity of so many notions and practices, long cherished in our country, are being challenged. When caught by parents or authorities, youths are no longer hanging their heads in shame. Instead, they are asserting the rightness, at least for themselves, of what they're doing. And they are asking what right do their elders have to put them down?

And not infrequently the irreverence takes a form which goes beyond this openly aggressive challenging. An increasing number of happeners have reached a level of disrespect so thoroughgoing that they don't even bother to "push their cause." Not only have they dropped their defensive posture, but their own assertiveness has become quiet, even urbane, in its detachment and indifference toward the "other morality." This withdrawal has aroused some of the greatest resentment and opposition since it is perhaps the gravest affront to an established ethic not to be taken seriously. To be defied is one thing; to be simply ignored and dismissed out of hand is something else. The spread of this more full-blown irreverence testifies to the fact that a good many happeners are managing to set up a life that is relatively independent of conventional society.

Another basic aspect of the hang-loose ethic is a diffuse and pervasive *humanism* which puts great store upon the value of human beings and human life. Adherents don't necessarily proclaim the rationality of men or their inherent "goodness," but they do claim that people are precious and that their full development is perhaps the most worthwhile of all things.

Killing is a heinous violation of this ethos and so is any action which puts others down, except under extreme circumstances. The most approved method of defense and retaliation is to turn one's oppressors onto the good life they're condemning and to help them resolve hang-ups which prevent this from happening. If this fails, one may attempt to "blow their minds," to shock their preconceptions and prejudices in some ways and hence force them to open their eyes, to re-evaluate, and hopefully to grow. The happeners refuse under most circumstances to employ the weapons of their adversaries because they feel that by so doing they would merely become like them. Instead, they try to transform their adversaries into fellows. The only really endorsed aggression is to try and force your enemies to become your friends. Only in extreme cases is putting down — the main strategy of the Establishment — even partly acceptable.

Ideally, the happeners do not fill the role of modern missionaries, though their practice in conversation and contact reminds one of historical attempts at persuasion and conversion. When approaching others, they welcome acceptance as well as adoption, but this does not imply that happeners resemble the adventurous, pioneering missionaries of established religions or ideologies. The few actual organizations existing in the happening world are there, first, to serve their "constituents" and, second, to espouse and inform.

This humanism, combined as it is with irreverence, produces a passive resistance toward the Establishment and the persuasive efforts of straights, rather than an active rebellion. The happeners are more transcendent than antagonistic; more indifferent and benevolently contemptuous than negative and bitter. Bitterness does occur over concrete immediate cases of harassment or "for your own good" busts, commitments, and putdowns. But it fades rather quickly again into the more general mood of simple wariness. The mood is not grim, although there is a diffuse paranoia toward the established social order which waxes and wanes as the scene gets hot and cools down again.

Another basic aspect of the hang-loose ethic is the pursuit of *experience* both as a thing in itself and as a means of learning and growing. The idea is that a great variety and depth of experience is beneficial and not at all harmful as long as you can handle it. This entails a heightened attention to the present ongoing moment and far less concern with the past or future. It also involves a mistrust of dogmas and principles which tend to obscure the richness of life. For this reason, they also often reject the categorizing and generalizing which is so rampant in our educational system. Within the drug scenes, for instance, there is full awareness that LSD-25 can trigger "bad trips," for some people. But, again the fact of experience alone, whether guided officially by researchers or informally by "guides," overrides the application of a generalized rule about the possible detrimental effects of such drugs.

This courting of raw experience is what gives many people the impression that those participating in the happenings are without any morals whatsoever; that they are selfishly pursuing swift gratification of their impulses. And it is true that the unabashed seeking of experiences will frequently lead the seeker to violate what other people consider proper. But such judgments are one-sided. Although they see that swingers are breaking standards, they entirely miss the point that swingers are following another, different set of standards; so that arguments between the camps are in reality debates between conflicting ideologies.

As part and parcel of the importance placed on directly experiencing oneself and the world, we find that *spontaneity*, the ability to groove with whatever is currently happening, is a highly valued personal trait. Spontaneity enables the person to give himself up to the existential here and now without dragging along poses and hangups and without playing investment games in hopes of possible future returns. The purest example of spontaneity is the jazz musician as he stands up and blows a cascade of swinging sounds.

Another facet of the hang-loose ethic is an untutored and unpretentious *tolerance*. Do whatever you want to as long as you don't step on other people while doing it. A girl is free to wet her pants or play with herself openly while she's up on an acid trip and no one will think less of her for it. A man can stand and stare at roadside grass blowing in the wind and no one will accuse him of being the village idiot. If you like something that I don't like, that's fine, that's your bag; just don't bring me down.

The swingers, when you come down to it, are anarchists in the fullest sense. They chafe at virtually all restrictions because they see most every restriction that modern man has devised as a limitation on directions people can travel and grow. They feel that the irony of contemporary society is that the very restrictions necessary to curb an immature populace prevent that same populace from becoming mature enough to live without restrictions, just as a girdle weakens the muscles it supports.

Even clothes are regarded by some as mostly a nuisance and swingers have led the whole Western world toward simplicity and ease in styles and makeup. And over weekends and vacations, small groups will often go up together to back country retreats where whoever wants to can run around naked.

Without the fuss or the self-righteousness so common among Establishment liberals, the happeners have come closer to integrating the races, religions, and the sexes than any other group one can think of. A fierce equality is practiced among them, which is appreciative of differences in backgrounds and temperaments. Equality and tolerance aren't abject attempts to make people feel comfortable or wanted; they are dispositions that permit things and relationships to just happen without deliberate forethought and planning. In most happening circles, a Negro is not the recipient of conscious liberal acceptance, but an individual in and of himself who may or may not be a "good" person. Acceptance and participation is based more on how the individual presents himself within the context of the scene, not by preconceived and nurtured stereotypes about the way he is expected to be.

One's past is not held against one and one's reputation is not spoiled by the fact that one might have served time in a prison or mental institution, had an abortion, or perhaps a homosexual affair.

This doesn't mean that the swingers will indiscriminately associate with anyone. Like everybody else, they choose their friends, their lovers, their acquaintances and the people they avoid by how well they get along with one another and enjoy doing things together. But they are less down on the people they don't choose to associate with than others generally are.

But the tolerance stops if somebody is stepping on other people. For instance, if a guy shows up in a particular scene and starts tooling around with other people's minds or bum tripping them just for his own kicks, several people are likely to get together and elect themselves to deal with him by busting *his* mind. And such a guy can quickly be shut out of virtually the entire happenings in that specific scene.

The ideal person in the hang-loose view embodies traits that are difficult to combine. Being as spontaneous as a child yet being sophisticated and worldwise; being fully self-expressive yet being always in control of oneself. This is the ambiguity of being cool. Being able to dig the ongoing present as it unfolds yet being able to get things done and maintain a competent life of fulfilled commitments and involvements. Being hang-loose from any constraining orthodoxy, yet being courageous enough to follow your own path wherever it may lead and whatever the travails it plunges you into.

The heroes are those who have managed to swing in some eminent way especially if they did so in spite of tough conditions. The distinguished outsiders of history, avant-garde artists, the leaders of unpopular social movements. The list of admirable people would include figures such as Aldous Huxley, Allen Ginsberg, Gandhi, John F. Kennedy, Fidel Castro, Alpert and Leary, and Bob Dylan. But such people are not so much heroes in the ordinary sense because, although they are much admired, they are not so much worshipped, and because they are critically discussed as well as fondly quoted.

The fact that swingers operate at least partly outside the Establishment and often even outside the law produces a certain admiration and sympathy among them for other categories of alienated and disaffiliated people, such as the Negroes, the poor, the mentally disturbed, the delinquent, the sexual deviant, and the peoples of under-developed countries. They do not necessarily approve of what these people do, but they do see them as victims of Establishments.

These sympathies, coupled with their tolerance and opposition to restrictiveness lead the happeners to take a "liberal" stand on almost every question and issue, from welfare measures to disarmament, to the legalization of pot and abortions, to racial integration and civil liberties generally, to recognition of Red China and negotiations with the Viet Cong, to sexual permissiveness and progressive education, to socialized medicine and the exploration of space.

But most of them are not self-conscious "liberals." They take these stands for granted as the only reasonable and sensible ones, but they usually don't work within organized political parties to bring them about and they are not very happy with the compromising Establishment liberals who do. They support such men as Governor Brown, Clark Kerr and Bobby Kennedy only as the best of the poor choices available, all of whom are really more alike than different, and none of whom are really worth a good God damn.

But they are not pro-Communist either, although sympathetic toward revolutionaries in under-developed countries. They see Communism as at least as odious and repressive as the societies of the West and probably a good deal more so.

The hang-loose people are not joiners; indeed this is one of their defining attributes. They tend to shy away from any kind of conventional ideologies or fanaticisms, seeing them as unfree compulsions and obsessions rather than noble dedications. They regard those who are too intensely and doggedly involved in even such highly approved causes as integration and peace, a little askance and happeners will sometimes describe their own past involvements in these movements as something of a psychological hangup.

The villains in the hang-loose view are people and social forces which put other people down and hang them up, which teach people to be stolid and dignified rather than swinging, self-righteous and moralistic rather than responsible, dutiful rather than devoted. Those who, for the sake of some ideology, will set fire to other peoples' kids; who, for the sake of some ideology, will slap their own children into becoming something less than they might have been. The villains are those who pass their own hangups onto those around them and thus propagate a sickness, "for your own good."

This seems to be the still amorphous and emerging ethos which is the basis of the happenings we're concerned with. Admirable in some ways, perhaps a bit idealistic and innocent and even silly in others, still in the process of forming and changing, and creating many problems for everyone. And perhaps as inevitable, given current conditions, as the spring winds which stir its adherents.

And it is a set of ideals which, like all people, the adherents are not able to live up to. Sometimes when things get uptight, they betray themselves and each other. Sometimes they can't resist selling out for a better package deal. Sometimes, despite their utterances, they can become as provincial and arrogant as any tribesman who thinks he has the monopoly on truth. And sometimes they are driven by other motives to cheat and exploit one another. But such shortcomings are panhuman and can be leveled at any group including the United States Senate or the medical profession. And this should not obscure the fact that ideals are a potent social force which have a major hand in making people what they are. Ideals, aside from having a part in making individual attitudes, attachments and adjustments, also serve to categorize people as runners along certain tracks of life. What is today called deviant is tomorrow only eccentric. What harps upon and tortures the older ethics and ideologies can eventually become an accepted, if not generally followed, belief system.

Like all ideologies, this ethos is sometimes used as a rationalization and justification. Irresponsibility can be excused as freedom. Apathy can be called being cool. Lack of dependability can be called spontaneity and so can boorishness and sloth. And virtually any behavior can be justified on the grounds that it is experience and will lead in some way to personal growth.

But then pointing out these blindspots may be a pot calling a kettle black for all ideologies are so misused and the misuse doesn't destroy the fact that they are also faithfully followed.

Those following under the banner of the hang-loose ethic are not of one stripe. Sometimes it is the spontaneous pose of a youth who is drunk on his own vaulting life-energy. Sometimes it is the final vision which has resulted from long training in some Eastern philosophy. Sometimes it is the whimsical realization that your hard work has produced a degree of comfort and success but that you're growing older and that things are perhaps just too uncertain to lay too much store upon the alleged joys of the future or the hereafter. Sometimes it is a temporary fling in what will prove to be an otherwise pedestrian life. Sometimes it is a later stage in a journey which has led a youth through romantic idealism, folksong clubs and science fiction, protest movements, a period of disenchantment, wandering, and psychedelic drugs while still in his teens. And sometimes it is the stony and even vicious hipsterism of the slum ghetto.

The hang-loose attitude is simply not a uniform thing. One can hang-loose happily or bitterly, stoically or desperately, wisely or floundering, as a posing actor or as a blithe spirit. Sometimes it is mixed with defiance; sometimes loving tolerance; and sometimes it embodies an indifference which smacks of callous unconcern for the fate of others. And sometimes it is tinged with the pathos of the feeling that in another, better world things would be different.

This ethos will have a somewhat different flavor in different groups and in different regions of the country. On the Eastern seaboard, it is likely to be more cosmopolitan and European in temperament. In the midwest it is more likely to be a reaction to the stolid Dirksonesque environment. In the South, it tends to combine the effete with the rustic. And in the West it is likely to be more gaudy and mystical. Among students it tends to be more self-reflective and among drop-outs it tends to be more starkly hedonistic. Among the lower classes it tends to be a proletarian disaffiliation, among the middle and upper classes it tends to combine the *Playboy* hipsterism with psychoanalytic self-realization. Among teenagers it is likely to be the following of fads, among youth it is more likely to be a search for meanings and recipes, among adults it is likely to be more cautious and more straight, and among older people it is likely to be hobbies and vitriolic conversations in the sun.

Among Negroes, Mexicans and Puerto Ricans it will tend to be more angry and physical and immediate, among whites it will probably be more sedentary and compromising and tolerant because it is more their society. Among Catholics it will involve "soul trouble"; among Protestants, a Nietzschean debate over whether God is dead; among Jews, an agnostic urbanity; and among the uncommitted, a search for alternative faiths.

In the urban slums it is explosive and a source of constant potential violence. Among middle class youth it is a source of scandals, a recruiting ground for protests of all kinds, and a susceptibility toward the milder, unharmful forms of deviance, and personal problems. And among suburban adults it is a careful but sometimes determined minority voice within the Establishment, and an "aw, come on!" ambivalence toward the Great Society bit.

American suburbs aren't the places of otherdirected conformity as Whyte and Reisman depicted them in the fifties. Perhaps they never altogether were. But the stereotype of the jovial empty-spirited organization man which may have had a good deal of truth a decade ago, now fits only a plurality at most — and a plurality that is no longer in the center of things, but off to the side as a disinherited conservatism.

In today's suburbs one finds a widespread diffidence toward job, background, and other external tags and badges. People are unwilling to think of themselves or others as merely the sum of their statuses and nothing more. A few years ago you might ask "what do you do?"; be answered, "I'm an accountant"; and say, "Oh, that's nice." But now you'd say, "Well, yes, but what do *you* do, who are *you*?"

Fromm's classic thesis that contemporary people are only using their freedom from the chains of tradition to package and sell their external selves until the package becomes the person and there's nothing left but a gaudy shell, is no longer so true either. In almost any neighborhood gathering, one can find plenty of evidence for a growing disaffection with external symbols (which were the main unit of currency in the heyday of the Sociable Ethic). Expressions of a certain distance from one's job and other positions and a conspiratorial show of fellow humanness have in fact become the newest gambit in advertising, salesmanship and interpersonal relations generally.

There is of course a good deal of the older ideologies still around and certain facets of them still ring faintly even among the most far out followers of the hang-loose view. Among those followers who are working within the Establishment there is still moderate disapproval of doing things just for kicks. Swinging should be "constructive," either by refreshing you so that you can return zestfully to the playful fray of your workaday world, or by helping you resolve psychoanalytic hang-ups so that you can move on to the next stage of growth.

And with a bit of pendulum swinging from the gregarious outward-ness of the Sociable Ethic to the fierce individualism of our puritan predecessors, the current swingers in schools and suburbs are less con-cerned with courting the offhand opinions and tepid acceptance of the crowds they encounter. They are not immune to the smiles and frowns of others, especially people they like, but they are not enslaved by them either, and much of the time they groove along with an inner-directed-ness that would delight Reisman.

There is also an appreciation of affluence as with the Sociable Ethic, and in fairly sharp distinction to the self-conscious poverty of most of the Beats during the fifties. But this is more of a taken-for-granted that the world is full of material baubles which can be very useful, than a deliberate striving to accumulate them. The current swingers take national affluence for granted and only strive to have it distributed more widely and with less necessity of selling oneself to get a part of it.

The modern happeners like many of the things which our shopping-center society produces in so great a quantity, such as cars and clothes and stereos and prints and books, and they do not share the anti-television stance of the intellectuals during the last decade. But they don't want to struggle too hard to get them and they will freely loan and borrow them. So this shared appreciation of affluence shouldn't lead us to neglect what is now so different — namely that swingers have broken away from the high valuation of property which has been the cornerstone of every Western society since the Reformation and the rise of the middle classes. Property is not something designed to domi-nate an individual's life; it is something to be lived with and used, not as a focus of existence, but as incidental to the fact that humans are alive and dynamic. A young man, who like many others is only involved in some of the happening scenes, once commented, "do you realize that legally we can kill for the sake of property? What gives us the right to say that if a burglar is stealing a damned TV set we can go ahead and blow his brains out. Property, not human life, has become the most sacred thing in our society."

Along with the repudiation of property as something to work and live for, the hang-loose people feel less honor bound to fulfill commitments unless they are coupled with personal involvements and attachments. This makes them less dependable workers and spouses, and their lack of steadfastness creates part of their bad reputation in a society which still harkens to the Calvinist idea of duty. But swingers will not discharge their duties as students, workers, lovers, or citizens just because someone else says they *should*. "Should" isn't good enough unless it is coupled with "want to," stemming either from personal desire or personal convictions. Concretely, this means that they will break a law they disagree with, will desert a spouse or friend they no longer love, will cheat on a test they feel is unjust, will walk off a job they find odious, and will speak against a war they feel is dishonorable. The swingers will, because of expediency, often cool it by fulfilling obligations they do not feel personally bound to, but if they don't have to, they frequently won't.

Hence, an obvious strategy for those in the opposition wishing the demise of happening scenes and their tangential attributes, would involve making these people "want to" do something or discharge some particular responsibility. Sadly it is too infrequently recognized that unless those with the hang-loose philosophy are, at a minimum, tolerated, little progress in the above direction can be made. You can't call somebody a lunatic, beatnik, dope addict, or radical and expect them to jump to your beck and call. Regardless of how much reason and substance are part of the opposition doctrines, they will get nowhere until debate goes beyond mutual debasement and vilification.

In the hang-loose view, the main problems besides hassles with the Establishment and its blue-frocked representatives, are the personal hang-ups which prevent people from living as fully and spontaneously as they otherwise might. This is a more general and extreme form of the ideals of individualism, self-determination and self-realization which have been kicking around Western Civilization for several centuries and which have been such a prominent part of psychoanalysis. These ideals, when carried to their logical extreme by the swingers, however, put them in opposition to a good many of the rules and practices of the Establishment, which, like societies everywhere grants personal freedom only within limits and which labels those who go beyond these limits, deviant.

And this is the dilemma of the swinger. In the very process of attempting to resolve his hang-ups, he will usually move further outside the pale of conventional society and will become more deviant, immoral and dangerous in the eyes of the general populace.

Happeners are aware of this dilemma and spend long hours talking with each other about how it might be resolved. An individual solution is to become exceedingly cool — to develop the skills and habits to swing yet evade the eye of the Establishment by being discreet and by being able to play straight when necessary.

But this is only a makeshift solution, temporary and high in personal cost. The longterm solution almost all swingers agree is to turn the world on. Their dream is to live in a world of beautiful people in which everyone grooves on their own things and doesn't interfere with anyone else in doing it. Where people will say "no" only because they want to and not because of fear or tie-ups. Where people don't make it their business to screw each other up over some decrepit dogma. Where children aren't stunted by "education" and "training" into growing up absurd, sad caricatures of their possible selves. Where people are free enough and fearless enough to grow their own trees.

If you think this dream is a little naive and foolish and fantastic, you are right. If you think it neglects and glosses over many of the realities of present world conditions and that it is a bit pretentious and unlikely, given the facts of history, you are right again. And if you find nothing good or true or beautiful about it, you can go to hell.

There is a storm of violent opposition to the hang-loose ethos and the behavior that stems from it. This storm of opposition seems to be of two kinds, and the first kind is moral.

A good many people feel that those participating in the happenings are morally depraved. Bratty overgrown kids crying for the freedom to play with each other underneath the streetlights. Arrogant but innocent youngsters who think they know more than they do and who are easy prey for dope peddlers, sexual perverts, and Communist agitators. A few more rapped knuckles, stiffer curfews and supervision, a few more jail sentences to set examples, and a stint in the army might make men (and women) out of them. But right now they're spoiled, oversexed, smart aleck brats who aren't worth their pay on a job of work and who are unfit to inherit our great country.

In the rush of controversy and opposition to what's happening, the swingers become *objects* for explanation, condescending sympathy, or condemnation. But because the happeners don't themselves own or have much access to communication channels for reaching the general public, the fact that they are active *subjects* who are in turn evaluating their evaluators is lost sight of. So their turnabout indictments seldom reach the ears of the general public, although they are widely circulated and discussed among the swingers themselves. When they are quoted by officials or the mass media, it is usually only to illustrate their alienation, willfulness, or delinquency. The quotes are treated only as graphic evidence of their sickness and depravity. Attempts, for example, to legalize the use of marijuana receive the sarcastic and superior attention of smiling commentators on the 11 o'clock news. But, for those even partially involved in the drug world such activity is serious business that is a frequent subject of conversation, if not direct action. Although they might discuss it with a measure of frivolity, fearful of taking themselves *too* seriously, marijuana legalization has become a meaningful aspect of personal commitment and not some deviant's practical joke.

Parents and other concerned adults are discussing and fretting over what is becoming of today's youth and turning to each other, to experts (usually self-proclaimed) and to their officials for advice.

And youth are discussing and fretting over their elders and they turn to each other and to those rare experts and officials who are in any sense "where it's at" for advice. Restless and uncertain they are; unsure of themselves, of their beliefs, and of their futures. But they are more self-assured in their feelings that parents and mentors, neighbors and newscasters, officials and Presidents of the United States cannot be taken at face-value. They suspect — dimly or consciously — that their elders are not altogether honest, wise or competent to run the world and give advice, though many sincerely wish they were.

To the widespread charges that they are being immoral, irresponsible, and irreverent, they turn about and reply: "Look at you, blowing up whole countries for the sake of some crazy ideologies that you don't live up to anyway. Look at you, mindfucking a whole generation of kids into getting a revolving charge account and buying your junk. (Who's a junkie?) Look at you, needing a couple of stiff drinks before you have the balls to talk with another human being. Look at you, making it with your neighbor's wife on the sly just to try and prove that you're really alive. Look at you, hooked on *your* cafeteria of pills, and making up dirty names for anybody who isn't in your bag, and screwing up the land and the water and the air for profit, and calling this nowhere scene the Great Society! *And you're gonna tell us how to live?* C'mon man, you've got to be kidding!"

(This collage was made from a multitude of remarks dropped in a wide variety of different scenes. The remarks were usually reactions to specific events such as McNamara's proposal to draft the world or

Reagan's promises of suppression, Dirkson's Biblical pronouncements or the sentencing of a youth for smoking a casual weekend joint. Ill-will is more of a temporary reaction than an intrinsic attitude among happeners.)

And the oldsters in their turn reply: "Well, what are you doing that's so meaningful? Aren't you maybe on a hundred roads to nowhere too?" And the host of individual debates that go to make up the Great Debate continue all over our country.

The other kind of opposition is a practical concern. Who's going to be left to run the world if everybody turns on? This question bothers many people who are otherwise not so concerned about the morality or immorality of what's happening. They fear that nobody will be left to mind the store, to do those thousand-and-one routine but necessary things that keep society's wheels turning, her goods flowing and her children growing. Who will hold the world together?

Maybe nobody will hold the *present* world together. Who wants to? How much of it do we really need? How many of our proud items are only consolation prizes? Maybe a newer social order could evolve in which we would have the real things that we talk about on rainy nights but never quite seem to achieve?

The worry that the present social order cannot continue unless the happenings are checked is counter-balanced by the worry among happeners that the present social order may well persist in spite of their wishes and efforts to change things, and that the current social order at the worst may destroy the world in a thermo-nuclear light that would dim any prospect of an enlightened future. Here we find a true opposition and conflict between those who want to preserve the present moral order and those who wish to transform it.

Many among the older cohort worry whether today's youth are training and preparing themselves for the adult roles they are soon to occupy. This worry contains some validity, for many swingers are pretty unimpressive even judged in terms of their own values and ideals. A three year collection of *Wonder Woman* comics is perhaps trippy but it doesn't make the world a cleaner, greener land.

But the worry is also ethnocentric and historically arrogant because the young needn't accept or strive to fill adult roles as the oldsters choose to define them — and it might even be best if they didn't. On this issue youth *is* rebellious as it tries to revamp the more traditional conceptions of a "man," a "woman," a "career," a "citizen," a "human being." In their uncertain experimentations some swingers are probably stumbling toward what will prove to be more realistic and effective roles which may better fit the upcoming times.

Perhaps the most curious irony about the hang-loose ethic is that it is distilled from many of the highest ideals of Western man and our national heritage, carried out to their logical conclusion. America is now, in a sense, confronted by a legion of youths who are trying in their own fumbling way to practice what generations of fatuous graduation speakers have been preaching. This emerging ethos which seems so heretical at first glance is partly a restatement of some of the highest ideals and values which the great middle classes struggled for during the Industrial Revolution and which have since served all-too-often as a covering rationalization for self-seeking exploitation; the ideals we learn to bend and compromise in the process of "growing up" and "learning the ropes" and becoming "mature." The irony is not that Americans have failed to teach the upcoming generation but that they have been perhaps too successful in their training and must now confront their fervent pupils.

RICHARD ROVERE
freedom: who needs it?

"Individuality is the aim of political liberty," James Fenimore Cooper wrote in 1838, in *The American Democrat,* and a decade later, in his *Civil Disobedience,* Henry David Thoreau insisted that "there will never be a really free and enlightened state until the state comes to recognize the individual as a higher and independent power, from which all its power and authority are derived, and treats him accordingly."

How wrong — how mistaken in prophecy — our American moralists have been! Had Cooper and Thoreau been right, the Great Society would be all around us, its every member happy and fulfilled. There would be no civil disorder, and of course no war in Vietnam. "Alienation" might be a legal and pathological term — but not a widespread social phenomenon and the fundamental "issue" in the presidential campaign of one aspirant, Senator Eugene McCarthy. Civility would prevail, and, the state having long since accommodated itself to the examined consciences of "individuals," there would be no point to the kind of civil disobedience to which Thoreau felt driven by the Mexican War. Thoreau was an eloquent man, a noble spirit in a mean time, but his logic was often flawed, and it was his proposition — one wonders if he could actually have believed it — that if the state liberated the individual, the individual would liberate the state, and everything would be just fine. Jefferson and Toqueville knew better, but they had known more of the world than Concord and did not think that all truth was contained in "the mind and heart of me."

It seems not to have dawned on Thoreau that the social whole might be something greater than — or at least something quite different from — the sum of its parts. With his view of man and the state, he would have had a hard time understanding what has happened in this republic in the century since his death, which is that the state has come to behave toward the individual pretty much as he thought it should but that it is still, alas, given to folly and wickedness, still very much in need of "enlightenment."

I am assuming that the individual *qua* individual (as distinct, be it clearly noted, from the individual as a member of the whole society or of any minority within it) has very little to complain about in the United States at the present time. Though a day may come, and before very long, when this will not be true, it seems to me clear beyond serious dispute that the liberties specified in the Bill of Rights are honored and in general vigorously upheld by the state. The government that Cooper distrusted and Thoreau despised imposes no effective limitations on speech or any other form of individual expression. I may say what I choose and disseminate it in any way I find possible, no matter how much offense I may give society in general or any of the groups that constitute it. In matters political, moral, and religious, my rights as an individual take precedence over any and every consensus of public opinion. I am seldom held to any test of factuality or damage. Indeed, the more powerful my adversary happens to be, the more unrestrained may I be in smiting him, for the courts have ruled that the bigger they are, the harder they may be hit. If I wish to proclaim my hatred and defiance of authority, constituted or otherwise, I can expect objection but not, as a rule, interference; should interference be attempted or proposed, I can demand and get the state's protection.

It may be objected that what I describe as rights and liberties are in fact privileges and immunities that are largely dependent on status — and, even at that, honored only in certain jurisdictions. Were I a black Mississippian not exercising but merely pleading for my "rights," I might be speaking my last words on earth. As a white New Yorker denouncing authority in Mississippi, I might meet the same fate. Status is important in this society — in fact, in any society — and if I threaten that of another man in certain circumstances, I may lose my right to live. But if I lost it in such circumstances, I would have lost it to another individual, not to the state, even if the individual happened to be an agent of some provincial government. For the individual, equal protection is assured by the state that exercises national sovereignty. In England, in November, 1967, a Black Muslim named Michael Abdul Malik was given a year's imprisonment for what the sentencing judge called "attempting to raise hostility" against white people — an offense under the Race Relations Act of 1965. A couple of weeks later, the London *Sunday Times* was fined $12,000 and court costs for having printed an unflattering but accurate description of the same Malik in a picture caption while his case was *sub judice*. But in the United States, Stokely Carmichael and H. Rap Brown, though they may encounter difficulties over passport regulation and statutes dealing with the possession of firearms, are as free as any benighted honky to preach hatred and incite others to civil disorder, and a journalist is free to use any language he chooses in describing them.

Is the individual as free to *do* what he wants as well as *say* what he wants? Of course not. No society can protect anyone's rights without a criminal code. However, my freedom of action is probably greater than any that has ever before existed in an organized society. I can adopt any style of living that does not interfere with the right of others to do the same. There are no limits to my freedom of association except the possible reluctance of others to associate with me. There are almost no remaining constraints on sexual activity between consenting adults. In recent years, there has been established a right unnamed and unclaimed seventy-five years ago — the right to privacy. The right to withhold support from and participation in certain undertakings of the state, such as war, no doubt falls short of what Thoreau wished, but it is vastly broader than it was in his day. Conscientious objection to military service is reported under a steadily broadening definition of "conscience," and it is conceivable that the courts will one day extend a similar respect to the kind of tax-withholding for which Thoreau spent a night in Concord jail. In ways too numerous to cite, the state has yielded to Thoreau's smug assertion that "any man more right than his neighbors constitutes a majority of one already."

The political order may accord liberties to the individual which the social or economic order may be said to nullify or to diminish in value. As the Marxists used to say, what good is freedom of the press to anyone who does not own a press? A man has to have a home before he can call it his castle. But to repeat, the early libertarians regarded the state — the central, sovereign state — as their antagonist and did not distinguish it from the social and economic orders. Their conflict was with government, and by all the measures most of them employed, the victory is already theirs. Furthermore, when the conflict has been with oppressive social and economic power, the state has as often as not been the ally of the abused individual. Thoreau's conditions for a "free and enlightened state" have been achieved.

Yet never in our history has the individual seemed as wretched and despairing as he is today; and seldom have free men anywhere felt so thwarted and powerless in their relations to government democratically chosen. I speak particularly, but by no means exclusively, of those who have sought and in some measure achieved "individuality." The conformists seem hardly less in revolt than the nonconformists. Never have disaffection, alienation, and frustration been more widespread. And, what is the most alarming thing of all, never has the kind of liberty the libertarians valued so greatly been held in such low esteem by those who possess and use it. Thoreau's hope for the redemption of the state was, of course, absurd. Liberty does not create enlightenment; it merely brings it within the realm of the possible. But at least one might suppose that liberty would be valued for its own sake and be seen by the individual as one means for building a society that would be somewhat closer to his heart's desire.

It is clear in 1968 that one can suppose no such thing. There now seems to be something new under the American sun — a disenchantment not only with the society in which individual liberty thrives as it seldom has in the past but with the idea of liberty itself. In a survey of attitudes among liberal and radical college students and teachers late in 1967, Nan Robertson, of the New York *Times*, found that those who have the most grandiose and in some ways the most humane visions of a different, better America place little value on their constitutional rights. "The most radical among them displayed total scorn for individual liberties," Miss Robertson reported. Nor, evidently, is this contempt limited to the very young, who — lacking much acquaintance with, to say nothing of respect for, history — take freedom very much for granted. Mary McCarthy, a writer with a richly informed sense of the past and an honorable record of libertarian activity, has lately described "freedom in the United States . . . simply as the right to self-expression, as in the dance, psychodrama, be-ins, kinky sex, and baking ceramics."

The disillusionment of the radical students and of such of their elders as Miss McCarthy has its origins — as what does not in this country today? — in the war in Vietnam. What they have all discovered, though it is hard to believe that Miss McCarthy did not know it all along, is that the war cannot be stopped by the individual's exercise of liberty. Miss McCarthy was quite explicit about this: "The uselessness of free institutions, pleasurable in themselves, to interpose any check on a war of this character, opposed, though not enough, by most so-called thinking persons, suggests that freedom . . . is no longer a political value." By "value" she means, I am sure, "weapon," or, better perhaps, "force." Certainly this is what Dwight Macdonald means when he explains that he took up "resistance" in the summer of 1967, when "it became evident to me that two years of writing, speaking, and demonstrating against the war had not got through to our President." (Macdonald is a man of awesome ingenuousness. He has been writing, speaking, and demonstrating for thirty-five years, through five presidencies, without, so far as is known, "getting through" to a Deputy Assistant Secretary of Anything. He must have rated Johnson as an especially quick study.)

The bitter truth is that we cannot use our liberty or our individuality to make the President cease and desist in Vietnam. Indeed, when we try, he insists on telling us that he is doing it all so that we can hold on to our right to dissent. Under the circumstances, the most we can do is vote against him when the proper time comes and in the meanwhile try to persuade others to do the same. This kind of activity, however, we undertake not really as individuals, as right-minded majorities of one, but as fragments of society.

I have suggested that there is something new to American experience in this disenchantment with individual liberty. I think it is without precedent. But I also think I detect a common element in the attitudes of Thoreau and Mary McCarthy. Neither is willing to accept liberty as an end in itself. The classic libertarian position, one has always supposed, is that the whole point of the struggle is to get the state off one's back

— to achieve individuality, as Cooper said, and to achieve it for exactly the purpose Miss McCarthy scorns, "self-expression." Kinky sex and ceramics could be part of it, as well as a man's right to hold and proclaim his own vision of God or of beauty. The idea was not to control the state, but to avoid being controlled by it, so that the individual, as Cooper put it, "is left to pursue his means of happiness in his own manner." But Cooper was a conservative, a right-winger of sorts, while Thoreau and Mary McCarthy represent another tradition — that of "social conscience" and political reform. They ask the state not to leave them alone but to give them power, to let them be part of the life of the state and have a share in what nowadays is called "decision-making" — so that, as Thoreau professed to hope, that state could be made "free and enlightened," and as Miss McCarthy would have it, freedom could be used to "interpose a check" on the war in Vietnam.

It is easy enough to say that they are mistaken as to the nature and value of individual liberty and have even turned inside out the classic defenses of it. But one is then compelled to ask if these arguments were ever themselves reasonable and honest. Has the desire for freedom ever been only a desire for self-expression or self-fulfillment? The great appeals for liberty have often stated the case in these terms — "Give *me* liberty or give *me* death" — but while there have been some valorous and lonely battles waged by individuals, the great crusades for liberty were collective undertakings (not for "me" but for "us") in which the aim was a collective liberation. Not many of those who have fought for liberty, if only in some bloodless demonstration against oppressive authority, have themselves had much to gain from destroying censorship or establishing the right to free scientific inquiry. No doubt there are in every society a few people who have faith, justified or otherwise, in their individual ability to create something of value or to uncover some hidden truth about the world and ask nothing of their fellowman but noninterference. But, as the cases of Henry Thoreau and Mary McCarthy so amply demonstrate, even among the most gifted there can be so powerful a yen to change the world that a devaluation of freedom seems called for when it develops that free speech and free thinking and free love are not particularly effective instruments of change. And among the less gifted, those who are incapable of using liberty in a solitary pursuit of truth or beauty, disillusionment is bound to be commensurately greater. Eric Hoffer long ago pointed out that mass movements are built and staffed by "uncreative men of words."

And so it may be idle, even stuffy and pedantic, to point out that some

Americans have misconstrued the nature of liberty and that they ask for more than can reasonably be expected of it. If this is a species of irrationality, it is only one of several that are to be found in this country today. To confront one's contemporaries with the ideals of the founders and early ideologues may be as irrelevant as attributing to the founders the present maladies of the nation they established. The fact is that the society in which we live is not the one the founders intended it to be or the one the ideologues hoped it would someday become. In it, the individual has a wide range of liberties and, thanks mainly to its affluence, a wide range of opportunities for self-fulfillment. But, as John Kenneth Galbraith has written, "the presumption of this society is no longer individualist but collectivist." He might have added that this is no recent development. Ours is a mass society in which ideas get lost or diluted or distorted in consensus — and this is not a word that Lyndon Johnson invented or gave currency to but one that Theodore Roosevelt selected as descriptive of the way it is in our political system. Universal education, perhaps the most distinctive of our institutions, created not a nation of individualists but a literate mass that formed itself into a market for mass culture and consensus politics.

It was doubtless inevitable — that is to say, predictable — that there would be extraordinary tensions between the free individual and the free but generally unresponsive society. For freedom and individuality are not sweet but galling when they cannot be put to good use, which for most men means some power to control events. This side of the New Jerusalem, there will always be a reformer of sorts dwelling in every sentient being. Each of us wishes that the mass would adopt at least some of our values, and some of us want a good deal more than reform. "Quite simply, I want a new civilization," said Ezra Pound, who went mad from wanting.

A classic instance of how galling a powerless freedom can be is to be found in the memoirs of George Kennan, perhaps the most brilliant diplomat of the century. Kennan entered the Foreign Service of the United States in 1925, and the government paid for an education that put him on the road to becoming our leading authority on Soviet affairs and about as well informed as anyone else on Germany and Eastern Europe. From the late twenties down to the end of the forties, he provided Washington with interpretations of men and events that can, in hindsight, be seen to have been almost spectacularly accurate. What use did his government make of the talent it had so wisely developed and of the analyses that might have saved it so much grief? Not until the very end of his career did his superiors — the ambassadors and Secretaries of State and Presidents he had served — trouble to listen to him.

In his memoirs are dozens of memoranda drawn from his and the Department's files; though some were written more than thirty years ago, they make compelling reading today. Had they been read upon receipt by those to whom they were addressed, this essay might bear happier tidings than it does. But many of them, in all probability, were never read by anyone before they were published by Kennan himself and, ironically, given mass distribution by the Book-of-the-Month Club. Though he is by temperament anything but a whiner, Kennan, as an autobiographer, is an aggrieved chronicler of rejection and of a frustration so deep that, having "no reason to believe that my views would be interesting or welcome in official Washington," toward the end he almost gave up trying; and, in the end, even after a brief period of belated recognition, he got out, hoping that he would have more impact on events by the writing of history than by writing policy recommendations that policy-makers never read. Out of public life, he has contributed much to enlightenment but discouragingly little to public policy.

George Kennan was not ignored because his views were radical — they were anything but that; he wanted no new civilization — or because he was held in low esteem. It would be closer to the truth to say that he was ignored because his views were complex, and despite the exemplary lucidity of the prose in which they were couched, not easily grasped. The views that Kennan advanced were those of an *individual,* an Emersonian Man Thinking — thinking as hard as he possibly could, thinking his way through illusions to what he perceived as reality. His views could seldom be reduced to slogans; indeed, they often ran counter to the slogans currently in vogue and obscuring hard truth. The consensus could not accommodate them.

We are, as I see it, in this fix: ours is probably the only kind of society which can liberate the individual, and it is at the same time a society in which he is less likely to find fulfillment than he might under certain kinds of authoritarian rule. Dissent is tolerated and at times encouraged, but unless and until it is organized on a mass scale — developing in the process a new orthodoxy, and inevitably, a new dissent — it is not more likely to influence events than it would be in the Soviet Union. Like the rich man with his money, the free individual learns that freedom cannot buy happiness. He suffers anxieties of a kind he would not know in a totalitarian country, where the notion that a few scattered voices might change national policy could no more take hold than the notion that a local astronomy club could send a rocket to Venus. The anxieties may be endurable when he differs with the society over matters that he regards as being at least debatable and subject to compromise; they become unendurable when he persuades himself that because of his powerlessness men and women in large numbers are dying in hideous ways each hour of every day.

When the failure to prevail through freedom becomes thus unendurable, it is only, one supposes, a short step to a renunciation of freedom itself. This would be particularly the case in a country in which not even the oldest citizens can recall a time when the individual *qua* individual was subject to the more severe forms of repression. In our time, the civil rights movement and the labor movement have had their martyrs, but even when Joseph McCarthy flourished, no one lost his life as a fighter for the freedom of the individual. (Some may say there were losses no less grave, and this may be true, but the sufferers who live in memory are those who have died or at least bled for a cause.) A right that has long been secured is less prized, and more easily despised, than a right won in our own or our father's time.

It is not, then, difficult to see how in this worst of American times, some of the young and some of the not so young can, as Miss Robertson put it, display "total scorn for individual liberties." But to understand is not to pardon. If individual liberties are held in contempt simply because they produce no quick political results, liberty of all kinds will be in jeopardy. Of course Dwight Macdonald cannot talk or write the President of the United States out of the war in two years. Nor can Stokely Carmichael create black power by extolling it before a thousand crowds.

The test of liberty can never be narrowly pragmatic. Freedom of expression does not assure greatness: it may, on the contrary, smother it in outpourings of mediocrity. But if for this or any other reason it is to be held in low esteem by those who wish to change society, they will soon enough find that the likeliest kind of change their attitude will promote is in the direction of reaction and regression.

We appear to have reached a point at which there can be no communication between the alienated and those who have, as I do, a continuing commitment not only to the professed ideals of this society, many of which are dishonored every day, but to its political and legal institutions. Alienation is not, I suppose, a point of view that can be dealt with by discourse of any kind. Still, it seems to me that those who are coming to perceive the limitations of liberty owe it to themselves to confront not only the disagreeable facts about those limitations but the facts, many of them no less disagreeable, about the nature of this society and its place in history and in the world.

Such a confrontation can be dispiriting indeed, for it can produce despair not only about American possibilities but about human possibilities in general. It must begin, I think, with an acknowledgment of the fact that the United States was born in a revolution led by men of uncommon intelligence and integrity, men whose ideals were of an elevation rare in the history of revolutions. They provided us with model charters of freedom and with a governmental structure that, whatever its defects, has been workable enough to endure for almost two centuries. They achieved a political unity that was in time, though not without strife, to become continental. The continent we claimed was enormously rich and fertile, and this made easier the maintenance of the liberties for which the charters provided. In the first century and a quarter of our national existence, we attracted from a Europe unable to achieve much in the way of either liberty or unity millions of settlers eager to share the opportunities our continent offered, and for the most part, eager to share our ideals. We enjoyed, in short, good fortune of a kind unknown in the past and unlikely to be known in the future. It is not, I think, chauvinistic to say that if in the end we prove unable to make a go of democracy, there is a fair presumption that no one else will be able to do so either.

The alienated feel that the evidence is already in, that we have compromised ourselves fatally, and that the role of the individual is either to destroy the society or drop out of it. In that case, if I am right, they must concede the futility of the very idea of human community and the fatuousness not only of change but of criticism. For myself, though I have not known a time of greater anguish over our possibilities, I want this society to be preserved, and I hope for the strength to maintain my own commitment to it. Despite the horror of Vietnam, despite the squalor and hopelessness to which we have condemned generation after generation of Negro Americans, despite the vulgarity of much of our culture, we have, I think, done much to keep hope alive in this world. Until the Negro is fully franchised and represented, we cannot rebut those who are cynical about our democratic professions. Nevertheless, our history has been one of a steady extension and strengthening of the democratic procedures — and this extension continues in this period. The rule of law has likewise been extended and strengthened, more in the last decade than in any period in the past. Though our economy can fairly be described as exploitative, we have, by the exercise of democracy on behalf of equality and compassion, compelled it to distribute the product of our agriculture and technology more equitably than many countries which claim to have institutionalized economic egalitarianism have distributed their products.

As for our failures, they seem to me — to use a phrase expressive of some of our shabbier values — about par for the course. The war in Vietnam is a monstrous miscarriage of a foreign policy that may very well have been ill-conceived to begin with, but I do not think it morally more odious than similar undertakings on the part of other great powers, most notably and most recently, the French in Indochina and Algeria, who now censure us. Among the alienated, it is terribly fashionable now to say that ours is a "racist" society. Of course it is. I should like to know of an organized society anywhere of which this cannot be said. I have yet to visit a country in which the dominant minority, even where it is physically indistinguishable from any of its majorities, is not persuaded of its own innate superiority. I think it far less remarkable that we can be accurately described as racist than that we can be described as a people who have shown some eagerness to be free of this condition and have elected leaders and representatives committed to this form of liberation.

Though I have been writing here of "this society" as if it were an entity that the individual can sensibly be "for" or "against," this way of approaching the problem has never made much sense to me. There are too many loose and loosely connected phenomena here, too many currents and cross-currents, too many forces in tension and contention, to speak of the whole thing as a machine in operation. There is plenty to be despised and rejected. There is much that stands in need of radical change or of destruction. There is at the same time much to be defended and preserved, the liberty of the individual being to my mind the first of these because it is the most needed for the realization of any possibilities. The work of any sentient individual, of anyone interested in appraising the utility or inutility of freedom, would seem to me to be to cast a discriminating eye on the nation — not to determine whether it is good or bad but to associate these qualities with the specific values and institutions that come within his field of vision. His judgment will not be reflected in cease-and-desist orders from the President or rewarded by vast transformations of the economic order. But the exercise of liberty will be a defense of liberty, while its disparagement will surely lead to its atrophy and disappearance and to the end of any talk about human possibilities.

DENNIS H. WRONG
identity: problem and catchword

Lionel Trilling's story "Of This Time, Of That Place" begins with a young English professor assigning to his freshman class as their first theme the writing of an essay on "Who I am and Why I came to Dwight College." The first of the student papers the professor examines is that of a tall, gawky, badly-dressed but passionately if confusedly eloquent boy who has previously caught his attention. It begins: "I think, therefore I am, but who am I? Tertan I am, but what is Tertan? Of this time, of that place, of some parentage, what does it matter?" After puzzling a few minutes over the strange mixture of fractured syntax and verbal richness of Tertan's essay, Professor Howe picks up a second student paper and proceeds to read: "I am Arthur J. Casebeer, Jr. My father is Arthur J. Casebeer and my grandfather was Arthur J. Casebeer before him. My mother is Nina Wimble Casebeer. Both of them are college graduates and my father is in insurance. I was born in St. Louis eighteen years ago and we still make our residence there."

Trilling's story was published in 1943 before the terms "identity" and "identity crisis" had joined "neurosis," "alienation," and "mass society" as semantic beacons of our time, verbal emblems expressing our discontent with modern life and modern society. In his latest book, Erik H. Erikson, the creator of "identity" as a distinctive psychoanalytic and social psychological concept, has brought together in revised and reworked form all of his major papers on the subject.[1] Commenting on the promiscuous popularity the concept has achieved, he observes that adolescents these days know that "they are supposed to have" an identity

From Dissent, Sept.–Oct., 1968. Copyright 1968 by Dissent. Reprinted by permission.
[1] Erik H. Erikson, Identity, Youth and Crisis, New York: W. W. Norton, 1968.

crisis and compares the "strenuous overtness" of their search for identity with the earlier emergence into general awareness of sexual wishes that formerly remained unconscious and gave rise to hysterical symptoms.[2] Almost unavoidably, one today sees Trilling's two student protagonists as having arrived, tentatively at least, at contrasting solutions to the problem of identity. Tertan rejects the socially established coordinates of time and place and even of family, and seeks a deeper, more individual and at the same time less history-bound definition of himself. Casebeer, while "less interesting" than Tertan, "at least knows who he is," reflects Trilling's professor. The contemporary reader is likely to see Tertan as a seeker after "authentic selfhood," a quest that for him, as Trilling brilliantly shows, verges on the psychotic; Casebeer, on the other hand, is obviously a conformist, a square, a budding "organization man," who buries his true self by identifying himself totally with his social roles as scion of the Casebeer family, son of college graduates and a potential graduate himself, heir of a respected businessman, urban Midwesterner.

Such a facile response to the contrast between the two students is little more than an ideological reflex that does scant justice to the subtlety and moral ambiguity of Trilling's fictional exploration of Tertan's fate in the prosaic setting of an American college. I call it "ideological," using the word pejoratively, because "identity crisis," "authentic selfhood," and "conformism" belong to a whole language of social criticism that has recently become widely diffused in our society, reaching well beyond academic, literary, and psychoanalytic circles. "Alienation," "anomie," "mass society," "the loss of community," "the overdeveloped society," "organization man," "status-seeking," "soulless bureaucracy" are other terms in this language. I am not objecting to these terms as such — we owe most of them to our very greatest thinkers in the social sciences and they have become popular precisely because they truly convey something of the quality of life in modern society and express live historical emotions. What E. V. Walter has said of the idea of mass society applies more broadly to our language of fundamental social criticism as a whole:

> It cultivates the muddle ground between fact and supposition that is frequently occupied by metaphysics and myth. . . . It is a sensitive indicator of changes dimly perceived, and perhaps it is a proto-scientific formulation of truth, bringing to consciousness features of

[2] *Ibid.*, pp. 28–29.

reality not yet substantial enough to be grasped by the methods of science.[3]

But this language is able, because of the very evocative power it possesses, to elicit indiscriminate negative responses to modern life. Nowadays its separate words frequently blur into a general hum of lamentation about the fate of man in modern society, in which each individual word loses its conceptual clarity in contributing to an overall tonal effect. Any stick to beat a dog with. That each concept has a rich and varied intellectual and ideological pedigree is forgotten. That the accusations leveled at modern society are inconsistent with each other is overlooked. Thus our society is charged with destroying the primordial bonds of community among men, while at the same time it is pilloried for promoting conformity and "togetherness"; man is said to be alienated, rootless, and drifting in contemporary America; but simultaneously he is too tightly controlled by giant bureaucracies and manipulated by the mass media. Our consumption-centered economy encourages Americans to retreat into a "privatized" life of affluence in which they are apathetic about public affairs, yet modern society is also seen as the seedbed of fanatical mass movements whose followers willingly submerge their private lives in dedication to a collective goal.

Now all of these charges may be true and their inconsistency apparent rather than real. Different charges may describe the behavior and attitudes of different segments of the population; or there may be a temporal dialectic in which a particular response when played out is succeeded by an alternative reaction to basically unchanged social conditions. But popular social criticism, indiscriminately brandishing as weapons such terms as "alienation" or "materialism," rarely dispels the impression of inconsistency by systematically analyzing these possible connections between the various counts of the indictment drawn up against American society. A word like "alienation" with its peculiarly rich sociological and philosophical heritage has become virtually shapeless in its current intellectual usage. And now the same fate threatens "identity" and "identity crisis," initially defined and analyzed so carefully and acutely by Erikson.

I do not think the solution is to abandon words that have become blurred as a result of wide and rapid circulation. The history of the social sciences sufficiently attests to the disastrous consequences of efforts

[3] E. V. Walter, "Mass Society: The Late Stages of an Idea," *Social Research*, XXXI (Winter, 1964), pp. 409–410.

to create a hygienic would-be "scientific" vocabulary free of all ideological overtones. And, anyway, communication between social scientists and a larger public is so rapid and extensive today that even the most arid neologisms quickly reach a wide audience. As Erikson notes, the classic psychoanalytic terms are themselves subject to changing historical connotations "which range from what Freud called the 'age-old ideologies of the Super-Ego' to the influence of contemporary ideologies."[4] Far from advocating the avoidance of "richly suggestive terms," he suggests that "an awareness of the changing connotation of its most important terms is one of the requirements of a 'self-analytic' psychosocial orientation."[5]

What we must try to do is restore something of the analytical precision of the original terms; while simultaneously taking into account the resonance they have acquired, as their creators obviously could not. By analyzing the very cheapening process to which the language has been subject as an intellectual and social phenomenon in its own right, we may be able to arrest it and thereby advance the debate over the situation of man in our time.

Why do people suffer from identity crisis or identity confusion in modern industrial society? One common answer is that society fails to provide them with stable social roles in which they can take pride and invest a large portion of their emotional energies and self-respect. Work roles are increasingly perceived as routines that fail to relate the worker to the larger community in any significant way; the emphasis on the consumption of trivia and the commercial provision of unimportant services and time-killing leisure pursuits that characterizes our advanced, "tertiary-stage" industrial economy, makes many occupational activities seem intrinsically debasing— one thinks of advertising executives, cocktail waitresses, or change-makers in Nevada gambling casinos. The difficulty of achieving stable identity is increased by the sharp discontinuities in the life-cycle of Americans that result from rapid social change, from mobility, and from an imposed age-graded schedule of involvement in successive specialized and segregated institutional milieus — school, college, military service, work. Moreover, exposure to the mass media means exposure to constantly shifting fashions in life-styles. Even traditional sexual and familial roles become ambiguous, while depressions, wars, and cold wars destroy continuity of understanding between generations.

[4] Erikson, *op. cit.*, p. 228.
[5] *Ibid.*, p. 230.

The diagnosis is familiar. In effect, it equates identity with *social identity* and delineates the features of modern industrial society that prevent the establishment of firm, preferably life-long, social identities. Social identity is the social psychological counterpart of social role — the role as viewed from the perspective of its incumbent rather than in relation to the larger system of roles to which it belongs. The failure of society to provide the individual with "secure anchorage," as it is often put, in a social role is seen as the cause of the anxieties and identity crises from which we suffer. True, it is a sociological commonplace that men play multiple social roles in modern society. But they are likely to lack firm attachment (or anchorage) to any one of them, nor do they possess a secure total status in society cutting across their various "situated,"[6] or segmental roles, such as that of "aristocrat" or "peasant" in the more rigidly stratified society of the past. Thus some social analysts have treated the decline of hereditary social classes and the increase in mobility aspirations as the major cause of the individual's uncertain and fluctuating identity in modern society.[7] Earlier writers, including Durkheim, more often stressed the decline of a common, deeply experienced religious faith uniting people who differed widely in status, wealth, occupation, and even language.

II

When viewed in this manner, the concept of identity becomes almost a synonym for "identification," with which it shares a common linguistic origin. At most, social identity is the result of successful identification with another person, group, social role, or movement. Sociologists have perhaps preferred to adopt the term identity, not merely because it is briefer and more economical — such considerations hardly seem to have influenced their terminological habits in general — but because it lacks the special psychoanalytic connotation of identification. However, even in psychoanalytic theory, identification is a socializing mechanism, in fact the primary socializing mechanism through which the superego itself is shaped and stabilized.

Yet Erikson rejects the equation of identity and identification from the standpoint of psychoanalytic theory.[8] He regards identity-formation

6 Erving Goffman uses the term "situated roles" in *Encounters*, Indianapolis: Bobbs-Merrill, 1961, p. 96.

7 Thomas Luckmann and Peter Berger, "Social Mobility and Personal Identity," *European Journal of Sociology*, V (1964), pp. 331–344.

8 Erikson, *op. cit.*, pp. 158–159.

as a distinct psychic mechanism that "begins where the usefulness of identification ends."[9] Identity is the unique selection made by the individual from all of the significant identifications of his past. "It arises from the selective repudiation and mutual assimilation of childhood identifications and their absorption in a new configuration."[10] Erikson goes on to observe that identity requires confirmation by the society to which the individual belongs. He makes it plain, however, that he does not mean confirmation of the individual's membership in a group or recognition that he has attained a new social role, but rather confirmation of the unique being that the individual has forged out of the identifications of his childhood and adolescence. Identity to Erikson means *personal* identity and is something more than mere social identity or the subjective reflection of a social role.

Personal identity is roughly synonymous with *individuality*. An important connotation that it has in common with individuality is that of referring to an objective attribute of the person rather than solely to the idea he has of himself. Identity, therefore, is not the same thing as "self-concept" or "self-image," although many writers have dealt with it as if it were. Self-image is more changeable than identity, lacking the "genetic continuity" Erikson ascribes to the latter.[11] Also, self-image is closer to consciousness, whereas identity, while including "the conscious sense of individual identity," refers also to an "unconscious striving for a continuity of experience."[12] If I understand Erikson correctly, identity includes both what the person really is — *how* in psychoanalytic terms his ego has synthesized his previous identifications and social roles — and his perception of himself, whether positive or negative.

That a sense of identity is something more than a favorable self-conception needs stressing because identity has tended to become a value-charged, almost a charismatic, term, with its secure achievement regarded as equivalent to personal salvation. It has acquired the same aura that clings to "mental health" or "normality" in popular usage. Even the experiencing of identity crisis is interpreted as a mark of spiritual depth: Erikson reports that "on occasion I find myself asking a student who claims that he is in an 'identity crisis' whether he is complaining or boasting."[13] Yet, surely, one may wryly or ruefully accept

9 *Ibid.*, p. 159.
10 *Ibid.*
11 *Ibid.*, p. 209.
12 *Ibid.*, p. 208.
13 *Ibid.*, p. 314.

one's identity. A sense of identity may include a regretful recognition of limits: recognition that the self one has become precludes some experiences, some kinds of mastery, has closed off what were once open possibilities as now lying beyond the range of personal capability. Opportunities for mobility and the array of life-styles popularized by the mass media are often held responsible for delaying the achievement of secure personal identity by keeping modern men in a state of perpetual adolescence, fostering an illusory sense of limitless possibilities that survives well into the adult years.

Existentialist discussions of identity appear to be at sharp variance with the sociological perspective that stresses the lack of consensus, the fragmented social structure, and the discontinuities in individual growth of modern society. Existentialist writers are primarily concerned with personal identity. Far from seeing identification with a social role as a prerequisite for identity, they see it as the ultimate death of authentic selfhood. To Sartre, the man who identifies himself totally with his social role is guilty of "bad faith" in seeking to destroy the freedom of his "being-for-itself" by grasping at an illusory "being-in-itself." Such men have handed their lives over to others when they imprison themselves in the "dance of the grocer, of the tailor, of the auctioneer, by which they endeavour to persuade their clientele that they are nothing but a grocer, an auctioneer, a tailor."[14] Their betrayal of identity lies in their effort to *be* their social role in the same way that "this inkwell is an inkwell, or the glass is a glass."[15] Sartre calls the man who thus tries to escape from his freedom and individuality a *"salaud"* — a French colloquialism which, it seems to me, is most accurately translated in this usage as "square." The square is he who fails to realize the arbitrariness, the humanly invented character, of all social codes. He is blind to the fact that his social role is truly a role in the theatrical sense — something one plays at, not something that exhausts the definition of what one is.

Writers influenced by existentialism complain that modern society, far from preventing identity-formation by failing to provide secure social roles, depersonalizes the individual by forcing him into standardized roles and treating him as an altogether replaceable integer in a mass. He becomes the mere appendage of a technical-bureaucratic machine. Political propaganda, mass production, and the mass media pre-

14 Jean-Paul Sartre, *Being and Nothingness*, New York: Philosophical Library, 1956, p. 59.
15 *Ibid.*

suppose a public that is merely an aggregate of identical consumers or "little men" and thus they promote conformism. Such protests are, of course, by no means confined to existentialists. Like existentialism, however, they stem from an antinomian, romantic individualist tradition that sees social controls and collectively-imposed patterns of conduct as the enemies of personal identity. This tradition appears to be directly at odds with the sociological critique that regards identity as the result of anchorage in a group or social role and condemns the atomization, rootlessness and anomie of modern life. Yet popular social criticism borrows freely from both perspectives, seemingly unaware of the contradictions between them. In its purer forms existentialism, however, purports to describe not merely man as victimized by modern society, but the human condition in general. Thus appropriations of the language of existentialism for attacks on the specifics of contemporary life are of doubtful justification. For to the existentialist *all* social roles, *all* institutions, mores, and group loyalties are threats to personal identity — the rituals of the tribesman and the allegiances of serf and nobleman as much as the "alienated" work routines of the organization man or the frantic sociability of the suburban housewife. All social identities are masks, false-faces that stifle the lonely freedom and uniqueness of the person. As John Schaar observes:

> With all its richness of sociological and psychological detail, the philosophical theory of alienation refuses to concede that alienation can be reduced to an exclusively sociological problem and understood solely in sociological terms.[16]

If one similarly pushes the sociological critique of modern society to its limits, it is hard to see why the writers who make use of it so frequently deplore conformism, organization men, and the search for roots in suburbia. For if identity is the result of firm group attachments and rootedness in established social roles, what is wrong with efforts to create a master loyalty to the corporation or the suburban community? Was the feudal vassal's loyalty to his liege different in kind from that of the modern executive to his company? For that matter, why object, now that religious faith has lost its hold over men, to establishing a new consensus based on a secular ideology interpreted by a priesthood of state officials? Indeed, both David Riesman and William H. Whyte have understood, unlike many of those who parrot

[16] John H. Schaar, *Escape from Authority*, New York: Harper Torchbooks, 1964, p. 225.

them, that other-direction as a way of life and managerial efforts to create loyal organization men owe a great deal to popularization and application of the findings and principles of modern social science.

III

Ultimately, there is a fundamental moral and philosophical conflict between the antinomian individualist and the sociological positions. But having drawn as sharply as possible the contrast between their critical perspectives on modern society, I shall now explore the sense in which both are true and complement one another.

Social analysts have often observed that greater individuality, a heightened sense of identity, and a richer inner life may flourish where social constraints are more binding and inescapable than under the regime of aimless freedom enjoyed by so many contemporary Americans. Maurice Stein, a sociologist, remarks that: "It almost seems as if community in the anthropological sense is necessary before human maturity or individuation can be achieved. . . ."[17] Although David Riesman has frequently protested such an interpretation, readers of *The Lonely Crowd* have often understood it as an attack on other-direction and a eulogy of inner-direction. Yet our Victorian grandfathers were models of inner-direction, while the entire modern movement in the arts, social sciences, psychiatry, education, child-rearing, and attitudes toward sexuality have been an assault on the repressiveness, narrowness, intolerance, and hypocrisy of the faiths and moral codes by which they lived.

Erikson observes that "the concept or at least the term identity seems to pervade much of the literature on the Negro Revolution in this country."[18] While he concerns himself chiefly with problems of Negro identity, he also recognizes that the survival of racial oppression poses a challenge to white identities and provides opportunities to reshape them: "there is, in fact, more than poetic justice in the historical fact that many young white people who feel deeply deprived *because* of their family's 'culture' find an identity and a solidarity in living and working with those who are said to be deprived for lack of such culture."[19] The attitude of some writers and intellectuals toward the Negro is also instructive. Norman Mailer and Jack Kerouac are only the most

[17] Maurice R. Stein, *The Eclipse of Community*, Princeton, N.J.: Princeton University Press, 1959, p. 248.
[18] Erikson, *op. cit.*, p. 295.
[19] *Ibid.*, p. 304.

extreme and most publicized celebrants of the greater vitality, inner freedom, and personal integrity often attributed to Negro life and personality.

Yet Negro writers have protested, like Ralph Ellison, that the Negro is the "invisible man," or, like James Baldwin, that "nobody knows my name." Negro identity in America is, of course, a negative identity in Erikson's terms, and without accepting the romanticism of Mailer and Kerouac, it may for that very reason be for some of its bearers less stifling of personal identity than approved roles. Under the worst conditions of oppression in the South it often became no more than a self-conscious mask worn in encounters with whites.

The fragmentation of the civil rights movement, however, reflects (among other things) growing conflict between the claims of personal and social identity among Negroes themselves. The civil rights movement initially seemed to promise viability and identity to Negroes as individual human beings. Its failures and the shift in the focus of protest from segregation in the South to conditions in the urban ghettos of the North have intensified efforts by Negroes to replace a negative group identity with a positive one, efforts that seemed exotic and cultist even a few years ago when the Black Muslims first received national publicity. Today someone like Ralph Ellison, with his passionate insistence on his right to his own individuality as it has been shaped by the cultural resources of Western civilization as a whole, strikes black power militants as being positively old-fashioned and out of touch — if they do not simply dismiss him as an Uncle Tom.[20]

Hereditary statuses, precisely because they represent an unalterable social fate for the individual, may threaten personal identity less than statuses that are subject to the tensions and agonies of choice and for which the individual, having chosen, must prepare himself in advance by what sociologists have called "anticipatory socialization." [21] Also, frequent and intimate personal contacts between members of different social classes and status groups have often been the rule where status rank is hereditary, as Philippe Ariès and Philip Mason have recently shown to have been the case in Medieval Europe and 18th-century England respectively.[22] Thus in contrast to the negative racial identities

[20] See Ellison's intense discussion of this issue in *Shadow and Act*, New York: Random House, 1964, especially in the essay "The World and the Jug," pp. 107–143.

[21] Luckmann and Berger, *op. cit.*, pp. 338–339.

[22] Phillipe Ariès, *Centuries of Childhood*, New York: Alfred A. Knopf, 1962, pp. 207, 411–415; Philip Mason, *Prospero's Magic: Some Thoughts on Class and Race*, New York and Toronto: Oxford University Press, 1962.

of modern times, the person of low social rank in these societies was less likely to become invisible and nameless behind a derogatory stereotype.

A sense of personal identity is more easily safeguarded by formal manners and strict rules of etiquette governing one's relations with others than by the ready friendliness, lack of reserve, and casual intimacy with strangers that have long been recognized as characteristically American. The very rigidity and artificiality of formal manners permits the individual to maintain his inner life intact behind the barrier they present and gives an unmistakable significance to breakthroughs to intimacy (recall the meaning of achieving a linguistic "thee-thou" relationship with someone in the great 19th-century European novels). In America, on the other hand, quite apart from the blatant commercial exploitation of pretended intimacy (pseudo-*Gemeinschaft*, as Merton has called it[23]), an apparently intimate rapport is established so quickly that one cannot be certain it means anything beyond the moment.

IV

Considerations such as these have been advanced by ideological conservatives in defense of hereditary social hierarchies and restrictions on personal freedom. As has often been pointed out, much of both the language and the substance of modern social criticism is derived from, or is at least continuous with, the conservative critique of democracy and equality developed in the aftermath of the French Revolution. And the usual riposte by defenders of contemporary American life is to label the critics reactionaries whose nostalgia for the past prevents them from enthusing over the vastly increased opportunities for freedom and individuality made available to all men, rather than to an upper-class elite alone, by democratization and technical progress. This rebuttal is unconvincing, not merely because analysts who hold a wide variety of theoretical and ideological positions agree on essentially the same diagnosis of the ills of American society, but because the fact that greater freedom and individuality are *possible* under conditions of relative classlessness, democratic culture, and high living standards is not the same thing as their *actual* realization. Moreover, if these values have truly been maximized, how account for the swelling chorus of discontent? To attribute complaints about modern life to disgruntled conservatives, disillusioned ex-Marxists, literary snobs, Europeans with

23 Robert K. Merton, *Mass Persuasion*, New York: Harper and Brothers, 1946, p. 142.

an aristocratic bias or, more generally, "alienated intellectuals," is to ignore the resonance of the complaints in much wider circles. After all, books of social criticism have been best-sellers and have often found an audience among the very groups whose way of life they attack — suburbanites, junior executives, the metropolitan middle class in general.

Conservatives and radicals, to be sure, often agree that equality of opportunity and material abundance have led to identity crisis, dehumanization, and cultural mediocrity rather than to freer, more creative, and more individualized lives for the majority of the population. Comparing two recent philosophical works analyzing modern technological society — Hannah Arendt's *The Human Condition* and Herbert Marcuse's *One-Dimensional Man* — one is struck by the underlying similarity of outlook by the authors in spite of obvious contrasts between their theoretical positions. Arendt is full of misgivings about the world created by modern science and technology when contrasted with the pre-industrial societies of classical antiquity and Medieval Christendom where men preserved a sense of limits in a world they did not regard as entirely of their own making; she fears that "it is quite conceivable that the modern age — which began with such an unprecedented and promising outburst of human activity — may end in the deadliest, most sterile passivity history has ever known." [24] Marcuse, too, is aware of the loss of psychological depth in our "one-dimensional" world dominated by a purely functional rationality of anonymous and impersonal social controls, in which even the formerly explosive, reality-transcending energies of sexuality and artistic creativity are tamed in the service of a system that becomes all the more difficult to challenge because it tolerates them. But Marcuse insists that man must complete his "technological project" by realizing the historical alternative to the present: "the planned utilization of resources for the satisfaction of vital needs with a minimum of toil, the transformation of leisure into free time, the pacification of the struggle for existence." [25]

Arendt is more concerned with what has been lost in the passage from the stable, stratified, faith-centered societies of the past, while Marcuse's central aim is to reassert the liberating potentialities of science and technology — including social science — that have been used to create

---

[24] Hannah Arendt, *The Human Condition*, New York: Doubleday Anchor Books, 1959, p. 295.
[25] Herbert Marcuse, *One-Dimensional Man*. Boston: Beacon Press, 1964, pp. 252–253.

weapons of destruction, useless consumers' goods, and bureaucratic monoliths. The thrust of Arendt's argument is "conservative" while Marcuse's is "radical," although such simplifying labels do both writers an injustice.

Personal identity may have been less threatened by the more custom-bound societies of the past in which social institutions and norms retained an aura of sacredness and "charisma" than by today's self-evidently man-made world of technological rationality and planned social organization. But we cannot — even if we wished to — restore the mystery and absolutism of social control for the sake of enhancing identity, nor for the sake of anything else. What Max Weber called the "disenchantment of the world" applies to the realm of society as well as to the realm of nature:

> There are no mysterious incalculable forces that come into play but rather ... one can, in principle, master all things by calculation. ... One need no longer have recourse to magical means in order to master or implore the spirits, as did the savage, for whom such mysterious powers existed. Technical means and calculations perform the service.[26]

Social science itself has made no small contribution to the de-mystification of social processes and, like the physical sciences, it has often been used to promote ends and to justify moral and political creeds at odds with those cherished by its creators. George Orwell once remarked that, even if one concedes the truth of the most extreme accusations of ugliness and human and natural destructiveness made against machine civilization, one nevertheless cannot travel to London by ox-cart with automobiles whizzing past and planes droning overhead, at least not in the same spirit that was possible before the invention of modern transportation. The very consciousness of the existence of alternatives that are faster and mechanically more efficient alters the experience, no matter how intensely the wider social consequences of the alternatives may be deplored. Thus, Orwell argued, the self-conscious effort of Medievalist and agrarian ideologues to eliminate modern technology from their lives and to live by handicrafts, relying only on human and animal labor power, is absurd.[27]

The same applies to efforts to recreate social ties and identities that

---

[26] Max Weber, "Science as a Vocation," in *From Max Weber: Essays in Sociology,* transl. and introd. by Hans Gerth and C. Wright Mills, New York: Oxford University Press, 1946, p. 139.

[27] George Orwell, *The Road to Wigan Pier,* New York: Berkeley Medallion Books, 1961, p. 167.

have the emotional power of the pre-bureaucratic past. Thus those sociologists, who argue for the necessity of stable social roles, binding consensus, and firm intermediate group loyalties, are not in the end inconsistent when many of them refuse to applaud contemporary conformism, organization men, suburban sociability, and the "engineered consent" of the mass media or of totalitarian methods of control. The loyalty of the executive to his company is ultimately either a compulsive, willed loyalty or a qualified and provisional one that is different in kind from the loyalty of the vassal to his liege. We have lost the capacity to believe, or even to achieve a "willing suspension of disbelief" in the transcendental authority of society, just as we some time ago lost the capacity to believe in supernatural authority — which Nietzsche understood when he proclaimed the death of God. Nor is the existentialist who asserts that all socially-imposed conduct is alienating as ahistorical as he appears to be. For he knows that only in the modern world of de-mystified instrumentalized social structures could he gain such insight into the human condition.

Social identity no longer provides a protective barrier for personal identity. Nor does it destroy personal identity by eliminating choice and the possibility of "role distance."[28] With the important exception of racially persecuted minorities and the underclass of the permanently poor and unemployed, the absorption of individuality by social role is not an irresistible process but one that depends on the complicity of the individual himself: he *chooses* to be an eager role-player, to wear the uniform of the organization man, the happy consumer, or the hippie. We know now that even totalitarian regimes are less successful in reshaping men in their own ideological image than we once thought. The existentialist insistence that man makes himself by his choices has never been more apposite than to the situation of modern man. Yet the existentialist, while actively engaging himself in protests against social injustice and political oppression, usually describes only in negaitve terms the social order that might encourage men to make the most authentic choices. The sociologist, on the other hand, has been unable to advance much beyond specifying the formal requirements such an order must meet: minimal consensus, a degree of continuity in socialization, the regulation of potentially destructive group conflicts, etc. Can we create a society that does not mythologize its own processes of social control and allows men to choose their own identities without making life appear a senseless routine?

28 Goffman, *op. cit.*, pp. 105–110.

chapter two

The Alienated Yet
Active Minority:
A Saving Remnant?

introduction

So much has been written about student activism on campus, dissent in America, and the radical new left that it would seem impossible for anyone to approach an analysis of the subject in a fresh, provocative way. But Theodore Roszak, professor of history at California State College at Hayward, has produced a synthesis which serves to integrate not only the essays in this chapter, but, in a sense, all the chapters of the text. He approaches, first, the problem of defining what in our society causes dissent; he labels the enemy "technocracy." Roszak is a man who desires social change, and his indictment of those in power who espouse technology and in turn exploit the public is savage, full of sarcasm, and ultimately, wholly sane. His decision to use *Playboy* sexuality as an example of "repressive desublimation" — a Marcusian term — is perceptive; the horror of this perception, coupled with his analysis of parental inability to act against technocracy, persuades the reader to hope along with Roszak that our youth can and will bring salvation. However, Roszak is not indiscriminately praising youthful activists; in fact, many critics will praise his discussion of the present "spoiled" generation. Yet he makes such a valid point about the "adolescentization of dissent" that even doubters must reassess their views. Roszak believes that "the alienated young are giving shape to something that looks like the saving vision our endangered civilization requires" but he also wants "to help educate them in what they are about."

There is no doubt that the late Robert F. Kennedy desired change and also shared the hope that a better future would come about through young people. His speech "What Can the Young Believe?" was given at an ADA dinner in Philadelphia in February, 1967. As a rhetorical form, speech-making demands of the writer and speaker a conscious effort to arouse the audience and to keep their attention. Language, phrasing, style, parallelism of thought become even more important when one can rely primarily upon only the listening habits of the audience. Kennedy's speech is an important example of how structure reinforces theme. He deliberately sets up contrasts between "us" and "them," "we" and "they" throughout. During the first part of the speech, the accumulation of such phrases as "they tell us," "they did not know," "they see the world" countered during the second half with "we are friends of education," "we seem headed toward," "and if we add to the insincerity" all point to the deliberate setting up of a confrontation theme. Such a theme reaches a peak when Kennedy recites a short declaration given by a student representative at a meeting of the Board of Regents of the University of California. The "we" shifts to the student voice here and the "you" becomes the adult listener. The techniques used in Kennedy's speech show us that structure (form) does reinforce theme (meaning) and that conscious effort does produce worthy results.

The companion piece, or properly, the counter-argument, to Robert Kennedy's speech appeared a month later in *The New Republic.* Henry Fairlie begins his essay, "How is Youth to be Served?", with quotations from Michael Oakeshott and C. H. Wilson, a technique which helps define the problem he sees in Kennedy's approach to youth. By using proper historical perspective, Fairlie demonstrates the use of what composition instructors refer to as "outside sources." Fairlie also shows his readers how to take materials from the opposing point of view and work them effectively into an argumentative essay. Many of his statements compare with some of Roszak's views and George Kennan's analysis of what is wrong with today's youth.

"Rebels Without a Program," first delivered by Kennan as a speech at the opening of a new library at Swarthmore College in December, 1967, and then published in the *New York Times Magazine* on January 21, 1968, brought such a response from both students and faculty, that the speech and their letters with a lengthy reply by Kennan have appeared in book form in *Democracy and the Student Left*. Kennan says in his later reply that he did not know his arguments would bring such criticism and opposition; but his condemnation of the radical left on campus for its "utter absorption in the affairs of this passing world," for its being full of passion but not much knowledge, and for lacking a program of political reform certainly opened the floodgates of counter-argument. Kennan is a scholar, a historian, and a man committed to preserving an ideal in the university which he felt was and is being attacked. His style is that of a concerned, intelligent man who voices long-accepted premises which require serious response.

The interview with Mrs. Del Behrend by T George Harris lets the reader hear what a one-time campus radical believes about infiltrating the system in order to work for change from within. This type of interview is built on a selection of questions by the interviewer to make the interviewee bear the main burden of the conversation. The interviewer can make various points by emphasizing the other person's remarks; hence he can show the absurdity or validity of that person's position, and by doing so, create what might be called an indirect counter-argument. Although much of what Mrs. Behrend says relates directly to the Roszak essay, in particular, one might ask whether she will succeed in "making an economically affluent society into a humane society" or will the technocracy Roszak describes sublimate her urges? Is she being deluded when she feels that top management sees eye to eye with young people on the "whole question of social change"? Is business really more "flexible"? Roszak would probably say no but would also wish Mrs. Behrend good luck in her efforts.

Richard Poirier's diagnosticians in his "technotronic society" (Brzezinski's term) are very much like Roszak's experts in the technocracy, and Poirier's fear at the end of the essay that adult society just wants to absorb youth is also a reminder of how Roszak analyzes the power of the state. Although, in "The War Against the Young," the image of war and of weapons is carried throughout the first two paragraphs, Poirier defines the struggle as a cultural one. His essay can be analyzed for transition techniques, allusions, analogies, sentence structure, and style. Poirier's direct attack on Kennan reveals that both men, even though they disagree, draw their ammunition from the same sources.

Kenneth Keniston, a psychology professor, shows this same interrelatedness when he refers to Poirier's essay and also labels Kennan's discussion a "moral condemnation of 'revolting students' rather than an effort to explain their behavior." He discusses two current analyses of student behavior: Feuer's "Oedipal Rebellion," a psychological approach, and Brzezinski's and Bell's "Historical Irrelevance," a sociological theory. He disputes both and then explains his own theory which centers around what he calls "youth," an extension between adolescence and adulthood. He discusses protest as a fusion of two revolutions, one quantitative, the other qualitative. Because the first revolution is already completed in Scarsdale, the more affluent students are asking, "Beyond freedom and affluence, what?" Keniston's essay is a model of lucid construction so skillfully engineered that it compels the reader to follow his thought. The letter to the editor written by Daniel Bell and Keniston's reply show us that two professional men, although trying to counter the other's position, end up sounding almost childish in their accusations and finger pointing. The moral here would seem to be that try as we might to practice craft and control in communication, we aren't always going to succeed.

THEODORE ROSZAK
youth and the great refusal

The struggle of the generations is one of the obvious constants of human affairs. One stands in peril of some presumption, therefore, to suggest that the rivalry between young and adult in Western society during the current decade is uniquely critical. And yet it is necessary to risk such presumption if one is not to lose sight of our most important contemporary source of radical dissent and cultural innovation. For better or worse, most of what is presently happening that is new, provocative, and engaging in politics, education, the arts, social relations (love, courtship, family, community), is the creation either of youth who are profoundly, even fanatically, alienated from the parental generation, or of those who address themselves primarily to the young. It is at the level of youth that significant social criticism now looks for a responsive hearing as, more and more, it grows to be the common expectation that the young should be those who act, who make things happen, who take the risks, who generally provide the ginger. It would be of interest in its own right that the age-old process of generational disaffiliation should now be transformed from a peripheral experience in the life of the individual and the family into a major lever of radical social change. But if one believes, as I do, that the alienated young are giving shape to something that looks like the saving vision our endangered civilization requires, then there is no avoiding the need to understand and to educate them in what they are about.

The reference . . . is primarily to America, but it is headline news that generational antagonism has achieved international dimensions. . . .

Over and again it is the same story throughout Western Europe: the students may rock their societies; but without the support of adult social forces, they cannot overturn the established order. And that support would seem to be nowhere in sight. On the contrary, the adult social forces — including those of the traditional left — are the lead-bottomed ballast of the status quo. The students march to the Internationale, they run up the red flag, they plaster the barricades with pictures of Marxist heroes old and new . . . but the situation they confront stubbornly refuses to yield to a conventional left-right analysis. Is it any wonder that, in despair, some French students begin to chalk up the disgruntled

from *The Making of a Counter Culture* by Theodore Roszak. Copyright © 1968, 1969 by Theodore Roszak. Reprinted by permission of Doubleday and Company, Inc.

slogan *"Je suis marxiste, tendance Groucho"* ("I'm a Marxist of the Groucho variety") ? At last they are forced to admit that the entrenched consensus which repels their dissent is the generational phenomenon which the French and German young have begun to call "daddy's politics."

If the experience of the American young has anything to contribute to our understanding of this dilemma, it stems precisely from the fact that the left-wing of our political spectrum has always been so pathetically foreshortened. Our young are therefore far less adept at wielding the vintage rhetoric of radicalism than their European counterparts. But where the old categories of social analysis have so little to tell us (or so I will argue here), it becomes a positive advantage to confront the novelty of daddy's politics free of outmoded ideological preconceptions. The result may then be a more flexible, more experimental, though perhaps also a more seemingly bizarre approach to our situation. Ironically, it is the American young, with their underdeveloped radical background, who seem to have grasped most clearly the fact that, while such immediate emergencies as the Vietnam war, racial injustice, and hard-core poverty demand a deal of old-style politicking, the paramount struggle of our day is against a far more formidable, because far less obvious, opponent, to which I will give the name "the technocracy" — a social form more highly developed in America than in any other society. The American young have been somewhat quicker to sense that in the struggle against *this* enemy, the conventional tactics of political resistance have only a marginal place, largely limited to meeting immediate life-and-death crises. Beyond such front-line issues, however, there lies the greater task of altering the total cultural context within which our daily politics takes place.

By the technocracy, I mean that social form in which an industrial society reaches the peak of its organizational integration. It is the ideal men usually have in mind when they speak of modernizing, up-dating, rationalizing, planning. Drawing upon such unquestionable imperatives as the demand for efficiency, for social security, for large-scale coordination of men and resources, for ever higher levels of affluence and ever more impressive manifestations of collective human power, the technocracy works to knit together the anachronistic gaps and fissures of the industrial society. The meticulous systematization Adam Smith once celebrated in his well-known pin factory now extends to all areas of life, giving us human organization that matches the precision of our mechanistic organization. So we arrive at the era of social engineering in which entrepreneurial talent broadens its province to orchestrate the total human context which surrounds the industrial complex. Politics, education, leisure, entertainment, culture as a whole, the unconscious drives, and even, as we shall see, protest against the technocracy itself: all these become the subjects of purely technical scrutiny and of purely technical manipulation. The effort is to create a new social organism whose health depends upon its capacity to keep the technological heart beating regularly. . . .

In the technocracy, nothing is any longer small or simple or readily apparent to the non-technical man. Instead, the scale and intricacy of all human activities — political, economic, cultural — transcends the competence of the amateurish citizen and inexorably demands the attention of specially trained experts. Further, around this central core of experts who deal with large-scale public necessities, there grows up a circle of subsidiary experts who, battening on the general social prestige of technical skill in the technocracy, assume authoritative influence over even the most seemingly personal aspects of life: sexual behavior, child-rearing, mental health, recreation, etc. In the technocracy everything aspires to become purely technical, the subject of professional attention. The technocracy is therefore the regime of experts — or of those who can employ the experts. Among its key institutions we find the "think-tank," in which is housed a multi-billion-dollar brainstorming industry that seeks to anticipate and integrate into the social planning quite simply everything on the scene. Thus, even before the general public has become fully aware of new developments, the technocracy has doped them out and laid its plans for adopting or rejecting, promoting or disparaging.[1]

Within such a society, the citizen, confronted by bewildering bigness and complexity, finds it necessary to defer on all matters to those who know better. Indeed, it would be a violation of reason to do otherwise, since it is universally agreed that the prime goal of the society is to keep the productive apparatus turning over efficiently. In the absence of expertise, the great mechanism would surely bog down, leaving us in the midst of chaos and poverty. . . . [T]he roots of the technocracy reach deep into our cultural past and are ultimately entangled in the

[1] For a report on the activities of a typical technocratic brain trust, Herman Kahn's Hudson Institute, see Bowen Northrup's "They Think For Pay" in *The Wall Street Journal*, September 20, 1967. Currently, the Institute is developing strategies to integrate hippies and to exploit the new possibilities of programmed dreams.

scientific world-view of the Western tradition. But for our purposes here it will be enough to define the technocracy as that society in which those who govern justify themselves by appeal to technical experts who, in turn, justify themselves by appeal to scientific forms of knowledge. And beyond the authority of science, there is no appeal. . . .

When any system of politics devours the surrounding culture, we have totalitarianism, the attempt to bring the whole of life under authoritarian control. We are bitterly familiar with totalitarian politics in the form of brutal regimes which achieve their integration by bludgeon and bayonet. But in the case of the technocracy, totalitarianism is perfected because its techniques become progressively more subliminal. The distinctive feature of the regime of experts lies in the fact that, while possessing ample power to coerce, it prefers to charm conformity from us by exploiting our deep-seated commitment to the scientific world-view and by manipulating the securities and creature comforts of the industrial affluence which science has given us.

So subtle and so well rationalized have the arts of technocratic domination become in our advanced industrial societies that even those in the state and/or corporate structure who dominate our lives must find it impossible to conceive of themselves as the agents of a totalitarian control. Rather, they easily see themselves as the conscientious managers of a munificent social system which is, by the very fact of its broadcast affluence, incompatible with any form of exploitation. At worst, the system may contain some distributive inefficiencies. But these are bound to be repaired . . . in time. And no doubt they will be. Those who gamble that either capitalism or collectivism is, by its very nature, incompatible with a totally efficient technocracy, one which will finally eliminate material poverty and gross physical exploitation, are making a risky wager. It is certainly one of the oldest, but one of the weakest radical arguments which insists stubbornly that capitalism is *inherently* incapable of laying golden eggs for everyone.

The great secret of the technocracy lies, then, in its capacity to convince us of three interlocking premises. They are:

1. That the vital needs of man are (contrary to everything the great souls of history have told us) purely technical in character. Meaning: the requirements of our humanity yield wholly to some manner of formal analysis which can be carried out by specialists possessing certain impenetrable skills and which can then be translated by them directly into a congeries of social and economic programs, personnel

management procedures, merchandise, and mechanical gadgetry. If a problem does not have such a technical solution, it must not be a *real* problem. It is but an illusion . . . a figment born of some regressive cultural tendency.

2. That this formal (and highly esoteric) analysis of our needs has now achieved 99 per cent completion. Thus, with minor hitches and snags on the part of irrational elements in our midst, the prerequisites of human fulfillment have all but been satisfied. It is this assumption which leads to the conclusion that wherever social friction appears in the technocracy, it must be due to what is called a "breakdown in communication." For where human happiness has been so precisely calibrated and where the powers that be are so utterly well intentioned, controversy could not possibly derive from a substantive issue, but only from misunderstanding. Thus we need only sit down and reason together and all will be well.

3. That the experts who have fathomed our heart's desires and who alone can continue providing for our needs, the experts who *really* know what they're talking about, all happen to be on the official payroll of the state and/or corporate structure. The experts who count are the certified experts. And the certified experts belong to headquarters. . . .

. . . The prime strategy of the technocracy . . . is to level life down to a standard of so-called living that technical expertise can cope with — and then, on that false and exclusive basis, to claim an intimidating omnicompetence over us by its monopoly of the experts. Such is the politics of our mature industrial societies, our truly *modern* societies, where two centuries of aggressive secular skepticism, after ruthlessly eroding the traditionally transcendent ends of life, have concomitantly given us a proficiency of technical means that now oscillates absurdly between the production of frivolous abundance and the production of genocidal munitions. Under the technocracy we become the most scientific of societies; yet, like Kafka's K., men throughout the "developed world" become more and more the bewildered dependents of inaccessible castles wherein inscrutable technicians conjure with their fate. True, the fool-proof system again and again bogs down in riot or apathetic rot or the miscalculations of overextended centralization; true, the chronic obscenity of thermonuclear war hovers over it like a gargantuan bird of prey feeding off the bulk of our affluence and intelligence. But the members of the parental generation, storm-tossed by depression, war, and protracted war-scare, cling fast to the technocracy for the myopic sense of prosperous security it allows. By what right would they complain against those who intend only the best, who purport to be the agents of democratic consensus, and who invoke the high rhetorical sanction of the scientific world view, our most unimpeachable mythology? How does one take issue with the paternal beneficence of such technocratic Grand Inquisitors? Not only do they provide bread aplenty, but the bread is soft as floss: it takes no effort to chew, and yet is vitamin-enriched.

To be sure, there are those who have not yet been cut in on the material advantages, such as the "other Americans" of our own country. Where this is the case, the result is, inevitably and justifiably, a forceful, indignant campaign fixated on the issue of integrating the excluded into the general affluence. Perhaps there is an exhausting struggle, in the course of which all other values are lost sight of. But, at last (why should we doubt it?), all the disadvantaged minorities are accommodated. And so the base of the technocracy is broadened as it assimilates its wearied challengers. It might almost be a trick, the way such politics works. It is rather like the ruse of inveigling someone you wish to capture to lean all his weight on a door you hold closed . . . and then, all of a sudden, throwing it open. He not only winds up inside, where you want him, but he comes crashing in full tilt.

In his analysis of this "new authoritarianism," Herbert Marcuse calls our attention especially to the technocracy's "absorbent power": its capacity to provide "satisfaction in a way which generates submission and weakens the rationality of protest." As it approaches maturity, the technocracy does indeed seem capable of anabolizing every form of discontent into its system.

Let us take the time to consider one significant example of such "repressive desublimation" (as Marcuse calls it). The problem is sexuality, traditionally one of the most potent sources of civilized man's discontent. To liberate sexuality would be to create a society in which technocratic discipline would be impossible. But to thwart sexuality outright would create a widespread, explosive resentment that required constant policing; and, besides, this would associate the technocracy with various puritanical traditions that enlightened men cannot but regard as superstitious. The strategy chosen, therefore, is not harsh repression, but rather the *Playboy* version of total permissiveness which now imposes its image upon us in every slick movie and posh magazine that comes along. In the affluent society, we have sex and sex galore — or so we are to believe. But when we look more closely we see that this sybaritic promiscuity wears a special social coloring. It has been assimilated to an income level and social status available only to our well-heeled junior executives and the jet set. After all, what does it cost to rent these yachts full of nymphomaniacal young things in which our playboys sail off for orgiastic swimming parties in the Bahamas? *Real* sex, we are led to believe, is something that goes with the best scotch, twenty-seven-dollar sunglasses, and platinum-tipped shoelaces. Anything less is a shabby substitute. Yes, there is permissiveness in the technocratic society; but it is only for the swingers and the big spenders. It is the reward that goes to reliable, politically safe henchmen of the status quo. Before our would-be playboy can be an assembly-line seducer, he must be a loyal employee.

Moreover, *Playboy* sexuality is, ideally, casual, frolicsome, and vastly promiscuous. It is the anonymous sex of the harem. It creates no binding loyalties, no personal attachments, no distractions from one's primary responsibilities — which are to the company, to one's career and social position, and to the system generally. The perfect playboy practices a career enveloped by noncommittal trivialities: there is no home, no family, no romance that divides the heart painfully. Life off the job exhausts itself in a constant run of imbecile affluence and impersonal orgasms.

Finally, as a neat little dividend, the ideal of the swinging life we find in *Playboy* gives us a conception of femininity which is indistinguishable from social idiocy. The woman becomes a mere playmate, a submissive bunny, a mindless decoration. At a stroke, half the population is reduced to being the inconsequential entertainment of the technocracy's pampered elite.

As with sexuality, so with every other aspect of life. The business of inventing and flourishing treacherous parodies of freedom, joy, and fulfillment becomes an indispensable form of social control under the technocracy. In all walks of life, image makers and public relations specialists assume greater and greater prominence. The regime of experts relies on a lieutenancy of counterfeiters who seek to integrate the discontent born of thwarted aspiration by way of clever falsification.

Thus:

We call it "education," the "life of the mind," the "pursuit of the truth." But it is a matter of machine-tooling the young to the needs of our various baroque bureaucracies: corporate, governmental, military, trade union, educational.

We call it "free enterprise." But it is a vastly restrictive system of oligopolistic market manipulation, tied by institutionalized corruption to the greatest munitions boondoggle in history and dedicated to infantilizing the public by turning it into a herd of compulsive consumers.

We call it "creative leisure": finger painting and ceramics in the university extension, tropic holidays, grand athletic excursions to the far mountains and the sunny beaches of the earth. But. it is, like our sexual longings, an expensive adjunct of careerist high-achievement: the prize that goes to the dependable hireling.

We call it "pluralism." But it is a matter of the public authorities solemnly affirming everybody's right to his own opinion as an excuse for ignoring anybody's troubling challenge. In such a pluralism, critical viewpoints become mere private prayers offered at the altar of an inconsequential conception of free speech.

We call it "democracy." But it is a matter of public opinion polling in which a "random sample" is asked to nod or wag the head in response to a set of prefabricated alternatives, usually related to the *faits accomplis* of decision makers, who can always construe the polls to serve their own ends. Thus, if 80 per cent think it is a "mistake" that we ever "went into" Vietnam, but 51 per cent think we would "lose prestige" if we "pulled out now," then the "people" have been "consulted" and the war goes on with their "approval."

We call it "debate." But it is a matter of arranging staged encounters between equally noncommittal candidates neatly tailored to fit thirty minutes of prime network time, the object of the exercise being to establish an "image" of competence. If there are interrogators present, they have been hand-picked and their questions rehearsed.

We call it "government by the consent of the governed." But even now, somewhere in the labyrinth of the paramilitary agencies an "area specialist" neither you nor I elected is dispatching "special advisors" to a distant "trouble spot" which will be the next Vietnam. And somewhere in the depths of the oceans a submarine commander neither you nor I elected is piloting a craft equipped with firepower capable of cataclysmic devastation and perhaps trying to decide if — for reasons neither you nor I know — the time has come to push the button.

It is all called being "free," being "happy," being the Great Society. . . .

It is essential to realize that the technocracy is not the exclusive product of that old devil capitalism. Rather, it is the product of a mature and accelerating industrialism. The profiteering could be eliminated: the technocracy would remain in force. The key problem we have to deal with is the paternalism of expertise within a socioeconomic system which is so organized that it is inextricably beholden to expertise. And, moreover, to an expertise which has learned a thousand ways to manipulate our acquiescence with an imperceptible subtlety. . . .

How do the traditional left-wing ideologies equip us to protest against such well-intentioned use of up-to-date technical expertise for the purpose of making our lives more comfortable and secure? The answer is: they don't. After all, locked into this leviathan industrial apparatus as we are, where shall we turn for solutions to our dilemmas if not to the experts? Or are we, at this late stage of the game, to relinquish our trust in science? in reason? in the technical intelligence that built the system in the first place?

It is precisely to questions of this order that the dissenting young address themselves in manifestoes like this one pinned to the main entrance of the embattled Sorbonne in May 1968:

> The revolution which is beginning will call in question not only capitalist society but industrial society. The consumer's society must perish of a violent death. The society of alienation must disappear from history. We are inventing a new and original world. Imagination is seizing power.[2]

Why should it be the young who rise most noticeably in protest against the expansion of the technocracy?

There is no way around the most obvious answer of all: the young stand forth so prominently because they act against a background of nearly pathological passivity on the part of the adult generation. It would only be by reducing our conception of citizenship to absolute zero that we could get our senior generation off the hook for its astonishing default. The adults of the World War II period, trapped as they have been in the frozen posture of befuddled docility — the condition Paul Goodman has called "the nothing can be done disease" — have in effect divested themselves of their adulthood, if that term means anything more than being tall and debt-worried and capable of buying liquor without having to show one's driver's license. Which is to say: they have surrendered their responsibility for making morally demanding decisions, for generating ideals, for controlling public authority, for safeguarding the society against its despoilers.

Why and how this generation lost control of the institutions that hold

[2] From *The Times* (London), May 17, 1968: Edward Mortimer's report from Paris.

sway over its life is more than we can go into here. The remembered
background of economic collapse in the thirties, the grand distraction
and fatigue of the war, the pathetic if understandable search for security
and relaxation afterwards, the bedazzlement of the new prosperity, a
sheer defensive numbness in the face of thermonuclear terror and the
protracted state of international emergency during the late forties and
fifties, the red-baiting and witch-hunting and out-and-out barbarism of
the McCarthy years . . . no doubt all these played their part. And there
is also the rapidity and momentum with which technocratic totalitarianism came rolling out of the war years and the early cold war era, drawing on heavy wartime industrial investments, the emergency centralization of decision making, and the awe-stricken public reverence for science.
The situation descended swiftly and ponderously. Perhaps no society
could have kept its presence of mind; certainly ours didn't. And the
failure was not only American. Nicola Chiaromonte, seeking to explain
the restiveness of Italian youth, observes,

> . . . the young — those born after 1940 — find themselves living in a
> society that neither commands nor deserves respect. . . . For has
> modern man, in his collective existence, laid claim to any god or ideal
> but the god of possession and enjoyment and the limitless satisfaction
> of material needs? Has he put forward any reason for working but
> the reward of pleasure and prosperity? Has he, in fact, evolved any-
> thing but this "consumer society" that is so easily and falsely
> repudiated? [3]

On the American scene, this was the parental generation whose god
Allen Ginsberg identified back in the mid-fifties as the sterile and
omnivorous "Moloch." It is the generation whose premature senility
Dwight Eisenhower so marvelously incarnated and the disease of whose
soul shone so lugubriously through the public obscenities that men like
John Foster Dulles and Herman Kahn and Edward Teller were prepared
to call "policy." There are never many clear landmarks in affairs of
the spirit, but Ginsberg's *Howl* may serve as the most public report
announcing the war of the generations. It can be coupled with a few

[3] The "falsely" in this quotation relates to Chiaromonte's very astute analysis of
a doctrinaire blind spot in the outlook of Italian youth — namely their tendency to
identify the technocracy with capitalism, which, as I have suggested, is a general
failing of European youth movements. This very shrewd article appears in *Encounter*, July 1968, pp. 25–27. Chiaromonte does not mention the factor of fascism
in Italy, but certainly in Germany the cleavage between young and old has been
driven deeper than anything we know in America by the older generation's complicity with Nazism.

other significant phenomena. One of them would be the appearance of *MAD* magazine, which has since become standard reading material for the junior high school population. True, the dissent of *MAD* often sticks at about the Katzenjammer Kids level; but nevertheless the nasty cynicism *MAD* began applying to the American way of life — politics, advertising, mass media, education — has had its effect. *MAD* brought into the malt shops the same angry abuse of middle-class America which comics like Mort Sahl and Lenny Bruce were to begin bringing into the night clubs of the mid-fifties. The kids who were twelve when *MAD* first appeared are in their early twenties now — and they have had a decade's experience in treating the stuff of their parents' lives as contemptible laughing stock.

At a more significant intellectual level, Ginsberg and the beatniks can be associated chronologically with the aggressively activist sociology of C. Wright Mills — let us say with the publication of Mills' *Causes of World War III* (1957), which is about the point at which Mills' writing turned from scholarship to first-class pamphleteering. Mills was by no means the first postwar figure who sought to tell it like it is about the state of American public life and culture; the valiant groups that maintained radical journals like *Liberation* and *Dissent* had been filling the wilderness with their cries for quite as long. And as far back as the end of the war, Paul Goodman and Dwight Macdonald were doing an even shrewder job of analyzing technocratic America than Mills was ever to do — and without relinquishing their humanitarian tone. But it was Mills who caught on. His tone was more blatant; his rhetoric, catchier. He was the successful academic who suddenly began to cry for action in a lethargic profession, in a lethargic society. He was prepared to step forth and brazenly pin his indictment like a target to the enemy's chest. And by the time he finished playing Emile Zola he had marked out just about everybody in sight for accusation.

Most important, Mills was lucky enough to discover ears that would hear: his indignation found an audience. But the New Left he was looking for when he died in 1961 did not appear among his peers. It appeared among the students — and just about nowhere else. If Mills were alive today, his following would still be among the under thirties (though the Vietnam war has brought a marvelous number of his academic colleagues out into open dissent — but will they stay out when the war finally grinds to its ambiguous finish?).

Admittedly, the dissent that began to simmer in the mid-fifties was not confined to the young. The year 1957 saw the creation at the adult level of resistance efforts like SANE and, a bit later, Turn Toward Peace. But precisely what do groups like SANE and TTP tell us about adult America, even where we are dealing with politically conscious elements? Looking back, one is struck by their absurd shallowness and conformism, their total unwillingness to raise fundamental issues about the quality of American life, their fastidious anti-communism, and above all their incapacity to sustain any significant initiative on the political landscape. Even the Committee of Correspondence, a promising effort on the part of senior academics (formed around 1961) quickly settled for publishing a new journal. Currently the diminishing remnants of SANE and TTP seem to have been reduced to the role of carping (often with a deal of justice) at the impetuous extremes and leftist flirtations of far more dynamic youth groups like the Students for a Democratic Society, or the Berkeley Vietnam Day Committee, or the 1967 Spring Mobilization. But avuncular carping is not initiative. And it is a bore, even if a well-intentioned bore, when it becomes a major preoccupation. Similarly, it is the younger Negro groups that have begun to steal the fire from adult organizations — but in this case with results that I feel are apt to be disastrous.

The fact is, it is the young who have in their own amateurish, even grotesque way, gotten dissent off the adult drawing board. They have torn it out of the books and journals an older generation of radicals authored, and they have fashioned it into a style of life. They have turned the hypotheses of disgruntled elders into experiments, though often without the willingness to admit that one may have to concede failure at the end of any true experiment.

When all is said and done, however, one cannot help being ambivalent toward this compensatory dynamism of the young. For it is, at last, symptomatic of a thoroughly diseased state of affairs. It is not ideal, it is probably not even good that the young should bear so great a responsibility for inventing or initiating for their society as a whole. It is too big a job for them to do successfully. It is indeed tragic that in a crisis that demands the tact and wisdom of maturity, everything that looks most hopeful in our culture should be building from scratch — as must be the case when the builders are absolute beginners.

Beyond the parental default, there are a number of social and psychic facts of life that help explain the prominence of the dissenting young in our culture. In a number of ways, this new generation happens to be particularly well placed and primed for action.

Most obviously, the society is getting younger — to the extent that in

America, as in a number of European countries, a bit more than 50 per cent of the population is under twenty-five years of age. Even if one grants that people in their mid-twenties have no business claiming, or letting themselves be claimed for the status of "youth," there still remains among the authentically young in the thirteen to nineteen bracket a small nation of twenty-five million people. (As we shall see below, however, there is good reason to group the mid-twenties with their adolescent juniors.)

But numbers alone do not account for the aggressive prominence of contemporary youth. More important, the young seem to *feel* the potential power of their numbers as never before. No doubt to a great extent this is because the market apparatus of our consumer society has devoted a deal of wit to cultivating the age-consciousness of old and young alike. Teen-agers alone control a stupendous amount of money and enjoy much leisure; so, inevitably, they have been turned into a self-conscious market. They have been pampered, exploited, idolized, and made almost nauseatingly much of. With the result that whatever the young have fashioned for themselves has rapidly been rendered grist for the commercial mill and cynically merchandised by assorted hucksters — *including* the new ethos of dissent, a fact that creates an agonizing disorientation for the dissenting young (and their critics) and to which we will return presently.

The force of the market has not been the only factor in intensifying age-consciousness, however. The expansion of higher education has done even more in this direction. In the United States we have a college population of nearly six million, an increase of more than double over 1950. And the expansion continues as college falls more and more into the standard educational pattern of the middle-class young.[4] Just as the

[4] The rapid growth of the college population is an international phenomenon, with Germany, Russia, France, Japan, and Czechoslovakia (among the developed countries) equaling or surpassing the increase of the United States. UNESCO statistics for the period 1950–64 are as follows:

	1950	1964	Increase
U.S.A.	2.3 million	5 million	2.2x
U.K.	133,000	211,000	1.6x
U.S.S.R.	1.2 million	3.6 million	3.0x
Italy	192,000	262,000	1.3x
France	140,000	455,000	3.3x
W. Germany	123,000	343,000	2.8x
W. Berlin	12,000	31,000	2.6x
Czechoslovakia	44,000	142,000	3.2x
Japan	391,000	917,000	2.3x
India	404,000	1.1 million	2.2x

dark satanic mills of early industrialism concentrated labor and helped create the class-consciousness of the proletariat, so the university campus, where up to thirty thousand students may be gathered, has served to crystallize the group identity of the young — with the important effect of mingling freshmen of seventeen and eighteen with graduate students well away in their twenties. On the major campuses, it is often enough the graduates who assume positions of leadership, contributing to student movements a degree of competence that the younger students could not muster. When one includes in this alliance that significant new entity, the non-student — the campus roustabout who may be in his late twenties — one sees why "youth" has become such a long-term career these days. The grads and the non-students easily come to identify their interests and allegiance with a distinctly younger age group. In previous generations, they would long since have left these youngsters behind. But now they and the freshmen just out of high school find themselves all together in one campus community.

The role of these campus elders is crucial, for they tend to be those who have the most vivid realization of the new economic role of the university. Being closer to the technocratic careers for which higher education is supposed to be grooming them in the Great Society, they have a delicate sensitivity to the social regimentation that imminently confronts them, and a stronger sense of the potential power with which the society's need for trained personnel endows them. In some cases their restiveness springs from a bread-and-butter awareness of the basic facts of educational life these days, for in England, Germany, and France the most troublesome students are those who have swelled the numbers in the humanities and social studies only to discover that what the society really wants out of its schools is technicians, not philosophers. In Britain, this strong trend away from the sciences over the past four years continues to provoke annoyed concern from public figures who are not the least bit embarrassed to reveal their good bourgeois philistinism by loudly observing that the country is not spending its money to produce poets and Egyptologists — and then demanding a sharp cut in university grants and stipends.[5]

Yet at the same time, these non-technicians know that the society cannot do without its universities, that it cannot shut them down or

[5] In his 1967 Reith Lectures, Dr. Edmund Leach seeks to account for the steady swing from the sciences. See his *Runaway World*, British Broadcasting Company, 1968. For reflections on the same phenomenon in Germany, see Max Beloff's article in *Encounter*, July 1968, pp. 28–33.

brutalize the students without limit. The universities produce the brains the technocracy needs; therefore, making trouble on the campus is making trouble in one of the economy's vital sectors. And once the graduate students — many of whom may be serving as low-level teaching assistants — have been infected with qualms and aggressive discontents, the junior faculty, with whom they overlap, may soon catch the fevers of dissent and find themselves drawn into the orbit of "youth."

The troubles at Berkeley in late 1966 illustrate the expansiveness of youthful protest. To begin with, a group of undergraduates stages a sit-in against naval recruiters at the Student Union. They are soon joined by a contingent of non-students, whom the administration then martyrs by selective arrest. A non-student of nearly thirty — Mario Savio, already married and a father — is quickly adopted as spokesman for the protest. Finally, the teaching assistants call a strike in support of the menaced demonstration. When at last the agitation comes to its ambiguous conclusion, a rally of thousands gathers outside Sproul Hall, the central administration building, to sing the Beatles' "Yellow Submarine" — which happens to be the current hit on all the local high-school campuses. If "youth" is not the word we are going to use to cover this obstreperous population, then we may have to coin another. But undeniably the social grouping exists with a self-conscious solidarity.

If we ask who is to blame for such troublesome children, there can be only one answer: it is the parents who have equipped them with an anemic superego. The current generation of students is the beneficiary of the particularly permissive child-rearing habits that have been a feature of our postwar society. Dr. Spock's endearing latitudinarianism (go easy on the toilet training, don't panic over masturbation, avoid the heavy discipline) is much more a reflection than a cause of the new (and wise) conception of proper parent-child relations that prevails in our middle class. A high-consumption, leisure-wealthy society simply doesn't need contingents of rigidly trained, "responsible" young workers. It cannot employ more than a fraction of untrained youngsters fresh out of high school. The middle class can therefore afford to prolong the ease and drift of childhood, and so it does. Since nobody expects a child to learn any marketable skills until he gets to college, high school becomes a country club for which the family pays one's dues. Thus the young are "spoiled," meaning they are influenced to believe that being human has something to do with pleasure and freedom. But unlike their parents, who are also avid for the plenty and leisure of the consumer society, the young have not had to sell themselves for their comforts or to accept them on a part-time basis. Economic security is something they can take for granted — and on it they build a new, uncompromised personality, flawed perhaps by irresponsible ease, but also touched with some outspoken spirit. Unlike their parents, who must kowtow to the organizations from which they win their bread, the youngsters can talk back at home with little fear of being thrown out in the cold. One of the pathetic, but, now we see, promising characteristics of postwar America has been the uppityness of adolescents and the concomitant reduction of the paterfamilias to the general ineffectuality of a Dagwood Bumstead. In every family comedy of the last twenty years, dad has been the buffoon.

The permissiveness of postwar child-rearing has probably seldom met A. S. Neill's standards — but it has been sufficient to arouse expectations. As babies, the middle-class young got picked up when they bawled. As children, they got their kindergarten finger paintings thumbtacked on the living room wall by mothers who knew better than to discourage incipient artistry. As adolescents, they perhaps even got a car of their own (or control of the family's), with all of the sexual privileges attending. They passed through school systems which, dismal as they all are in so many respects, have nevertheless prided themselves since World War II on the introduction of "progressive" classes having to do with "creativity" and "self-expression." These are also the years that saw the proliferation of all the mickey mouse courses which take the self-indulgence of adolescent "life problems" so seriously. Such scholastic pap mixes easily with the commercial world's effort to elaborate a total culture of adolescence based on nothing but fun and games. (What else could a culture of adolescence be based on?) The result has been to make of adolescence, not the beginning of adulthood, but a status in its own right: a limbo that is nothing so much as the prolongation of an already permissive infancy.

To be sure, such an infantization of the middle-class young has a corrupting effect. It ill prepares them for the real world and its unrelenting if ever more subtle disciplines. It allows them to nurse childish fantasies until too late in life; until there comes the inevitable crunch. For as life in the multiversity wears on for these pampered youngsters, the technocratic reality principle begins grimly to demand its concessions. The young get told they are now officially "grown up," but they have been left too long without any taste for the rigidities and hypocrisies that adulthood is supposed to be all about. General Motors all of a sudden wants barbered hair, punctuality, and an appropriate reverence for the conformities of the organizational hierarchy. Washington wants patriotic cannon fodder with no questions asked. Such prospects do not look like fun from the vantage point of between eighteen and twenty years of relatively carefree drifting.[6]

Some of the young (most of them, in fact) summon up the proper sense of responsibility to adjust to the prescribed patterns of adulthood; others, being incorrigibly childish, do not. They continue to assert pleasure and freedom as human rights and begin to ask aggressive questions of those forces that insist, amid obvious affluence, on the continued necessity of discipline, no matter how subliminal. This is why, for example, university administrators are forced to play such a false game with their students, insisting on the one hand that the students are "grown-up, responsible men and women," but on the other hand knowing full well that they dare not entrust such erratic children with any power over their own education. For what can one rely upon them to do that will suit the needs of technocratic regimentation?

The incorrigibles either turn political or drop out. Or perhaps they fluctuate between the two, restless, bewildered, hungry for better ideas about grown-upness than GM and IBM or LBJ seem able to offer. Since they are improvising their own ideal of adulthood — a task akin to lifting oneself by one's bootstraps — it is all too easy to go pathetically wrong. Some become ne'er-do-well dependents, bumming about the bohemias of America and Europe on money from home; others simply bolt. The FBI reports the arrest of over ninety thousand juvenile runaways in 1966; most of those who flee well-off middle-class homes get picked up by the thousands each current year in the big-city bohemias, fending off malnutrition and venereal disease. The immigration departments of Europe record a constant level over the past few years of something like ten thousand disheveled "flower children" (mostly American, British, German, and Scandinavian) migrating to the Near East and India — usually toward Katmandu (where drugs are cheap and legal) and a deal of hard knocks along the way. The influx has been sufficient to force Iran and Afghanistan to substantially boost the "cash in hand" requirements of prospective tourists. And the British counsel-general in Istanbul officially requested Parliament in late 1967 to grant him increased accommodations for the "swarm" of penniless

---

[6] Even the Young Americans for Freedom, who staunchly champion the disciplined virtues of the corporate structure, have become too restive to put up with the indignity of conscription. With full support from Ayn Rand, they have set the draft down as "selective slavery." How long will it be before a conservatism that perceptive recognizes that the ideal of free enterprise has nothing to do with technocratic capitalism?

young Englishmen who have been cropping up at the consulate on their way east, seeking temporary lodgings or perhaps shelter from Turkish narcotics authorities.[7]

One can flippantly construe this exodus as the contemporary version of running off with the circus; but the more apt parallel might be with the quest of third-century Christians (a similarly scruffy, uncouth, and often half-mad lot) for escape from the corruptions of Hellenistic society: it is much more a flight *from* than *toward*. Certainly for a youngster of seventeen, clearing out of the comfortable bosom of the middle-class family to become a beggar is a formidable gesture of dissent. One makes light of it at the expense of ignoring a significant measure of our social health.

So, by way of a dialectic Marx could never have imagined, technocratic America produced a potentially revolutionary element among its own youth. The bourgeoisie, instead of discovering the class enemy in its factories, finds it across the breakfast table in the person of its own pampered children. To be sure, by themselves the young might drift into hopeless confusion and despair. But now we must add one final ingredient to this ebullient culture of youthful dissent, which gives it some chance of achieving form and direction. This is the adult radical who finds himself in a plight which much resembles that of the bourgeois intellectual in Marxist theory. In despair for the timidity and lethargy of his own class, Marx's middle-class revolutionary was supposed at last to turn renegade and defect to the proletariat. So in postwar America, the adult radical, confronted with a diminishing public among the "cheerful robots" of his own generation, naturally gravitates to the restless middle-class young. Where else is he to find an audience? The working class, which provided the traditional following for radical ideology, now neither leads nor follows, but sits tight and plays safe: the stoutest prop of the established order. If the adult radical is white, the ideal of Black Power progressively seals off his entrée to Negro organizations. As for the exploited masses of the Third World, they have as little use for white Western ideologues as our native blacks — and in any case they are far distant. Unless he follows the strenuous example of a Regis Debray, the white American radical can do little more than sympathize from afar with the revolutionary movements of Asia, Africa, and Latin America.

[7] For the statistics mentioned, see *Time*, September 15, 1967, pp. 47–49; *The Observer* (London), September 24, 1967; and *The Guardian* (London), November 18, 1967.

On the other hand, the disaffected middle-class young are at hand, suffering a strange new kind of "immiserization" that comes of being stranded between a permissive childhood and an obnoxiously conformist adulthood, experimenting desperately with new ways of growing up self-respectfully into a world they despise, calling for help. So the radical adults bid to become gurus to the alienated young or perhaps the young draft them into service.

Of course, the young do not win over all the liberal and radical adults in sight. From more than a few their readiness to experiment with a variety of dissenting life styles comes in for severe stricture — which is bound to be exasperating for the young. What are they to think? For generations, left-wing intellectuals have lambasted the bad habits of bourgeois society. "The bourgeoisie" they have insisted, "is obsessed by greed; its sex life is insipid and prudish; its family patterns are debased; its slavish conformities of dress and grooming are degrading; its mercenary routinization of existence is intolerable; its vision of life is drab and joyless; etc., etc." So the restive young, believing what they hear, begin to try this and that, and one by one they discard the vices of their parents, preferring the less structured ways of their own childhood and adolescence — only to discover many an old-line dissenter, embarrassed by the brazen sexuality and unwashed feet, the disheveled dress and playful ways, taking up the chorus, "No, that is not what I meant. That is not what I meant at all."

For example, a good liberal like Hans Toch invokes the Protestant work ethic to give the hippies a fatherly tongue-lashing for their "consuming but noncontributing" ways. They are being "parasitic," Professor Toch observes, for "the hippies, after all accept — even demand — social services, while rejecting the desirability of making a contribution to the economy."[8] But *of course* they do. Because we have an economy of cybernated abundance that does not need their labor, that is rapidly severing the tie between work and wages, that suffers from hard-core poverty due to maldistribution, not scarcity. From this point of view, why is the voluntary dropping-out of the hip young any more "parasitic" than the enforced dropping-out of impoverished ghetto dwellers? The economy can do abundantly without all this labor. How

[8] Hans Toch, "The Last Word on the Hippies," *The Nation*, December 4, 1967. See also the jaundiced remarks of Eric Hoffer in the New York *Post Magazine*, September 23, 1967, pp. 32–33; Milton Mayer writing in *The Progressive*, October 1967; and Arnold Wesker's "Delusions of Floral Grandeur" in the English magazine *Envoy*, December 1967.

better, then, to spend our affluence than on those minimal goods and services that will support leisure for as many of us as possible? Or are these hippies reprehensible because they seem to enjoy their mendicant idleness, rather than feeling, as the poor apparently should, indignant and fighting mad to get a good respectable forty-hour-week job? There are criticisms to be made of the beat-hip bohemian fringe of our youth culture — but this is surely not one of them.

It would be a better general criticism to make of the young that they have done a miserably bad job of dealing with the distortive publicity with which the mass media have burdened their embryonic experiments. Too often they fall into the trap of reacting narcissistically or defensively to their own image in the fun-house mirror of the media. Whatever these things called "beatniks" and "hippies" originally were, or still are, may have nothing to do with what *Time, Esquire, Cheeta,* CBSNBCABC, Broadway comedy, and Hollywood have decided to make of them. Dissent, the press has clearly decided, is hot copy. But if anything, the media tend to isolate the weirdest aberrations *and* consequently to attract to the movement many extroverted poseurs. But what does bohemia do when it finds itself massively infiltrated by well-intentioned sociologists (and we now all of a sudden have specialized "sociologists of adolescence"), sensationalizing journalists, curious tourists, and weekend fellow travelers? What doors does one close on them? The problem is a new and tough one: a kind of cynical smothering of dissent by saturation coverage, and it begins to look like a far more formidable weapon in the hands of the establishment than outright suppression.

Again, in his excellent article on the Italian students quoted above, Nicola Chiaromonte tells us that dissenters

> must detach themselves, must become resolute "heretics." They must detach themselves quietly, without shouting or riots, indeed in silence and secrecy; not alone but in groups, in real "societies" that will create, as far as possible, a life that is independent and wise.... It would be ... a nonrhetorical form of "total rejection."

But how is one to develop such strategies of dignified secrecy when the establishment has discovered exactly the weapon with which to defeat one's purposes: the omniscient mass media? The only way anybody or anything stays underground these days is by trying outlandishly hard — as when Ed Saunders and a group of New York poets titled a private publication *Fuck You* to make sure it stayed off the newsstands. But it can be quite as distortive to spend all one's time evading the electronic eyes and ears of the world as to let oneself be inaccurately reported by them.

Yet to grant the fact that the media distort is not the same as saying that the young have evolved no life style of their own, or that they are unserious about it. We would be surrendering to admass an absolutely destructive potential if we were to take the tack that whatever it touches is automatically debased or perhaps has no reality at all. In London today at some of the better shops one can buy a Chinese Army-style jacket, advertised as "Mao Thoughts in Burberry Country: elegant navy flannel, revolutionary with brass buttons and Mao collar." The cost: £28 . . . a mere $68. Do Mao and the cultural revolution suddenly become mere figments by virtue of such admass larks?

Commercial vulgarization is one of the endemic pests of twentieth-century Western life, like the flies that swarm to sweets in the summer. But the flies don't create the sweets (though they may make them less palatable) ; nor do they make the summer happen. It will be my contention that there is, despite the fraudulence and folly that collects around its edges, a significant new culture a-borning among our youth, and that this culture deserves careful understanding, if for no other reason than the sheer size of the population it potentially involves.

But there *are* other reasons, namely, the intrinsic value of what the young are making happen. If, however, we want to achieve that understanding, we must insist on passing over the exotic tidbits and sensational case histories the media offer us. Nor should we resort to the superficial snooping that comes of cruising bohemia for a few exciting days in search of local color and the inside dope, often with the intention of writing it all up for the slick magazines. Rather, we should look for major trends that seem to outlast the current fashion. We should try to find the most articulate public statements of belief and value the young have made or have given ear to; the thoughtful formulations, rather than the off-hand gossip. Above all, we must be willing, in a spirit of critical helpfulness, to sort out what seems valuable and promising in this dissenting culture, as if indeed it mattered to us whether the alienated young succeeded in their project.

Granted this requires a deal of patience. For what we are confronted with is a progressive "adolescentization" of dissenting thought and culture, if not on the part of its creators, then on the part of much of its audience. And we should make no mistake about how far back into the early years of adolescence these tastes now reach. Let me offer one illuminating example. In December of 1967, I watched a group of

thirteen-year-olds from a London settlement house perform an improvised Christmas play as part of a therapeutic theater program. The kids
had concocted a show in which Santa Claus had been imprisoned by
the immigration authorities for entering the country without proper
permission. The knock at official society was especially stinging, coming
as it did instinctively from some very ordinary youngsters who had
scarcely been exposed to any advanced intellectual influences. And
whom did the thirteen-year-olds decide to introduce as Santa's libera-
tors? An exotic species of being known to them as "the hippies," who
shiva-danced to the jailhouse and magically released Father Christmas,
accompanied by strobelights and jangling sitars.

However lacking older radicals may find the hippies in authenticity
or revolutionary potential, they have clearly succeeded in embodying
radical disaffiliation — what Herbert Marcuse has called the Great
Refusal — in a form that captures the need of the young for unrestricted
joy. The hippy, real or as imagined, now seems to stand as one of the
few images toward which the very young can grow without having to
give up the childish sense of enchantment and playfulness, perhaps
because the hippy keeps one foot in his childhood. Hippies who may
be pushing thirty wear buttons that read "Frodo Lives" and decorate
their pads with maps of Middle Earth (which happens to be the name
of one of London's current rock clubs). Is it any wonder that the best
and brightest youngsters at Berkeley High School (just to choose the
school that happens to be in my neighborhood) are already coming to
class barefoot, with flowers in their hair, and ringing with cowbells?

Such developments make clear that the generational revolt is not
likely to pass over in a few years' time. The ethos of disaffiliation is
still in the process of broadening down through the adolescent years,
picking up numbers as time goes on. With the present situation we are
perhaps at a stage comparable to the Chartist phase of trade unionism
in Great Britain, when the ideals and spirit of a labor movement had
been formulated but had not reached anything like class-wide dimensions. Similarly, it is still a small, if boisterous minority of the young
who now define the generational conflict. But the conflict will not
vanish when those who are now twenty reach thirty; it may only reach
its peak when those who are now eleven and twelve reach their late
twenties. (Say, about 1984.) We then may discover that what a mere
handful of beatniks pioneered in Allen Ginsberg's youth will have
become the life style of millions of college-age young. Is there any

other ideal toward which the young can grow that looks half so appealing?

"Nothing," Goethe observed, "is more inadequate than a mature judgment when adopted by an immature mind." When radical intellectuals have to deal with a dissenting public that becomes this young, all kinds of problems accrue. The adolescentization of dissent poses dilemmas as perplexing as the proletarianization of dissent that bedeviled left-wing theorists when it was the working class they had to ally with in their effort to reclaim our culture for the good, the true, and the beautiful. Then it was the horny-handed virtues of the beer hall and the trade union that had to serve as the medium of radical thought. Now it is the youthful exuberance of the rock club, the love-in, the teach-in.

The young, miserably educated as they are, bring with them almost nothing but healthy instincts. The project of building a sophisticated framework of thought atop those instincts is rather like trying to graft an oak tree upon a wildflower. How to sustain the oak tree? More important, how to avoid crushing the wildflower? And yet such is the project that confronts those of us who are concerned with radical social change. For the young have become one of the very few social levers dissent has to work with. This is that "significant soil" in which the Great Refusal has begun to take root. If we reject it in frustration for the youthful follies that also sprout there, where then do we turn?

ROBERT F. KENNEDY
what can the young believe?

More and more of our children are almost unreachable by the familiar premises and arguments of our adult world. The first task of concerned people is not to castigate or deplore — it is to search out the reason for disillusionment and alienation, the rationale of protest and dissent —

From *The New Republic*, March 11, 1967.

perhaps, indeed, to learn from it. What are they dissenting from — and what do they tell us about ourselves?

They begin, of course, with the war in Vietnam. We are not talking about all our young people; after all, Vietnam is a young man's war. The men who fight and die there, with bravery and endurance equal to any in our history, are young. There are others, as I have seen on many campuses, who are in favor of escalation — though many who favor escalation also favor continuation of the student deferment, their seeming slogan: "Escalation without Participation." But when a hundred student body presidents and editors of college newspapers; hundreds of former Peace Corps volunteers; dozens of present Rhodes scholars question the basic premises of the war, they should not and cannot be ignored.

These students oppose the war for the brutality and the horror of all wars, and for the particular terror of this one. But for our young people, I suspect, Vietnam is a shock as it cannot be to us. They did not know World War II, or even Korea. And this is a war surrounded by rhetoric they do not understand or accept; these are the children not of the cold war, but of the thaw. Their memories of communism are not of Stalin's purges and death camps, not even the terrible revelations of the Twentieth Party Congress, or the streets of Hungary. They see the world as one in which communist states can be each others' deadliest enemies or even friends of the West, in which communism is certainly no better, but perhaps no worse, than many other evil and repressive dictatorships all around the world — with which we conclude alliances when that is felt to be in our interest.

Even as the declared foreign policy of our government is to "build bridges" to this new communist world, they see us, in the name of anti-communism, devastating the land of those we call our friends. However the war may seem to us, they see it as one in which the largest and most powerful nation on earth is killing children (they do not care if accidentally) in a remote and insignificant land. We speak of past commitments, of the burden of past mistakes; and they ask why they should now atone for mistakes made before many of them were born, before almost any could vote. They see us spend billions on armaments while poverty and ignorance continue at home; they see us willing to fight a war for freedom in Vietnam, but unwilling to fight with one-hundredth the money or force or effort to secure freedom in Mississippi or Alabama or the ghettos of the North. And they see, perhaps most disturbing of all, that they are remote from the decisions of policy; that they themselves frequently do not, by the nature of our political system, share in the power of choice on great questions shaping their lives.

It would be tempting — but it would be wrong and self-deluding — to trace to the war all the problems of our disaffected youth. Nor can this problem be traced to any individual, or to any Administration, or to a political party; the challenge is deeper and broader.

Consider for example our economy: the wondrous production machine which has made us richer, as we count, than any people in history, within which we all find sustenance and support. It is a business economy — which is to say, that most Americans are engaged in some form of business. Yet in a survey last year, only 12 percent of all graduating college seniors hoped for a career in business, or thought such a career would be worthwhile and satisfying.

Why? Part of the answer is that the great corporations which are so large a part of American life, play so small a role in the solution of its vital problems. Civil rights, poverty, unemployment, health, education — these are but a few of the deep crises in which business participation, with a few important exceptions, has been far less than might be expected from such an important part of the society. We can recognize, and applaud, the work of the NAM in job training, or the work of foundations like Ford and Rockefeller, or the efforts of individuals like Paul Hoffman or Thomas Watson, or corporations like Smith, Kline and French. But certainly business as a whole has not sought out the challenges of the nation's frontier. Of course, it may well be argued that the business of business is to make a profit, that to attempt more is to do less than its stockholders deserve. But does such an argument have relevance, ask the young, when a single company, like General Motors or IT&T, has annual profits greater than the gross national product of any one of 70 nations in the world?

Nor — painful as it may be for liberals to acknowledge — are these young people enchanted with liberal institutions. Labor has been in the forefront of many a great battle. But youth looks with other eyes, and their view is very different: They think of labor as grown sleek and bureaucratic with power, sometimes frankly discriminatory, occasionally even corrupt and exploitative; a force not for change but for the status quo, unwilling or unable to organize new groups of members, indifferent to the men who once worked the coal mines of Appalachia, a late-comer to the struggles of the grape pickers of California or the farm laborers of the Mississippi Delta. This is a one-sided picture, without the dimensions of 50 years' struggle, and the undramatic yet vital work of labor in many parts of the nation today. But there is too much truth in it for us not to understand our children's view — or to ignore the need for change.

We are friends of education, especially of universities; our friends and allies teach there, they are a major force in the liberal community. But listen: "Education [is] by its very nature an individual matter . . . not geared to mass production. It does not produce people who instinctively go the same way. . . . [Yet] our millions learn the same lessons and spend hours before television sets looking at exactly the same thing at exactly the same time. For one reason and another we are more and more ignoring differences, if not trying to obliterate them. We seem headed toward a standardization of the mind, what Goethe called 'The deadly commonplace that fetters us all'." That might well have been, but it was not, a speaker at a Berkeley rally; it was Edith Hamilton, one of our greatest classicists.

And now listen to a student representative, speaking to a meeting of the Board of Regents of the University of California: "We have asked to be heard. You have refused. We have asked for justice. You have called it anarchy. We have asked for freedom. You have called it license. Rather than face the fear and hopelessness you have created, you have called it communistic. You have accused us of failing to use legitimate channels. But you have closed those channels to us. You, and not us, have built a university based on distrust and dishonesty."

It is impossible to mistake the anguish of that voice. There may be many things in that cry, but one of them is surely a protest of individuality — against the university as corporate bureaucracy, against the dull sameness Miss Hamilton saw also — for in bureaucracy and sameness is the denial of individuality, and the denial that human beings matter; if all are the same, why listen to what anyone says? And if we are not prepared to listen, then men cannot be recognized as more than numbers in statistical collections, a part of the gross national product like so many coffee cups or carpet sweepers.

The nonrecognition of individuality — the sense that no one is listening — is even more pronounced in our politics. Television, newspapers, magazines, are a cascade of words, official statements, policies, explanations and declarations; all flow from the height of government, down to the passive citizen; the young must feel, in their efforts to speak back, like solitary salmon trying to breast Grand Coulee Dam. The words which submerge us, all too often, speak the language of a day irrelevant to our young. And the language of politics is too often insincerity. And if we add to the insincerity, and the absence of dialogue, the absurdity of a politics in which a Byron de la Beckwith can declare as a candidate for lieutenant governor of Mississippi, we can understand why so many of our young people have turned from engagement to disengagement.

It is not enough to understand, or to see clearly. Whatever their differences with us, whatever the depth of their dissent, it is vital — for us as much as for them — that our young feel that change is possible; that they will be heard; that the cruelties and follies and injustices of the world will yield, however grudgingly, to the sweat and sacrifice they are so ready to give. If we cannot help open to them this sense of possibility, we will have only ourselves to blame for the disillusionment that will surely come. And more than disillusionment, danger; for we rely on these young people more than we know: not just in the Peace Corps, though the Peace Corps has done more for our position around the world than all our armed forces and foreign aid; not just in civil rights, though our youth have done more toward a solution of that problem than all the power and panoply of government; we rely on our youth for all our hopes of a better future — and thus, in a real and direct sense, for the very meaning of our own lives.

HENRY FAIRLIE
how is youth to be served?

Michael Oakeshott — whose conservative political philosophy is so characteristically English and so individually his own that one can understand why it is so little appreciated in America — once said that the reason the young should not be allowed to participate in politics was "not because of their vices, but because of their virtues." And C. H. Wilson has written: "The first object of a political education is to dispel in the citizen's mind the manifold Utopian notions of man's nature and of the nature of the world with which he emerges from the arduous experience of adolescence. He has to learn that men are moved not only by principle but by interest, that their actions are aimed not only at the

From *The New Republic*, April 8, 1967. Copyright 1967 by Harrison-Blaine of New Jersey, Inc. Reprinted by permission of *The New Republic*.

discharge of duty but also at the satisfaction of passion, appetite and unreflecting habit. He has to learn that the world in which he acts is a world of scarcity and that all the resources at his disposal are limited, both material resources of wealth and immaterial ones of time and political support. He must learn that all these resources have alternative uses between which he must choose, and that generally his choice is irrevocable."

Both of these quotations came to my mind as I read the remarks of Senator Robert Kennedy in *The New Republic* of March 11 under the title: "What Can the Young Believe?" I am interested in Senator Kennedy's remarks only because he is one of the most active and most publicized spokesmen of those who insist that the young are today in some unique situation, which demands from their elders some equally unique response.

We are in danger of becoming obsessed by the young: in our lives, in our thinking, in our politics. "The first task of concerned people," says Senator Kennedy, "is not to castigate or deplore — it is to search out the reason for disillusionment and alienation, the rationale of protest." By and large, this has been *one* of the first tasks of "concerned people" — who, by the way, are not? — in most ages. But they have not made so much fuss about it. We should be careful not to spoil the young by a false, and condescending, obsequiousness or flattery. We should not, by taking them too seriously, invite them too early to take themselves too seriously as well. When Henry Fox found his son being chastised by his nurse for breaking some priceless ornament, he reproved, not his son, but the nurse. "Do not punish the boy. The world will break his spirit soon enough." We cannot all adopt such a lofty Whig attitude, but we can help to prevent their youthful spirit from being broken by a premature and inappropriate responsibility.

The kind of attitudes which lie behind Senator Kennedy's remarks start from a serious confusion about the nature of "generations." As far as my knowledge goes, I do not think that any philosopher or sociologist or anthropologist has yet satisfactorily explained the nature of a "generation." The farthest we have got is to make the kind of distinction which has been succinctly summarized in a recent essay by Arno J. Mayer: "There can be little doubt that 'static conditions make for attitudes of piety,' and that within static societies — especially but not exclusively within static agrarian societies — the tensions and conflicts between generations are essentially nonpolitical, nonideological and nonintellectual. But under the impact of a quickening tempo and exploding scale of social change the almost automatic adaptation to 'traditional patterns of experience, thought and expression' ceases to be possible. A social-political — rather than a biological — generation emerges when its members, following exposure to . . . change, develop a distinctive style and outlook."

None of it is very new. Walter Bagehot, in the introduction to the second edition of his essays on the English constitution, pointed out that there was a generational change in English politics when those who had entered politics after the Reform Act of 1832 replaced in *office* those who had entered politics before it. Senator Kennedy points to another (I am less certain that it is such a generational watershed), when he says: "These are the children, not of the cold war, but of the thaw."

It is worth noticing one important difference. Bagehot assumed a generational change only when an age group which had enjoyed some common experience at last occupied positions of power and responsibility. Senator Kennedy, true to the spirit of the age, assumes a generational change when all the evidence we have is the attitudes of youth itself. This assumption that generational changes can be observed before a generation has been submitted to the test of responsibility is, of course, one of the more widely accepted, and less convincing, assumptions made by Marshall McLuhan. We would do well to set against it Ortega y Gasset's remark that a man's historical activity really begins at the age of 30.

THE DANGER OF SYMBOLS

We would also do well to remember that, although "social-political" generations are not to be confused with "biological" or family generations, they cannot be entirely separated from them. It is here that we encounter a warning not to be too solemn. I remember asking John Strachey why he and so many like him — brought up in upper-class, conservative, English homes — became socialists after the 1914-18 war. "Because I was not given my place in the First XI in cricket at Eton," he replied. I demurred: there must have been more to it than that. "I am not sure," he said. "I am aware that I wished to revolt against my father and all that he and his generation seemed to me to stand for, and therefore looked for some 'world-picture' to set against his. That is where socialism — or, rather, Marxism — came in. But the occasion of my revolt was being denied my place in the First XI at Eton when I knew that my accomplishment as a batsman entitled me to one."

That Strachey — one of the most habitually honest political minds of his generation — recalled, 40 years later, his exclusion from the cricket team at Eton (because he was an intellectual; because he looked like a Jew) ought to remind us not to erect symbols like the "Berkeley student." The intellectually adventurous and intellectually sensitive have always had a difficult time when they are young, and some kind of "alienation" has normally (even hopefully) been the result. But the sources of that "alienation" are as mixed and puzzling as Strachey suggested. We should be able to retain some good humor about the young, so that they may retain it about themselves. From the flat and decent plateau of middle age, we can envy them many of their opportunities, material and immaterial. But what one cannot envy them is the syrup of "understanding" in which their elders seem determined to drown them. This "understanding" goes so far that I do not believe, from my own observation, that the young today are in revolt against the values and standards of their elders, which would be normal and healthy, for the simple reason that their elders have offered them precious few standards and values against which they can revolt. Their elders could, indeed, be accused of betraying them by abdicating.

Nevertheless, most of the attitudes of the young which Senator Kennedy describes are recognizable, even across 20 years. He makes much, for example, of the fact that few graduating college seniors today hope for a career in business, or think that such a career would be worthwhile or satisfying. "Why? Part of the answer is that the great corporations, which are so large a part of American life, play so small a role in the solution of its vital problems." I think this is hocus-pocus.

The young today, on the whole, despise business for the same reason that the young of my own day despised it: that it *seems* to be concerned only with making money by processes which *seem* to be intellectually and emotionally unsatisfying; and, if the young do not despise the making of money, at an age when they have no responsibilities, then God (although not very hopefully) have mercy on us.

I am not, therefore, surprised that the young should display some "disillusionment" with, and "alienation" from, the big corporations. But it bothers Senator Kennedy, and he thinks that part of the solution is for the big corporations to become more socially conscious. As a conservative (in an English sense) I am extremely suspicious of big business when it becomes socially conscious. One advantage, after all, of being a conservative is that one knows to whom, with however much fastidious disdain, one must look for support.

But Senator Kennedy, while rightly pointing out that the young today are disturbed by the huge "corporate bureaucracy" which seems to control so much of American life, himself applauds precisely those organizations which have made this "corporate bureaucracy" almost respectable: "the work of the NAM in job training, or the work of foundations like Ford and Rockefeller, or the efforts of individuals like Paul Hoffman or Thomas Watson, or corporations like Smith, Kline and French." The hope is to make big business — the actual world — seem respectable, so that the young may accept it: a world which they can understand, and in which they will be understood. But the glory of the young is that they have not yet met the world. They have not yet had to come to terms with it and, in their ignorance and their arrogance, they can reject it, and hope to remake it in their own image.

Anyone who has observed the impact of Camus on the intellectually adventurous and sensitive among the young must know what the liturgy of NAM, Hoffman, Smith, Kline and French will mean to them. The title of Camus' novel which has the most immediate impact on them is, in the American edition, mistranslated as *The Rebel;* in the English edition, more accurately translated as *The Outsider.* The young are the only natural Outsiders. They should be allowed to be so as long as possible. "The world will break their spirit soon enough."

The activities of the young, which we are today always being asked to consider so novel, seem to be much the same as those in which the young in my day indulged, and to have their source in the same anxiety: the desire for immediate experience. Of course, there are new factors, although they may not be as exciting as Marshall McLuhan would have us believe. The young today are more numerous and more articulate. They show more signs of intelligence than previous generations of the young — not all previous generations: the young of the 16th century were wonderfully endowed — but fewer signs of disciplined intelligence likely to grow. They have money in their pockets, and therefore are more courted, more publicized, and more presumptuous. But the only new factors which seem to me to introduce any real novelty into their situation are the scientific aids, from records to contraceptives, from travel to LSD, which provide both the temptation and the opporunity to satisfy, far more fully than before, the desire for immediate experience which is the source of the young's impatience.

THE ADULT INVASION

It is here that one is tempted to try to restrain the young: to suggest to them that they are seeking short cuts to kinds of experience which are only satisfying after considerably more varied efforts and experimentation than are possible by the age of 25, or even 30. Some of the statements made by those who take LSD remind me of the statements made by young girls in previous centuries who claimed they had enjoyed some exceptional visitation from God. Most of these were put through a rigorous examination by the church which, with very little alteration, might profitably be used today.

But even as I write these words I am aware that the inward concentration of the young — whether with the aid of LSD, or of Zen, or of both — may produce a remarkable generation, by the time they are equipped and ready to assume responsibility. I am certainly not prepared to treat their preoccupations (the ordinary preoccupations of the young in any period) as evidence of "disillusionment and alienation." Nor am I prepared to cross the fences which they erect to keep adults out.

But crossing these fences is precisely what our own generation of adults seems most determined to do. Anxious not to be thought "square," they steal the music, imitate the dance, adopt the dress, of the young. Anxious to be thought "understanding," they anxiously follow all that the young do, and, with a giggle, applaud it. This adult invasion of the world of the young is, committed against themselves, a banal act — committed against the young, almost criminal. It is as if the adults today are searching for some kind of reassurance from the young, which is exactly where they have no right to look for it. Generations should keep their fences in good repair.

It is this attitude which I find most displeasing of all those of which Senator Kennedy's remarks are representative. What he, in effect, says is that big business, or the liberals, or the trade unions — the groups which he specifically mentions — must somehow arrange themselves and their activities so that the young will reassure them that they have done a reasonable job, have passed on a reasonable heritage. This is not the test which adult institutions should have to pass. There is one which is much more serious: the test which we ourselves set, with our knowledge of the actual world, our perception of where the sources of corruption lie, and what, immediately, may be done about them.

The protest that matters is that which we manage to sustain, as we outgrow the arduous experience of adolescence, as our knowledge of the real world accumulates, and we suffer the painful process of reconciling ourselves to it. If, when we have learned that the walls of Jericho will not fall at the sound of a trumpet, that Jerusalem will not be built in a day, that Camelot in any age is a frail flower of chivalry — when we have learned how strong are the forces of evil and inaction in the world — if, then, we have still managed to sustain a spirit of protest, it will be worth attention, and it will educate and reform.

It is the knowledge of the adult — *and his survival of that knowledge* — which makes him important. It is too easy to satisfy the protest of the young by offering them hopes: the reflections of their own hopes. By paying too much attention to the young, we try to escape from the stern knowledge which we have gathered, and the stern opportunities (because limited) with which that knowledge endows us. We should leave the young alone until, in time, they can bring their own perceptions to what Robert Ardrey, in *The Territorial Imperative*, calls "our negotiations with the human circumstance."

GEORGE F. KENNAN
rebels without a program

There is an ideal that has long been basic to the learning process as we have known it, one that stands at the very center of our modern institutions of higher education and that had its origin, I suppose, in the clerical and monastic character of the medieval university. It is the ideal of the association of the process of learning with a certain remoteness from the contemporary scene — a certain detachment and seclusion, a certain voluntary withdrawal and renunciation of participation in contemporary life in the interests of the achievement of a better perspective on that life when the period of withdrawal is over. It is an ideal that does not predicate any total conflict between thought and action, but recognizes that there is a time for each.

No more striking, or moving, description of this ideal has ever come to my attention than that which was given by Woodrow Wilson in 1896 at the time of the Princeton Sesquicentennial.

"I have had sight," Wilson said, "of the perfect place of learning in my thought: a free place, and a various, where no man could be and not know with how great a destiny knowledge had come into the world — itself a little world; but not perplexed, living with a singleness of aim not known without; the home of sagacious men, hardheaded and with a will to know, debaters of the world's questions every day and used to the rough ways of democracy; and yet a place removed — calm Science seated there, recluse, ascetic, like a nun; not knowing that the world passes, not caring, if the truth but come in answer to her prayer. . . . A place where ideals are kept in heart in an air they can breathe; but no fool's paradise. A place where to hear the truth about the past and hold debate about the affairs of the present, with knowledge and without passion; like the world in having all men's life at heart, a place for men and all that concerns them; but unlike the world in its self-possession, its thorough way of talk, its care to know more than the moment brings to light; slow to take excitement, its air pure and wholesome with a breath of faith; every eye within it bright in the clear day and quick to look toward heaven for the confirmation of its hope. Who shall show us the way to this place?"

There is a dreadful incongruity between this vision and the state of mind — and behavior — of the radical left on the American campus today. In place of a calm science, "recluse, ascetic, like a nun," not knowing or caring that the world passes "if the truth but come in answer to her prayer," we have people utterly absorbed in the affairs of this passing world. And instead of these affairs being discussed with knowledge and without passion, we find them treated with transports of passion and with a minimum, I fear, of knowledge. In place of slowness to take excitement, we have a readiness to react emotionally, and at once, to a great variety of issues. In place of self-possession, we have screaming tantrums and brawling in the streets. In place of the "thorough way of talk" that Wilson envisaged, we have banners and epithets and obscenities and virtually meaningless slogans. And in place of bright eyes "looking to heaven for the confirmation of their hope," we have eyes glazed with anger and passion, too often dimmed as well by artificial abuse of the psychic structure that lies behind them, and looking almost everywhere else but to heaven for the satisfaction of their aspirations.

I quite understand that those who espouse this flagrant repudiation of the Wilsonian ideal constitute only a minority on any campus. But tendencies that represent the obsession of only a few may not be without partial appeal, at certain times, and within certain limits, to many others. If my own analysis is correct, there are a great many students who may resist any complete surrender to these tendencies, but who nevertheless find them intensely interesting, are to some extent attracted or morally bewildered by them, find themselves driven, in confrontation with them, either into various forms of pleasing temptation, on the one hand, or into crises of conscience, on the other.

If I see them correctly (and I have no pretensions to authority on this subject), there are two dominant tendencies among the people I have here in mind, and superficially they would seem to be in conflict one with the other. On the one side there is angry militancy, full of hatred and intolerance and often quite prepared to embrace violence as a source of change. On the other side there is gentleness, passivity, quietism — ostensibly a yearning for detachment from the affairs of the world, not the detachment Woodrow Wilson had in mind, for that was one intimately and sternly related to the real world, the objective, external world, whereas this one takes the form of an attempt to escape into a world which is altogether illusory and subjective.

What strikes one first about the angry militancy is the extraordinary degree of certainty by which it is inspired: certainty of one's own rectitude, certainty of the accuracy and profundity of one's own analysis of the problems of contemporary society, certainty as to the iniquity of those who disagree. Of course, vehemence of feeling and a conviction that right is on one's side have seldom been absent from the feelings of politically excited youth. But somehow or other they seem particularly out of place at just this time. Never has there been an era when the problems of public policy even approached in their complexity those by which our society is confronted today, in this age of technical innovation and the explosion of knowledge. The understanding of these problems is something to which one could well give years of disciplined and restrained study, years of the scholar's detachment, years of readiness to reserve judgment while evidence is being accumulated. And this being so, one is struck to see such massive certainties already present in the minds of people who not only *have not* studied very much but presumably *are not* studying a great deal, because it is hard to imagine that the activities to which this aroused portion of our student population gives itself are ones readily compatible with quiet and successful study.

The world seems to be full, today, of embattled students. The public prints are seldom devoid of the record of their activities. Photographs of them may be seen daily: screaming, throwing stones, breaking windows, overturning cars, being beaten or dragged about by police and, in the case of those on other continents, burning libraries. That these people are embattled is unquestionable. That they are really students, I must be permitted to doubt. I have heard it freely confessed by members of the revolutionary student generation of Tsarist Russia that, proud as they were of the revolutionary exploits of their youth, they never really learned anything in their university years; they were too busy with politics. The fact of the matter is that the state of being *enragé* is simply incompatible with fruitful study. It implies a degree of existing emotional and intellectual commitment which leaves little room for open-minded curiosity.

I am not saying that students should not be concerned, should not have views, should not question what goes on in the field of national policy and should not voice their questions about it. Some of us, who are older, share many of their misgivings, many of their impulses. Some of us have no less lively a sense of the dangers of the time, and are no happier than they are about a great many things that are now going on. But it lies within the power as well as the duty of all of us to recognize not only the possibility that we might be wrong but the virtual certainty that on some occasions we are bound to be. The fact that this is so does not absolve us from the duty of having views and putting them forward. But it does make it incumbent upon us to recognize the element of doubt that still surrounds the correctness of these views. And if we do that, we will not be able to lose ourselves in transports of moral indignation against those who are of opposite opinion and follow a different line; we will put our views forward only with a prayer for forgiveness for the event that we prove to be mistaken.

I am aware that inhibitions and restraints of this sort on the part of us older people would be attributed by many members of the student left to a sweeping corruption of our moral integrity. Life, they would hold, has impelled us to the making of compromises; and these compromises have destroyed the usefulness of our contribution. Crippled by our own cowardice, prisoners of the seamy adjustments we have made in order to be successfully a part of the American establishment, we are regarded as no longer capable of looking steadily into the strong clear light of truth.

In this, as in most of the reproaches with which our children shower us, there is of course an element of justification. There is a point somewhere along the way in most of our adult lives, admittedly, when enthusiasms flag, when idealism becomes tempered, when responsibility to others, and even affection for others, compels greater attention to the mundane demands of private life. There is a point when we are even impelled to place the needs of children ahead of the dictates of a defiant idealism, and to devote ourselves, pusillanimously, if you will, to the support and rearing of these same children — precisely in order that at some future date they may have the privilege of turning upon us and despising us for the materialistic faintheartedness that made their maturity possible. This, no doubt, is the nature of the compromise that millions of us make with the imperfections of government and society in our time. Many of us could wish that it might have been otherwise — that the idealistic pursuit of public causes might have remained our exclusive dedication down into later life.

But for the fact that this is not so I cannot shower myself or others with reproaches. I have seen more harm done in this world by those who tried to storm the bastions of society in the name of utopian beliefs, who were determined to achieve the elimination of all evil and the realization of the millennium within their own time, than by all the humble efforts of those who have tried to create a little order and civility and affection within their own intimate entourage, even at the cost of tolerating a great deal of evil in the public domain. Behind the modesty, after all, there has been the recognition of a vitally important truth — a truth that the Marxists, among others, have never brought themselves to recognize — namely, that the decisive seat of evil in this world is not in social and political institutions, and not even, as a rule, in the will or iniquities of statesmen, but simply in the weakness and imperfection of the human soul itself, and by that I mean literally every soul, including my own and that of the student militant at the gates. For this reason, as Tocqueville so clearly perceived when he visited this country a hundred and thirty years ago, the success of a society may be said, like charity, to begin at home.

So much, then, for the angry ones. Now, a word about the others; the quiescent ones, the hippies and the flower people.

In one sense, my feeling for these people is one of pity, not unmixed, in some instances, with horror. I am sure that they want none of this pity. They would feel that it comes to them for the wrong reasons. If they feel sorry for themselves, it is because they see themselves as the victims of a harsh, hypocritical and unworthy adult society. If I feel sorry for them, it is because I see them as the victims of certain great and destructive philosophic errors.

One of these errors — and it is one that affects particularly those who take drugs, but not those alone — is the belief that the human being has marvelous resources within himself that can be released and made available to him merely by the passive submission to certain sorts of stimuli: by letting esthetic impressions of one sort or another roll over him or by letting his psychic equilibrium be disoriented by chemical agencies that give him the sensation of experiencing tremendous things. Well, it is true that human beings sometimes have marvelous resources within themselves. It is also true that these resources are capable, ideally, of being released and made available to the man that harbors them and through him to others, and sometimes are so released. But it is not true that they can be released by hippie means.

It is only through effort, through doing, through action — never through passive experience — that man grows creatively. It is only by volition and effort that he becomes fully aware of what he has in him of creativity and becomes capable of embodying it, of making it a part of himself, of communicating it to others. There is no pose more fraudulent — and students would do well to remember this when they look at each other — than that of the individual who pretends to have been exalted and rendered more impressive by his communion with some sort of inner voice whose revelations he is unable to describe or to enact. And particularly is this pose fraudulent when the means he has chosen to render himself susceptible to this alleged revelation is the deliberate disorientation of his own psychic system; for it may be said with surety that any artificial intervention of this sort — into the infinitely delicate balance that nature created in the form of man's psychic makeup — produces its own revenge, takes its own toll, proceeds at the cost of the true creative faculties and weakens rather than strengthens.

The second error I see in the outlook of these people is the belief in the possibility and validity of a total permissiveness. They are misjudging, here, the innermost nature of man's estate. There is not, and cannot be, such a thing as total freedom. The normal needs and frailties of the body, not to mention the elementary demands of the soul itself, would rule that out if nothing else did. But beyond that, any freedom *from* something implies a freedom to something. And because our reality is a complex one, in which conflicts of values are never absent, there can be no advance toward any particular objective, not even the pursuit of pleasure, that does not imply the sacrifice of other possible objectives. Freedom, for this reason, is definable only in terms of the obligations and restraints and sacrifices it accepts. It exists, as a concept, only in relationship to something else which is by definition its opposite; and that means commitment, duty, self-restraint.

Every great artist has known this. Every great philosopher has recognized it. It has lain at the basis of Judaic-Christian teaching. Tell me what framework of discipline you are prepared to accept, and I will attempt to tell you what freedom might mean for you. But if you tell me that you are prepared to accept no framework of discipline at all, then I will tell you, as Dostoevski told his readers, that you are destined to become the most unfree of men; for freedom begins only with the humble acceptance of membership in, and subordination to, a natural order of things, and it grows only with struggle, and self-discipline, and faith.

To shun the cruelty and corruption of this world is one thing. It is not always unjustifiable. Not everyone is made to endure these things. There is something to be said for the cultivation, by the right people, and in the right way, of the virtues of detachment, of withdrawal, of unworldliness, of innocence and purity, if you will. That, as a phase of life, is just what Wilson was talking about. In an earlier age, those who are now the flower children and the hippies would perhaps have entered monastic life or scholarly life or both. But there, be it noted, they would very definitely have accepted a framework of discipline, and it would normally have been a very strict one. If it was a monastic order, their lives would have been devoted to the service of God and of other men, not of themselves and their senses. If it was the world of scholarship, their lives would have been devoted to the pursuit of truth, which never comes easily or without discipline and sacrifice. They would have accepted an obligation to cultivate order, not chaos; cleanliness, not filth; self-abnegation, not self-indulgence; health, not demoralization.

Now I have indicated that I pity these people, and in general I do. But sometimes I find it hard to pity them, because they themselves are sometimes so pitiless. There is, in this cultivation of an absolute freedom, and above all in the very self-destructiveness with which it often expresses itself, a selfishness, a hardheartedness, a callousness, an irresponsibility, an indifference to the feelings of others, that is its own condemnation. No one ever destroys just himself alone. Such is the network of intimacy in which every one of us is somehow embraced, that whoever destroys himself destroys to some extent others as well. Many of these people prattle about the principle of love; but their behavior betrays this principle in the most elementary way. Love — and by that I mean the receiving of love as well as the bestowal of it — is itself an obligation, and as such is incompatible with the quest for a perfect freedom. Just the cruelty to parents alone, which is implicit in much of this behavior, is destructive of the purest and most creative form of love that does exist or could exist in this mortal state.

And one would like to warn these young people that in distancing themselves so recklessly not only from the wisdom but from the feelings of parents, they are hacking at their own underpinnings — and even those of people as yet unborn. There could be no greater illusion than the belief that one can treat one's parents unfeelingly and with contempt and yet expect that one's own children will some day treat one otherwise; for such people break the golden chain of affection that binds the generations and gives continuity and meaning to life.

One cannot, therefore, on looking at these young people in all the glory of their defiant rags and hairdos, always just say, with tears in one's eyes: "There goes a tragically wayward youth, striving romantically to document his rebellion against the hypocrisies of the age." One has sometimes to say, and not without indignation: "There goes a perverted and willful and stony-hearted youth by whose destructiveness we are all, in the end, to be damaged and diminished."

These people also pose a problem in the quality of their citizenship. One thing they all seem to have in common — the angry ones as well as the quiet ones — is a complete rejection of, or indifference to, the political system of this country. The quiet ones turn their backs upon it, as though it did not concern them. The angry ones reject it by implication, insofar as they refuse to recognize the validity of its workings or to respect the discipline which, as a system of authority, it unavoidably entails.

I think there is a real error or misunderstanding here. If you accept a democratic system, this means that you are prepared to put up with those of its workings, legislative or administrative, with which you do not agree as well as with those that meet with your concurrence. This willingness to accept, in principle, the workings of a system based on the will of the majority, even when you yourself are in the minority, is simply the essence of democracy. Without it there could be no system of representative self-government at all. When you attempt to alter the workings of the system by means of violence or civil disobedience, this, it seems to me, can have only one of two implications: either you do not believe in democracy at all and consider that society ought to be governed by enlightened minorities such as the one to which you, of course, belong; or you consider that the present system is so imperfect that it is not truly representative, that it no longer serves adequately as a vehicle for the will of the majority, and that this leaves to the unsatisfied no adequate means of self-expression other than the primitive one of calling attention to themselves and their emotions by mass demonstrations and mass defiance of established authority. It is surely the latter of these two implications which we must read from the overwhelming majority of the demonstrations that have recently taken place.

I would submit that if you find a system inadequate, it is not enough simply to demonstrate indignation and anger over individual workings of it, such as the persistence of the Vietnam war, or individual situations it tolerates or fails to correct, such as the condition of the Negroes in our great cities. If one finds these conditions intolerable, and if one considers that they reflect no adequate expression either of the will of the majority or of that respect for the rights of minorities which is no less essential to the success of any democratic system, then one places upon one's self, it seems to me, the obligation of saying in what way this political system should be modified, or what should be established in the place of it, to assure that its workings would bear a better relationship to people's needs and people's feelings.

If the student left had a program of constitutional amendment or political reform — if it had proposals for the constructive adaptation of this political system to the needs of our age — if it was *this* that it was agitating for, and if its agitation took the form of reasoned argument and discussion, or even peaceful demonstration accompanied by reasoned argument and discussion — then many of us, I am sure, could view its protests with respect, and we would not shirk the obligation either to speak up in defense of institutions and national practices which we have tolerated all our lives, or to join these young people in the quest for better ones.

But when we are confronted only with violence for violence's sake, and with attempts to frighten or intimidate an administration into doing things for which it can itself see neither the rationale nor the electoral mandate; when we are offered, as the only argument for change, the fact that a number of people are themselves very angry and excited; and when we are presented with a violent objection to what exists, unaccompanied by any constructive concept of what, ideally, ought to exist in its place — then we of my generation can only recognize that such behavior bears a disconcerting resemblance to phenomena we have witnessed within our own time in the origins of totalitarianism in other countries, and then we have no choice but to rally to the defense of a public authority with which we may not be in agreement but which is the only one we've got and with which, in some form or another, we cannot conceivably dispense. People should bear in mind that if this — namely noise, violence and lawlessness — is the way they are going to put their case, then many of us who are no happier than they are about some of the policies that arouse their indignation will have no choice but to place ourselves on the other side of the barricades.

These observations reflect a serious doubt whether civil disobedience has any place in a democratic society. But there is one objection I know will be offered to this view. Some people, who accept our political system, believe that they have a right to disregard it and to violate the laws that have flowed from it so long as they are prepared, as a matter of conscience, to accept the penalties established for such behavior.

I am sorry; I cannot agree. The violation of law is not, in the moral and philosophic sense, a privilege that lies offered for sale with a given price tag, like an object in a supermarket, available to anyone who has the price and is willing to pay for it. It is not like the privilege of breaking crockery in a tent at the county fair for a quarter a shot. Respect for the law is not an obligation which is exhausted or obliterated by willingness to accept the penalty for breaking it.

To hold otherwise would be to place the privilege of lawbreaking preferentially in the hands of the affluent, to make respect for law a commercial proposition rather than a civic duty and to deny any authority of law independent of the sanctions established against its violation. It would then be all right for a man to create false fire alarms or frivolously to pull the emergency cord on the train, or to do any number of other things that endangered or inconvenienced other people, provided only he was prepared to accept the penalties of so doing. Surely, lawlessness and civil disobedience cannot be condoned or tolerated on this ground; and those of us who care for the good order of society have no choice but to resist attempts at its violation, when this is their only justification.

Now, being myself a father, I am only too well aware that people of my generation cannot absolve ourselves of a heavy responsibility for the state of mind in which these young people find themselves. We are obliged to recognize here, in the myopia and the crudities of *their* extremism, the reflection of our own failings: our faintheartedness and in some instances our weariness, our apathy in the face of great and obvious evils.

I am also aware that, while their methods may not be the right ones, and while their discontent may suffer in its effectiveness from the concentration on negative goals, the degree of their concern over the present state of our country and the dangers implicit in certain of its involvements is by no means exaggerated. This is a time in our national life more serious, more menacing, more crucial, than any I have ever experienced or ever hoped to experience. Not since the civil conflict of a century ago has this country, as I see it, been in such great danger; and the most excruciating aspect of this tragic state of affairs is that so much of this danger comes so largely from within, where we are giving it relatively little official attention, and so little of it comes, relatively speaking, from the swamps and jungles of Southeast Asia into which we are pouring our treasure of young blood and physical resources.

For these reasons, I do not mean to make light of the intensity of feeling by which this student left is seized. Nor do I mean to imply that people like myself can view this discontent from some sort of smug Olympian detachment, as though it were not our responsibility, as though it were not in part our own ugly and decadent face that we see in this distorted mirror. None of us could have any justification for attempting to enter into communication with these people if we did not recognize, along with the justification for their unhappiness, our own responsibility in the creation of it, and if we did not accompany our appeal to them with a profession of readiness to join them, where they want us to, in the attempt to find better answers to many of these problems.

I am well aware that in approaching them in this way and in taking issue as I have with elements of their outlook and their behavior, it is primarily myself that I have committed, not them. I know that behind all the extremisms — all the philosophical errors, all the egocentricities and all the oddities of dress and deportment — we have to do here with troubled and often pathetically appealing people, acting, however wisely or unwisely, out of sincerity and idealism, out of the unwillingness to accept a meaningless life and a purposeless society.

Well, this is not the life, and not the sort of society, that many of us would like to leave behind us in this country when our work is done. How wonderful it would be, I sometimes think to myself, if we and they — experience on the one hand, strength and enthusiasm on the other — could join forces.

T GEORGE HARRIS
infiltrate the structures:
interview with Mrs. Del Behrend

T GEORGE HARRIS: You were involved with the first rumbles of student revolt, Del, and now you turn up as an officer in the world's biggest bank, the Bank of America. Do you expect most students now in protest to settle down, perhaps be more like their parents?

MRS. DEL BEHREND: If by "settle down" you mean will they accept the system as it is, the answer is no. We've got to change it from within. I feel very strongly that most parents sold out. There are basic reasons, economic and intellectual, why the people my age and younger will not.

HARRIS: Let's get at your economic reasons first.

BEHREND: Look, people really know things only out of their personal experience — out of what has already happened to them. The previous generation went through the Depression, which reduced what few economic options they had. Then came the World War II necessities, which were total, and a postwar period of extreme uncertainty followed by rapid economic expansion. So you have many older people who don't know what's going to hit them next. Even after they reach economic security, they don't feel secure. It's too good to last.

But my generation, most of us, have never been deprived or put upon. We know nothing but a consistent pattern of affluence. We aren't bothered by those economic hang-ups. We know we aren't going to starve, and we know that if we lose one job, we'll find another. So instead of adjusting ourselves to institutions as they are, trying to fit in, we can work to make them serve our values. We are the beginning of a big population group who know what we know out of a unique experience.

From *Careers Today* Magazine, Charter Issue 1968. Copyright © 1968 by Communication/Research/Machines/Inc. Reprinted by permission.

HARRIS: How does this make you any better than the parent generation?

BEHREND: Not better, but very different. I don't get any Brownie points for growing up in the affluent era, and I'm not putting down my own father and mother. They're beautiful. I might have done the same as most parents did if I'd been in their shoes. What matters is that the two generations tend to act in opposite ways.

HARRIS: The New Left argues that society is too corrupt to save, except by revolution, and urges young people to fight "the Establishment" from outside.

BEHREND: You can't just sit on the outside and bitch. If you don't like something, by God, go in and change it. Activists like me need to infiltrate the system and work from within. I could cop out. But the problem is here. We have the job of making an economically affluent society into a humane society.

HARRIS: You don't sound very pessimistic, which puts you out of fashion with both generations nowadays.

BEHREND: I'm no optimist, but I've seen too much happen to be a dogmatic pessimist. People who really get involved feel that way. Some of the most fantastic changes in history have come in very recent years. And it keeps accelerating.

That's part of the point about what is called the generation gap. Many of the older people can't cope with this kind of rapid social change. The kids can. They have been systematically exposed to the information explosion, to fast growth, to technology. The institutions are geared to yesterday; my group and those younger live in tomorrow. We can make it work, though there are still too few of us.

HARRIS: How? One person tends to get lost.

BEHREND: I am only one, but I *am* one. The more intensely I live my life, and by the daily things I do, I can make a difference. I may be fighting all by myself, but I hear through the media about somebody else. People today are better educated and more articulate, so there is far more communication among us. By being like-minded, those my age and younger can be more effective and scratch each other's backs. Get more and more thinking together, and pretty soon you've got a movement.

Teddy Kennedy said it: "It is from numberless diverse acts of courage and belief that human history is shaped. Each time a man stands up for an ideal or acts to improve the lot of others, or strikes out against injustice, he sends forth a tiny ripple of hope, and crossing each other from a million different centers of energy and daring, those ripples build a current that can sweep down the mightiest walls of oppression and resistance."

HARRIS: How does that kind of stuff go in banking?

BEHREND: The bank is getting things done that need to be done, and doing them a lot faster than the Federal Government. When you work for the world's biggest bank, and are effective, people listen to you. As you know, I am editorial officer for B of A's Area Development Division, a unique service among banks. We fight for the full development of any community. On the national level, I work with a catalyst group of business organizations, white and black, to expand Negro capital — Green Power.

Throughout business, there is a potential alliance that not many people know about. Top management, surprisingly enough, sees pretty much eye to eye with the youngest group coming into business. This is especially true on racial policy, as well as on the whole question of social change. The action is speeding up so much that it's hard to remember where the struggles were a couple of years ago. In a company I once worked for, my boss ordered me to fire a Negro nurse I had hired. I told him that I wouldn't, and if he insisted, I'd go, too. That particular issue would not arise at many places today. Quite the opposite.

HARRIS: You feel that business needs new-generation people because they are at home in the present environment, and sense the future. But the big institutions of business and government look, to some, terrifyingly formidable and rigid.

BEHREND: Many are. It all depends on where you go, and what strategy you use. Everything in our society is structurally defined. You can't get a certain type of job if you don't have at least a Bachelor's degree. So you get it. Or a Master's. Every Monday, I put on my monkey suit, like this gray flannel lady banker's dress, and drive off to work. These are the criteria you have to meet to get inside — like the degree, the suit, the short hair, the conformist behavior. We've got to be wolves in sheep's clothing.

HARRIS: Your hippy friends disagree. Aren't you being a hypocrite? Playing roles?

BEHREND: Not me. The hippies are overreacting to their parents. Daddy said, "You ought to go out and suffer the way I did," so they do the deprivation bit. After a while, most discover that deprivation is not ennobling. The concept of love, of community, is the main insight we can get from the hippy movement. But the hippies themselves are the role-players and the label-makers. They're hung-up with the cosmetics. They ask me, who is the real you? and aren't you selling out during the week? But me is me, and I'm all me. Who I am is a function of what I believe and what I do.

HARRIS: Are you free to say and be what you believe at the bank? Every place has its bureaucracy.

BEHREND: Being big, we have bureaucracy, of course, but we also have what I call the Magna Carta. Any employee can go to his superior's superior without sanctions being applied. It works, in most areas, and I can compare us with what happens with other banks. When the newspapers ran articles on one of my reports, a friend in Brand-X bank came and said, Gee whizz, how did this happen? His name had once been mentioned, when his boss's wasn't, and he was called on the carpet. But my bosses encourage me to speak on my own. Nobody is responsible for what I say but me. Del Behrend is talking to you, George, not the Bank of America.

Several social critics are looking at the prospects for more democratic forms of corporate organization. Our Magna Carta is an idea that gives tangible freedom. When I'm angry, not a rare event, I do something about what bugs me.

HARRIS: Did you find much less freedom in school? You dropped out of a suburban high school and quit Ohio State for a year.

BEHREND: Yes, I was asked to leave. The teachers called me a rabble-rouser. I later took my degree in Political Science. I got out just in time because I helped in a student demonstration for freedom of speech. We were trying to get rid of the president because he put on too many restrictions. My husband, Dwight, had already been kicked out of Bowling Green State University for organizing a protest. I now have graduate credits from Western Reserve and have done some work in the University of California at Berkeley, but I'd hate to go after my Ph.D. now. Doctorate study is still too much of a Mickey Mouse thing.

HARRIS: Does Dwight mind you working?

BEHREND: We operate as a team. Both of us even race the Formula Vee sports car that he built. When both a husband and a wife work, each has more freedom on the job. If one gets canned, the money doesn't stop. Dwight is really great on cars, and he has been working for Volkswagen. But he quit his job when Senator Kennedy was shot. That hit us both very hard. He decided that if he's going to get into social-action work, he'd better start soon, so he plans to go on to law school.

HARRIS: Yes, he told me. But neither you nor Dwight have quite said how the freedom of affluence changes your social values.

BEHREND: Isn't it obvious? Abraham Maslow, the psychologist, talks about two kinds of human needs: the A-value needs like food and shelter, and the B-value needs like self-fulfillment. Our country has advanced to the point that we can satisfy the first set; now we have to learn to satisfy the second set. Work is not just a way of getting income to buy something; what you do has to be intrinsically satisfying.

HARRIS: Does that mean that it has to change society?

BEHREND: For some of us, yes. I'm not interested in change for its own sake. But you either confront real problems, like race, or you have revolution. The university riots have given us a taste of what can happen in rigid institutions. I don't think anything like that will happen in business, because it is more flexible. And you are getting millions of young people who can stand for their values every day. I've found that if you make it clear from the beginning that you will not prostitute yourself, people will look to you for leadership.

RICHARD POIRIER
the war against the young

The social systems which organize and rationalize contemporary life have always been ingeniously armed for the day when youth would rebel against the essentially pastoral status assigned to it. Despite pamperings until recently unimaginable, despite economic briberies and various psychological coercions, the rebellion has broken out. Predictably, the response to it is a gradual escalation involving a more naked use of the tactics that were supposed to prevent, but which also helped to provoke, the crisis in the first place: patronizations, putdowns, and tongue-lashings, along with offers of a place in the governing system if only the system is left intact and promises that in any

From *The Atlantic Monthly*, October, 1968. Copyright © 1968, by The Atlantic Monthly Company, Boston, Mass. Reprinted by permission.

case the future itself holds the solution to whatever now seems to be the trouble. If this technique sounds familiar in its mixture of brutality and pacification, in its combination of aggression and absorption, noted by Edgar Freidenberg in his brilliant analysis of the adult treatment of the adolescent minority, if it sounds vaguely like methods used in other and related domestic and foreign conflicts, then the point is obvious: our society is unfortunately structured, in the prevalent forms of its language and thinking, in ways designed to suppress some of the most vital elements now struggling into consciousness and toward some awareness of their frustrated powers.

This struggle is essentially a cultural one, regardless of the efforts by older people to make political use of it or to place it, unflatteringly, within the terms of traditional politics, particularly cold-war politics. The intellectual weapons used in the war against youth are from the same arsenal — and the young know this — from which war is being waged against other revolutionary movements, against Vietnam, against any effective justice, as distinguished from legislative melodrama, in matters of race and poverty. These weapons, as I've suggested, are by no means crude. They scarcely look at times like weapons at all, and many of the people most adroit in handling them, writers and teachers as well as politicians, aren't even aware that they are directing against youth arguments of a kind used also to rationalize other policies which they consider senseless and immoral. Aside from the political necessities of candidates, why is it that people who can be tough-mindedly idealistic in opposition to our actions in Vietnam or to our treatment of the powerless, talk about youth and think about the rebellion of youth in a manner implicit in the mentality that produces and excuses these other barbarities? The reason, I think, is that most people don't want to face the possibility that each of these troubles grows from the same root and can be traced back to the same murky recesses within each of us and within the social organisms to which we have lent ourselves. They prefer isolated and relatively visible sources for such difficulties, along with the illusion that each of them is susceptible to accredited forms of political or economic cleansing. By contrast, it is the conviction of the most militant young people, and of some older ones, that any solutions will require a radical change in the historical, philosophical, and psychological assumptions that are the foundations of any political or economic system. Some kind of cultural revolution is therefore the necessary prelude even to our capacity to think intelligently about political reformation.

Oddly enough, the young are proved right, in this supposition at least, by the nature of the attacks made against them. I don't mean attacks from the like of Reagan and Wallace, but those coming from becalmed and sensible men, whose moderation is of a piece with their desire to increase the efficiency of the present system. At work in these attacks are the same tendencies of thought and language that shape the moderate, rationalizing analyses of the other nightmares I've mentioned. They help us to sleep through them during the night and during most of the day.

Maybe the most prevalent of these tendencies is the insistence on a language that is intellectually "cool," a language aloof from militant or revolutionary vocabularies, which in their exclusion sound excessive, exaggerated, and unserviceable. This cool language is not at all dull or plodding. On the contrary, it's full of social flair; it swings with big words, slang words, naughty words, leaping nimbly from the "way out" to the "way in" — it really holds the world together, hips and squares alike. The best working example is the style of *Time* magazine, and it wasn't surprising in a recent issue to find a piece full of compliments to what were titularly called "Anti-Revolutionaries." With the suave observation that writers like these "who prefer rationality to revolution are by no means conservative," they honored three distinguished commentators on youth and other scenes. One of the three, Benjamin DeMott, a professor of English at Amherst, diversely active as a novelist, critic, and educational innovator, had earlier written an essay in the Sunday New York *Times Magazine* on the style of what he called the "spirit of over-kill" among some of his fellow writers, especially those of the revolutionary fringe like Paul Goodman, Andrew Kopkind, and Susan Sontag.

According to DeMott, the verbal violence of this decade "was" (and I'll get to the significance of this past tense in a moment) "pressed not at new 'enemies' but at old ones already in tatters." Just at a glance one had to wonder why "enemies," new or old, were assigned the unreality of quotation marks. Has the semblance of negotiations made the war in Vietnam disappear as an "enemy"? Does he mean racial injustice? the horrors of urban life? the smothering effects of educational institutions of which he is himself one of the most active critics? I'm afraid these enemies aren't so easily dispelled. The degree to which they press against DeMott's own "cool" dismissal of them is in fact made evident, with engaging innocence, in the very form of his essay. In order to find a requisite dispassion for his own style, as against what he mistakenly takes for the dominant style of this decade, he must project himself to the end of the century and then look back at us. Like other critics of our violence, he is himself already visiting the famous year 2000, programming for which, as we are cautioned by a number of distinguished economists, sociologists, and technicians, will only be disrupted by people who fail to remain politely soft-spoken amid the accumulating squalor, blood, and suffering of their lives.

This peculiar form of address, by which we are asked to hear our present as if it were our past, suggests yet another and more subtle method of repression — the futuristic — now especially popular in the social sciences. A notably unembarrassed practitioner, and yet another writer commended by the article in *Time* magazine, is Zbigniew Brzezinski, director of the Research Institute on Communist Affairs at Columbia, recently a member of the Policy Planning Staff of the State Department, and now head of Hubert Humphrey's "task force" on foreign affairs. Also concerned because revolutionary loudmouths and their young adherents are incited by the past rather than the future — keep in mind that there is no present, in case you thought it was hurting someone — Brzezinski has published two futuristic position papers in the *New Republic:* "The American Transition," and more recently, "Revolution and Counterrevolution (But Not Necessarily About Columbia!)." Happily bounding over invisible rainbows, Brzezinski lets us know that, like it or not, we are already becoming a "technetronic society," and any old-fashioned doctrinal or ideological habits — as if ideology wouldn't be inherent in his imagined social systems — will get us into real, permanent troubles instead of temporary ones. We'll fail to adapt, that is, to "the requirements of the metamorphic age," and thus miss the chance of creating a "meritocratic democracy" in which "a community of organization-oriented application-minded intellectuals [can relate] itself more effectively to the political system than their predecessors." We need only stay calm, and admittedly such language is not designed to excite us, since "improved governmental performance, and its increased sensitivity to social needs is being stimulated by the growing involvement in national affairs of what Kenneth Boulding has called the Educational and Scientific Establishment (EASE)."

Deifications have of course always been announced by capitalization. As in religion, so in politics: an "excessive" concern for the present is a sure way of impairing your future. If, in the one case, you might as well surrender your will to God, in the other you might as well surrender it to EASE, or, getting back to DeMott patiently waiting there at the turn of the century, to "the architects of the Great Disengagement," with "their determination to negotiate the defusing of The Words as well as of The Bombs." But I'm afraid it's merely symptomatic of how bad things are now that many of those who want the young and the rebellious to be more quiet follow the advice of Hubert Humphrey: they speak to the young not about the past, not even about the present, but about some future, which, as prognosticators, they're already privileged to know. They are There; the revolutionists are living in the Past. And who is here and now, living, suffering, and impassioned in the present? Apparently no one, except maybe a few of what Brzezinski likes to call the "historical irrelevants."

If the young are inarticulate, if, when they do try to expound their views, they sound foolish, are these, and other examples of adult thinking and writing which I'll get to presently, somehow evidences of superior civilization, something to be emulated, the emanations of a system worth saving from revolution? Such arguments and such uses of language — almost wholly abstracted from the stuff of daily life as it is lived in this year, these months, this week — do not define but rather exemplify the cultural and linguistic crisis to which the young are responding with silence even more than with other demonstrations of their nearly helpless discontent. "Power, or the shadow cast by power, always ends in creating an axiological writing," as the French critic Roland Barth puts it, "in which the distance which usually separates fact from value disappears within the space of a word." To prefer "rationality" to "revolution" is good *Time* magazine language. It can't be faulted except by those who feel, as I do, that a revolution is probably necessary if rationality is to be restored to a society that thinks it has been operating rationally. If the young are "revolutionary," and if this is the reverse of "rational," what, then, is the nature of the rationality they're attacking? Quite aside from science fiction passing for history in the writings we've just looked at, are the practices of the United States government with regard to most issues of race, poverty, the war, the gun laws, or even the postal service rational? Is it rational to vote an increase of money for Vietnam, and on the same hot day in July, cut appropriations for the summer employment of young Negroes and Puerto Ricans, thus helping to encourage a bloody summer at home while assuring one abroad?

These are all, as Brzezinski would point out, complex issues, and according to him, they will not be solved by "historical irrelevants," by those who, with revolutionary fervor, are yearning, as he would have it, for the simplicities of the past and who therefore "will have no role to play in the new technetronic society." But what has decided, since I know no people who have, that we want his "technetronic society," that it is desirable or inevitable? Who decides that it is necessary or even good for certain issues to be construed as complex and therefore susceptible only to the diagnosticians who could lead such a society? Why have certain issues become complex and who is served by this complexity? Why is the life we already lead, mysterious and frightening as it is, to be made even more so by the ridiculous shapes conjured up in Brzezinski's jaw-breaking terminologies? Some issues are not simple, which does not mean that others are not unnecessarily complex. It is clear to everyone that Vietnam is "complex." But it is equally clear that it need not, for us, have become complex; that it might not even have existed as an issue, except for those members of EASE who helped justify our continued presence there. Maybe the secret is that it is really "easy" to be complex.

The funniest and in a way the most innocent example of this kind of no-thinking passing in sound and cadence for responsible, grown-up good sense is offered by George Kennan. The third figure heralded for his rationality in the *Time* article, Kennan is a renowned historian, a former ambassador to the Soviet Union, and the author of yet another containment policy, this one for youth. Kennan's specialty is what might be called "the argument from experience," easily slipping into "the argument from original sin." "The decisive seat of evil in this world," he tells us in *Democracy and the Student Left*, a just-published debate between him and nearly forty students and teachers, "is not in social and political institutions, and not even, as a rule, in the ill-will or iniquities of statesmen, but simply in the weakness and imperfection of the human soul itself." No one can deny a proposition so general, but surely only someone who likes for other reasons to plead the inescapable complexity of issues could propose such an idea to people wondering how the hell we got into Vietnam or why millions of poor in a country so rich must go hungry every day.

Kennan has, of course, had direct experience with other revolutions and with other people who have ignored the imperfections of the human soul simply by denying its existence. No wonder it often sounds, then, as if the militant young are merely his chance at last to give a proper dressing-down to the kind of fellows who brought on the Russian Revolution, his historical analogies being to that extent, at least, more complimentary to the young than Brzezinski's evocation of Luddites and Chartists. "I have heard it freely confessed by members of the revolutionary student generation of Tsarist Russia," Kennan rather huffily reports, "that, proud as they were of the revolutionary exploits of their youth, they never really learned anything in their university years; they were too busy with politics." Earlier, from Woodrow Wilson at his prissiest, he describes an ideal "at the very center of our modern institutions of higher learning": it is a "free place," in Wilson's words, "itself a little world; but not perplexed, living with a singleness of aim not known without; the home of sagacious men."

Was it such sagacious men, one must ask, since it surely was not the rampaging students, who assumed that this ideal place should also house ROTC units, defense projects, recruiters from Dow Chemical, and agents of the CIA? An ideal institution freed of *those* perplexities — which evidently do not bother Mr. Kennan — is precisely what the students have been agitating for. It is not possible to think about learning now without being, as he pejoratively puts it, "busy with politics." The university officials and the government have seen to that. But again, Kennan probably doesn't regard ROTC as a political presence on campus, and students are "busy with politics" not in the precious hours wasted on drill and military science, but only while agitating against these activities, which are mostly useless even from a military point of view. Out of this mess of verbal and moral assumptions, the finest and stiffest blossom is the phrase "freely confessed": imagine having the gall to tell someone outright that as a student you hadn't even done your assignments while trying to overthrow a corrupt and despotic government. Doubtless that government also preferred its universities "not perplexed" by anything related to the conduct of public affairs.

Compared with the futuristic modes of Brzezinski and DeMott, Kennan's mode of argument is at least honest about seeing the present only as if it were the past. In its rather ancient charm it isn't nearly so dangerously effective as still other less explicitly theological, less passionate, more academically systematized methods now in vogue for abridging youthful radicalism or transcendentalism. Consider for example what might be called the tight-contextual method. This is particularly useful in putting assassinations in their place, or rather in no-place ("it was not Dallas that curled a finger round that trigger and pulled it; it was a sad and sick individual," one informant irrefutably told me), and in explaining why we cannot withdraw from Vietnam. That country gets reduced, in this form of argument, to some thousands of vaguely identified friends whom we cannot desert, even though their worth is even more difficult to locate than is their presence during combat operations. Of course this kind of analysis works wonders on anything as worldwide and variously motivated as student or youth protest. Unanswerably the students at Columbia are not the students in Paris or Czechoslovakia or even Berkeley. Like the leaders in any generation, the rebellious students are only a small minority of the young, a minority even of the student bodies they belong to. There are local, very special reasons not only for the motivations of each group but for each of the different acts of each group. What is astonishing, however, is that they all do act, that they are all acting now, that the youth of the world almost on signal have found local causes — economic, social, political, academic ones — to fit an apparently general need to rebel. So universal and simultaneous a response to scarcely new causes reveals in the young an imaginative largeness about the interconnection of issues, an awareness of their wider context, of a world in which what in former decades would have been a local war is now symptomatic, as is poverty and the quality of life in our cities, of where the dominant forms of thinking have taken us. Again, it can be said that the young are in effect rebelling against precisely the kinds of analysis that are inadequate to explain what the young are up to. More terrifying than the disorder in the streets is the disorder in our heads; the rebellion of youth, far from being a cause of disorder, is rather a reaction, a rebellion against the disorder we call order, against our failure to make sense of the way we live now and have lived since 1945.

Yet another form of restrictive or deflationary analysis — and appropriately the last I'll consider — is a special favorite of literary critics and historians as well as politicians: the anti-apocalyptic. Implicit in some of the methods we've already looked at, this one dampens revolutionary enthusiasms with the information that history has recorded such efforts before and also recorded their failure — the Abolitionists, the young Bolsheviks, the Luddites. All claims to uniqueness are either tarnished by precedent or doomed to meaninglessness. We've been through it all, and are now doing the best we can, given — and here we're back at the borders of Original Sin — our imperfect state of being. In the treatment of militant youth, this type of argument is especially anxious to expose any elitist or fascist tinge in the young, with their stress on chimerical "participatory democracy" or their infantile assumption that the worst must be allowed to happen — let us say the election of George Wallace — if ever the inherent horrors of the "System," and thus the necessities of revolution, are to become apparent to everyone. Some people do talk this way; some people always have. But only a minority of the articulate and protesting young lend themselves to anything so politically programmatic. Such arguments are wholly peripheral to the emergence of youth as a truly unique historical force for which there are no precedents. Youth is an essentially nonpolitical force, a cultural force, that signals, while it can't by itself initiate, the probable beginnings of a new millennium, though hardly the one described in the Book of Revelations. If only because of its continuously fluid, continuously disappearing and emerging, membership, it is incapable of organizing itself into shapes suitable to the political alliances that can be made by other, more stable minority groups like the blacks. It has no history; it may never have one, but it is that shared experience of all races which may come finally to dominate our imagination of what we are.

What is happening to the youth of the world deserves the freest imagination, the freest attention that older people are capable of giving. It requires an enormously strenuous, and for most people, probably impossible, intellectual effort. Working within the verbal and conceptual frames — a sadly appropriate word — against which the rebellion of youth is in large part directed, we must try to invent quite different ways of seeing, imagining, and describing. So complicated is the task linguistically that it is possible to fail merely because of the vocabulary with which, from the best intentions, we decide to try. It is perhaps already irrelevant, for example, to discuss the so-called student revolt as if it were an expression of "youth." The revolt might more properly be taken as a repudiation by the young of what adults call "youth." It may be an attempt to cast aside the strangely exploitative and at once cloying, the protective and impotizing concept of "youth" which society foists on people who often want to consider themselves adults. Is it youth or is it the economic and sexual design of adult society that is being served by what Erik Erikson calls the "moratorium," the period when people under twenty-one are "allowed" to discover their identities without at the same time having to assume adult responsibilities? Quite painfully, the young have suddenly made us aware that the world we have been seeing isn't necessarily the world at all. Not only that France wasn't France, but that even the young weren't necessarily that thing we call "young." It is no longer a matter of choice therefore: we must learn to know the world differently, including the young, or we may not know it until it explodes, thus showing forth its true nature, to follow the logic of Marx, only in the act and at the moment of breakdown.

Before asking questions about the propriety and programs of young militants who occupy buildings, burn cars, and fight the police, let's first ask what kind of world surrounds these acts. Let's not conceive of the world as a place accidentally controlled by certain people whose wickedness or stupidity has been made evident by disaster, or as the scene of injustices whose existence was hidden from us. Because to do so implies that we are beguiled rather than responsible even for specific things that we do not know are happening. We're in danger of becoming like the Germans before the war who afterward turned to their children with dismay, then surprise, then amnesia. Such analogies to our present situation, and even more to an anticipated one, are not exact, but neither are they remote.

The world we now live in cannot get any better merely by changing its managers or improving some of its circumstances. It exists as it does because of the way we think about one another and because of our incapacity, so far at least, to learn to think differently. For those who fought in it and who are now the middle generation and parents of the young, World War II gave absolutely the worst kind of schooling. It trained us to think in extraordinarily simplistic terms about politics and history. One might even say that it made people my age strangely apolitical and ahistorical. We were convinced that evil resided in Nazism and Fascism, and that against these nothing less than total victory was acceptable. The very concept of total victory or unconditional surrender was part of a larger illusion that all wickedness was entrenched in certain places, circumstances, and persons, and very subtly these were differentiated from the people or the nations where they found hospitality. The Morgenthau plan had no chance of success, and not simply because it was economically unfeasible in proposing the creation of an agrarian state between the West and the East. It would have had the even more tactically dangerous effect of blaming a *people* for a war. Thereby two embarrassing questions would have been raised: either that the Germans were really a separate kind of people, or if not, that they were like us, and must therefore have had some understandable provocation for acting as they did. And what could that provocation have been if not something for which we too had a responsibility? No — better just talk about the eradication of Nazism and warlords.

Like all wars, World War II blinded us to the conditions at home that required our attention, and so did the cold war that followed: for nearly twenty-five years we looked at foreign devils rather than domestic ills. The consequences were even worse in our thinking, however, or rather in our not thinking, about the true sources and locations of our trouble. They are within ourselves and within the mechanisms of our own society. One reason why those in the parental generation cannot understand the rebellion of the young is that our own "rebellion" was managed for us, while for the young now it is instinctive and invented and unprogrammed. Our protest movement was the war itself, the crusade against Nazism, Fascism, and Japanese imperialism. In many ways our youth didn't matter to the world. I went into the infantry in 1943 at seventeen, fought in Germany, and came out in 1946 imagining that I'd helped cleanse the globe and could therefore proceed to make up for lost personal time at the university, where a grateful government paid my expenses.

If the war absorbed and homogenized the political feelings of the millions like me who are now the parents of people nearly old enough to be drafted for a quite different kind of war, the G.I. Bill of Rights gave us an experience of college and university life different from any before or since. The G.I. Bill was legislation of enormous political and social importance. It allowed the first huge influx into colleges, universities, and later into the academic profession, of people, who for financial and social reasons weren't before recognized as belonging to the group which represents youth as our society likes to imagine it — the students. But, given their backgrounds, which made them poignantly anxious to take advantage of an opportunity they never thought available, much less a right, given their age, service experience, sexual maturity, and often marriage, this influx of a new kind of student had a stabilizing rather than a disrupting effect. We were maybe the first really serious mass of students who ever entered the academy, designed up till then, and still designed, to prolong immaturity until the ridiculous age of twenty-one or later.

If we were serious, it was in a bad sense, I'm afraid: we wanted so much to make it that we didn't much question the value of what we were doing. I'm not surprised that so few people my age are radical even in temperament. My fellow academicians who came through the process I've described have fitted all too nicely into the Anglophilic gentility of most areas of academic life, into the death-dealing social manners promoted by people who before the war could afford the long haul of graduate as well as undergraduate education. For how many families did the fact that "my boy" is a professor, especially a professor in English, mean the final completion of citizenship papers? Because that's what most of the proliferation of exams, graduate or otherwise, really add up to. Much more than the reputed and exaggerated effect of television and other media in creating a self-conscious community of the young (effects shared, after all, by people in their thirties and early forties), it is the peculiar nature of World War II and of subsequent schooling experience which separates the older from the younger but still contiguous groups.

In thinking about the so-called generation gap, then, I suggest that people my age think not so much about the strangeness of the young but about their own strangeness. Why is it "they" rather than "we" who are unique? By what astonishing arrogance do people my age propose to themselves the program described recently in the New York *Times* Sunday Book Review by a critic who wrote that during the summer he would support McCarthy and that "beyond that, full-time opposition to radical or reactionary excesses in the arts and criticism strikes me as proper and sufficient activity for a critic. And political enough, too, in its ultimate implications." The ultimate implications are dead center. Dead because what can anyone mean now by an "excess," and from where does one measure it unless, like the person in question, he entertains, as do most of my contemporaries, the paranoiac illusion that he has emerged a representative of True Nature?

Only when the adult world begins to think of itself as strange, as having a shape that is not entirely necessary, much less lovely, only when it begins to see that the world, as it has now been made visible to us in forms and institutions, isn't all *there*, maybe less than half of it — only then can we begin to meet the legitimate anguish of the young with something better than the cliché that they have no program. Revolutionaries seldom do. One can be sick and want health, jailed and want freedom, inwardly dying and want a second birth without a program. For what the radical youth want to do is to expose the mere contingency of facts which have been considered essential. That is a marvelous thing to do, the necessary prelude to our being able, any of us, to think of a program which is more than merely the patching up of social systems that were never adequate to the people they were meant to serve.

Liberal reformers, no matter how tough, won't effect and might even forestall the necessary changes. In our universities, for example, there is no point in removing symptoms and leaving the germs. It is true, as the young have let us know with an energy that isn't always convenient even to sympathizers like myself, that our universities are too often run by fat cats, that renowned professors are bribed by no or little teaching, that a disproportionate amount of teaching is done by half-educated, miserably underpaid, and distracted graduate assistants, that, as a consequence of this imbalance, research of the most exciting kind has very little immediate bearing on curriculum, which remains much as it has for the past fifty years, and that, as Martin Duberman eloquently showed in a recent issue of *Daedalus*, authoritarianism in curriculum and in teaching, not to be confused with being an authority in a subject, is so much a part of our educational system that university students arrive already crippled even for the freedom one is prepared to give them. These conditions exist in a pattern of idiotic requirements and childish, corrupting emoluments not simply because our universities are mismanaged. The mismanagement has itself a prior cause which is to be found in the way most people think about scholarship and its relation to teaching — a question which is a kind of metaphor for the larger one of the relations between the generations: what conditions permit the most profitable engagements between an older mind that is trained and knowledgeable and a younger one anxious to discover itself but preconditioned by quite different cultural circumstances?

These circumstances have, of course, always differed between one generation and another, but never so radically as now. Never before have so many revered subjects, like literature itself, seemed obsolete in any strict compartmental form; never before have the divisions between such subjects as anthropology, sociology, and languages seemed more arbitrary and harmful to intelligent inquiry; and seldom in the history of modern civilization has there been a greater need felt by everyone for a new key to our mythologies, a key that we nervously feel is about to be found. For if we are at a moment of terror we are also at a moment of great expectation and wonder, for which the young have a special appetite. To meet this challenge, the universities need to dismantle their entire academic structure, their systems of courses and requirements, their notion of what constitutes the proper fields and subjects of academic inquiry.

Most people who teach have in their heads some ideal university, and mine would be governed by a single rule: there is nothing that does not need to be studied in class, including, of course, the oddity of studying *in* a class. Everything and everybody, the more randomly selected the better, has to be subjected to questions, especially dumb questions, and to the elicitation of answers. The point is that nothing must be taken for other than "strange," nothing must be left alone. Study the morning paper, study the teacher, study the listless slouching of some students — half-dead already at eighteen. But above all, those working in advanced research sponsored at any university would also let capable students study that research and ask questions about it. And if in fact some things cannot be taught, then that in itself should be the subject of inquiry. The hierarchies that might evolve. would be determined on a wholly pragmatic basis: for subjects, by the amount of effort and time needed to make something yield up the dimensions of its mystery; for any way of thinking, by the degree to which it raises a student to eye level with the potentialities of a subject, the degree to which it can tune his ears into it. Above all, the university would be a place where curricula are discovered anew perhaps every year or so. The argument that the demands of an existing student body cannot be allowed to determine policy for succeeding ones would mean the reverse of what it now means: not that changes are difficult to effect, but that they would be effected year after year, if necessary, to meet the combined changes of interest in student and faculty. Given the sluggishness of most people, the results of such a policy would not be nearly as chaotic or exciting as one might imagine. Indeed, what would be hoped for is *more* disruption, and therefore more questioning and answering than one would ever get.

In confronting oppositions from youth as in other matters short of Vietnam, Lyndon Johnson is a genius in that his most decent impulses, and he has some, don't merely serve, aren't merely synchronized with, but are indistinguishable from his often uncanny political instinct for pacifying any opposition, for castrating any force that threatens to move the system off the center track which carried him to power. While demonstrations at Columbia were making Hubert Humphrey sick "deep inside," and Nixon was reportedly saying that if there were a second Columbia he wouldn't have to care *whom* he had to run against, LBJ was proposing that the vote be given to all people between eighteen and twenty-one. But the terrible price of the political logic he so masterfully handles is at once made evident if we ask what many of the young, and not simply the militant ones, would find to vote for in this election. They would be joining the electorate just when it is at last stagnating from our national satisfaction with the mere manipulation and redistribution of the poisons within us. So ingeniously is the center still in control of the manipulative forces that there will not be a turn to the right *within* our political system, not one with any more chance of success than Goldwater, at least, and no one within the system represents the left. The danger sign will be abstention, political indifference, a decision not to care very much who wins, not to participate in a process that affords only a negative choice.

When any large number of people demonstrate their indifference to the choices offered them, they tend to invent others that exist outside the going "democratic" system. They tend to gravitate toward some species of the "participatory democracy" for which the elitist young are most severely criticized. It's fortunate that Johnson's voting-age proposal can't be enacted in time for the young people of eighteen to twenty-one to enter a political imbroglio so contemptibly arranged as this one. It could only further convince them of the necessity for some kind of nondemocratic movement to replace the farce of democracy in which they'd have been asked to take part, and it would allow their critics to assign to them some blame for the consequences of the indifference among the older electorate. The indifference grows on the momentum supplied not by the young but by the nature of our public life. The now not uncommon proposition that our problems are no longer manageable within existing political systems, and that we need an Authority empowered to decide what is best for us, cannot be ascribed merely to youth, Herbert Marcuse, Vietnam, race, violence, or any combination of these. The emerging failure of confidence in our way of managing ourselves and our interests in the world is the consequence of a political process now overwhelmed by the realities it has tried to hide, realities that have grown like cancer cells treated by pain-killers.

Instinctively, the militant young are involved less in a political rebellion, where demands for their "program" would be relevant, than in an attack on the foundations of all of our current political programming. The issues they raise and the issues they personify are essentially anthropological, which brings us to the cultural rather than the political importance of the President's proposal to move the voting age back from twenty-one to eighteen. The importance can be dramatized, with no intention of melodrama, by predicting that within twenty years or so it will be necessary to propose, if not to pass, a voting age of sixteen. Like other mere changes of policy, changes in voting age should not be taken as a sign that we are suddenly to be governed by new or radical modes of thinking. Rather, such reforms signal the accumulated power of forces which our operative modes of thinking have before tried to ignore and which they will now try to make invisible by absorption.

But with the mass of youth — nearly half the population is now under twenty-five — our society is faced with an unprecedented difficulty in the application of this essentially social technique. For when it comes to the young, society is not simply absorbing a group who, like the Irish or labor, duplicate in their social organization each part of the dominant group. To give something like adult or historic identity to a mass that has up to now been relegated to the position of "youth" means a disruptive change in the concept of human identity, of when that identity is achieved, of what it properly should contribute to history. The time scheme that governs our ideas of adolescence, youth, and maturity has changed many times in history since the sixteenth century — Juliet was fourteen, and early in the eighteenth century the age of consent was ten — but it was adjusted to the convenience of an extraordinarily small ruling minority which was in turn submissive to familial regulations. For the first time in history a change of this kind is being made on demand from a powerful mass of young people freed of familial pieties, and never before has a society worked as strenuously as ours, through a mesh of mythologies, to hold these young people back, in an unmercifully prolonged state of adolescence and of what we call "youth." Especially in the United States, the representative and most talented young — the students — have for generations been forced *not* to take themselves seriously as men and women.

So far, the rebellion has accomplished at least one thing: it has succeeded in demoting "collegiate types" (and the sickly reminiscent values that they injected into later life) from glamour to absurdity. The change is not complete, and it never will be. Whole campuses are holdouts, some quite distinguished ones, like Yale and Stanford, where the prep-school ethos remains dominant, while at others the overwhelming number of young clods makes it difficult for the few students who really are alive even to find one another, much less establish an *esprit* that can irradiate more than a small circle. Still, recent agitations have confirmed some of the advances made by the earlier generation of students under the G.I. Bill and cleared still more room on American campuses for the kind of young person who does want to enter history at eighteen, and who is therefore contemptuous of society's cute and reassuring idea of the collegiate — with Lucille Ball as ideal House Mother. Such historical self-consciousness on the part of university students has been fairly common in Europe and in England, where, as shown by Peter Stansky and William Abrahams in *Journey to the Frontier*, students in the thirties could feel that the "journey" to the

Spanish Civil War did not follow but rather began at Oxford and Cambridge. But the differences are obvious, and again, relate to class and family: children of the English upper classes were educated to feel historical, and what distinguished them from lower-class boys was that from boyhood their "careers" *meant* something to the political and historical career of England. Only rarely, and almost exclusively at Harvard, does this phenomenon occur in American universities. Education in American universities has generally been a combination of utilitarian course work and play-acting, "getting ready" to be an adult, even if it meant still getting ready at twenty-two.

The shattering of this pattern has been the work of a complex of forces that include students within the larger power bloc of youth, with its enormous influence on dress and mores, and, perhaps above all, its success in the fields of entertainment. By force of numbers and energy alone, the young have created images which older people are now quite anxious to endow with a sexual-social significance that they before refused to find in the activity of "kids." Put another way, youth has ceased to fulfill the "literary" role which American society has been anxious to assign them. They no longer supply us with a pastoral, any more than the "darkies" do, and this is a serious cultural deprivation for which we have yet to discover a replacement.

Every civilization has to invent a pastoral for itself, and ours has been an idea of youth and of adolescence that has become socially and economically unprofitable, demographically unmanageable, and biologically comic. By a pastoral I mean any form of life that has, by common consent, been secured from the realities of time and history. Some form of pastoral is absolutely essential: it helps stabilize the cycles of individual lives and of civilizations. Its function is an idealizing, simplifying one: it secures certain elemental human attributes from the contaminations of time and of historical involvement. But if the logic of pastoral is to protect certain attributes, its ulterior motive is to keep the human embodiment of these attributes in their proper place, servants rather than participants in daily business where real men really face complex reality.

Insofar as America's imagination of itself can be inferred from literature, from popular entertainment, from fashions, conventions, and educational theory, it can be said that we have used youth as a revenge upon history, as the sacrificial expression of our self-contempt. Youth has been the hero of our civilization, but only so long as it has remained antagonistic to history, only so long as it has remained a literary or mythological metaphor. War, the slaughter of youth at the apparent behest of history, is the ultimate expression of this feeling. The American hatred of history, of what it does to us, gets expressed in a preposterous and crippling idealization of youth as a state as yet untouched by history, except as a killer, and in a corresponding incapacity to understand the demand, now, by the best of the young, to be admitted into it. More hung up on youth than any nation on earth, we are also more determined that youth is not to enter into history without paying the price of that adulteration we call adulthood. To justify what grownups have made of our young, virgin, uncontaminated land, it's as if we are compelled to show that what happened was necessary. Exceptions would prove our human culpability for what is otherwise ascribed to history, and so all that is best in our land must either be kept out of history or tarnished by it. Like our natural wonders, youth will be allowed to exist only on condition that it remain, like some natural preserve, outside the processes that transform everything else into waste.

Surely the destination of our assets needn't be so bleak, so inexorable, so neurotically determined. It will now be seen whether or not we are to exhaust our youth, whether or not in its vulnerability, its continually evaporating and exposed condition, it can resist being made grist for the mill. Because youth is not a historically grounded pressure group, aware of its history, jealous of its progress, continuous and evolving. It is rather what we, all of us, sometimes are. I have avoided any precise definition of youth because it refers to the rare human condition of exuberance, expectation, impulsiveness, and above all, of freedom from believing that all the so-called "necessities" of life and thought are in fact necessities. This condition exists most usefully, for the nation and the world, in people of a certain age, specifically in those who have attained the physical being that makes them wonderfully anxious to create life, to shape life, to enter into life rather than have it fed into them. It is the people of this age, members of what Freidenberg calls the "hot-blooded minority," who are in danger of obliteration as representatives of youth. It is impossible for them to remain youth, in any sense that would profit the rest of society, and also enter into history on the hateful terms now offered them by our political, economic, and technological system. Lyndon Johnson knew instinctively what he was up to when, calling for a vote for people of this age, he remarked that they deserved it because they are "adults in every sense."

Fine, if that means we now change our concept of adulthood to include an eighteen-year-old Bob Dylan rather than an eighteen-year-old Nixon, some creep valedictorian. But that isn't what he has in mind. LBJ has not changed his way of thinking about youth, adulthood, or anything else. He has merely responded to this fantastic cultural opportunity the way our leaders respond to any such opportunity for change: they merely make more room in the house with as little inconvenience as possible to the settled inhabitants. All he proposes to do, and this will have some amusing as well as sad consequences, is lift the term youth from those who threatened us with it, and then hold it in reserve for the time, not far off, when it can be quietly left on the narrow shoulders of what we now call adolescents. Some tinkering will be necessary here and there, of course. The Adolescent Clinic at Children's Hospital in Boston chooses the ages thirteen to nineteen for its patients, but those who've seen some of the ten-to-twelve-year-olds who sneak in tell me that if the ranks of adolescence are to be depleted to fill the vacated positions of youth, these in turn will be quickly occupied by Robert Coles's children of crisis. This will seem a facetious prediction to people who like to think they are reasonable.

So, what I'm saying is that if young people are freeing themselves from a repressive myth of youth only to be absorbed into a repressive myth of adulthood, then youth in its best and truest form, of rebellion and hope, will have been lost to us, and we will have exhausted the best of our natural resources.

KENNETH KENISTON
you have to grow up in scarsdale to know
how bad things really are

The recent events at Harvard are the culmination of a long year of unprecedented student unrest in the advanced nations of the world. We have learned to expect students in underdeveloped countries to lead unruly demonstrations against the status quo, but what is new, unexpected and upsetting to many is that an apparently similar mood is

Text from *The New York Times Magazine*, April 27, 1969; letters from *The New York Times Magazine*, June 8, 1969. Copyright © 1969, by The New York Times Company. Reprinted by permission.

sweeping across America, France, Germany, Italy and even Eastern European nations like Czechoslovakia and Poland. Furthermore, the revolts occur, not at the most backward universities, but at the most distinguished, liberal and enlightened — Berkeley, the Sorbonne, Tokyo, Columbia, the Free University of Berlin, Rome and now Harvard.

This development has taken almost everyone by surprise. The American public is clearly puzzled, frightened and often outraged by the behavior of its most privileged youth. The scholarly world, including many who have devoted their lives to the study of student protest, has been caught off guard as well. For many years, American analysts of student movements have been busy demonstrating that "it can't happen here." Student political activity abroad has been seen as a reaction to modernization, industrialization and the demise of traditional or tribal societies. In an already modern, industrialized, detribalized and "stable" nation like America, it was argued, student protests are naturally absent.

Another explanation had tied student protests abroad to bad living conditions in some universities and to the unemployability of their graduates. Student revolts, it was argued, spring partly from the misery of student life in countries like India and Indonesia. Students who must live in penury and squalor naturally turn against their universities and societies. And if, as in many developing nations, hundreds of thousands of university graduates can find no work commensurate with their skills, the chances for student militancy are further increased.

These arguments helped explain the "silent generation" of the nineteen-fifties and the absence of protest, during that period, in American universities, where students are often "indulged" with good living conditions, close student-faculty contact and considerable freedom of speech. And they helped explain why "super-employable" American college graduates, especially the much-sought-after ones from colleges like Columbia and Harvard, seemed so contented with their lot.

But such arguments do not help us understand today's noisy, angry and militant students in the advanced countries. Nor do they explain why students who enjoy the greatest advantages — those at the leading universities — are often found in the revolts. As a result, several new interpretations of student protest are currently being put forward, interpretations that ultimately form part of what Richard Poirier has termed "the war against the young."

Many reactions to student unrest, of course, spring primarily from fear, anger, confusion or envy, rather than from theoretical analysis. Governor Wallace's attacks on student "anarchists" and other "pin-headed intellectuals," for example, were hardly coherent explanations of protest. Many of the bills aimed at punishing student protesters being proposed in Congress and state legislatures reflect similar feelings of anger and outrage. Similarly, the presumption that student unrest *must* be part of an international conspiracy is based on emotion rather than fact. Even George F. Kennan's recent discussion of the American student left is essentially a moral condemnation of "revolting students," rather than an effort to explain their behavior.

If we turn to more thoughtful analyses of the current student mood we find two general theories gaining widespread acceptance. The first, articulately expressed by Lewis S. Feuer in his recent book on student movements, "The Conflict of Generations," might be termed the "Oedipal Rebellion" interpretation. The second, cogently stated by Zbigniew Brzezinski and Daniel Bell, can be called the theory of "Historical Irrelevance."

The explanation of Oedipal Rebellion sees the underlying force in all student revolts as blind, unconscious Oedipal hatred of fathers and the older generation. Feuer, for example, finds in all student movements an inevitable tendency toward violence and a combination of "regicide, parricide and suicide." A decline in respect for the authority of the older generation is needed to trigger a student movement, but the force behind it comes from "obscure" and "unconscious" forces in the child's early life, including both intense death wishes against his father and the enormous guilt and self-hatred that such wishes inspire in the child.

The idealism of student movements is thus, in many respects, only a "front" for the latent unconscious destructiveness and self-destructiveness of underlying motivations. Even the expressed desire of these movements to help the poor and exploited is explained psychoanalytically by Feuer: Empathy for the disadvantaged is traced to "traumatic" encounters with parental bigotry in the students' childhoods, when their parents forbade them to play with children of other races or lower social classes. The identification of today's new left with blacks is thus interpreted as an unconscious effort to "abreact and undo this original trauma."

There are two basic problems with the Oedipal Rebellion theory, however. First, although it uses psychoanalytic terms, it is bad psychoanalysis. The real psychoanalytic account insists that the Oedipus complex is universal in all normally developing children. To point to this complex in explaining student rebellion is, therefore, like pointing to the fact that all children learn to walk. Since both characteristics are said to be universal, neither helps us understand why, at some historical moments, students are restive and rebellious, while at others they are not. Second, the theory does not help us explain why some students (especially those from middle-class, affluent and idealistic families) are most inclined to rebel, while others (especially those from working-class and deprived families) are less so.

In order really to explain anything, the Oedipal Rebellion hypothesis would have to be modified to point to an unusually *severe* Oedipus complex, involving especially *intense* and unresolved feelings of father-hatred in student rebels. But much is now known about the lives and backgrounds of these rebels — at least those in the United States — and this evidence does not support even the modified theory. On the contrary, it indicates that most student protesters are relatively *close* to their parents, that the values they profess are usually the ones they learned at the family dinner table, and that their parents tend to be highly educated, liberal or left-wing and politically active.

Furthermore, psychological studies of student radicals indicate that they are no more neurotic, suicidal, enraged or disturbed than are non-radicals. Indeed, most studies find them to be rather more integrated, self-accepting and "advanced," in a psychological sense, than their politically inactive contemporaries. In general, research on American student rebels supports a "Generational Solidarity" (or chip-off-the-old-block) theory, rather than one of Oedipal Rebellion.

The second theory of student revolts now being advanced asserts that they are a reaction against "historical irrelevance." Rebellion springs from the unconscious awareness of some students that society has left them and their values behind. According to this view, the ultimate causes of student dissent are sociological rather than psychological. They lie in fundamental changes in the nature of the advanced societies — especially, in the change from industrial to post-industrial society. The student revolution is seen not as a true revolution, but as a counter-revolution — what Daniel Bell has called "the guttering last gasp of a romanticism soured by rancor and impotence."

This theory assumes that we are moving rapidly into a new age in which technology will dominate, an age whose real rulers will be men like computer experts, systems analysts and technobureaucrats. Students who are attached to outmoded and obsolescent values like humanism and romanticism unconsciously feel they have no place in this post-industrial world. When they rebel they are like the Luddites of the past — workers who smashed machines to protest the inevitable industrial revolution. Today's student revolt reflects what Brzezinski terms "an unconscious realization that they [the rebels] are themselves becoming historically obsolete"; it is nothing but the "death rattle of the historical irrelevants."

This theory is also inadequate. It assumes that the shape of the future is already technologically determined, and that protesting students unconsciously "know" that it will offer them no real reward, honor or power. But the idea that the future can be accurately predicted is open to fundamental objection. Every past attempt at prophecy has turned out to be grievously incorrect. Extrapolations from the past, while sometimes useful in the short run, are usually fundamentally wrong in the long run, especially when they attempt to predict the quality of human life, the nature of political and social organization, international relations or the shape of future culture.

The future is, of course, made by men. Technology is not an inevitable master of man and history, but merely provides the possibility of applying scientific knowledge to specific problems. Men may identify with it or refuse to, use it or be used by it for good or evil, apply it humanely or destructively. Thus, there is no real evidence that student protest will emerge as the "death rattle of the historical irrelevants." It could equally well be the "first spark of a new historical era." No one today can be sure of the outcome, and people who feel certain that the future will bring the obsolescence and death of those whom they dislike are often merely expressing their fond hope.

The fact that today's students invoke "old" humanistic and romantic ideas in no way proves that student protests are a "last gasp" of a dying order. Quite the contrary: *All* revolutions draw upon older values and visions. Many of the ideals of the French Revolution, for example, originated in Periclean Athens. Revolutions do not occur because new ideas suddenly develop, but because a new generation begins to take *old* ideas seriously — not merely as interesting theoretical views, but as the basis for political action and social change. Until recently, the humanistic vision of human fulfillment and the romantic vision of an expressive, imaginative and passionate life were taken seriously only by small aristocratic or Bohemian groups. The fact that they are today taken as real goals by millions of students in many nations does not mean that these students are "counterrevolutionaries," but merely that their ideas follow the pattern of every major revolution.

Indeed, today's student rebels are rarely opposed to technology *per se*. On the contrary, they take the high technology of their societies completely for granted, and concern themselves with it very little. What they *are* opposed to is, in essence, the worship of Technology, the tendency to treat people as "inputs" or "outputs" of a technological system, the subordination of human needs to technological programs. The essential conflict between the minority of students who make up the student revolt and the existing order is a conflict over the future direction of technological society, not a counterrevolutionary protest against technology.

In short, both the Oedipal Rebellion and the Historical Irrelevance theories are what students would call "put-downs." If we accept either, we are encouraged not to listen to protests, or to explain them away or reject them as either the "acting out" of destructive Oedipal feelings or the blind reaction of an obsolescent group to the awareness of its obsolescence. But if, as I have argued, neither of these theories is adequate to explain the current "wave" of student protest here and abroad, how can we understand it?

One factor often cited to explain student unrest is the large number of people in the world under 30 — today the critical dividing line between generations. But this explanation alone, like the theories just discussed, is not adequate, for in all historical eras the vast portion of the population has always been under 30. Indeed, in primitive societies most people die before they reach that age. If chronological youth alone was enough to insure rebellion, the advanced societies — where a greater proportion of the population reaches old age than ever before in history — should be the *least* revolutionary, and primitive societies the *most*. This is not the case.

More relevant factors are the relationship of those under 30 to the established institutions of society (that is, whether they are engaged in them or not) ; and the opportunities that society provides for their continuing intellectual, ethical and emotional development. In both cases the present situation in the advanced nations is without precedent.

Philippe Aries, in his remarkable book, "Centuries of Childhood," points out that, until the end of the Middle Ages, no separate stage of childhood was recognized in Western societies. Infancy ended at approximately 6 or 7, whereupon most children were integrated into adult life, treated as small men and women and expected to work as junior partners of the adult world. Only later was childhood recognized as a separate stage of life, and our own century is the first to "guarantee" it by requiring universal primary education.

The recognition of adolescence as a stage of life is of even more

recent origin, the product of the 19th and 20th centuries. Only as industrial societies became prosperous enough to defer adult work until after
puberty could they create institutions — like widespread secondary-
school education — that would extend adolescence to virtually all young
people. Recognition of adolescence also arose from the vocational and
psychological requirements of these societies, which needed much higher
levels of training and psychological development than could be guaran-
teed through primary education alone. There is, in general, an intimate
relationship between the way a society defines the stages of life and
its economic, political and social characteristics.

Today, in more developed nations, we are beginning to witness the
recognition of still another stage of life. Like childhood and adolescence,
it was initially granted only to a small minority, but is now being
rapidly extended to an ever-larger group. I will call this the stage of
"youth," and by that I mean both a further phase of disengagement from
society and the period of psychological development that intervenes
between adolescence and adulthood. This stage, which continues into
the 20's and sometimes into the 30's, provides opportunities for intellectual, emotional and moral development that were never afforded to
any other large group in history. In the student revolts we are seeing
one result of this advance.

I call the extension of youth an advance advisedly. Attendance at a
college or university is a major part of this extension, and there is
growing evidence that this is, other things being equal, a good thing
for the student. Put in an oversimplified phrase, it tends to free him —
to free him from swallowing unexamined the assumptions of the past,
to free him from the superstitions of his childhood, to free him to
express his feelings more openly and to free him from irrational
bondage to authority.

I do not mean to suggest, of course, that all college graduates are
free and liberated spirits, unencumbered by irrationality, superstition,
authoritarianism or blind adherence to tradition. But these findings do
indicate that our colleges, far from cranking out only machinelike robots
who will provide skilled manpower for the economy, are also producing
an increasing number of highly critical citizens — young men and
women who have the opportunity, the leisure, the affluence and the
educational resources to continue their development beyond the point
where most people in the past were required to stop it.

So, one part of what we are seeing on campuses throughout the world
is not a reflection of how bad higher education is, but rather of its

extraordinary accomplishments. Even the moral righteousness of the student rebels, a quality both endearing and infuriating to their elders, must be judged at least partially a consequence of the privilege of an extended youth; for a prolonged development, we know, encourages the individual to elaborate a more personal, less purely conventional sense of ethics.

What the advanced nations have done is to create their own critics on a mass basis — that is, to create an ever-larger group of young people who take the highest values of their societies as their own, who internalize these values and identify them with their own best selves, and who are willing to struggle to implement them. At the same time, the extension of youth has lessened the personal risks of dissent: These young people have been freed from the requirements of work, gainful employment and even marriage, which permits them to criticize their society from a protected position of disengagement.

But the mere prolongation of development need not automatically lead to unrest. To be sure, we have granted to millions the opportunity to examine their societies, to compare them with their values and to come to a reasoned judgment of the existing order. But why should their judgment today be so unenthusiastic?

What protesting students throughout the world share is a mood more than an ideology or a program, a mood that says the existing system — the power structure — is hypocritical, unworthy of respect, outmoded and in urgent need of reform. In addition, students everywhere speak of repression, manipulation and authoritarianism. (This is paradoxical, considering the apparently great freedoms given them in many nations. In America, for example, those who complain most loudly about being suffocated by the subtle tyranny of the Establishment usually attend the institutions where student freedom is greatest.) Around this general mood, specific complaints arrange themselves as symptoms of what students often call the "exhaustion of the existing society."

To understand this phenomenon we must recognize that, since the Second World War, some societies have indeed begun to move past the industrial era into a new world that is post-industrial, technological, post-modern, post-historic or, in Brzezinski's term, "technectronic." In Western Europe, the United States, Canada and Japan, the first contours of this new society are already apparent. And, in many other less-developed countries, middle-class professionals (whose children become activists) often live in post-industrial enclaves within pre-industrial societies. Whatever we call the post-industrial world, it has demonstrated that, for the first time, man can produce more than enough to meet his material needs.

This accomplishment is admittedly blemished by enormous problems of economic distribution in the advanced nations, and it is in terrifying contrast to the overwhelming poverty of the Third World. Nevertheless, it is clear that what might be called "the problem of production" *can*, in principle, be solved. If all members of American society, for example, do not have enough material goods, it is because the system of distribution is flawed. The same is true, or will soon be true, in many other nations that are approaching advanced states of industrialization. Characteristically, these nations, along with the most technological, are those where student unrest has recently been most prominent.

The transition from industrial to post-industrial society brings with it a major shift in social emphases and values. Industrializing and industrial societies tend to be oriented toward solving the problem of production. An industrial ethic — sometimes Protestant, sometimes Socialist, sometimes Communist — tends to emphasize psychological qualities like self-discipline, delay of gratification, achievement-orientation and a strong emphasis on economic success and productivity. The social, political and economic institutions of these societies tend to be organized in a way that is consistent with the goal of increasing production. And industrial societies tend to apply relatively uniform standards, to reward achievement rather than status acquired by birth, to emphasize emotional neutrality ("coolness") and rationality in work and public life.

The emergence of post-industrial societies, however, means that growing numbers of the young are brought up in family environments where abundance, relative economic security, political freedom and affluence are simply facts of life, not goals to be striven for. To such people the psychological imperatives, social institutions and cultural values of the industrial ethic seem largely outdated and irrelevant to their own lives.

Once it has been demonstrated that a society *can* produce enough for all of its members, at least some of the young turn to other goals: for example, trying to make sure that society *does* produce enough and distributes it fairly, or searching for ways to live meaningfully with the goods and the leisure they *already* have. The problem is that our society has, in some realms, exceeded its earlier targets. Lacking new ones, it has become exhausted by its success.

When the values of industrial society become devitalized, the élite sectors of youth — the most affluent, intelligent, privileged and so on — come to feel that they live in institutions whose demands lack moral authority or, in the current jargon, "credibility." Today, the moral imperative and urgency behind production, acquisition, materialism and abundance has been lost.

Furthermore, with the lack of moral legitimacy felt in "the System," the least request for loyalty, restraint or conformity by its representatives — for example, by college presidents and deans — can easily be seen as a moral outrage, an authoritarian repression, a manipulative effort to "co-opt" students into joining the Establishment and an exercise in "illegitimate authority" that must be resisted. From this conception springs at least part of the students' vague sense of oppression. And, indeed, perhaps their peculiar feeling of suffocation arises ultimately from living in societies without vital ethical claims.

Given such a situation, it does not take a clear-cut issue to trigger a major protest. I doubt, for example, that college and university administrators are in fact *more* hypocritical and dishonest than they were in the past. American intervention in Vietnam, while many of us find it unjust and cruel, is not inherently *more* outrageous than other similar imperialistic interventions by America and other nations within the last century. And the position of blacks in this country, although disastrously and unjustifiably disadvantaged, is, in some economic and legal respects, better than ever before. Similarly, the conditions for students in America have never been as good, especially, as I have noted, at those élite colleges where student protests are most common.

But this is *precisely* the point: It is *because* so many of the *other* problems of American society seem to have been resolved, or to be resolvable in principle, that students now react with new indignation to old problems, turn to new goals and propose radical reforms.

So far I have emphasized the moral exhaustion of the old order and the fact that, for the children of post-industrial affluence, the once-revolutionary claims of the industrial society have lost much of their validity. I now want to argue that we are witnessing on the campuses of the world a fusion of *two revolutions* with distinct historical origins. One is a continuation of the old and familiar revolution of the industrial society, the liberal-democratic-egalitarian revolution that started in America and France at the turn of the 18th century and spread to virtually every nation in the world. (Not completed in any of them, its contemporary American form is, above all, to be found in the increased militancy of blacks.) The other is the new revolution, the post-industrial one, which seeks to define new goals relevant to the 20th and 21st centuries.

In its social and political aspects, the first revolution has been one of universalization, to use the sociologist's awkward term. It has involved the progressive extension to more and more people of economic, political and social rights, privileges and opportunities originally available only to the aristocracy, then to the middle class, and now in America to the relatively affluent white working class. It is, in many respects, a *quantitative* revolution. That is, it concerns itself less with the quality of life than with the amount of political freedom, the quantity and distribution of goods or the amount and level of injustice.

As the United States approaches the targets of the first revolution, on which this society was built, to be poor shifts from being an unfortunate fact of life to being an outrage. And, for the many who have never experienced poverty, discrimination, exploitation or oppression, even to *witness* the existence of these evils in the lives of others suddenly becomes intolerable. In our own time the impatience to complete the first revolution has grown apace, and we find less willingness to compromise, wait and forgive among the young, especially among those who now take the values of the old revolution for granted — seeing them not as goals, but as *rights*.

A subtle change has thus occurred. What used to be utopian ideals — like equality, abundance and freedom from discrimination — have now become demands, inalienable rights upon which one can insist without brooking any compromise. It is noteworthy that, in today's student confrontations, no one requests anything. Students present their "demands."

So, on the one hand, we see a growing impatience to complete the first revolution. But, on the other, there is a newer revolution concerned with newer issues, a revolution that is less social, economic or political than psychological, historical and cultural. It is less concerned with the quantities of things than with their qualities, and it judges the virtually complete liberal revolution and finds it still wanting.

"You have to have grown up in Scarsdale to know how bad things really are," said one radical student. This comment would probably sound arrogant, heartless and insensitive to a poor black, much less to a citizen of the Third World. But he meant something important by it. He meant that *even* in the Scarsdales of America, with their affluence, their upper-middle-class security and abundance, their well-fed, well-heeled children and their excellent schools, something is wrong. Economic affluence does not guarantee a feeling of personal fulfillment;

political freedom does not always yield an inner sense of liberation and cultural freedom; social justice and equality may leave one with a feeling that something else is missing in life. "No to the consumer society!" shouted the bourgeois students of the Sorbonne during May and June of 1968 — a cry that understandably alienated French workers, for whom affluence and the consumer society are still central goals.

What, then, are the targets of the new revolution? As is often noted, students themselves don't know. They speak vaguely of "a society that has never existed," of "new values," of a "more humane world," of "liberation" in some psychological, cultural and historical sense. Their rhetoric is largely negative; they are stronger in opposition than in proposals for reform; their diagnoses often seem accurate, but their prescriptions are vague; and they are far more articulate in urging the immediate completion of the first revolution than in defining the goals of the second. Thus, we can only indirectly discern trends that point to the still-undefined targets of the new revolution.

What are these trends and targets?

First, there is a revulsion against the notion of quantity, particularly economic quantity and materialism, and a turn toward concepts of quality. One of the most delightful slogans of the French student revolt was, "Long live the passionate revolution of creative intelligence!" In a sense, the achievement of abundance may allow millions of contemporary men and women to examine, as only a few artists and madmen have examined in the past, the quality, joyfulness and zestfulness of experience. The "expansion of consciousness"; the stress on the expressive, the aesthetic and the creative; the emphasis on imagination, direct perception and fantasy — all are part of the effort to enhance the quality of this experience.

Another goal of the new revolution involves a revolt against uniformity, equalization, standardization and homogenization — not against technology itself, but against the "technologization of man." At times, this revolt approaches anarchic quaintness, but it has a positive core as well — the demand that individuals be appreciated, not because of their similarities or despite their differences, but because they *are* different, diverse, unique and noninterchangeable. This attitude is evident in many areas: for example, the insistence upon a cultivation of personal idiosyncrasy, mannerism and unique aptitude. Intellectually, it is expressed in the rejection of the melting-pot and consensus-politics view of American life in favor of a post-homogeneous America in which cultural diversity and conflict are underlined rather than denied.

The new revolution also involves a continuing struggle against psychological or institutional closure or rigidity in any form, even the rigidity of a definite adult role. Positively, it extols the virtues of openness, motion and continuing human development. What Robert J. Lifton has termed the protean style is clearly in evidence. There is emerging a concept of a lifetime of personal change, of an adulthood of continuing self-transformation, of an adaptability and an openness to the revolutionary modern world that will enable the individual to remain "with it" — psychologically youthful and on top of the present.

Another characteristic is the revolt against centralized power and the complementary demand for participation. What is demanded is not merely the consent of the governed, but the involvement of the governed. "Participatory democracy" summarizes this aspiration, but it extends far beyond the phrase and the rudimentary social forms that have sprung up around it. It extends to the demand for relevance in education — that is, for a chance for the student to participate in his own educational experience in a way that involves all of his faculties, emotional and moral as well as intellectual. The demand for "student power" (or, in Europe, "co-determination") is an aspect of the same theme: At Nanterre, Columbia, Frankfurt and Harvard, students increasingly seek to participate in making the policies of their universities.

This demand for participation is also embodied in the new ethic of "meaningful human relationships," in which individuals confront each other without masks, pretenses and games. They "relate" to each other as unique and irreplaceable human beings, and develop new forms of relationships from which all participants will grow.

In distinguishing between the old and the new revolutions, and in attempting to define the targets of the new, I am, of course, making distinctions that students themselves rarely make. In any one situation the two revolutions are joined and fused, if not confused. For example, the Harvard students' demand for "restructuring the university" is essentially the second revolution's demand for participation; but their demand for an end to university "exploitation" of the surrounding community is tied to the more traditional goals of the first revolution. In most radical groups there is a range of opinion that starts with the issues of the first (racism, imperialism, exploitation, war) and runs to the concerns of the second (experiential education, new life styles, meaningful participation, consciousness-expansion, relatedness, encounter and community). The first revolution is personified by Maoist-oriented Progressive Labor party factions within the student left, while the second is represented by hippies, the "acid left," and the Yippies. In any individual, and in all student movements, these revolutions coexist in uneasy and often abrasive tension.

Furthermore, one of the central problems for student movements today is the absence of any theory of society that does justice to the new world in which we of the most industrialized nations live. In their search for rational critiques of present societies, students turn to theories like Marxism that are intricately bound up with the old revolution.

Such theories make the ending of economic exploitation, the achievement of social justice, the abolition of racial discrimination and the development of political participation and freedom central, but they rarely deal adequately with the issues of the second revolution. Students inevitably try to adapt the rhetoric of the first to the problems of the second, using concepts that are often blatantly inadequate to today's world.

Even the concept of "revolution" itself is so heavily laden with images of political, economic and social upheaval that it hardly seems to characterize the equally radical but more social-psychological and cultural transformations involved in the new revolution. One student, recognizing this, called the changes occurring in his California student group, "too radical to be called a revolution." Students are thus often misled by their borrowed vocabulary, but most adults are even more confused, and many are quickly led to the mistaken conclusion that today's student revolt is nothing more than a repetition of Communism's in the past.

Failure to distinguish between the old and new revolutions also makes it impossible to consider the critical question of how compatible they are with each other. Does it make sense— or is it morally right — for today's affluent American students to seek imagination, self-actualization, individuality, openness and relevance when most of the world and many in America live in deprivation, oppression and misery?

The fact that the first revolution is "completed" in Scarsdale does not mean that it is (or soon will be) in Harlem or Appalachia — to say nothing of Bogotá or Calcutta. For many children of the second revolution, the meaning of life may be found in completing the first — that is, in extending to others the "rights" they have always taken for granted.

For others the second revolution will not wait; the question, "What lies beyond affluence?" demands an answer now. Thus, although we may deem it self-indulgent to pursue the goals of the new revolution in a world where so much misery exists, the fact is that in the advanced nations it is upon us, and we must at least learn to recognize it.

Finally, beneath my analysis lies an assumption I had best make explicit. Many student critics argue that their societies have failed miserably. My argument, a more historical one perhaps, suggests that our problem is not only that industrial societies have failed to keep all their promises, but that they have succeeded in some ways beyond all expectations. Abundance was once a distant dream, to be postponed to a hereafter of milk and honey; today, most Americans are affluent. Universal mass education was once a Utopian goal; today in America almost the entire population completes high school, and almost half enters colleges and universities.

The notion that individuals might be free, en masse, to continue their psychological, intellectual, moral and cognitive development through their teens and into their 20's would have been laughed out of court in any century other than our own; today, that opportunity is open to millions of young Americans. Student unrest is a reflection not only of the failures, but of the extraordinary successes of the liberal-industrial revolution. It therefore occurs in the nations and in the colleges where, according to traditional standards, conditions are best.

But for many of today's students who have never experienced anything but affluence, political freedom and social equality, the old vision is dead or dying. It may inspire bitterness and outrage when it is not achieved, but it no longer animates or guides. In place of it, students (and many who are not students) are searching for a new vision, a new set of values, a new set of targets appropriate to the post-industrial era — a myth, an ideology or a set of goals that will concern itself with the quality of life and answer the question, "Beyond freedom and affluence, what?"

What characterizes student unrest in the developed nations is this peculiar mixture of the old and the new, the urgent need to fulfill the promises of the past and, at the same time, to define the possibilities of the future.

TO THE EDITOR:

How does one deal with a hopelessly vulgarized version, and consequent distortion of, one's views? In his essay on explanation of youth movements, Kenneth Keniston ascribed to me a view that youth is "historically irrelevant" in a "post-industrial society" for holding "outmoded humanist values." I have *never* said that youth is "historically irrelevant": I did coin the concept of a "post-industrial society" but did not use it in the way Keniston ascribes, and I have never said that humanist values are "outmoded." (The entire point of my book on "The Reforming of General Education" — one of the places where the concept of the post-industrial society is elaborated — is to argue that humanistic studies can be one of the ways of dealing with the tension of the technocratic and apocalyptic moods which wrack the university.)

I have never said that the post-industrial society is "technologically determined." The entire thrust of the Commission on the Year 2000, of the American Academy of Arts and Sciences, which I chair, has been against that view. I have said that the post-industrial society is one of the major structural changes already taking place in the society, in that we are now a service economy, that innovation is increasingly dependent on theoretical knowledge, etc. But there is no one-to-one correspondence between these structural changes and political and cultural forms, as there has not been a one-to-one correspondence between an industrial society and its variant political forms — the United States, the Soviet Union, Nazi Germany and the like. The effort to describe an emerging post-industrial society is to allow us to make choices and redirect the social forms in accordance with our values.

I could not say that the youth protests were "historically irrelevant." Indeed, I have characterized them, perhaps somewhat facilely, as the "beginning class struggles of the post-industrial society." By this I mean that education becomes the determinant of the stratification system of the society, so that control of education becomes crucial for such a society. One of the sources of the present-day youth protest is that, because society has become more technical and specialized, an "organizational harness" has been dropped on young people at an earlier and earlier age. In short, youths begin to worry at an early age whether they will get into a good college, what major to take, whether they will get into graduate school and the like. And just as a rural artisan force rebelled at the industrial discipline imposed by the factory revolution, so the youth have kicked against the organizational harness that has dropped today. When I talked about the romanticism of the S.D.S., I was describing their tactics and their primitive, stilted conspiratorial theories of power. Instead of trying to deal with the problem of the university, the worst among them, in their nihilism, simply seek to destroy the university. What I don't think Mr. Keniston has seen is the trajectory of that nihilism.

That question aside, I return to the problem of intellectual probity. For the consequence of Mr. Keniston's distortion of my views is to take an effort which seeks to chart a direction of social change, to argue, as I have in several papers that the technocratic view will probably not prevail, and to seek to modify and deflect some of the course of that change, and to twist it into a justification of that change. If the intention was polemical, it is irresponsible argument.

DANIEL BELL
Columbia University, New York

The Author Replies:

"How does one deal with a heated defense against an attack one did not make? Professor Bell seems to have interpreted my brief comment upon the theory of 'historical irrelevance' as a 'hopelessly vulgarized version and consequent distortion' of his entire collected works. I did not even discuss, much less criticize, Professor Bell's general views on social change, general education, humanist studies or the future. And I am astounded that Professor Bell could have misread my comments as an effort to 'twist' his views into a 'justification' of technocracy. Thus, I find Professor Bell's letter interesting but scarcely related to my essay.

"In my article, I maintained that the description of protesting students as historically irrelevant presupposes a certain foreknowledge of the future. To speak of student radicals as an obsolescent group — or for that matter, to describe them (in Professor Bell's phrase) as the 'guttering last gasp of a romanticism soured by rancor and impotence' — implies that one *knows* who is about to die, and who will live. In his letter, however, Professor Bell makes clear that he wishes to dissociate himself from the implications of his own vivid phrase, and I am delighted to learn that we now both agree on that point.

"There are nonetheless substantive issues that divide Professor Bell and myself. In discussing the student movement, Professor Bell stresses the nihilism of the 'worst among them,' whereas I stress the idealism of the 'best among them' — who seem to me the majority. The extensive literature on the characteristics of American student activists, radicals and protesters supports my emphasis rather than his. Thus, while we both agree that destructiveness is dangerous in any movement, we disagree on its prevalence in the student movement.

"Professor Bell believes that what he calls the 'organizational harness' dropped upon today's youth provides a useful explanation of student discontent; he seems partially to share the student radical view that modern American society is organizationally oppressive. Here, too, I disagree. To me it seems that today's students are incomparably less 'in harness' and 'oppressed' than those of 50, 100 or 200 years ago. I view the relative *absence* of institutional constraints as a factor that permits more of today's youth to take seriously humanist and romantic ideals that formerly were relegated largely to the realm of abstract theory.

"I will assume that the intent of Professor Bell's letter was polemical. I regret that he did not choose to discuss further the issues I raised in my article; such a discussion would surely have been more enlightening than his self-justification. It would be impertinent of me to raise of his letter the questions of 'intellectual probity,' 'vulgarization,' 'irresponsibility' and 'distortion' that he raises in his reaction to mine."

chapter three

The University:
Embattled Citadel
or
Final Betrayal?

introduction

The student unrest and agitation discussed in the last chapter
clearly reveal that something is wrong in the American university
system, and the essays in this chapter attempt to define what is
wrong. Can we talk about purpose and mean the same thing for all
segments of a university? What is the role of the university? What
should be taught at the university level: the discipline of a profession or life adjustment courses? What should be the relationship between students and teachers? Since all of the essays are
analytical and argumentative, they are so arranged that the reader
can experience cogent forms of argument and counter-argument.

For example, Michael O'Neil, a student, in a formal essay
analyzes the role of American education and then sets up criteria
for an ideal undergraduate college which would help students
educate themselves as human beings. Robert Nisbet, a sociologist,

argues that the problem, if there is one, may lie in certain parts of the liberal arts colleges of universities, but, unlike O'Neil, he is highly skeptical of "individual development" as the aim of the university. He ends with a description of what students should want from their professors: preparation and communication in the classroom, not fatherhood and friendship.

In "The Student and Teacher: Face to Face," Stephen Shapiro describes a shattering personal experience to support his thesis that depersonalization has occurred on campus. Students need to reclaim and sustain their teachers, to make them see what is human in themselves, while teachers, to liberate students, must not only show them that knowledge affects action, but also must motivate them to reshape society. In place of more formal persuasive techniques, Shapiro writes from personal experience and uses narration which emotionally involves the reader.

Shapiro's definition of knowledge and research and the role of the professor leads directly into the essay, "Politics and Morality in Academe." In the face of demands for involvement, for bringing real-life situations into the classroom, Elayne and Leonard Rapping, both university teachers, make a strong case for moral detachment as the "necessary prerequisite for any intellectual activity." The purpose of a professor, his moral responsibility to his students, is to teach an "intellectual method or style of apprehending the world." There is a time for commitment and, of greater importance, a time for scholarly objectivity. This well-organized essay retraces major points for emphasis and moves the reader along by thought transitions, not by gimmicks. The essay culminates fully in the last paragraph and illustrates the aim of all good writing: solid unity.

Irving Kristol's essay is also highly organized. He discusses each of the three parts of the university — faculty, administration, and students — to show that nothing will be done to institute change simply because each segment is deficient in will, in power, and in ideas. This leads to his own proposal for "A Different Way to Restructure the University" which would take federal grants out of the hands of conventional administrative bureaus and turn them into student loans, giving students more buying power that would in turn revitalize higher education. Mr. Kristol then attempts to look at both the advantages and the risks in his plan. His arguments are challenged in the letters that follow his essay.

How effective as counter-argument are these responses of anger, personal attack, reasonable objection, and new insight?

The last three essays in Chapter Three are also argumentative but take up a new issue in the discussion of purpose in the university: what is the place of black studies? DeVere Pentony, college dean, first describes the black man's historical role in America in order to make a case for black leadership. He discusses a series of pros and cons of black studies programs, all in very gentle language, and uses large questions as transition techniques. Obviously, he has no clear-cut solutions to any of the questions he raises because black studies programs are too new. His essay is helpful, however, as a basis for exploration. Here is a man trying to project possible results and asking his reader for tolerance and broad-mindedness. For those who want hard answers and proofs, he may seem to equivocate.

To historian Eugene Genovese the demand for black studies needs no elaborate defense. In "Black Studies: Trouble Ahead," he sees the problem as recklessness and possible corruption of the meaning of black studies by nihilistic white radicals and many black militants. Mr. Genovese is against the demands for all black faculties, departmental autonomy, and student power, but he insists that the university does owe the black as well as the white students "an atmosphere of freedom and dissent for the pursuit of higher education." He is in favor of black studies programs if they have two tasks in mind: providing a setting and professional training for black intellectuals to become leaders on various levels of political and cultural action, and helping combat the racism of white students. Because he is aware of the controversial nature of his statements, Mr. Genovese occasionally uses an interesting persuasive technique: he labels anything that blacks would normally find objectionable in his thinking as the influence of white racism on them. For example, blacks who demand that SNCC training is better than a Ph.D. as a requirement for hiring faculty really reflect white racism because they, in effect, show contempt for black studies as a field requiring discipline and intellectual effort.

Agreeing in some parts with Genovese's article, Elliott Duane Moorman, a black student and president of the class of 1971 at Princeton, issues a plea for sanity in dealing with black demands. He defends black anger and asks that universities use it constructively. He does not use the language of the radical nor make terse demanding statements. His sentences are long, complex, often periodic. He seems at home with formal language and enjoys using qualifying statements. In short, here is a well-reasoned, organized (notice how the word "anger" operates as unifier), intelligent assessment of a new issue now challenging our universities.

MICHAEL O'NEIL
a case for humane intelligence

One of the purposes of this collection of essays is to help persuade the American community to re-examine some of its conventional ideas about higher education. In addressing ourselves to this task we are thus making at least two assumptions. We believe that as presently conceived and constituted American higher education is not adequately meeting the challenges of today's evolving world. And we are assuming that if we convincingly demonstrate why and how American higher education ought to be altered, we will, in fact, make a difference. I personally share this faith — both in our ability to make a cogent case in this regard, and in our fellow citizens' willingness to give us a sympathetic hearing. In the course of my own essay, indeed, I will present a plea for the revitalization of faith in general.

Education cannot be considered apart from the society it expresses and serves — local, national, and today increasingly global. To talk meaningfully about American higher education one must therefore also concern oneself with the nature of the contemporary world. And since this world is undergoing a major transition, one must examine the dominant trends that seem to be at work. These trends can be analyzed in many ways, but as I see it, they are most fundamentally twofold. The world is moving toward increasing centralization. And there is a universal striving for mankind's material betterment.

On the surface of it, global integration seems a remote prospect indeed. Intensely nationalistic forces appear to be pulling mankind

From *To Make A Difference*, edited by Otto Butz. Copyright 1967. Reprinted by permission of Harper and Row, Publishers, Inc.

further and further apart. Yet these forces, no matter how disruptive, are in fact responses to the very kinds of long-range cultural, economic and technological developments that in the end cannot but eliminate them. The centralizing process in our world is taking place almost completely below the level of our awareness. It is largely ignored by our newspapers, our public opinion, and even in the statements and actions of our political leaders. But its roots run deeply and someday it will sprout a tree hitherto seen only in the dreams — or nightmares — of men. For someday some kind of centralizing order and authority are going to have to cope effectively with irreversible changes in human aspirations and techniques that even now greatly affect the lives of people all over the globe. International order and mutual responsibility are clearly called for when a fluctuation on the New York Stock Exchange has world-wide economic repercussions, when a railway jam on Switzerland's St. Gotthard line backs up freight in Scandinavia, when mass communications take the story of Selma, Alabama, to Monrovia, West Africa, and when the industrially advanced nations have the know-how and resources to produce increasingly worrisome surpluses while much of the rest of the world remains on the edge of starvation.

Some interpreters of today's world claim that the trend of centralization is leading toward either a bipolar mobilization of whites versus coloreds, of haves versus have-nots, or of one ideological bloc against another. But these are not realistic alternatives. The logic of contemporary socioeconomic ideas, industrial techniques and military weapons requires nothing less than global world order. Either sovereign nation states are dead or mankind is dead.

I suggested that the second main trend in today's world is the universal drive for material betterment. I realize that there is currently more talk of raising physical standards than there are tangible results in that direction. The gap between rich and poor nations has, in fact, been increasing. Yet even though it suffers temporary setbacks, the battle for a decent standard of living for all peoples cannot be halted. The hearts and minds of human beings everywhere are set on it. In the short run, the frustrations that this quest engenders are bound to be highly explosive. But eventually it is certain to be accomplished. For where there is all this will, it is unthinkable that there is not going to be found a way.

Given these trends, the key questions facing contemporary man concern what *kind* of world order he is going to build, and what he is going to do with himself as *more* than a mere physical organism. On the answers he works out for these questions hangs the future not necessarily of life, but certainly of what we call civilization. And for these answers, we are ourselves responsible.

There are many who claim that science is incompatible with the idea of free will. Perhaps such a view seemed plausible in the past. But it certainly is not today. For today science and technology not only are satisfied to coexist with the notion of free will; their high degree of development and the powers they have unleashed make it absolutely essential that we subscribe to the precepts of free will and personal responsibility. The frontiers of science are theoretically unlimited. Whereas natural catastrophes, disease and starvation were once fatalistically accepted, science and technology now strongly indicate that there will be a day when nothing in the physical life of man, not even death, will be inevitable. We are truly becoming the masters of our physical fate. If we do not soon solve our physical problems, it will be because of our own stupidity and wickedness, not because we do not have the opportunity. Can we intelligently apply the unprecedented knowledge at our command? Can we place it in the service of the ideals of human worth, brotherhood and dignity? Or will we misuse it merely to exploit and manipulate one another?

The trends and circumstances which are reshaping today's world are so vast and complex that in their presence man often stands confused and troubled. He asks questions which his traditional concepts and institutions can no longer answer. In such a transitional world of troubled man, there is great danger that the forces of our age will become the tools of those who want to use their fellows for their own cause or profit. For taken together, our widespread uncertainties along with the nature of today's technology and psychological skills constitute a greater potential for human enslavement than has ever before existed.

At the root of the contemporary threat to our freedom is a very old and much-used conception of man. It is the misanthropic idea that human beings are innately too selfish, stupid, belligerent and divided to willingly join together in mutual advantage and harmony. Applied to today, this Hobbesian argument maintains that the world has become so crowded and complex that men can no longer be effectively coordinated save through some kind of systematic coercion.

Opposed to the pessimistic view of man and its accompanying threat to his freedom is a dynamic conception of the practicability of libertarian and democratic ideals. It is a conception which strives to put in man's service the powers of our age. It is the belief that with these powers man can pull upward his society as he himself ascends. It is a conception which claims that man can remake his institutions and concepts in such a way that they will shape a humane world order.

Above all, the conception of libertarian and democratic ideals is an expression of faith in man, a faith based not on the dictates of an authority or majority but in the creative potentialities of man himself. It is the belief that if you put faith in man, man will be deserving of this faith and will justify it in practice. It is analogous to the faith that underlies scientific research.

To paraphrase and grossly oversimplify the philosopher of science Charles Sanders Peirce,[1] scientific inquiry, because of man's human limitations, cannot properly start with a priori notions of Truth. That is, because man is not one and the same with the Real, he cannot know Reality. However, to start scientific research, man, whether he realizes and admits it or not, must believe that there *is* a Reality and that it is regular. Otherwise, inquiry is futile; and, indeed, as Jean Paul Sartre tells us, life itself is then absurd. Our best scientists, while not knowing the Real, have nevertheless believed in its existence. And for this reason they have found much of that small part of Reality which we *can* know — namely, the shared opinion of what are conceivable practical consequences in our experiential realm of living. On the basis of their faith, and because of a willingness to constantly test their beliefs or hypotheses about Reality, scientists have, for example, launched Mariner IV.

The conclusion to be drawn here concerns the logical imperative of faith. In science we have believed, and hence we have achieved. What now remains is to extend logical faith beyond science. We need to humbly recognize that man has not yet been seen in the fullness of his being, that there is a Reality about him which has so far escaped us. In order to develop the potentialities of man, we must put faith in man. To launch mankind's beauty and creativity, we must believe in him and be willing to work by trial and error toward his ever greater improvement. We can best do this by constantly improving the implementation of democratic and libertarian ideals. And to effectively implement these ideals, we must develop a practical dedication

[1] Charles Sanders Peirce, *Essays in the Philosophy of Science*, New York, Bobbs-Merrill, 1957.

to them which is as deep as is our dedication to the scientific method.

I do not define libertarian and democratic ideals in accordance with any ideology. I define them experientially. That is, I mean by them those concepts and practices which further the development and realization of the faith in man which underlies them. Thus, for example, the proposal to institute world peace by subjugating man to a coercively ordered world society is anathema to libertarian and democratic ideals; for, to name only a few of its gross faults, it admits lack of faith in the potential for ever higher good in mankind; it repels the logic of man's opportunity to participate in the building of an ever greater society; and it refutes the plainly indicated potential of truly free men.

If the forces of our age are put in the service of man, and, directly related to this, if libertarian and democratic ideals are made the guiding principles of the future one world, mankind will enter an unprecedented age of humaneness, abundance, and peace. However, such a world society is a questionable aspect of our future. Its development is dependent upon that more-than-material betterment of man which I earlier mentioned.

Both prerequisite and supplementary to continuous progress toward a humane world order is what I shall call the development of metatelic values and aspirations. I refer to man's need for a conception of human perfectness that is so open-ended, self-transcending and dynamically formative that it can never be claimed to have been fully realized. I mean an abstract, limitless ideal of human potentialities which can serve man as his ultimate inspiration and which he will feel impelled always to redefine and more fully to actualize as he moves from one successful experience to another. I believe such an ideal inspiration and reference for human strivings is essential for two reasons. It implies that no existing set of objectives and arrangements is ever finally sufficient. And it thereby provides a thrust to human unfolding that transcends the cultural expectations of any particular situation. By virtue of this fact, it also provides justification for the libertarian and democratic ideals of which I have spoken. And it at the same time requires that man operate in terms of these ideals if the never-consummated search for his full being is to be possible.

Unfortunately, we live in an age when faith both in the instrumental ideals of liberty and democracy and in the more abstract notion of infinite human perfectability is neither strong nor widespread. Faith of any kind — in the abstract, in ideals, in man himself — is badly languishing. Nor is our current anti-faith the rational, faith-inspired and creative reaction against dogmatism that earlier in Western history produced many of mankind's greatest moments. Instead, it is an expression of normlessness, confusion, despair, and extreme fear — fear of self, fear of the future, fear of all life. It is a rationalization for inactivity, for failure to sacrifice and plan, for failure to dream. It is rooted in more than the death of *a* God; it stems from the belief that "God is dead" and that no metaphysical orientation is possible or permissible. It is the reason contemporary man finds it so difficult to make moral choices and formulate clear purposes. Contemporary anti-faith is the reason modern man, when not standing inert, is reaching committee-type decisions with his psychiatrist, or finding direction in a bottle of liquor, tranquilizers or pep pills.

We cannot long endure the highly demoralized state which results from anti-faith. This is the major threat to our future in one world. If man too long lives in mental, moral, and social chaos, he inevitably turns to irrational faith. He turns to faith in extremist leaders, material success, scientism, or some other "ism" which, because it eliminates faith in man, leads to tyranny. This is to say that mankind is entirely capable of enslaving himself, of voluntarily committing himself to the collective security, order, and purpose of a tyrannical world state. And given the forces of our age, I am saying that we are entirely capable of developing ourselves into a race of human automatons, eugenically shaped, bureaucratically organized, technologically brainwashed, scientifically coerced, and completely subservient to a pseudo divine collective.

If the foregoing view is correct, it is clear that our most urgent task is the rebuilding of man's faith in man. Yet this is bound to be a most difficult undertaking. We cannot hope to create the kind of faith in man I am talking about overnight. At least for the time being we must work toward this objective indirectly — by demonstrating to all men everywhere the practical and personal benefits of liberalism and democracy. It must be shown what liberal and democratic institutions can do — that they provide the best possible answer to man's need for a coordinating social principle and that they therefore best facilitate his quest freely to participate in the shaping of his own destiny.

Despite all her shortcomings, I believe that the role of demonstrator in the task of restoring faith in man through the effective practice of liberalism and democracy falls to the United States. America commands the greatest force, power and influence in the world today. Also, at least in principle if not always in practice, the United States remains the world's most libertarian and democratic country. It is therefore America's opportunity and duty to exemplify to the world dynamic actualizations of libertarian and democratic ideals. Unless the United States assumes this duty, all that is humane and promising about this country will be lost. America, the idea, will perish.

To call on America for world involvement is not to call on her for world crusade. One does not spread ideals and institutions by exporting economic exploitation and armies. We must give up our obsession with force and power. We must be self-confident enough to enter into relationships on all levels with all peoples, currently friends or foes; and, even more important, after exemplifying the self-evident advantages of our ideals, and while yet engaged in the continuing development of these ideals at home, we Americans must be intelligent enough to realize that all peoples must be free to interpret and institute faith in mankind in accordance with their own indigenous circumstances and values. We must, then, be dedicated not to universally instituting our specific way of life, but to sharing with all the ideals which underlie our way of life.

To be an international exemplar, America must undergo reform at home. Our country has too long held on to outworn and even erroneous ideas which no longer, if ever they did, serve libertarian and democratic ideals. We have too long believed that irresponsible self-interests would automatically produce a progressive, harmonious society. We have relied on a mechanistically conceived market which, even if it ever did promote goods, always ignored men. We have practiced an amoral, anti-leadership politics which has too often responded to conflicting special interests and too seldom to community needs. By moral and intellectual default, we have allowed injustice and poverty to survive in our very midst.

Because many of the concepts by which we are guided have become outdated (if they ever were humanly appropriate), we face an unprecedented challenge to our highest faculty, our creative reason. Whereas in the past we have needed mainly our backs, hands, and practical good sense, today, more than anything else, we must call upon our powers to think penetratingly and imaginatively. To understand and guide the vast forces transforming today's world, to map out our new possibilities and goals, to implement a dynamic conception of libertarian and democratic ideals — to respond to these tremendous challenges we must bring to bear every bit of constructive intelligence we can muster. All our ideas and institutions must be honestly and critically evaluated and all of them must pass the test of appropriateness and, where necessary, be updated or replaced.

The task of providing this infusion of critical and creative reason cannot but fall mainly to our intellectual centers, our American colleges and universities. Of all our institutions, the one that holds the greatest promise and faces the greatest challenges is higher education. It is hardly too much to say that the future of the world depends in important measure on the kind of influences upon American society that can emanate from our colleges and universities.

America is today experiencing an educational revolution. One of the two main aspects of this revolution is the increasingly pivotal role being played by our institutions of higher learning in furnishing the scientific and organizational know-how to operate our industrially based, mass society. America is today turning its higher education into a knowledge industry that is becoming the fulcrum of its national growth. The chief reason for this is that the technical and organizational problems we face are too large and complex to be dealt with by uncoordinated conferences, isolated surveys, governmental studies, and individual research projects. What is needed instead are cooperative, planned syntheses of knowledge and expertise from a wide range of disciplines, which must then be focused on specific problems. And it is mainly by our colleges and universities that this service is being provided. It today constitutes the principal source of their status with the general public and accounts for the biggest portion of their financing.

The other major aspect of America's current educational revolution lies in the fact that more and more of our people are going to college. As one of the consequences of this, almost all of our future leaders — as well as the people who elect them — will have experienced higher education. This means that the quality of their response to our society's problems will depend in large measure on the quality of the education that our colleges and universities have been able to provide them.

It goes without saying that we must make higher education as effective in preparing us for this philosophical and political function as we can. *America's higher learning must concern itself with the continuous redevelopment of ideas, values and institutions which are*

*applicable to our ever changing conditions and inspired by the faith in
mankind that underlies liberalism and democracy.* I would call this a
third major aspect of our educational revolution. To date, however,
this further function of higher education is on the whole little recognized. And it is seriously endangered by the other two developments
I have cited — by the development of our colleges and universities into
centers of operational know-how, and by their absorption in the job of
educating ever greater numbers.

In itself, the application of knowledge for the more efficient operation of our society through our colleges and universities is undoubtedly a good thing. Yet it must be recognized that to provide
expertise is not the same thing as significantly to evaluate and alter.
That is, it is not adequate to meet the total challenge that education
today faces. Moreover, these two distinct functions require different
kinds of people and organizations. One cannot expect a force whose
business is to help run a system, at the same time also to question its
basic assumptions. Indeed, as has become increasingly evident, the
more energies our colleges and universities have devoted to solving
our society's technical problems, the less they have been concerned
with evaluating and recreating its foundations.

The ever larger numbers being handled by our institutions of
higher learning also retard the development of the creative function
of education. While mass education is certainly a worthy ideal, it is
not a sufficient educational achievement by itself. Since many students continue to attend college for economically and socially "practical" reasons, the function of mass education in effect converges with
that of servicing the society with expertise. It is then these simultaneous and mutually reinforcing activities that tend to make American
institutions of higher learning into the businesslike treadmills whose
biggest net contribution is to perpetuate the status quo.

It seems to me a first precondition for the fundamental re-evalua-
tion of our society's current directions that what I am calling the
purely educational function of colleges and universities and their
role as institutions for specialized training be organizationally separated. Our graduate and professional schools could then be oriented
to turning out experts, not claiming at the same time also to be concerned with education in the traditional humanistic sense. And our
undergraduate schools could devote themselves to pure education,
without feeling it necessary to seek status and financing by pretending
to be doing more than that — as is all too often the case at present.

If we utilize our undergraduate schools for general education and creative thinking, and if we gear our graduate and professional schools for training people in the mastery of our physical environment, we would only be taking a further step in a trend already in progress. We would be admitting and coping with the fact that our graduate and professional schools have more and more become training grounds for business and government; that they have contributed very little by way of understanding of our civilization's total situation; and that with their emphasis on highly specialized academic research, they have in fact discouraged the many gifted people on their payrolls from concerning themselves with the new horizons and problems of our age as a whole.

Far too many of our educated people have no idea of the larger assumptions and implications of the expertises they practice. Having been trained in what in effect are vocational studies, they take the existence and morality of the status quo entirely for granted. To remedy this we must make certain that everyone is first exposed to a general education in the complexities of life in their full dimensions, and that during this educational experience they hear not only from expert scholars but also from teachers who will encourage them to think for themselves. Only after they have passed through this truly liberal phase of their education ought they to be admitted to graduate and professional schools. While the purpose of the undergraduate schools should thus be to help people educate themselves as human beings, the chief work of graduate and professional institutions should be to provide the intellectual tools for the society's day-to-day functioning. And contrary to what is now generally the case, the job of teaching and creative thinking should not be rated as any less important and prestigious than that of producing academic or scientific experts. For if anything, the concern with man's needs and life as a whole is a humanly more actualizing and dignifying activity than is the task of training him for specialized roles.

The actual establishment of the kind of division of labor between undergraduate and graduate learning that I am proposing would require a number of basic changes in both types of institutions. To list specific reforms for our graduate schools must fall to someone more qualified than I. At my present level of experience I feel I should confine myself to some of the alterations badly needed in our undergraduate education.

The ideal undergraduate college would not have a program of

required courses. It would recognize that a highly structured curriculum is a sign of educational weakness. Its aim would be to help each student develop his individual potential rather than memorize information and work chiefly for grades. It would not conceive of the student's mind as a receptacle into which must be poured a certain volume of facts and figures. It would trust the student to decide for himself what is educationally relevant and what extracurricular activities are worth-while or not. With a basic faith in man, the ideal college would view the student's mind as something individually alive and would try to stimulate it and judge its performance according to its own unique dispositions.

The ideal undergraduate college would recognize that students come to it with their own innate gifts, needs and interests. It would accept and retain only those students who feel genuinely excited by intellectual activity, a criterion that has nothing at all to do with what is called "I.Q." And it would operate on the premise that if given enough time and if appropriately stimulated by their academic environment, most students can be counted on to find their own intellectual challenges and to pursue their studies with their own, self-imposed discipline.

There would be many more kinds of course offerings in the ideal undergraduate college. Especially emphasized would be courses in social and group processes as well as in the various arts — all areas of relevance for our changing and increasingly affluent society. And even more important than the expansion of the number of courses offered would be a radical alteration in the way they are taught and organized. The introductory course in biology, currently a very unpopular subject required at most colleges, provides a good example. In addition to the standard survey course which teaches a mass of biological definitions, the ideal college would offer another course which considers the personal and social implications of the biological knowledge presented and which traces the relationships of this knowledge to all other realms of human experience. All survey courses that concentrate on a mass of data, and all courses designed to force students to "appreciate" something or other, would be limited to future experts in those fields. Only future biologists, for example, would be required to learn a textbook-full of biological definitions. Other students would take a course designed to open to them the wonders that biology is exploring and to enable them to absorb these discoveries into their lives as a whole.

All survey courses in the ideal undergraduate college would be interdisciplinary. It would be realized that the ultimate subject of study is the whole human being in his total context and that every aspect of this subject is inseparably involved in every other. In place of today's one-year, specialized course in United States history, for example, the ideal college would offer a three- or four-year course in American civilization, a course which would bring together and transcend all conventional academic disciplines to present a unified, organic conception of America in its full dynamism and complexity.

As I mentioned earlier, today's teaching methods would be radically altered by the ideal undergraduate college. The teaching process would rely heavily upon dialogue between students and professors. Professors will have realized that straight lecturing quickly reaches a point of diminishing returns, that students can be talked at for only a limited span of time, and that they respond best when part of a barely organized, two-way conversation. Being a breeding ground for democratic methods, and posited on the libertarian faith in mankind, the ideal undergraduate college would provide continuous opportunity for teachers and students to cooperatively work out solutions both to academic questions and to the wider range of contemporary and perennial problems of human existence. This, far more than student government, will make students feel part of their education; this, far more than freshman orientation programs, will awaken their intellectual abilities; and this — a simple change in classroom procedure — will do more than any number of speeches by college deans and presidents to overcome the common view among today's students that college means impersonality, futility, intellectual suffocation, and bureaucratic regimentation.

To help make students free to learn, the ideal undergraduate college will have abolished the grading system. It will have realized that the highly competitive grading system of today is detrimental to learning; that it focuses students' attention on grades and not on knowledge; that it too often rewards those regimented students who perfectly distribute their time and effort over a wide, shallow area to produce a good grade point average, and not often enough those creative few who get thoroughly wrapped up in one or two courses. It will have realized that the grading system too often rewards those students who unquestioningly accept the material presented to them as fact and who are intellectually cautious or indeed dead; and not often enough those students who think freely and independently, who deal with problems for which the answers are ambiguous or unknown, and who discover not answers, but new and greater questions. The ideal undergraduate college, then, would determine who stays and who leaves, and who goes to graduate school and who doesn't, and who graduates with honors and who doesn't, and who gets what kind of job recommendation, by means and measurements other than the traditional grading system. Once during each school year, and twice during the freshman year, all students would appear individually before a panel of faculty members. By submitting a written paper, research project or work of art, or by presenting himself orally, or by agreeing to take written examinations, or by any other reasonable means chosen by himself, the student would seek to convince the faculty panel that he has been using well the college's opportunities. Any means of testing that the student chooses would examine his understanding and insight, not his ability to regurgitate "factual" material.

Students would be encouraged to engage in independent research projects and studies. Indeed, entire semesters could be devoted to one wide-ranging and preferably interdisciplinary project or study.

Almost all classes would meet only once a week. This would enable students not only to read, but also to think about assignments before discussing them in class. Some formal class sessions would be canceled and the saved time would be used for scheduled, but informal, meetings between individual students and their professors. Teachers and students would be free not only to discuss the student's academic work, but also to let a spontaneous conversation wander freely.

Courses would be concerned much more with the caliber of the material covered and the quality of student work than with the quantity of either. Busy-work would be eliminated. Compared to today's undergraduate, tomorrow's student would read less, write less, and take fewer exams; but he would converse more, think more, understand more, create more, write better, and deal with far more sophisticated materials.

The ideal undergraduate college would be concerned with expanding man's knowledge of man, not with expanding man's mastery over other men. Existing in an age of intellectual crisis, it would realize that to develop man's mind, it must restore those powers of contemplation which have too long been greatly weakened by Western man's devotion to political, economic, and technological conquest. It would realize that in a quest for rather blind and pure power, we have lost sight of the ends of man, of what man is, of how he should live, and of how our various power achievements could and should serve him.

A major concern of the ideal undergraduate college would be that its graduates enter the world with guiding principles, with a general orientation to life. But despite this fact, the college would not try to force any specific principles upon its students. Instead, it would leave students free to develop their own values. Indeed, the ideal college would strongly encourage students to do so. It would point out to students that they do inevitably have values and that, therefore, they should always admit their presence, and always stand ready both to defend and change them. It would point out to students that failing to admit and practice values leads to a normlessness which inhibits full intellectual and moral development, and that unless one eventually proceeds with clear purposes and goals, he proceeds too long by a wasteful, frustrating, and self-destroying system of trial and error.

The ideal college would teach students that while learning how to think is very important, realizing for what they should think and why, is even more important. It would point out to students that too often pure, unguided reason is used to vanquish, dehumanize, and devour man. It would point out that a humane orientation to life must be more than one of pure reason, that true intelligence is a synthesis of purposes, values, emotions, and reason; and that, therefore, true intelligence is a system of deep and guiding intellectual beliefs. In helping students to develop their own intellectual beliefs, the ideal college would be preparing them to seek constant improvement of society, of mankind, and of themselves.

The ideal undergraduate college would strive to develop in its students a capacity for creativity. Rather than fearing those inner forces which are today very little understood and are called irrational and nonrational, the ideal college would see them as composing a realm of preconsciousness which can lead man to an intuitive knowledge very often more rational than the knowledge which is produced by a simple retracing of intellectual steps already taken. Furthermore, the ideal college would realize that to create is to expand one's mind and release one's inner energies in a constructive direction, and that, therefore, to create is to give one faith in mankind.

Although delightful to attend, the ideal undergraduate college would make exacting demands on its students. It would force them to see social reality not as something affording them justification for self-pity, but as a realm for great opportunity, challenge, and excitement. Even more important, students would be expected to push themselves to the limits of their own powers. The college would know that as society grows more complicated, increasingly stronger men are required to hold it together; and thus the college would practice not equality of education, but equality of educational opportunity for each individual to achieve as far as possible that personal intellectual excellence which this democracy must have from many men in order to survive. Students, then, would be forced to test themselves within themselves. But compared to the labor of today's student, tomorrow's would be far more pleasant; it would be exciting and indeed heroic. For instead of competing against his classmates, the system, and the grading scale, tomorrow's student would reach for the utmost development of his own potentialities. Occasionally, in the pursuit, he might even wreck himself upon something deserving of his effort.

I have established very high ideals for the undergraduate college of tomorrow. I have done this because one must set his ideals high in order to reach the level of bare necessity. I have done this because America must set her educational ideals high in order to stand a chance of surviving her present intellectual crisis. The American college must ask itself what kind of world can be, what kind of world it wants to help build, and how it can best do so. The American college must clearly formulate our world's problems and then it must find, test, develop, and apply solutions. It must send to the world's leadership posts truly educated, not just trained, men. And, of course, to adequately do all this, it must constantly strive to perfect the internal actualizations of its own democratic and libertarian ideals.

Past generations of Westerners and Americans have given the Americans of our generation the blind powers we need in order to fulfill our opportunity to help build that humane world order which is now required. To respond successfully to that opportunity is the tremendous challenge of our generation. If the colleges fail, we all will fail. And if all fail, a humane one world will not materialize, and civilization, both as we've known and envisioned it, will fall.

Challenges are not new in human history. All generations have been required to meet the crisis of their age, and, of course, some generations have met their requirements more effectively than others. Thus it is not true that our age is faced with the crisis of mankind. It is faced with *a* crisis. However, it is true that our age is challenged to an extent never exceeded and rarely equaled, in mankind's life on this planet. And it is also true that in order to successfully meet our challenge, man's mind, more than ever before, must reign supreme.

To the American colleges and universities has fallen the task of playing the world's most significant part in making man's mind supreme. Western civilization has already deeply touched the lives of nearly all the peoples of the earth. America is already a world leader in possession of great powers. Therefore, as civilizations before us, we can, if we complement our power with an overriding intellectual development, become the foremost cultural influence of the emerging world. Out of the ferment of Hellenic Greece came some of Western civilization's most important roots. Out of the ferment of twentieth-century America can come some of the ethical and cosmological visions so essential for the shaping of our evolving global civilization. We need but make humane intelligence supreme in our own country to help make it supreme in the coming world order. The opportunity and responsibility are ours; for our own sake and for the sake of mankind — past, present and future.

I should conclude these thoughts about education in the context of America and the world at large with at least a few words about my own personal relationship to what I have said. I have served three years and nine months in this country's Marine Corps. I believe I served well. I was awarded military commendations. And I was proud to be a member of a force that has played such an important part in meeting some of the *external* threats to this nation and the promise that it has historically represented. From 1959 until 1963 I saw no contradiction between my ideals and military service. But it is now 1966. My country is part of a nightmare as old as man, and thus so am I. I see it as my duty to help abolish that nightmare. And as I now more fully understand it, this cannot be accomplished through the use of military force. Not only does the intrusion of force into today's infinitely complex and deeply felt human developments fail to reach the springs of people's actions. It also cannot but damage the quest for a common, universal human purpose that is the unique opportunity and imperative of our age. More than that, the preoccupation with force leads to an aggravation and mobilization of our anxieties, causes us to regress to a myopic nationalism, and so diverts us both from the great promise of today's world and from the inescapable problems that must be faced if that promise is to be made a reality. It is to that promise that I will look in future for my inspiration. And it is to the analysis and solution of the problems involved in its actualization — problems requiring above all what I have called the application of humane intelligence — that I hope to devote my energies.

ROBERT A. NISBET
crisis in the university?

Is there one? Quite a few intellectuals think so, but this in itself is not a sure guide. Intellectuals are often prone to see "crisis" in circumstances that for other persons merely range from good to bad, desirable to undesirable. In medicine, a crisis is the point in a disease where what follows is either recovery or death. In politics, crisis is the point in the career of a specific government where what follows is either downfall or renewed strength. Some degree of precision attaches to the word in these uses. But what is meant when "crisis" is applied to, say, modern culture, democracy, religion, the family, Western civilization — or higher education?

The contemporary university has become, almost in the measure that "capitalism" once was, a cherished setting for diagnoses of "crisis" — not to mention decadence, sickness, moribundity, and so on. Rare is the month in which some outburst of student activity, or some revelation of the incidence of "pot" and LSD, does not produce fresh apprehensions. Think only of Berkeley and the immediate aftermath of the student demonstrations of late 1964: there isn't space enough in this issue of *The Public Interest* to reprint the reactions of those who saw in these unhappy events, not a complex problem in local administration, but instead a fevered symptom of nation-wide student malaise, revolt, and alienation or, changing the perspective, a crisis in the purposes of higher education in America. I would be the last to minimize the gravity and personal agony of the two years that followed the student demonstrations at Berkeley. It was, in every sense, a time of troubles. But a crisis of the university in America? What, precisely, is meant?

From *The Public Interest*, Winter, 1967. Copyright 1967 by National Affairs, Inc.

Clark Kerr has recently dealt with the subject in masterly fashion. If anyone is entitled, by intellectual gifts and searing personal experience, to see crisis in the university, it is he. But he doesn't. In an address at a major convocation in Los Angeles last year, called by Robert Hutchins and the staff at his Center (including such distinguished participants as Sir Eric Ashby, Rosemary Parks, Jacques Barzun), Mr. Kerr made so bold as to ask: where is the crisis? Certainly not, he said, in the professional schools, which manifestly are flowering. Not in the graduate schools, which are booming. Not in research. Not in the centers and institutes from which scholarly and scientific, as well as creative and imaginative works pour forth annually. These areas have their problems, but crisis is hardly the word to describe their overall state.

Where, then, *is* the crisis, asks Kerr? In the undergraduate area alone. Kerr's answer leaves the prophets of crisis a few *fleurs du mal* to be sure. But, in an analysis as relentless as it is unemotional, he emphasizes that even in the undergraduate sphere the fevered unrest taken for "crisis" is rather limited: not to be found, for example in such broad areas of undergraduate education as engineering, agriculture, and business administration. To the extent that it exists at all, Kerr concludes, "crisis" is to be found in a few, but by no means all, areas of the humanities and social sciences. Mr. Kerr does not minimize what he finds in these areas; their problems can be serious to a university and they must be met — chiefly, he believes, through the instituting of smaller "cluster" colleges. I will come back to this point in a moment.

A PAINFUL DISCREPANCY

To many of us, Kerr's dispassionate view of the university has the ring of expert acquaintance and sharp insight. But not to W. H. Ferry, Vice President of the Hutchins' Center for the Study of Democratic Institutions at Santa Barbara, who, judging from the convocation proceedings, could scarcely contain himself at Kerr's *lèse majesté*. "The university crisis," Mr. Ferry thundered, "is not partial but general." Student disturbances should be seen "as symptomatic of deeper-lying troubles that [Kerr] either passes by or mis-identifies as evidence of health." Then Mr. Ferry adds: "I would think it far more advisable to break up the system than to continue patching its defects, no matter how ingeniously." Mr. Ferry, in short, like most of his associates at the Center in Santa Barbara, simply will not settle for less than total crisis — and, of course, total reformation.

For most of us, as I say, Clark Kerr's words on crisis will seem authoritative. But what, then, is the source of all the *intimations* of crisis? Student demonstrations? In one form or other, these have always been with the university. Read only Hastings Rashdall's stirring accounts, in his great history of the founding of the European universities, of early student riots and insurrections, not to mention alcoholic bouts. If such activities — along with student malaise and anomie (called *acedia* in the Middle Ages) — bespeak crisis, well, all one can say is that it has been a long crisis.

The real source of intimations of academic crisis does not lie here. The source is, as one would expect, the pain that arises from discrepancy between the City of God and the City of Man. At its most exalted, this pain lies behind the works of Plato, St. Augustine, Rousseau, and Marx. At its less exalted, however, it is the source of the captious and niggling criticism that forms the fringe of the rationalist tradition. Exalted or not, the discrepancy is closely related to what Michael Oakeshott calls, in his classic essay, "Rationalism in Politics," the "sovereignty of the felt need." Political life, says Professor Oakeshott (and we will include the university in this) "is resolved into a succession of crises, each to be surmounted by the applications of 'reason.' " Or faith. And, of course, through dialogue. Nothing is more repugnant to this type of rationalist (a type that flourishes at the Santa Barbara Center) than the thought that any institution cannot be ceaselessly endowed with new purpose to assuage the pain of the felt need.

Purpose! Here, I think, we come to the nub of the matter. The contemporary university in America is guilty, so the indictment goes, because it lacks purpose. "Purpose" is another word dearly loved by a certain type of intellectual, both in and outside the academy. A few years ago there was much written about America needing "to find" a new purpose. As I recall, President Eisenhower actually appointed a committee on the subject. The Luce papers took it up, and for a number of months one couldn't open *Life* or *Time* without running smack into some new variant of the American Dream, Destiny, or Purpose. Most of this is now absent from the national arena, but it is not dead; it has only moved, like "crisis," to the university.

THE SEARCH FOR "PURPOSE"

No university, no college, it is said, can be legitimate until its functions are clearly translatable into explicit, verbalized *purpose*. There is enough truth in this to make it plausible. But there is also enough latent futility in it to make it inane, especially when the subject is something as large and complex as is the state, the economy, the family, or the university. Here, what Karl Popper has written on the subject of definitions is applicable. To those who argue that clarity of definition is indispensable to science, Popper replies: If so, there will be no science (ever an untidy business), only an infinite regression of definitions. So, I fear, with purpose. When I am told that I must make my own individual purposes clear in a given enterprise, I can understand that. But the mind boggles at the prospect of making the legitimacy of major institutions depend upon agreement of purpose to be reached by conference or committee.

All of this is not to imply that there is no purpose in the contemporary university, no common idea that gives it distinctiveness. I am only suggesting that in a large-scale historic institution such as the university, purpose is given, not by rationalist assent, arrived at on the basis of "dialogue" in conferences, but by continuous historical function, through common, if diversified, effort over long periods of time (subject always, of course, to experimental and pragmatic changes that are the result of new ideas) and, often, through collisions between the university and other institutions.

There is indeed a purpose, a central idea, in the contemporary university — in America as well as in Europe. President Pusey has recently given it expression. To the question, is there a central idea in the American university?, Mr. Pusey said: "The answer is, most certainly, yes. For such an idea is found in the devotion to learning which permeates the whole community and in the recognition of learning's importance for the full manner of life. . . . Though scholars today often appear to pursue separate ways within universities — quite unaware of their colleagues' existence . . . still, by and large, they all are, and know they are, working in a common vineyard. They know it is not their specialties but 'learning' . . . that they have in common."

To most of us this would seem an admirable and sufficient statement of university purpose: drawn, as are all purposes in large institutions, not from conference but from observation of history and of continuing function. Devotion to learning and to learning's importance for the full manner of life. Is this not a purpose? Mr. Hutchins is one of those who thinks it is not. He says that in other countries today there is a better sense of what a university is. This may be. If so, it is because in these countries the professional character of the university, for the most part, is taken for granted. Several years ago I taught at the University of Bologna, the oldest of European universities and still one of the greatest. I was amused to discover that curricular issues which burn in the

American academic community — sanctity of liberal arts, general education, self-realization — simply did not exist for my colleagues on the Bologna faculty. For them, the answer to the question — what is a university? — was simple, if profound. The university is a place for scholarship in the learned disciplines; teaching, of course, but teaching within the disciplines. What comes out of the university? Professionals: professional scholars in the humanities as well as lawyers, physicians, and engineers.

But, I asked, do you not care whether students emerge from the university experience possessed of intellectual leadership, wisdom, character, and a sense of life's wonder and challenge? Certainly, they replied, and students (or some students) do emerge from the university with these qualities. And this is no doubt good. But the purpose, the distinctive and guiding purpose of the university, is none of these. It is what it has been for many centuries: scholarship and teaching in the learned and professional disciplines.

THE SPECTER OF "PROFESSIONALISM"

Now, I certainly don't want to imply that the good is only what is or has been; in higher education or elsewhere. And if others want to use the word "university" differently, well, we have Humpty Dumpty's (if not Alice's) authority for one's right to make a word mean just what he chooses it to mean — neither more nor less. I do not scorn the establishment of what Mr. Hutchins lovingly calls an "autonomous thinking community." (Still: "You came to think?" Jowett once snapped at a Balliol student; "About what, pray?") I think there is also room in our affluent society for institutes for the cultivation of wisdom ("Why not take direct aim at it," asks the Center's Commodore Ferry), of "individual development," of techniques of political action, of reading dynamics, and so on. I question none of these. If funds for them can be raised, fine. But, with all possible sympathy for the pain of felt need that gnaws at these critics, I nevertheless think it is unworthy of them to imply, not merely that the university *should* dedicate itself to one or all of their proffered aims, but that, in *not* doing so, the university is betraying its trust.

What really irritates the prophets of academic crisis as they look at the university is its "professionalism." So far as I can tell, professionalism, for most of them, is anything that can't be reduced to instant dialogue. Mr. Hutchins, for several decades, has used the stick of "professionalism" to clout the university in America. He has always confined his thwacks, of course, to the more extreme examples. His target used to be schools of administration, but now that some of these have become important centers of basic research, he has had to look elsewhere. In his address at the convocation in Los Angeles, he used schools of embalming. It seems that at the last meeting he attended of Big Ten presidents, the question of a proposed school of embalming came up. One gathers from the context that this is just about what Mr. Hutchins thinks the university in America — Harvard, Berkeley, Columbia, as well as the Big Ten — has come to.

Speaking for myself, I wouldn't particularly care to see a school of embalming on any university campus. And I don't expect to. But if I had to choose between a university in which there was the slight danger of such a school being added — as the result of the university's general commitment to professional education — in society's service — and a so-called university made aseptically safe from schools of embalming by its consecration to the type of thought that flows so effortlessly at the Center in Santa Barbara, I would unhesitatingly choose the first. In it, at least, embalming would be "narrow," "specialized," and even "fragmented."

Lest I seem uncritically and unwontedly adulatory of an institution that requires all the informed criticism it can get, I do want to pinpoint one tendency in the American university that bodes ill for both its unity and autonomy in society. It has nothing to do with "professionalism," for it is to be found in the basic areas of the university, and it is as easy to imagine it in the humanities, given suitable funding, as in the sciences. I am referring to a novel and rapidly spreading pattern of research: project research.

Research as such is, of course, the life blood of the university. Without it — and I mean *visible* research — university teaching would degenerate in a decade to the kind of thing that goes on piously in Great Books circles and dialogue-seminars. But the indispensability of research does not mean *all types and structures* of research. The genius of the university has been its capacity to unite teaching with research, to make the former a part of the latter. That is, research and teaching were (and still are generally) united in the carrying-on of research with students *as students*.

What we are beginning to witness today, however, and on a steadily widening front, is the acceptance by universities (with the all too eager acquiescence, even initiative, of faculty members) of types of research that not only could be done more appropriately by agencies outside the university — industrial and governmental — but have the effect within the university of destroying the time-honored union of research and teaching. Both in scale and in nature, this research seems to me fundamentally incompatible with the demands of teaching. To be sure, such research uses students; but there lies the rub. For with rising frequency one hears the complaints of students that they are being "used" rather than taught; used as technicians, as employees, as spectators, but not as students. There is also the structural character of much of this project research; it looms up as a kind of *imperium in imperio*. That grantsmanship has already shown signs of replacing scholarship is perhaps important enough. But of greater long run importance, it seems to me, is the sheer impact upon university unity — and then university autonomy in society — that organized research of this scale and entrepreneurial type represents. But, as I say, this has almost nothing to do with professionalism. Recent informal inquiry into one large area of professionalism in the American university — law schools — convinces me that here at least, and certainly in the best ones, there is a better union of teaching and research, greater dedication to teaching, than one finds in many of the nonprofessional fields.

LIFE ADJUSTMENT

But let us go back to the single area of the university that even the temperate Clark Kerr concedes may have some crisis in it: the undergraduate levels of *some* of the social sciences and humanities. Mr. Kerr, as I noted earlier, believes that the turbulence of this area could be offset in considerable part by the establishment of "cluster colleges" such as those to be found in the new Santa Cruz campus of the University of California. I wish I could agree, but I don't think they would really affect the matter. The essence of the problem does not seem to me to lie in large classes and corps of teaching assistants. After all, as Mr. Kerr has noted, there are large areas of the sciences and social sciences at Berkeley in which these conditions existed but out of whose ranks came few if any of the students in revolt.

More important, the cluster college would not be exempt, I think, from that larger problem that today besets the liberal arts college everywhere: the attraction to it of first rank intellects and scholars; those whom, quite frankly, the best students are eager to work under, even to simply listen to, irrespective of curricular context.

If there is one single part of the contemporary university in America that deserves the word "crisis" for its present condition, it is the historic liberal arts college within the university (I am not here referring to the separate liberal arts colleges — the Swarthmores and Amhersts — about which I know little). The trouble with this venerable institution is that its function has become increasingly unclear and, taken simply as a curricular fastness, less and less challenging to faculty members and students alike. It is easy to blame a crass and unfeeling society for this, to invoke the familiar demon of professionalism. But the sad and distasteful fact seems to be that its moribundity arises from its own nature. The corporate atmosphere of *in loco parentis* is of diminishing appeal to students and faculty. The effort to find in curriculum alone — bank upon bank of requirements that "everybody should have," to quote the familiar phrase from the catalogue — a substitute corporatism is ever more obviously unavailing. This is in part because many students (coming from secondary schools that have become immeasurably better in recent decades) find the work in this area too often repetitive and ritualistic; after all, there can be cross-*sterilization* as well as fertilization. In larger part, however, the cause lies in the unwillingness of faculty — and I mean, with the rarest exceptions, the best faculty — to participate. Vigorous minds are too busy being intellectually vigorous to suffer gladly the countless hours of teaching *and non-teaching* that the liberal arts college calls for. Over and over in American universities faculty members produce plans for model colleges. But over and over the same faculty members then manifest small inclination to participate in what they have helped to create. The best usually flee, the worst stay on, engaged in endless curriculum-tinkering or rearrangement of icons. My clear impression is that this situation is better on the whole in the Ivy-league universities than in the others. But even at a Harvard or Columbia the state of the college would not appear rugged.

One of the consequences of the moribundity of the college within the university is a desperate turning to other missions, and here we run smack into what I can only call "life adjustment." It may well be that the greater sense of unease and frustration that one finds in undergraduate psychology, sociology, political science, and also philosophy and literature today in the American university stems from trying to make these disciplines serve two rather different functions: on the one hand, *scholarship in learned disciplines* and, on the other, *life adjustment* or, as the case more often is, *adjustment of life*. Ever since the Jacobs study years ago revealed, to the author's evident dismay, that many students in college were graduating with their social values unchanged, there has been a constantly accumulating interest in the college as a *place primarily for the radical dislocation of old values and the radical adoption of new ones.* (Cluster colleges, of course, would make *this* function vastly more successful of achievement.)

The burden typically falls on the social sciences and humanities, or some of them, for the other learned disciplines simply won't play this life-adjustment game. They say — in mathematics, biology, Oriental languages, physics, etc. — that they have other and vitally necessary ends in view: preparing students for the hard work of scholarship in these disciplines. But, as is all too evident, there are many in the social sciences and humanities who will play the life-adjustment game and who, moreover, begin to think of it as the primary, even exclusive, purpose of a university or college education. What, it is asked — sometimes passionately, sometimes solemnly — could be more important than making what students learn seem "meaningful" to their social and political activities? This leads inexorably, of course, to the now widely popular concept of the college as a setting for "individual development." A few decades ago, when the exponents of life adjustment in the secondary schools threatened to drive out the disciplines of mathematics, English, and history in favor of courses organized around the theme of individual and social development, most of us in the universities rolled up our sleeves and went into battle. And, with the aid of Sputnik, we won. But now life adjustment has come to the university. What else is one to make of the following passage, taken from the preface of Nevitt Sanford's recent book, *Where Colleges Fail?*

"My aim," writes Mr. Sanford, who is Professor of Psychology and Director of the Institute for the Study of Human Problems at Stanford University, "is to help restore the student to his rightful place at the center of the college's activities. I state the case for individual development as the primary aim of education, present a theory of how students actually develop, and then apply it to various aspects of the student's development and the college's educational procedures."

It should be understood that Professor Sanford is very serious about this aim of individual development. He continues: "If the development of the individual is the primary aim, then colleges should organize all their resources in efforts to achieve it. Such planning of a *total* educational environment must be guided by a theory of personality . . ." (italics in the original).

Just what is to become of the learned disciplines in the setting envisaged by Professor Sanford, where the *total* aim is individual development, guided by *a* theory of personality, is not clear. But we can guess.

May I say here, as I did earlier about some other objectives for the university, that there is nothing intrinsically wrong with Professor Sanford's objective. And, as I noted in reporting my conversation with Bologna faculty members, individual development is indeed to be admired when one finds it. But made the aim of a university? Or, for that matter, of undergraduate social sciences and humanities? What happens, in that case, to sociology, political science, and other fields if we conceive them also as (what they are in fact) complex and abstract disciplines, fully as demanding in intellectual terms, as chemistry or biology? Is it really possible to organize, say, sociology at one and the same time around the kind of objectives that Professor Sanford has in mind and also those peculiar to a science? I know it is possible in the form of ringing declarations at conferences on student alienation. But I mean in actual courses, and in curricula.

I would like to say again that I am deeply mindful of the fact that individual development, the transvaluation of student values, the emergence of wisdom and leadership have ever been among the consequences of university student life — and nowhere more resplendently than at Oxford and Cambridge. But if one read correctly the histories, memoirs, and published letters that tell us about these great universities, it was scholarship and teaching-within-scholarship that were nonetheless held to be the central purposes. No one, surely, imagined that you could, in Mr. Ferry's or Professor Sanford's words, take direct aim at wisdom or individual development.

Or at leadership. When Macaulay, no idle worshipper of a classical education, was asked why he chose so many students of the classics for the civil service, his answer was: Because classics is where the brightest minds are. And he went on to say: If astrology were the preferred subject at oxford and Cambridge, I shouldn't mind; I would select those best at casting nativities; the results, for my purposes, would be the same. Macaulay was, in short, under no illusion that curriculum creates leaders.

A QUESTION OF LEGITIMACY

This leads us to one final aspect of the matter; the *legitimacy* of individual development, or personal values, as an aim of the university. Quite a few faculty members think they are legitimate; and a very wise young man, Michael Drosnin, only recently graduated from Columbia College, where he was editor of the student newspaper, has told us in an important article, that many of his college teachers made no bones about declaring that "it is the college's role to substitute a new set of values for those the student has inherited from his previous environment." Mr. Drosnin, however, disagrees. He writes (his article is to be found in *The Educational Record*, Summer, 1966, and also in a volume just published by the American Council on Education) :

"But this, I believe is a misunderstanding of both the college's responsibility and the student's desire. . . . . Recent campus protests criticising the impersonality of the modern university have led many concerned faculty members to adopt the mistaken notion that undergraduates are seeking in the professor both a father and a friend. Actually, most students want neither; they are quite happy to have finally escaped parental domination and even parental guidance, and would rather find their friends among their contemporaries. *What they want in a professor is, quite simply, a professor.* . . . When today's student decries the lack of communication between teacher and student, he is likely to be attacking the breakdown within, rather than outside, the classroom. The lack of concern he finds disturbing inheres not in the limited nature of extra classroom contact, but in the limited interest the professor displays in his classroom performance" [italics mine].

Well! This is unexpected counsel indeed. What this wise Columbia student is saying, very respectfully but firmly, is: please don't bother with all the palliatives now being worked out in faculty and administrative committees across the land. Just come to class — prepared! What we want in a professor is, quite simply, a professor — neither a life adjuster, nor an adjuster of life.

Somehow, as I think of all the faculty members who are getting leaves from the classroom these days to work out solutions to restlessness among students, it seems to me that the best commentary is contained in an old, now famous, Herblock cartoon. It was drawn when the late John Foster Dulles was incessantly engaged in missions outside Washington, D.C. It showed President Eisenhower sitting at the telephone saying: "Foster, don't just *do* something; *stand* there."

STEPHEN A. SHAPIRO
the student and the teacher: face to face

Recently, an "A" student of mine, a freshman, telephoned me at my home on a Friday evening. I say "an 'A' student" quite deliberately, because teachers tend to think of students not as individuals but as slots — A mind, B mind, C mind, D mind, No mind — which are filled and refilled by rank after rank of students, just the way slots in the Automat are refilled by identical egg salad, ham, and cheese sand-wiches. But this particular student, as I was to discover, was deter-mined to become visible, to be recognized as an individual, not just processed and graded. Nearly choking on her words, she asked me if I was busy. I replied that I was working. What did she want? She wanted to talk to me. Could she and her friend come over? I had talked with her for an hour in my office that afternoon. Perhaps fright-ened, certainly indignant, I said no, she could see me in my office on Monday. Apologizing for having bothered me, she stammered into silence.

I had not even bothered to find out what my student really wanted. Perhaps it was urgent. Was I so in love with my image of myself as a professional scholar that I could no longer remember what it feels like to need attention and to be rejected? I do care about my students, don't I? I recalled her tone of voice as she said to me that afternoon, "But you're my teacher," as if pleading with me to realize something that was perfectly apparent to her but which I could not see. True, she was in my class; I taught her a subject. But that was not what she meant. She meant I was *her* teacher; I taught *her*. She belonged to me and I belonged to her. What did she want from me?

I

Some obscure mixture of shame, responsibility, curiosity, and love compelled me to call the girl and ask her to come over. But before I reveal the nature of our conversation, let me place my question in the general context of the current uproar over education at the Big Campuses. "What does a student want from his teacher? What does it mean to be a teacher?" About two years ago, I was confident that these questions were going to be asked and answered on every cam-pus in the country. At Berkeley, students rebelled against the faceless,

From *Motive*, February, 1968. Copyright 1968 by *Motive*. Reprinted by permission.

bureaucratic, educational machine. "Do not fold or mutilate." Students demanded that a human face replace the metal smile of efficient administration. This image, of course, simplifies the complex uprising at Berkeley. But surely no one could deny that Berkeley students were frustrated by the mechanism of an education that served the needs of the Establishment rather than the needs of individual students who hungered to connect what they learned with how they lived. Recently Martin Meyerson wrote:

> The more I met with discontented students the more I realized that they were... objecting to being neglected. This was true for graduates as well as undergraduates... they did not have an opportunity to discuss the new ideas that were troubling them... they felt that they never got to know their teachers as persons and were not known as persons to their teachers.[1]

Surely no one could deny that the professional concerns of graduate education, publication, specialization, *are* indeed monopolizing the time and energy of professors, and that students, especially freshmen and sophomores, are becoming invisible to their teachers.

But Vice Chancellor Robert E. Connick of Berkeley did deny that professor-student relationships, or the lack of them, were a significant cause of discontent (L. A. *Times*, August 20, 1966, p. 24). He chanted the ritual response of all administrators on this subject: 1) research is an integral part of teaching; 2) teaching methods are being improved constantly; 3) professor-student relationships are not "as close as they might be," but a poll shows students think X is a good place. Events like the UCLA Conference on Undergraduate Education, which I attended last year as a representative of the Faculty Senate of the Irvine campus of the University of California, clearly operate as safety valves for the *status quo*. The feeling that something is happening is an illusion — nothing essential changes.

Much has been written on the Publish or Perish syndrome, and it should be clear by now that the Research fetish has done much harm, especially in the humanities, where teachers no longer *read* widely in order to become (to use a taboo word) *wiser* men — they do research on smaller and smaller subjects in order to become experts. Scientists normally publish their research because research in the sciences means discovery, but in the humanities, research can legitimately mean passionately learning the best that has been thought and said in order to participate in the perpetuation and transformation

<hr>

[1] "The Ethos of the American College Student: Beyond the Protests," *Daedalus*, Summer 1966.

of our culture. Humanists publish *and* perish when they substitute expertise for perspective and participation. However, those who oppose Research frequently do so in the name of Teaching — without bothering to define what teaching involves. Indeed, at third-rate colleges, teachers and administrators have smugly begun to be *proud* of the fact that they do not do research, refusing to realize that many among them are not intellectuals or genuine teachers, but merely philistines who indifferently expound various subjects.

The technology of teaching is becoming more refined: we now use slides, tape recorders, television, etc. Also, there is a confused and potentially tyrannical administrative campaign being launched to evaluate teaching ability — utilizing some refined form of spy or squealer system. More anxiety for the professor. Now he can worry about his rating as well as about whether his article is going to be accepted. But the most bizarre feature of the new concern with teaching, from the point of view of anyone concerned about student-teacher relationships, is the host of articles about teaching appearing in professional journals. The writers *think* they are discussing teaching, but their overwhelming concern is with methodology, texts, their "discipline" — rarely do we hear even a word about teaching as a complex and perilous relationship between a teacher and his students. Everyone pays lips service to the ideal of a "close" student-teacher relationship — but only at a safe distance of abstraction. My purpose is not to define or prescribe "the ideal" student-teacher relationship — it should be idiosyncratic, personal — but to move up close to what happens between students and their teachers so that we can see what we are talking about.

I am a professor of literature, but the crisis in values and attitudes which concerns me extends along a broad front, certainly involving history, philosophy, and the social sciences. Scientists concerned with human ecology have also begun to insist that since the acquisition of knowledge is inseparable from technological applications and social goals, scientists must become responsible for the consequences of their research. Rene Dubos keeps warning us that specialization could endanger man's adaptive capacities:

> The more civilization increases in complexity and the more it compels its members to become specialized the more it is necessary to maintain a certain number of human activities in a primitive, unorganized state.[2]

Teachers must safeguard the notion of the whole person.

[2] *Mirage of Health*, Anchor Book, 1962.

Ironically, professors are under pressure to consider themselves "professionals" whose primary concern is to become specialists and thereby to rise in their disciplines and in the university hierarchy as rapidly as possible. Paul Goodman frequently has satirized the new species, Academic Man. The academic world is growing steadily more pernicious, and protests like "The Shame of The Graduate Schools," by William Arrowsmith, do not even begin to evoke the full horror of what is happening.[3] "It does no good to exhort multiversity professors to take an interest in undergraduates and at the same time make it clear that appointments and promotions and increases in salary depend on the prosecution and publication of research in which undergraduates take no part. In many multiversity departments an interest in undergraduates is a positively harmful eccentricity."[4] Academic Man can only sneer at the notion of the university as a community. The New Professors, especially those under 30, know that only one thing pays — publication. Mobility and prestige are the way to "the top." Gazing toward the top of the pyramid, the professor cannot see the insect-like undergraduate hauling his burden of confusion. "Communicate with students?" One of my professors once said, with an urbane chuckle, "Why, what does one *say* to a freshman?"

That is the question, but it is not so amusing when a freshman marches into your home one evening and *you* do not know what to say. We know how to lecture to students, and how to speak *of* them, but *to* them — that is different. Recently, a professor-become-department-chairman-become-dean declared, with a familiar tone of smug, idealistic vagueness, that "our problem with [freshmen and sophomores] is to find ways to teach them whatever they must know of literature in order not to be crippled as human beings." My experience is that *despite* the literature they teach, professors of literature, themselves misshapen by graduate school and hardened by the impersonality of the institutional struggle for survival, help to *do* the crippling.

And they don't even know it. They hide behind words. Such self-deception is common among "humanists." Recently, I was present at a lecture given by one of America's most distinguished academic psychologists on the occasion of an administration-engineered scheme to furnish instant student-faculty togetherness. (After attending a lecture, students and faculty are supposed to draw together in small

[3] *Harper's*, March 1966.
[4] Robert Maynard Hutchins, *The New Republic*, April 1, 1967.

groups. These gatherings have shown that students and teachers *do not know how* to gather in small groups — especially when intimacy is the official policy of the occasion.) The professor gave a very edifying lecture — a little general, of course — on the subject of the "uses and abuses" of human beings, exhorting us to "Do not unto people as you would unto things." Unfortunately, there was no question period, so one could not ask how exactly one does unto people, but afterward I hopefully asked the speaker to characterize the student-teacher relationship in concrete terms, as an example of the I-Thou relationship he evidently had in mind. He said "It should be a very intense intellectual relationship." All his years as a teacher and a psychologist combined to produce this magnificent cliché. How can you dissociate the intellectual part of a student from the rest of his personality?

This psychologist, like most "humanists," was quite ready to launch a jeremiad against the isolation, alienation, and impersonality so prevalent in our bureaucratic world, and to announce the need to be human, to sustain I-Thou relationships, but he was also quite prepared to treat students as things with intellects. Perhaps, he is "too busy" to do what he says we should do. But, to paraphrase Dostoyevsky's Father Zossima, it is very easy to feel a sublime love for all mankind, but it is very difficult to love the student who calls you at your home, not because he or she has discovered an article you might want to read, but because . . . because. Students never know why they "must talk to you." But teachers should know why.

One problem is that while most teachers are hypocrites, few undergraduates are cynics. They don't realize that teachers are only playing a game when they talk about, say, D. H. Lawrence and the necessity of rebelling against a stifling environment, of expressing what one really feels. They don't realize that although the teacher talks as if he cares intensely about people, he really spends his time worrying about whether the chairman ignored him in the corridor, writing memos, worrying about publishing. Students are lovers, hungry for attention, for recognition, for encouragement and confirmation. They are experimenting with "roles," and they need models to identify with, as any good book on the psychology of adolescence can tell any teacher. So an excited student resents the impersonality of office conferences: he wants more than the small square of space-time allowed for in the teacher's appointment book. What does he want? He wants to talk to you — he wants you to see him and he wants you to show yourself to him. Whether you are dealing with a boy or girl, intellectual problems are never distinct from problems of identity formation and more or less sublimated sexual desires and fears. It is not only the relationships between students and teachers of opposite sexes that become intense and problematic. When a male student casts a male teacher in the role of his father, the ambivalent ramifications can create an explosive situation. Teachers must accept occasional shrapnel wounds.

There is plainly a great need for students and professors to become unashamedly aware of the nature of the adolescent psyche, and even for "the university experience" to adapt to the needs and anxieties of adolescents, instead of ramming them through a meatgrinder on the assumption that students are rational animals; but this is not the place to argue about such Utopian schemes. My more immediate aim here is to hold a mirror up to what is happening now.

II

The worst thing you can say to a young girl who is bewildered by the obscure forces that drive her to do impulsive things is, "What do you want?" I know this to be so because the first thing I said to my student when she seated herself in my living room was, "What do you want?" Well, she and her friend had been discussing Dostoyevsky, and I had said in class . . .

Then she was crying, and it was quite plain that she had not come here to discuss Dostoyevsky.

"I don't know why I'm crying . . . Whenever I talk to you, I cry. Why is that?"

I answered something stupid, undoubtedly. But how can you answer such a question? This girl had been in my class for three weeks. She is clearly sensitive, intelligent, and curiously mature and immature in her preoccupation with herself. Her father died recently; her mother is domineering; she has a boyfriend at another school. All this I learned that afternoon, in the course of exploring why her first essay got a B. She was bored by her essay and began talking about herself. But like many other fragile and insecure young girls I have spoken with, she got so upset just because she *was* talking about her own inadequacies and confusions that she began weeping and then grew outraged at herself for crying "for no reason."

That evening, despite the presence of her friend, she evidently wanted to continue her "confessions." Soon I lost patience. I could not find the right tone of voice, so I mechanically began to lecture —

in my own living room. I knew that these girls had come not because they had a burning desire to be English majors and to discuss books, but because they thought I could help them understand everything in general by being friendly and conversing with them for several hours.

However, instead of responding to these girls as individuals, I lectured in a stern, hard tone about how difficult it was for students and teachers to become friends. (Students frequently ask why teachers do not become friends with their students.)

First of all, there are so many more students than teachers that it would be impossible for a teacher to get to know all of his students, just as impossible as it would be for a girl who was asked out on a date by twenty boys to go out with all of them on the same evening. So a student must earn attention by merit.

Second, students must have interests and temperaments that harmonize with those of the teacher. Third, students must be patient; friendships do not develop overnight. Fourth, the teacher must not undermine his authority by revealing all kinds of potentially damaging bits of personal information to a student. Students gossip about teachers.

Fifth, the age gap between students and teachers is a complicated barrier. Sixth, students cannot expect to *bleed* before teachers and receive endless bandages of gauzy sympathy and encouragement.

Disregarding my "hypothetical case," the girl indignantly denied that she had come "to bleed"; then she burst out crying and said yes, it was true; all she wanted was attention; she had come to bleed. Then she said, still bawling, that she would leave now and was sorry she had bothered me, and it was terrible that it was so hard for students to get to know their teachers.

But I could not let her go now. I was ready to climb the wall with exasperation. "What *do* you want?" I kept asking. "Shall we just sit and chat? I have work to do. No, I mean . . . Well, you have a mother, a boyfriend, and friends. Don't they give you the attention you need?"

"Yes," she said, "but." But what? But when I had told her that she was in love with her style, it was so true — but so cruel and impersonal that she felt that nothing was left. She wanted to be a writer. I assured her that she was very gifted, that I was trying to help her improve, that she could be a fine writer. Yes, but I didn't understand. She wanted to show me her poetry and her journal, but she was afraid I would criticize that, too. I thought of Elizabeth Bowen's *The Death of the Heart,* and I tried to explain how cruel her innocent demands were, how frightening. She only wanted *attention,* but could she understand how brutal the competition for attention is in our world?

And yet, the more I protested that teachers are workers, not substitute parents, that students cannot expect teachers to be emotional service centers, the more I defended the values of distance, formality, privacy, fair and equal treatment for all students, the more I came to feel hollow and ready to condemn what I was defending. I began to really see the girl sitting there. She was not "a student." She was a person. And I? I was a professor. Was I a person?

In a strange dreamlike moment, I felt myself transformed into this girl. Or rather, I incorporated her into a memory of myself sitting in the office of one of my teachers (I never got as far as their homes). I kept demanding that they recognize me, make me visible and real with a word of understanding. Now I finally got to see my teacher, and I turned into my teacher and saw myself sitting before me, but I was mute and blind.

"I don't know how to talk to you," I said. I had talked too much and listened too little. It was then that I realized with a sense of desperation and near panic that I could not wrench off my mask and confront this girl face to face. I was lost, unable to hear myself in my voice. Very dimly, then, I began to see what has become blazingly clear today: students must help their teachers, must keep them in touch with what is human in themselves, keep them from losing the faces they saw in the mirror when they were young — just as teachers must help students realize and refine their own resources and motivate them to reshape the world in their own image. If the students fail to reclaim and sustain their teachers, the teachers will fail to liberate their students, and the cycle of depersonalization will be perpetuated.

The girl kept apologizing for bothering me, in a tone of voice that said, "It is too bad you are so inhuman." She was impertinent, and I was annoyed, but I was also grateful. She did not realize that there comes a time when you discover that your parents cannot understand you and that they require your understanding. But she helped me to perceive that I was becoming a machine with a facelike mask, and that it was time to revolt and reform. I was a success. That was the trouble.

In graduate school I had learned to subordinate all human impulses into a disciplined drive to produce, to produce first a Ph.D., and then articles, and then books. What Herbert Marcuse, in *Eros and Civilization*, terms "the performance principle": that is reality in the university, as well as in our entire society. Production is the only thing that matters. Everything is a means toward that end. Production, promotion, prestige — this is our trinitarian God. I and my successful colleagues have become streamlined projectiles — dead and deathdealing because we have forgotten that people are not means. Students and teachers cannot meet face to face until we realize that it is not the structure of our universities alone, but our sense of reality, our value system that is freezing faces into masks. We will not have time for students until we have time for ourselves.

The most horrifying aspect of my experience with this one student did not appear until about a week after our encounter in my home. First she wrote a very powerful essay on Camus and "the absurd," saying that in my home she had realized the meaning of isolation and absurdity. Then we had another talk. It was a genuine conversation, but I was stunned to discover that she decided that she had been romanticizing herself, that I was right; people do not have time for one another. That is the way things are. Alienation is inevitable. Now I tried to persuade her and myself that this was just sane-sounding insanity. We must not resign ourselves to a situation that can be transformed. But (and this seems to me to be very significant) my conversation with this girl will not resume in the fall because she has transferred to another university — not because of our relationship, I hasten to add. Students are almost as mobile as professors. Faces disappear.

III

One thing that this girl said to me I find especially haunting. She said that she wanted to know what it was like to be an adult, that she would like to be invisible so that she could watch my wife and me eat breakfast. There is clearly an element of sexual infatuation and voyeurism involved in the wish to be an invisible observer of intimate behavior. So what? Students are starving for genuine information about what it is like to live in this world, not just generalization or even insight, but actual, sensual, "existential" experience. Am I saying that teachers should lead guided tours through their own bathrooms? No, but I think we should examine our notion of privacy. Whom are we protecting —

for and from what? Does a teacher who changes the lives of his students by what he says in class — and this is what a good teacher does — does he have the right to disclaim all responsibility for his actions once he has left the classroom?

Today many teachers would insist that they do not teach students, they teach subjects. They are choosing blindness. The terrible power they have, the power to approve or disapprove, to form or deform, is always exercised, whether they get actively "involved" with their students' private lives or not. A teacher cannot escape action, choice, or responsibility. Silence, coldness, and withdrawal are actions that have consequences. It is dangerous to "play God" with the lives of students, but it is more dangerous to play Mephistopheles, the Denier. We cannot engage with all our students, but we need not worry about that. Not all our students will want to engage with us. What I am suggesting is that teachers must risk human relationships with the few students who are bold enough to assert themselves and tough enough to endure us.

Our society must cease being hypocritical about the role of sex in teaching. It is always present. Teachers are exhibitionists. The rhetoric of the learning process is sexual. Students are "receptive"; we "penetrate" their minds and "fertilize" them. We plant seeds, and so on. Students idealize teachers and cast them in sexual fantasy roles. A marriage of minds is always erotically charged. But when I say that a teacher must risk a human relationship with students, I do not mean to suggest that I approve of teachers or students using sex or grades as a bribe. That is an *economic* relationship. However, any teacher who risks involvement with a student risks an intensification of the erotic elements already in play, risks falling in love, risks despair, risks suffering, frustration, and personal revolution. If we teach our students that they must be ready to change their lives, then we must be ready to change our lives. A Ph.D. is not a certificate of immunity or invulnerability. Of course, we cannot and should not attempt to become Miss Lonelyhearts, bearing the weight of all our students' burdens. That is simply self-destructive. But if we withdraw into the autistic realms of pure research, we are buying the kind of security that will eventually make us all bankrupt. If professors are so insecure and anxious that they cannot spend an evening in the company of a few students, informally discussing what the students want to know, because such time spent with people seems wasted, because they feel guilty about not working (and this is indeed the situation that exists in academia today), then teachers can only teach one thing — how students can avoid becoming like their teachers.

Normally, students look to their teachers for models. Adolescents need models because this is part of the process of identity formation. But teachers also need to feel they are being taken as models, because this confirms them in their sense of identity and value, and this gives students great potential power. They can refuse to accept the models they are offered; they can reject teachers whose values are destructive, or whose lives mock the ideals they are paid to profess. "Jesus was a dropout," says a bumpersticker sold by the Los Angeles "Underground." But I urge students who hate the system not to drop out, but to stay in and fight to change the lives of the research zombies and other academic vampires and to persuade other students to do likewise. Students who conform to present demands are sustaining a system that will suck their blood and cripple them. I have encountered undergraduates who deliberately decided to enroll in a course given by a teacher they hated — and who was worthy of their contempt — just because a letter of recommendation from this person would help them get into a prestigious graduate school. Where are they going?

Anyone who understands how powerful the need to feel oneself a model actually is, will not think that it is quixotic to appeal to the students to change their professors, especially the younger ones. Hemingway's very popular *The Old Man and the Sea* demonstrates quite clearly how heroically a man will struggle if he knows a boy is watching him. Paradoxically, however, the task of teachers today is not to learn how to struggle, but to learn how to relate to people. This is much harder to do. Santiago's model, Joe DiMaggio, suffered and endured. The heroes of Western Civilization all suffer nobly in isolation, crucify themselves. Now, when we are "threatened" by a leisure-time revolution, it is time to ask why we are fanatically producing research that is not consumed and refusing to satisfy the societal and sensual impulses that are becoming twisted and destructive from frustration. Teachers must now be forced to ask *why* they are working, what they are working *for*. Means must not be confused with ends. I have heard professors respond to William Arrowsmith's claim that humanists must not divorce knowledge from action, by sneering that he was confusing humanism with humanitarianism. Confusion, self-deception, and cowardice can go no further than this. There is only one aim for all study — the amelioration of human life.

A professor is expected to extend, coordinate, and transmit knowledge. But he is also expected to influence the character and values of his students. I am not arguing that research is "no good." I am arguing that even trivial research has become sacred, an end in itself, and that this has frequently operated against the willingness or ability of the professor to coordinate and transmit knowledge, and has in fact replaced the intellectual with the specialist, the professional who simply does not care about "other fields," or students, or the responsibility of the intellectual to criticize and help reshape his society. If a teacher does not make some effort to show his students how knowledge affects action, and what knowledge is for, by getting involved with them as people, then he has not only abdicated his role as a teacher, but contributed toward a very ominous situation that was clearly exposed during the trials of Nazis. The specialist disavows responsibility for anything outside his specialty. People are not his business.

In *The Human Use of Human Beings*, Norbert Wiener tried to warn us that we must revere the difference between human beings and ants: ants are specialized creatures; we are not. But the Academic Man is a kind of ant, and he trains others to be ants. In 1939, at the end of his *Autobiography*, R. G. Collingwood wrote: "I know now that the minute philosophers of my youth, for all their profession of a purely scientific detachment from practical affairs, were the propagandists of a coming Fascism." In the endless corridors of our universities, you can sense the future being born in the classrooms, laboratories, and offices of specialists. Down those corridors march millions of invisible students. The teachers cannot see them, do not know how to speak with them, do not care about them. The teachers do their jobs. Kafka knew how it would happen. One morning, the world was an anthill.

This must not happen. We must join in the deepening revolt, whether SDS or LSD inspired, against a social order dominated by an ideology of production, aggression, competition, and self-destruction. Efficiency is the virtue of machines; not of men. Emotional starvation is not "normal." Students who demand personal attention will get it, and may transform the lives of their teachers. Knock on their doors. The walls of our prisons are not as solid as they seem. Frightened students can only feel locked out by frightened teachers who feel locked in. I say again that the university is the seedground of the future. This machine can become a garden. Knock on the doors. Become visible.

ELAYNE ANTLER RAPPING
LEONARD A. RAPPING
politics and morality in academe

Surely everyone is convinced by now that there is some kind of trouble afoot in the American university system. After Berkeley there was talk of disinterested professors, irrelevant courses, and dehumanized bureaucracies. After Columbia the political implications of these charges are clearer, and while there is still considerable faculty sympathy and support for the protesters, it appears that some backlash is building up. On the one hand, some professors who ignored or were bewildered by the issues involved — until the sight of blood on young middle-class faces hurled them into the radical camp — are as ignorant and bewildered as before, but are now staunchly committed to the wounded oppressed. On the other hand, less sympathetic statements by eminent intellectuals assert that the function of the university is to pursue and impart knowledge and that it cannot possibly get on with its business unless law and order is maintained. This is undoubtedly true, but it may well be beside the point. For at least one thing the protesters seem to be trying to tell us is that the university has been pursuing a lot of things besides knowledge lately, and as a result it has been making a hash of its traditional function.

Having spent many years around various universities, we tend to believe that what the students smell within the halls of ivy is an authentic rat. However, we are distressed by the response of the academic community itself to this "crisis in the university." The faculty seems to see itself as having only two options: to turn their classrooms into instruments of political agitation, or to defend the pristine purity of their disciplines against the corruption of political ideas in any form. But the moral and political aspects of the relationship between the university and the community, between politics and education in general, are more complicated than this. The university and its faculty have traditionally upheld certain standards of objectivity and noncommitment in their observations and judgments about the world. They have had a definite moral and political responsibility to do so. And it is this very commitment to objectivity which is now so bitterly attacked and so embarrassingly undefended on moral or political grounds.

From *Saturday Review*, October 19, 1968. Copyright © 1968 by Saturday Review, Inc. Reprinted by permission.

Professors are apparently so anxious to be morally engaging, and to eliminate dry abstraction from their classes, that they are incorporating everything from group therapy to civil disobedience into the curriculum. But they miss the point. And they miss it because, like many of their students, most faculty members do not assume that "the academic life is the good life" at all. They themselves have lost sight of the true relationship between intellectual and social matters, and they themselves no longer see the relevance of the intellectual disciplines to life. This is a devastating loss, for it implies that the intellectual life is as spiritually dead as God himself, and that higher education is not merely apolitical or amoral — it is mad. For if academic economics is not about poverty, and academic criticism not about the substance of literature, what in the world are they about and why would anyone bother with them?

So the professors are madly trying to put as much "real life" as possible into their classes. But "real life" will not survive in a classroom environment; it will wither and die if not quickly transformed into abstract thought, which is the only "real" thing that can thrive and bear fruit in such a climate. The fate of "real life experience," once it gets trapped in a college bulletin, can be glimpsed in this excerpt from an innovative English course description:

> The course will confront the student with the literary work as an image.... The student should live with a literary image and in it for a time, and learn to talk about it meaningfully and without cant or pedantry. The course should provide a vital and dramatic experience of coming to terms with literature. In a sense it should be a course in learning to read, in the fullest sense of the term. The student should become free within the work of literature....

The person who wrote this was clearly disenchanted with the academic approach to literature (which we know can be very disenchanting). But, no doubt having a family to support, he decided to say that there was some other, groovier way of teaching literature, without abstraction or rational analysis. But one cannot do away with abstraction or reason and still communicate meaningfully in a classroom, and the idealistic attempt to deny this leads to the garbled and muddleheaded jargon of statements like the one above, full of empty clichés and intellectualisms that betray the failure to think through one's problems clearly. The particular course described above might even be dangerous in operation. Its attempts to communicate the direct, visceral experience of art could lead to the frustration with the inadequacies of language that helped drive Billy Budd to murder.

But what is most disturbing about these proposals is not that they are doomed to fail, but that they subvert the truly exciting and morally relevant aspects of the scholarly tradition. Reason, abstraction, and moral detachment are not the sources of evil in our society. In fact, Victorian as it may sound, they are among the few useful tools we have devised for identifying and dealing with evil. Neither are they opposed to the warmer human instincts. John Stuart Mill (himself unfortunately misread and out of fashion these days) understood this when he advised the St. Andrews School boys to learn logic and political economy, as well as poetry, in spite of the general belief that the first two are "unfeeling." He said:

> For my part, the most unfeeling thing I know of is the law of gravitation: it breaks the neck of the best and most amiable person without scruples, if he forgets for a single moment to give heed to it. The winds and waves too are very unfeeling. Would you advise those who go to sea to deny ... or make use of them? ... My advice to you is to study [these subjects] and hold firmly by whatever in them you find true; and depend upon it that if you are not selfish or hard-hearted already [they] will not make you so.

If we doubt the value of this advice for anyone whose "primary concerns are political and moral," we need only recall Mill's own character and the humane and liberal works to which he dedicated his own life.

The point is that one need not deny or destroy the emotional or moral response to experience in the process of analyzing it. In fact, one can think of any number of cases in which a thorough analysis of a problem can lead to a fuller, more useful emotional response. Let us take an example from the dismal science. Most of us who support the idea of state-subsidized higher education do so in part because it is a way of redistributing income from rich to poor. Theoretically, we assume that those who can best afford it will be paying the most "tuition" in the form of taxes, while those who can least afford to pay will be able to send their children to college for a truly nominal fee.

We approve of this scheme because we believe in equality of opportunity regardless of family background and we want each child to be given the same educational and cultural training, insofar as this does not interfere in another democratic value, that of individual freedom. And yet in California, known for its liberal and progressive tuition-free university system, a 1964 survey reported that while 60 per cent of the system's undergraduates came from families with over $12,000 annual income, only 5 per cent were from families with less than $5,000 income. While tuition-free education seems to benefit high-income groups in disproportionately large numbers, the costs of the university system are widely shared because it is supported in most part by a state sales tax which, in percentage terms, affects all families equally.

The political rhetoric on this issue is quite simply meaningless — or should be to men of goodwill. The voter is presented with a false and simplistic choice between a reactionary anti-intellectual who simply cuts the education budget, and a "liberal," vaguely in favor of free education for all.

There is no reason why the facts of such issues should not be demanded by the public or why the public should not be educated to interpret them. But a quantitative approach to any social issue, even a financial one, is often viewed with the kind of hostility commonly expressed toward "computer analysis"; for intellectuals are often lulled to sleep with humanistic fairy tales in which the villian computer transforms the man of pure feeling to stone. Now there is no doubt that computer analysis can be an expensive and pointless academic game. But for those of us with serious social concerns, a more subtle view of computers, statistics, and numbers themselves might be more useful.

For example, the public animosity toward Robert McNamara was based on a naïve and inflated image of him as an omnipotent master of men and machines. But what was really frightening about Secretary McNamara's manipulation of facts and figures before Congress was not his transformation of human lives into bits of data, but the fact that the Congressmen were apparently unable to judge whether his conclusions were valid or invalid; or worse, whether the questions he answered should ever have been asked. Moral outrage has always been easy to incite. What is difficult, tedious, but increasingly important, is to teach people to make careful and accurate distinctions between the cops and the robbers, and then to know enough about thievery to be able to catch a thief.

We would not wish to be misinterpreted as making too strong a claim for human reason. We are well aware of the dark forces of irrationality affecting our lives from within and without, even as we are writing. But we *are* writing — all of us *do* read, write, think, and vote; and if we are not always wholly rational when we do these things, it is not for lack of trying. There are people of course who truly prefer what Keats called "a life of Sensation rather than of Thought." But it is the paradox of such discussions as this one (as Keats well knew) that these people will never tell us their side of the argument because they do not argue. All of us who do argue, however, are united on the side of reason, whether we like it or not, and no matter how embarrassing our teams' losses may become, we are always disingenuous when we pretend otherwise. For no matter how profound our anguish and compassion for the poor, there is no meaningful way of dealing with the problem of poverty which does not at some point become a method of manipulating symbols.

And this is as true of esthetic problems as of social ones. For, as a well known critic recently pointed out (after all these centuries of confusion), it is not "literature" that we teach, but a more or less conscious, more or less coherent, method of literary criticism, which is knowledge *about* literature in the same sense that physics is knowledge about nature. That is, the direct experience of literature is as inescapably real as the direct experience of sunlight, and as unteachable. For literature is not a direct imitation of or comment upon life. If it were, it would deserve the suspicion it arouses in pragmatic hearts; for it is clumsy and inaccurate as imitation and commonplace, when not hopelessly obscure, as philosophy.

The real reason we study literature is that we suspect that it is life that imitates art; that is, that literature may provide us with myths and metaphors which we learn to impose on the chaos of events to endow them with human significance. If it is so, then the study of literature should be an inquiry into workings of the poetic and myth-making faculties, as revealed in the structural and thematic elements, formal rules and strategies, that distinguish strictly imaginative literature from expository prose.

This question of what is teachable and what is worth teaching should be at the heart of all discussions of education, but instead we still have tiresome and misleading polemics about teaching and research, scientific detachment and moral engagement. And this, in spite of the fact that we know almost nothing about the real qualities that make for effective teaching. Even terms such as "irresponsibility" are ambiguous at best. There are, after all, all kinds of irresponsible teachers, and those who do not prepare or even show up for class are not necessarily the worst. What is really wrong with most undergraduate education is that it is boring, and even the most conscientious teacher is likely to bore his students to death with a lot of dry facts which they rightly judge useless and immediately forget.

And the popular idea of good teaching is often as smugly simplistic as that of bad. For example, good teaching is often associated with the Socratic method which draws the student into active participation in the learning process rather than making him a passive receiver of the lecturer's own conclusions. But this dichotomy is as false as the others, for what most of his modern followers tend to forget is that Socrates believed in innate ideas, and he never asked a question to which he himself did not know the objective, unique answer. He believed that there was something real beyond the chaos of subjective impressions, and he demonstrated to his students a rational method of discovering it.

Few of us worry much about innate ideas any longer. In fact, we tend to view our various methodological models as hypothetical and meta-phoric, so intellectually jaded have we become. To put the matter simply, what we call truth, knowledge, or meaning is not some essential reality we discover in the external world; it is something we create ourselves, because it is contained within, and emerges out of our own process of investigation.

Once we see this, we also see the importance of the rigorous method-ology Socrates employed in his dialogues. For if we know now that serendipity will not send us stumbling upon what he thought was an innate idea, then we also know that we can only understand what he was getting at by adopting his method of thinking about things. From this point of view, knowledge becomes a way of thinking rather than a thought, and it becomes clear that there is only one really useful thing a teacher can communicate — not a set of facts, or formulae, or the "true meaning" of a poem, but an intellectual method or style of appre-hending the world. (We could even say, if we wanted to be cute about it, that in education the method is the message.)

If that is so, and we think for the most part it is, then it seems obvious that research is an essential part of a teacher's responsibility. He need not ever publish anything of course, but anyone who does not use the methods of his discipline regularly, or find them relevant to his own deepest interests, is not likely to maintain his ability to teach them for long.

It should be clear by now that we believe the teacher has a strong moral responsibility to his students. On the simplest level, he must show them that what he does is meaningful and useful to them as citizens and human beings. And unless he is shamefully hypocritical and exploitative, he will be exposing his own view of the world and his own life style to their judgment in every class presentation.

We do not mean to imply that every discipline is informed by a world view or an attitude toward life which has broad moral implications. The important point is that the scholarly activity is itself informed by a clear moral attitude, that of scientific detachment and objectivity, and it is as rigorous and demanding as any other moral discipline which has proved socially valuable. It insists that one stand back from his own interests, prejudices, and desires in order to free himself from the stock responses his personality, society, and culture impose upon him. It demands that he be skeptical of received opinions and accepted values, and alert to the processes which gradually transform truth and honesty into cliché and sham.

This kind of morality does not incorporate such Christian virtues as love, tolerance, and forgiveness. But it does have one great virtue: it is not as easily perverted as the more tender-hearted varieties, and it therefore has its own place of importance in the conscience of a citizen. It may seem a bit cold-blooded, but it is not inhumane, and it is much too straightforward to produce the institutionalized evil and exploitation that smile up at us from posters and magazines all the time. For there is surely a subtle but grotesque inhumanity in a photograph of a Congressman smiling at a bleeding Vietnamese child, and a healthy antidote to such deepseated disingenuousness might be a public trained to see beyond rhetoric and sentimentality to a clear analysis of social problems. We might begin with defense spending in general, and then perhaps dig beneath the slogans that obscure the human aspects of such issues as urban renewal, manpower retraining, the organization of the welfare system, and the waste and oppressiveness of compulsory conscription.

Not everyone will have a stomach for this kind of morality, with its emphasis on detachment, and its eagerness to reduce the agony of Dostoevsky to matters of literary convention, and the sufferings of the unemployed to binary digits. But before one rejects it, he should be very clear about how much of human endeavor he is rejecting. Dostoevsky himself could not communicate his suffering except through the abstractions of language and the gross lies of fiction. For the immediate effect of intense suffering is to destroy all other thoughts and perceptions, and ultimately to destroy human dignity itself, as we in the twentieth century have ample reason to know. It is only those of us who survive our moments of suffering, then, who can indulge in the luxury of reading, writing, or even thinking about them. Once we admit this, we must see that moral detachment is not required only of the scientists; it is equally essential to the humanistic scholar and to the artist himself, because it is a necessary prerequisite to any intellectual activity. For one must stand back a bit from life itself in order to find meaning in it, and anyone who does not understand or appreciate the moral value of such a position would be well advised to give up not only statistics, but art itself, which is, of course, what Jean-Paul Sartre has recently done.

The general failure to recognize the political and moral importance of scientific detachment has, by the way, led to great confusion over the role of the social sciences. We have all seen scholarly journals full of formalistic exercises in methodology, and we would all probably agree with critics who say that the authors have carried their detachment to the point of disinterest, and are dabbling in useless trivia. But there is another, more serious criticism of American social science which says that it is not detached at all; that it is morally committed not to the truth, but to the status quo. It says that government agencies and large industries exercise great financial control over the universities and thereby influence faculty and students to learn those skills and engage in those research projects which serve the political and financial ends of the powers that be.

This is a very serious charge indeed, and it should alert every university professor to the dangers of committing himself to any set of goals or values except the truth. It is no small thing to teach students to make objective judgments about what the world is like. And if large numbers of professors are spending large amounts of time helping various agencies achieve their own desired ends, then it is surely more important than ever to maintain a hard core of truly objective scholars, to make public what their colleagues are up to, if nothing else.

We have recently had a gratifying example of just such an activity in Noam Chomsky's article about "The Responsibility of Intellectuals." In it Chomsky upheld the highest academic standards of truth and objectivity in exposing certain false and biased statements about our foreign policy by various intellectuals associated with the government. Since then Chomsky has written other pieces which are not objective but politically committed, as is his right. But we must be careful to see the great distinction between these two positions. A political decision to picket, withhold taxes, or resist the law does not require academic competence; any citizen is capable of making it. What was truly courageous and significant about the academic role in the Vietnam war controversy was not that professors marched, but that some of them first stood back from the goals and interests of their government in order to analyze the world situation objectively and fairly. It was professional historians and political scientists, for the most part, who had the skill and knowledge to make such analyses, and therefore gave themselves and others a clear, rational basis for political action.

And isn't this, at bottom, the function of education in a democracy? What intellectuals know how to do best is to discover what the world is like, and the reason we send our children through years of school is that we believe it is meaningless to talk of changing things for the better if we don't know how to tell what they are like in the first place.

It is itself a cliché to say that we live in a world of clichés, managed news, and self-perpetuating bureaucracies, in which even politicians have taken to persuading us that what they and the world are really like is best expressed in a Madison Avenue commercial. But it is this very situation which makes it more important than ever that the moral and political values of science and scholarship be properly understood and appreciated by every citizen. We can no longer afford the myths of the ivory tower and the absent-minded professor. It is too important that we, as intellectuals, are reminded of how our traditional activities do affect the world, and how our way of life does set a moral example.

IRVING KRISTOL
a different way to restructure the university

I have the gravest doubts that, out of all the current agitation for a "restructuring" of the university, very much of substance will come. There are a great many reasons why this is so, among them the fact that practically no one any longer has a clear notion of what a "university" is supposed to be, or do, or mean. We are, all of us, equally vague as to what the term "higher education" signifies, or what functions and purposes are properly included in the categories of "student" or "professor." But in addition to such basic problems, there is a simple and proximate obstacle: all of the groups — professors, administrators and students — now engaged in this enterprise of "restructuring" are deficient in the will to do anything, or the power to do anything, or ideas about what might be done.

Let us begin with the faculty, since they are indeed, as they claim ("Sir, the faculty *is* the university"), the preponderant estate of this realm. In most universities, it is the faculty that controls the educational functions and defines the educational purposes of the institution. It is the faculty that usually arranges the curriculum, makes staff appointments, etc. It is the faculty that has the moral authority, the mental capacity, and a sufficiently intimate knowledge of the realities of the educational system to operate upon it. Unfortunately, these virtues are far outweighed by an all too human defect — a limited imagination which leads to a lack of objective insight into its own position. What faculty members of our universities fail to see is that any meaningful restructuring will not only have to be done *by* the faculty, but will also have to be done *to* the faculty. And to ask the American professoriat to restructure itself is as sensible as if one had asked Marie Antoinette to establish a republican government in France. Whether or not it coincided with her long-term interests was immaterial; the poor woman couldn't even conceive of the possibility.

Now, I don't mean to suggest that there is anything especially shortsighted or selfish about the American professor. Some of my best friends are professors, and I can testify that they are every bit as broadminded, every bit as capable of disinterested action, as the average business executive or higher civil servant. Nor are they particularly smug and complacent. On the contrary, they are all keenly aware of the crisis that has befallen them, while many have long been discontented with their lot and full of haunting insecurities. Nevertheless, they do have one peculiar and notable flaw: being generally liberal and reformist in their political predisposition, they believe themselves able to have a truly liberal and reformist perspective on themselves. This is, of course, an idle fancy. No social group really possesses the imaginative capacity to have a liberal and reformist perspective on itself; individual members of the group may and do — but the group as a whole cannot. Otherwise the history of human society would be what it is not: an amiable progression of thoughtful self-reformations by classes and institutions.

So the beginning of wisdom, in thinking about our universities, is to assume that the professors are a class with a vested interest in, and an implicit ideological commitment to, the *status quo* broadly defined, and that reform will have to be imposed upon them as upon everyone else. If any empirical proof were required of the validity of these assumptions, one need only cast a glance over the various proposals for university reform that have been made by faculty committees at Berkeley and elsewhere.

These proposals have one distinguishing characteristic: at no point, and in no way, do they cost the faculty anything — not money, not time, not power over their conditions of employment. They liberally impose inconveniences upon the administration, upon the taxpayers, upon the secondary schools, upon the community. But they never inconvenience the faculty. They never, for instance, increase its teaching load. (On the contrary: after four years of "restructuring" at Berkeley, professors there now spend *less* time in the classroom than they used to.) They never suggest anything that would intrude on those four months' vacations; they never interfere with such off-campus activities as consultancies, the writing of textbooks, traveling fellowships, etc.; they never discourage the expensive — but convenient — proliferation of courses in their specialized areas; they never even make attendance at committee meetings compulsory. This is precisely what one would expect when one asks a privileged class to reform the institution which is its very *raison d'être*. It is rather like asking corporation executives or trade union leaders or officials of a government agency, all of whom have been given lifelong tenure in their present positions, to "restructure" the institutions and redefine their positions.

I have touched upon this question of tenure because of its symbolic significance. Few professors, in conversation, will defend the present tenure system, whereby senior- and middle-level faculty are given a personal, lifelong monopoly on their positions. They will accept the criticisms of it by Robert Nisbet and others as largely valid. They will concede that it could be substantially modified — via long-term contracts, generous severance agreements, etc. — without any danger to academic freedom and with obvious benefits to everyone. They will agree that the "controversial" professor, whom tenure was supposed to protect, is today in great demand and short supply, whereas the mediocre professor is its prime beneficiary. They may even admit that the presence of a tenured faculty is one of the reasons that the university has been — with the possible exception of the post office — the least inventive (or even adaptive) of our social institutions since the end of World War II. They will allow that tenure in the university, like seniority in a craft union, makes for all sorts of counter-productive rigidities. But they will then go on to dismiss the whole issue as utterly "academic."

To tamper with tenure, they argue, would produce fits and convulsions throughout their well-ordered universe. Nothing can or will be done, and they themselves could not be counted on to try. Even those economists who argue in favor of a free market for labor everywhere else somehow never think of applying this doctrine to themselves.

So when these same people announce that, to cope with the crisis in that university, they are going to "restructure" the institution, one has the right to be skeptical. To suppose that they actually will do any such thing is probably the most "academic" idea of all.

Nor is the administration going to "restructure" the university. It couldn't do it if it tried; and it is not going to try because it doesn't regard itself as competent even to think about the problem. University administration in the United States today combines relative powerlessness with near-absolute mindlessness on the subject of education.

That statement about powerlessness needs to be qualified in one respect. Though a great many people are under the impression that the boards of trustees are the "real" power structure of the university, this is in fact the one group over which the administration does wield considerable influence. The trustees of a modern university are rather like the boards of directors of a modern corporation. They represent a kind of "stand-by" authority, ready to take over if the executive officers lead the organization into a scandalous mess. (Having little first-hand knowledge of educational institutions, they will then usually make the mess even worse than it was; but that's another story.)

They also may — repeat: *may* — intervene in certain broad economic decisions, such as the construction of a new campus, the launching of a major fund-raising drive, etc. But on the whole, and in the ordinary course of events, they solemnly rubber-stamp whatever the administration has done or proposes to do.

And that's about the sum and substance of "administrative power." True, a determined administration can badger and bribe and blackmail the faculty into marginal revisions of the curriculum, just as a determined administration can have some influence over senior appointments. But most administrations are not all that determined — like everyone else, university administrators prefer an untroubled life. And even where they are determined, it doesn't make all that much difference, from an outsider's point of view. Within the institution, of course, even small differences can cause great anguish and excitement.

As for the administration's power over students, that hardly seems worth discussing at a time when the issue being debated is the students' power over the administration. Suffice it to say that, where disciplinary power does exist on paper, it is rarely used; and it is now in the process of ceasing to exist even on paper.[1] In this respect, university administrators are ironically very much *in loco parentis*. They have about as much control over their 19- and 20-year-old charges as the parents do.

There might be something to deplore in this situation if one had reason to think that university administrators could wisely use power, did they have it. But there is no such reason, if what we are interested in is higher education. University administrators have long since ceased to have anything to say about education. By general consent, their job is administration, not education.

When was the last time a university president came forth with a new idea about education? When was the last time a university president wrote a significant book about the education of — as distinct from the government of — "his" students? Robert M. Hutchins was the last of that breed; he has had no noteworthy successors. Indeed, the surest way for an ambitious man never to become a university president is to let it be known that he actually has a philosophy of education. The faculty, suspicious of possible interference, will rise up in rebellion.

The university president today is primarily the chief executive of a corporate institution, not an educator. Unfortunately, he usually is also a poor executive, for various reasons. To begin with, he is almost invariably a professor, with no demonstrated managerial experience. More important, there are few meaningful standards against which to judge his performance, as distinct from his popularity. Since most university administrators have no clear idea of what they are supposed to be doing, they end up furiously imitating one another, on the

[1] "Colleges are not churches, clinics, or even parents. Whether or not a student burns a draft card, participates in a civil rights march, engages in premarital or extramarital sexual activity, becomes pregnant, attends church, sleeps all day or drinks all night, is not really the concern of an educational institution." — The president of the American Association for Higher Education as reported in *Time*, July 11, 1968.

assumption — doubtless correct — that to be immune from invidious comparisons is to be largely exempt from criticism.

Thus, at the moment, all administrations are proudly expanding the size of their plant, their facilities and their student bodies. An outsider might wonder: Why should any single institution feel that it has to train scholars in all disciplines? Why can't there be a division of labor among the graduate schools? Aren't our universities perhaps too big already? Such questions are occasionally raised at conferences of educators — but, since every administrator has no other criterion for "success" than the quantitative increase in students, faculty, campus grounds, etc., these questions spark no debate at all.

As a matter of fact, university administrators never get much criticism — though, of course, they are convenient scapegoats who are instantly *blamed* for anything that goes wrong. The professors are just too busy and self-preoccupied, and in the ordinary course of events are perfectly content to leave the government of the university to the administration — even when they have a low opinion of the administration. (This has been the story at Columbia these past 10 years.)

It is interesting to note that, despite the fact that our best economists are all professors, there has been little public criticism from them on the grotesquely conservative way in which universities invest their endowment funds. It was not until the Ford Foundation's McGeorge Bundy made an issue of it, that the universities began to bestir themselves. Similarly, it was an off-campus man, Beardsley Ruml, who, some 15 years ago, pointed out that it was wasteful to leave campus facilities unused for months at a time, because of the vacation schedule. One would have thought that this idea could have passed through the minds of professors of management, or city planning, or something.

An interesting instance of the charmed life of university administrators is a recent report of the Carnegie Commission on the Future of Higher Education. Written by an economist, it delicately refuses to raise any interesting questions and limits itself to arguing for the need of ever greater government subsidies. After pointing out that the deficit in university budgets is largely incurred by the graduate divisions — a graduate student costs about three or four times as much as an undergraduate — the Carnegie report offers by way of explanation of the costliness of graduate education the following: "The conscientious supervision of a student's independent work is the essence of high-level graduate education. . . ."

What this means in practice, as everyone knows, is that the only way a university can attract big faculty names away from other places is by offering them minimal teaching loads in the graduate division, and the only way it can attract the brightest graduate students away from other schools is by offering them attractive (i.e., expensive) fellowships. Whether or not it makes sense for each institution of higher learning to adopt such a competitive policy would seem to be an important problem; but the Carnegie Commission loyally refrained from exploring it. Nor did it show any interest in whether in fact there is "conscientious supervision" in graduate schools, and if so how extensive or effective it is. From casual conversation with graduate students, one gets the impression that such supervision is not all that common, to put it mildly.

In short and in sum: university administrations have neither the power, nor the inclination, nor the stimulus of informed criticism which would result in any serious efforts at "restructuring" their institutions.

And the students? They, alas, are indeed for the most part rebels without a cause — and without a hope of accomplishing anything except mischief and ruin.

In our society and in our culture, with its pathetic belief in progress and its grotesque accent on youth, it is almost impossible to speak candidly about the students. Thus, though most thoughtful people will condemn the "excesses" committed by rebellious students, they will in the same breath pay tribute to their "idealism" and their sense of "commitment." I find this sort of cant to be preposterous and disgusting. It seems to me that a professor whose students have spat at him and called a "mother————" (it happened at Columbia) ought to be moved to more serious and more manly reflection on what his students are really like, as against what popular mythology says they are supposed to be like.

My own view is that a significant minority of today's student body obviously consists of a mob who have no real interest in higher education or in the life of the mind, and whose passions are inflamed by a debased popular culture that prevails unchallenged on the campus. We are reluctant to believe this because so many of the young people who constitute this mob have high I.Q.'s, received good academic grades in high school, and because their popular culture is chic rather than philistine in an old-fashioned way. Which is to say: we are reluctant to believe that youngsters of a certain social class, assembled on the grounds of an educational institution, can be a "mob," in the authentic sociological sense of that term. (We are also reluctant to believe it because many of these students are our children, and we love them regardless of what they do. Such love is, of course, natural and proper. On the other hand, it is worth reminding oneself that members of lower-class lynch mobs have loving fathers and mothers too.)

The really interesting question is: How did they get that way? After all, we do assume that young people of a certain intelligence, provided with a decent education, will be more rational — and therefore more immune to mob instincts — as they near the end of their education than they were at the beginning. The assumption is plausible; but it also patently fails to hold in many instances, and this can only represent a terrible judgment on our system of education.

How is it possible for a Columbia or Berkeley sophomore, junior or even graduate student to believe in the kinds of absurd simplicities they mouth at their rallies — especially when, before entering college, many of these youngsters would have been quick to recognize them as nothing but absurd simplicities? How is it possible for a radical university student — and there is no reason why a university student shouldn't be radical — to take Che Guevara or Chairman Mao seriously when, in his various courses, he is supposed to have read Marx, Max Weber, Tocqueville, has been examined on them, and has passed the examination?

When I discuss this problem with my professor friends, I am informed that I display a naive faith in the power of formal instruction as against the force of the *Zeitgeist*. And there is a measure of justice in this rejoinder. There can be no doubt that we are witnessing, all over the world, a kind of generational spasm — a sociological convulsion whose roots must go deep and far back and must involve the totality of our culture rather than merely the educational parts of it. It is fairly clear, for example, that many of the students are actually revolting against the bourgeois social and moral order as a whole, and are merely using the university as a convenient point of departure. Whether their contempt for this order is justified is a topic worthy of serious discussion — which, curiously enough, it hardly ever receives in the university. But, in any case, this question ought not to distract us from the fact that those radical students who are most vociferous about the iniquities of the university are the least interested in any productive "restructuring."

On the other hand, not all of the rebellious students are all that radical politically; and it does seem to me that, in these cases, it ought to be possible for a university education to countervail against the mish-mash of half-baked and semiliterate ideologies that so many students so effortlessly absorb within a few months of arriving on campus. My own opinion, for what it's worth, is that the college and the university fail to educate their students because they have long since ceased trying to do so.

The university has become very good at training its students for the various professions; and it is noteworthy that, within the university, the professional schools and divisions have been the least turbulent. But for the ordinary college student — majoring in the humanities or in the social sciences — the university has become little more than an elegant "pad," with bull-sessions that have course numbers or with mass lectures that mumble into one ear and ramble out the other.[2]

The entire conception of a liberal education — of the most serious ideas of our civilization being taught by professors who took them seriously — has disappeared, under pressure of one kind or another. The graduate divisions, with their insistence on preprofessional training, have done their part; but so has the whole temper of our educational system over the past decades, with its skepticism toward "great ideas" in general and toward great ideas of the past in particular.

I believe that, when students demand that their studies be "relevant," this is what they are unwittingly demanding. After all, what could be more "relevant" today than the idea of "political obligation" — a central theme in the history of Western political philosophy — or the meaning of "justice"? And, in fact, on the few campuses where such teaching still exists, the students do find it "relevant," and exciting, and illuminating.

But, whether I am right or wrong in this appraisal, the whole issue is, like so many others, "academic." The students think they are rebelling against the university as a "bureaucratic" institution, and they think it so powerfully that they are not likely to listen to anyone who informs

[2] A special word is necessary about sociology departments, whose students play a leading — perhaps critical — role in the current rebellion. Sociology is an odd kind of hybrid: a profession many of whose members are completely unprofessional in outlook, temperament, and intellectual rigor. When I was in New York's City College in the late nineteen-thirties, most students majored in sociology because it was the closest thing to a major in current social problems that the curriculum offered — and majoring in such problems was what they really wanted to do. In the end, most of them did become professional sociologists; and if they remained interested in social problems and social reform, their interest was anything but simple-minded. But these days, though the motivation for majoring in sociology is still a heightened concern with social problems, the number of sociology majors is so large, the departments so amorphous, the curriculum so sprawling, that it is quite easy for a student to move through his courses with his passions never being seriously disturbed by a sociological idea.

them that they are really rebelling against a soulless institution — one that has been emptied of its ideal content. So those who are not set upon destroying the university will be permitted to tinker at "restructuring" it. They will serve on committees that define the curriculum; they will help enforce a dwindling minimum of student discipline; they will be solemnly listened to instead of being solemnly preached at.

But you can't reform an institution unless you know what you want; and though our university students have always been encouraged to want the true, the good, and the beautiful, they have never been taught how to think about the conditions and consequences of such desires. To date, most of the reforms sponsored by students have been in the direction of removing their obligation to get any kind of education at all. It is not surprising that harassed administrators and preoccupied professors are quick to find such proposals perfectly "reasonable."[3]

So where are we? In an impasse, it would appear. Here we have a major social institution in a flagrant condition of crisis, and not one of the natural social forces involved with this institution can be relied upon to do any of the necessary work of reformation. In situations of this kind, the tradition is for the governmental authorities to step in and fill the power vacuum. And such, I think, will again have to be the case this time.

That last sentence made even me, its author, shudder as it was written. The spectacle of state or Federal legislators invading the campus en masse for solemn investigation of deliberation is the kind of tragic farce we can do without. And the idea of state legislators or Congressmen trying to impose educational reforms by legislation is as fantastic as it is horrifying. Still, the fact remains that there is a genuine "public interest" at issue here, and there is no one except government who can be asked to defend it. Fortunately, I believe that for once we are in luck, in that the particular circumstances of the moment permit government to act in an indirect, noncoercive, prudent, yet possibly effective way.

The first such particular circumstance is the fact that the very idea of "higher education" has become so devoid of specific meaning that there is little danger of government, or anyone else, imposing some

[3] Jacques Barzun, in his recently published "The American University," points out that it has long been common in many universities for students, at the end of a course, to hand in written critiques of its form and substance. He also points out that, if one surveys these critiques over a period of time, one discovers that the most recent will be demanding a return to what was rejected by students only a few years back.

kind of orthodox straitjacket on the prevailing chaos. There just aren't any such orthodoxies available. Indeed, the very reason we have a crisis in the universities is because all such traditional notions about the function and ends of higher education have, during these past three decades, become otiose.

The real problem at the moment is that no one — not the faculty, not the administration, not the students — has any kind of clear idea of what any "institution of higher learning" is supposed to be accomplishing. It is even beginning to be suspected by many that such phrases as "the university" or "higher education" have acquired different and contradictory meanings, that the vast number of young people now moving onto the campuses are too diverse in their interests and talents to be contained within the old category of "university students," and that the root cause of our distemper is our failure to sort out all these meanings and people, and to make suitable institutional adjustments.

In other words, the situation seems to be such that what we need is a huge injection of pluralism into an educational system that has, through the working out of natural forces, become homogeneous and meaningless at the same time. No one can presume to say what the future pattern of higher education in America should look like. Not until we have far more experimentation — not until we have tried out different kinds of "universities" for different kinds of "students" — can we even hope to know what the real options are. In the ordinary course of events the prospects for this kind of pluralism would be so dim as to be utopian: none of the existing institutions can be counted on to cooperate except in a ritualistic and rather hypocritical way. But this leads me to the second "particular circumstance," which gives the prospect an honest dimension of reality.

This second particular circumstance is the fact that government — especially the Federal Government — is going to be pouring more and more money into the universities. This is inevitable, and I am willing to persuade myself that it is desirable. But it is neither inevitable nor desirable that the money should flow through the conventional channels — i.e., directly from the public treasury to the bursar's office. Understandably enough, college presidents cannot imagine it proceeding otherwise — higher education is "their" province, and they feel strongly that the money should be "theirs" to expend as administrative discretion and wisdom prescribe.

But the citizens of this republic have a claim to assert that higher education is "their" province, too; and they have a right to insist that public monies be expended in such a manner as might overcome the crisis in our universities, instead of deepening it.

What I would therefore like to see — and the idea is one that is slowly gaining favor with many observers; it is not original with me — is something along these lines: (a) State expenditures for higher public education should be frozen at the present level, and all increases in this budget should take the form of loans to qualifying students — these loans being valid for out-of-state institutions as well as in-state ones[4]; (b) Federal grants to institutions of higher learning (excepting research grants) should be slowly phased out entirely, and this money — together with new appropriations, which are to be expected — should also be replaced by loans to the qualifying student. This means, in brief, that our universities should have a minimum of direct access to public funds to spend as they see fit, since their vision in this matter has turned out to be too imperfect. It also means that students will have more of the only kind of "student power" that counts: the freedom to purchase the kind of education they want, on terms acceptable to them.

There are potential benefits and risks attendant on this proposal, and they merit a listing. But, first, one must face the frequently heard objection to student loans — that their repayment may place too great a burden on a student, especially the student from a poor family, after his graduation. This objection can be surmounted. To begin with, not all students would need loans, and many would need only small ones. There are plenty of well-to-do parents who would still want to pay for their children's education. In addition, repayment plans can be — have been — calculated so as to be proportionate to the student's average income during his working life, and to exempt those whose average income would be below a fixed level; and the burden on both student and taxpayer (for a subsidy would still be necessary, especially for women) could be made perfectly tolerable.

If one wished to be more egalitarian, one could augment a loan program with a part-scholarship program for those from low-income families. When all is said and done, however, the university graduate

---

[4] Ideally, the entire state budget for higher education should, in my opinion, take the form of student loans. But so radical a measure has little chance of getting through — the state universities would lobby it to death. Besides, so radical a measure is not really necessary. With a ceiling on their budgets and with inevitably increasing costs, the state universities will be constrained gradually to compete for students in terms of the education they offer, as against the low fees they charge, and their position will become a little less privileged with every passing year.

is the prime beneficiary, in dollars and cents, of his education; he ought to be the prime taxpayer for it. There is no such thing as "free" higher education. Someone is paying for it and, as things now stand, it is the working class of this country that is paying taxes to send the sons and daughters of the middle class — and of the wealthy, too — through state colleges. (Some 60 per cent of the students at Berkeley come from families with incomes of over $12,000.) It is not an easily defensible state of affairs, though we are now so accustomed to it that it seems the only "natural" one.

Now, as to benefits and risks:

[1] A possible benefit that might realistically be expected is that college students would take a more serious and responsible view of their reasons for being on the campus. To the extent that they would disrupt their own education, they would be paying for this out of their own pockets. As a consequence, there would certainly be less casual or playful or faddish disruption. One does get the impression that for many students the university is now, like the elementary and high schools, a place of compulsory attendance, and that the occupation of a campus building is a welcome lark and frolic. If these students were called upon to pay for their frolics, some of them at least might go back to swallowing goldfish. This would be bad for the goldfish but good for the rest of us.

[2] Another potential benefit is that the large state universities, denied the subsidy which permits them to set very low tuition rates for state residents, would find it difficult to grow larger than they are; the college population would probably become more widely distributed, with the smaller and medium-sized institutions in a position to attract more students. This would be a good thing. It is clearly foolish to assemble huge and potentially riotous mobs in one place — and to provide them with room, board, a newspaper, and perhaps a radio station to boot. This violates the basic principles of riot control. We should aim at the "scatteration" of the student population, so as to decrease their capacity to cause significant trouble. I would also argue there are likely to be some educational gains from this process.

[3] An obvious risk is that a great many of the radical and dissenting students would use their money to attend newly founded "anti-universities." And many of the black students would veer off into black nationalist institutions of higher learning. Something like this is bound to happen, I suppose, though to what extent is unpredictable. It would,

beyond question, create bad publicity for the whole student loan program. On the other hand, it would take the pressure off existing institutions to be both universities and "anti-universities" — as well as "integrated" and "black nationalist" universities — at the same time. The degree to which such pressure has already been effective would shock parents, state legislators, and public opinion generally, were the facts more widely known.

Quite a few of our universities have already decided that the only way to avoid on-campus riots is to give students academic credit for off-campus rioting ("field work" in the ghettos, among migrant workers, etc.). And at Harvard — of all places! — there is now a course (Social Relations 148), which enrolls several hundred students and is given for credit, whose curriculum is devised by the S.D.S., whose classes are taught by S.D.S. sympathizers, and whose avowed aim is "radicalization" of the students.

[4] As a corollary to this last risk, there is the possibility that more new, "good" (in my sense of that term) colleges would also be founded. I'm not too sanguine about this — a fair portion of the academic community would surely look more benevolently on a new college whose curriculum made ample provision for instruction in the theory of guerrilla warfare than one that made a knowledge of classical political philosophy compulsory. Besides, it would be much easier to find "qualified" faculty for the first type than the second. Nevertheless, it is conceivable that the "traditionalists," as well as the academic hipsters, could take advantage of the new state of affairs. And among the students they attract there might be quite a few blacks who are not really interested in studying Swahili or Afro-American culture or "black economics," but who — as things are now moving on the campus — are pretty much forced to do so by their black nationalist fellow students.

[5] The greatest benefit of all, however, is that the new mode of financing higher education will "shake things up." Both university administrators and faculty will have to think seriously about the education of the students — and about their own professional integrity as teachers. This shake-up is bound to have both bad and good consequences. Some universities, for instance, will simply try to reckon how they can best pander to what they take to be student sentiment, and many professors will doubtless pay undue attention to their "popularity" among students. On the other hand, it is reasonable to assume that you can't fool all the students — and their parents — all of the

time; and if students are paying for their education, most of them will want to be getting their money's worth.

So, at long last, the academic community, and the rest of us as well, will have to engage in sober self-examination, and address ourselves to such questions as: What *is* this "college" of ours, or this "university" of ours? What *is* the "higher education" we offer? What do we parents expect from a particular "institution of higher learning" when we send our children there? The answers will certainly be too various to be pleasing to everyone. But at least they will be authentic answers, representing authentic choices.

It would be ridiculous to expect that, during this period of "shake-up," calm will descend upon our campuses. As I have already said, the roots of the student rebellion go very deep, and very far back. I recall Leo Rosten observing long before Columbia that, so far as he could see, what the dissatisfied students were looking for were: adults — adults to confront, to oppose, to emulate.

It is not going to be easy to satisfy this quest, since our culture for many decades now has been ploughing under its adults. But I agree with Mr. Rosten that this is what is wanted, and I am certain it will not be achieved until our institutions of higher education reach some kind of common understanding on what kind of adult a young man is ideally supposed to become. This understanding — involving a scrutiny of the values of our civilization — will not come soon or easily, if it ever comes at all. But we must begin to move toward it — and the first step, paradoxically, is to allow a variety of meanings to emerge from our existing, petrified institutions of higher learning.

campus confusion

TO THE EDITOR:

Kudos for Irving Kristol and his amusing lampoon of "old-time" education, "A Different Way to Restructure the University," Dec. 8. Kristol effectively impersonates a cryptopopulist demi-intellectual who suddenly emerges, unbidden and unqualified, from an off-campus trade to pronounce judgment on academia. His pretended alarm over the imminent anarchization of Columbia, Berkeley and Harvard has just the right mixture of misinformation and unction to make it true to life. The crocodilian concern with the lower classes and their subsidy of middle-class students (who are fighting to extend such subsidies to lower-class children) is authentic "old-time" common sense at the zenith of coherence. There are many fine touches like this throughout the piece.

More the pity, therefore, that Kristol's ending is too wildly hilarious to be credible. No doubt there are many friends of academia who advocate longer jail sentences, summary expulsion and the draft as cures for campus unrest. But most readers will just be confused when it comes to the idea that the way to stop the student movement is to raise tuition and force the kids to mortgage themselves for the rest of their lives. Kristol's attempt to pass this off as a rather common suggestion for which he claims no credit is highly unconvincing. It is hard to believe that there is more than one Strangelove in the universe who would say: "We'll teach 'em the value of education. No more getting off with bloody heads and jail sentences. Wait till they see how much this is going to cost them per month after they graduate. So learn, baby, learn!" Kristol's imagination seems to have gotten just a little out of control. After all, it doesn't require very much innuendo to get people to realize that the establishment intellectuals, whom the students properly hold in greatest contempt, are those who measure the quality of education by its value in the market place.

MARVIN HARRIS
Professor of Anthropology
Columbia University, New York

TO THE EDITOR:

Irving Kristol's comments on the university are amusing, but his own "ideal solution" — to channel all public funds for education into student loans — is laughably naive.

What sustains his hope that "universities will be constrained gradually to compete for students *in terms of the education they offer*"? More likely, students will be cynical (or realistic?) enough to decide that they are paying not for an education, but for a diploma, and they will go comparison shopping accordingly.

The resulting economic pressure on the university will have to be relieved in one of two ways: (1) lowering the cost of the product, or (2) lowering the quality of the product.

The first must lead to efficiency measures of the Beardsley Ruml variety. Assembly-line techniques are fine for making cars or television sets, but whatever a university may be, it is *not* a factory.

The second is even more disastrous. It may not turn Harvard into a diploma mill, but it will certainly erode the educational demands which any but the most prestigious universities will be able to make upon its students.

Consumer control is probably the best way to get the most for the least in the supermarket. Surely the events of the past years are hard evidence that it is singularly inappropriate in the classroom.

DR. CURT W. BECK
Professor of Chemistry
Vassar College, Poughkeepsie, New York

TO THE EDITOR:

I found myself in surprising agreement with much of Irving Kristol's analysis of the malaise on college campuses, but I also found some of his arguments wholly untenable.

In trying to please everyone, a college — which has sadly limited resources — is doomed to failure. The preaching of high ideals (usually by administrators) is offset by the practices of everyday college administration. A college president who is trying to raise money (a good and necessary thing to be done) sounds like a fool when he tries to defend R.O.T.C. and free contemplative inquiry in the same breath. That may be good fund-raising; it is rotten educational leadership. It is piteously soulless.

What annoys me about Mr. Kristol's article, though, is his apparent belief that order (as in "law and order") is the essential foundation stone of our society and of higher education. In fact, it is only when order prevails that incompetent administrators can hold onto real power. What is wrong with a curriculum that fluctuates frequently? What is wrong with teaching the views of S.D.S. in the hallowed halls of Harvard (of all places)?

As someone who has never rioted and never been a member of a mob, I resent Mr. Kristol's insinuation that what happened at Columbia can be equated with the goldfish swallowing of an earlier generation. Perhaps it is because we really are more intelligent, more mature, more concerned, and more upset about soullessness that Mr. Kristol and others hate our generation. Perhaps it is his basic lack of sensitivity. Having one's head busted by Mr. Kristol's defenders of order is not a lark. It is a desperate attempt to awaken those who run our soulless institutions that time is running short. If Mr. Kristol could draw the conclusions he did from the evidence he cited, it is too late for him. But perhaps for others it is not.

ROBERT E. FEIR
Bucknell, 1969
Lewisburg, Pennsylvania

The Author Replies:

"It seems to be very difficult for some people — even some professors of anthropology — to understand that there is no such thing as 'free' higher education. Someone has to pay for it. Professor Harris resists the idea that college students should, in effect, take a mortgage on a portion of their future income in order to pay for their education. But he apparently sees nothing wrong with the present situation, in which those taxpayers who have not gone to college mortgage *their* modest earnings to pay (in taxes) for the college education of others — these others usually coming from families with above-average incomes.

"Professor Beck assumes that, if college students are free to shop around for the kind of higher education they prefer, they will all opt for the cheapest and easiest degree. I'm sure that *some* will — just as they do now. But a 'cheap' degree will not — and does not — have either the same market value or the same intellectual value as a 'good' degree which has been truly earned. College students understand this perfectly well, and I would expect them to buy the college education that best suits their ambitions and talents.

"There is nothing wrong with teaching the views of S.D.S., at Harvard or anywhere else. I do think it wrong, however, to turn over a course to S.D.S., or to any other private group on the campus. This may buy a temporary respite from organized 'confrontation,' but it cheapens the academic value of the degree and is unfair to the majority of students. On the other hand, I have no objection whatsoever to S.D.S. starting its own college and to permitting students to obtain government loans if they wish to pay tuition to study there. What a degree from such a college could be worth is, of course, another question — and one that prospective students would have to contemplate."

TO THE EDITOR:

If Irving Kristol were actively engaged in teaching, he should have been able to answer most of the questions he poses. For example, he alludes to the number of students with high I.Q.'s who turn from academics to revolution. Has he ever wondered why gifted students would seek to destroy the only structure that offers them a temporary solace from a society that loathes the exceptional? In speaking with a number of such students, I have noted a frighteningly consistent educational pattern.

They are, for the most part, brilliant but undisciplined — highly articulate on matters they consider "relevant" (Vietnam, civil rights, sex), but the passion with which they speak dissipates on paper into tortured fragments conveying all the elegance of a telegram. In sociology and political science they excel; in languages and literature prior to 1960 they exhibit a Neanderthal apathy. And why?

In grammar school, many of them were never taught the parts of speech formally, but rather were exposed immediately to block paragraphs with the idea that they would learn the grammar "inductively." Consequently, they cannot distinguish adverbs from adjectives or "there" from "their" (the relative pronoun is *terra incognita* to most). They learned foreign languages from overhead projectors, transparencies, and the aural-oral method which taught them to say, "I want to go to the bathroom" in French and Spanish but never to translate the first sentence of "Les Misérables" or "Don Quixote."

In high school, they were given teachers who discreetly skirted a curriculum that required ancient history and moved as rapidly as possible to contemporary problems, with the genuine conviction that "the student is more interested in the present than the past." "Wuthering Heights" and "Pride and Prejudice" were bypassed in an effort to get to "Lord of the Flies" and "The Fall." The high-school student identifies the teacher with his material; if the teacher requires "Another Country" and uses Beatles records to explain prosody, he is a swinger, not a square. But what these students never realize is that they have been used by their teachers, who have relied on the oldest device in the profession to gain a class's acceptance—catering to adolescent immaturity by being immature themselves.

Thus, young people nurtured on the present come to a college that requires written expression, memorization and a foundation in the past. Of course their frustration grows when they are confronted with works like "The Republic" and "Utopia" which must be read slowly and digested; anyone would resent studying the grammar of a foreign language when he does not even know his own, although he presumably studied it for twelve years. But then for 12 years he was also told that understanding is far superior to the baser faculty of memory. Compared to Golding, Dickens is irrelevant and Homer passé.

Academic revolution stems from frustration and resentment. Who would not want a continuation of a high-school curriculum that pandered to every conceivable student urge — relevance, contemporaneity and the burial of the past? And who would not want to destroy the institution that destroys the dream?

BERNARD F. DICK
Chairman, Classics Department
Iona College, New Rochelle, New York

DeVERE E. PENTONY
the case for black studies

The history of the development of various American groups into an
integrated culture is a complex story, but there is one simple fact that
seems germane to the problems of black-white integration in the United
States. This obvious fact is that almost every immigrant group with the
major exception of the blacks came to these shores because they wanted
to come. America was to be the land of opportunity, the land where
the rigidities for social mobility would be relaxed, and the land where
a man could be free. That these expectations were not quickly fulfilled
is a cloudy part of the political and social history of the United States,
but in retrospect the members of most of these groups, the Irish, the
Germans, the Dutch, the Scotch, the Italians now view the story of their
ethnic past in the United States as a reasonably successful one.

No similar memories have been available to the black man and
woman. Brought to this country in chains, torn from family and tribal
past, physically and psychologically enslaved, taught by lash and
example to be subservient, forced to suffer indignities to their basic
humanity, and instantly categorized by the accident of color, black
people have all too often found the American dream a nightmare.
Instead of joining the dominant culture, many have learned to exist in
the psychologically bewildering atmosphere neither slave nor free.
That they have survived at all is tribute to their magnificent resiliency
and basic toughness; but that some carry with them a heavy baggage
of hate and rage is not surprising.

While many whites in America have congratulated themselves upon
the progress toward freedom and equality that has recently been made,
a number of black intellectuals are eloquently questioning whether,
indeed, meaningful progress has been made. Perhaps blacks are all too
familiar with the ability of white people to dash black hopes for
freedom and dignity on rocks of intransigence and patience. Witness
the rise and fall of hope in the story of black men in America: in the
aftermath of the Civil War they were told that they were freed from
slavery only to find that they were not free — not free to be treated as
individuals, not free to eat, or sleep, or live, or go to school, or drink
from the same fountain, or ride the same conveyance, or enjoy the same

political and economic privileges as people of "white" skin. And when in the twentieth century they had their hopes raised by long overdue court decisions and civil rights legislation finally demanding integration, these hopes were once again shattered as blacks found that significant segments of the white culture often lagged far behind the basic justice of these acts.

This has led some of the black community to question whether integration was not just another scheme to preserve the dominance of the whites, seducing blacks to give up their black identities and to copy the speech, manner, hair, dress, and style of the whites, and to accept the myths, heroes, and historical judgment of white America without reciprocity or without appreciation of, or respect for, black experience. Moreover, this estimate has been coupled with the hunch that in any significant way, only the "talented tenth" of the black community could really hope to overcome the monetary, social, and psychological barriers to true integration with whites. The remaining 90 percent would, therefore, be left in poverty and psychological degradation, doomed to an almost motiveless, hopeless existence, forever on the dole, forever caught in hate of self and of others. Thus has been posed a transcendent dilemma for the black man and woman: to succeed in the white world is to fail, to overcome the outrageous obstacles thrown in their way by white society seems partially to deny their black experience. Above all, to integrate on an individual basis in a society that makes this increasingly possible for the fortunate may well mean an exodus of the talented tenth from the black community, with the consequent decimation of the ranks of potential leaders whose commitment to the whole community could help set their people free.

Seen in this light, the demand for black studies is a call for black leadership. The argument is that if there is to be an exodus from the land of physical and psychological bondage, an informed and dedicated leadership is needed to help bring about individual and group pride and a sense of cohesive community. To accomplish this, black people, like all people, need to know that they are not alone. They need to know that their ancestors were not just slaves laboring under the white man's sun but that their lineage can be traced to important kingdoms and significant civilizations. They need to be familiar with the black man's contribution to the arts and sciences. They need to know of black heroes and of the noble deeds of black men. They need to know that black, too, is beautiful, and that under the African sky people are at proud ease with their blackness. In historical perspective they need to know the whole story of white oppression and of the struggles of some blacks, and some whites too, to overcome that oppression. They need to find sympathetic encouragement to move successfully into the socio-economic arenas of American life.

To help fulfill all these needs, the contention is, a black studies effort must be launched. At the beginning, it must be staffed by black faculty, who must have the time and resources to prepare a solid curriculum for college students and to get the new knowledge and new perspectives into the community as quickly as possible. In a situation somewhat similar to the tremendous efforts at adult education in some of the less developed societies, the advocates of black studies press to get on with the urgent tasks.

It is in this context that a basic challenge is made to many of the traditional values of the college or university. Important critical questions arise: Will black studies be merely an exchange of old lies for new myths? Is it the work of the college to provide an ideological underpinning for social movement? Will the traditional search for the truth be subordinated to the goal of building a particular group identity? Is the ideal of the brotherhood of all men to be sacrificed to the brotherhood of some men and the hatred of others? Can the college teach group solidarity for some groups and not for others? Will the results of separatist studies be a heightening of group tensions and a reactive enlarging of the forces of racism? Will standards of excellence for students and faculty alike be cast aside in the interest of meeting student and community needs? Will anti-intellectualism run rampant? Will constitutional and other legal provisions be violated by this new version of "separate if not equal"?

A REMEDY FOR WHITE STUDIES

It seems clear that the advocates of a black studies program see it as a remedy for "white studies" programs that they have been subjected to all their lives and as a way to bring pride, dignity, and community to black people. They are questioning the relevance of the style and content of education designed to meet the needs and expectations of the dominant white culture, and some seem to be suggesting that the lifestyles and ways of perceiving the world in much of the black community are sufficiently different to justify a new, almost bicultural approach to educating the members of the community who are at once a part of, yet apart from, the general American culture. While they hope that this effort will range over the whole educational experience from childhood through adulthood, they seem to view the college or university as the place where talents can be gathered and resources mobilized to provide intellectual leadership and academic respectability to their efforts. The college is to be the place for the writing of books, the providing of information, and the training of students to help with the critical tasks. It is to be one of the testing grounds for the idea that black people need to have control of their own destiny.

But what of the outcome? There is obvious concern that efforts to focus on blackness as one of the answers to white racism will result in an equally virulent black racism. Black "nationalism," with its glorifying of the black ingroup, may have powerful meaning only when it focuses on the hate object of whiteness. Indeed, it is painfully true that whites through their words and deeds over many generations have provided the black nationalists with all the bitter evidence they need for building a negative nationalism based mainly on hatred and rage. Thus we should expect that a significant ingredient in constructing black unity and group dignity would be an antiwhiteness.

Increasingly, the black intellectual is drawing a colonial analogy to the situation of the black community in the United States. Like people in the colonized lands of Asia, Africa, and Latin America, some black men look at their rather systematic exclusion from first-class citizenship in the United States as a close parallel to the exploitation and subjugation perpetrated by those who shouldered the "white man's burden" during the high tide of imperialism. Thus the focus on black culture and black history is to prepare the black community to be as free and proud as anyone in the newly emerging states. And the outcome of that may be the growth of the self-confidence and sense of personal dignity that pave the way for an easier integration into a common culture on the basis of feelings of real equality.

While it would be foolish to deny that ugly and self-defeating racism may be the fruits of the black studies movement, we should not forget that a sense of deep compassion and intense concern for all humanity has often shone through the rage and hate of such prophets of the movement as Malcolm X, Stokely Carmichael, and W. E. B. Dubois. Whether that hopeful strain of compassion and human concern will gain the upper hand in the days that lie ahead may well depend on the degree of understanding and tenderness with which the white community is able to react to these efforts.

There is the possibility that an emphasis on blackness, black dignity, black contributions, and black history will provide whites with new perspectives about the black man and woman. In turn, these new perspectives may indicate what clues of behavior and guides to proper responsiveness are necessary to enable whites to relate to blacks in something other than a patronizing or deprecating fashion. Through black studies there may be opportunities for whites to enrich their understanding of the black man and thus, perhaps, to help build more meaningful bridges of mutual respect and obligation. Moreover, if the truth can make blacks free and open, it may also free the whites from their ignorant stereotypes of the black man and his culture. Unfortunately, it may also be possible for those who teach black studies to reinforce those stereotypes by aping the worst features of the white society and becoming merely a mirror image of that aspect of white society that is insensitive and inhuman.

STANDARDS AND SCHOLARSHIP

Will accepted standards and scholarship be maintained in the black studies program? When any new program is proposed, a question of this sort is certainly appropriate for members of the academic community. However, it is an extremely difficult one to answer for a black studies program or for any other new program. All that can be safely said is that the pressures for respectable scholarly performance and for recognized achievements will be at least as great for black studies as for any other new programs.

In the performance and evaluation of students, we can probably expect the same ferment over learning, grading, and evaluative practices that perturbs the rest of the academic world. But academicians who are pushing the black studies idea give no indication that they will be content with a half-hearted, sloppy, shoddy intellectual effort on the part of themselves or their students. Indeed, one of the underlying assumptions of black studies seems to be that students who become involved in it will become highly motivated toward academic success not only in black studies but in the rest of the curriculum as well. Out of the black studies experience are to come black students, committed, socially aware, ambitious, devoted to the welfare of black people, and equipped for helping the black community assume its rightful place in American society. These are high ambitions which are not likely to be fulfilled immediately by a black studies program, but which deserve to be given the same benefit of doubt and the same opportunities for growth by trial and error that most new programs are given.

Will black studies scholars manipulate data, bias their studies, and create towering myths which bear little resemblance to the shifting realities of human existence? The answer is difficult to assess.

In one respect the quest for pristine outside objectivity may miss the point. A distinguished philosopher has argued that the search for intergroup accommodation must be based upon what he terms the discovery of the normative inner order — that is, the values, assumptions, and world views or images of various societies or cultures. It may be that one of the most important roles that the black scholar can play is to share in the discovery and articulation of this normative inner order of the black community, with the possible result of improving the chances for mutually beneficial black-white interaction.

In this process we should expect that there will be black professors who profess a certain "ideology" just as white professors do. We can even expect a case for racial superiority of blacks, but surely this is not a reason for opposing black studies. To do so on those grounds would be analogous to opposing the teaching of biology because a certain biologist has attempted to make a case for a black inferiority based on some of his genetic investigations, or of economics because certain economists continue to adhere to pre-Keynesian economic principles.

Moreover, the ideology argument may mean no more than that black scholars will attempt to emphasize common assumptions about American society from the perspective of the black experience. But this kind of "indoctrination" is not essentially different from what is found, for example, in many college textbooks in American government which rest on some value-laden assumptions about the American political system. A more serious charge would be that black professors may insist that their students follow some "party line" as they examine the various facets of the black situation. But students are not as gullible as we sometimes imagine and are generally quite capable of resisting efforts at indoctrination.

Closely allied to the questions of standards and scholarship are questions of curriculum. What is an appropriate beginning curriculum for a black studies effort? The unspoken consensus seems to be that an area studies program should dig as deeply as possible into the history, the culture, the language, the politics, the economics, the geography, the literature, the arts, the life-styles, and the world views of the people in the area concerned. How this is all put together in a way that students will understand and benefit from is a significant organizing problem for all area studies programs, including black studies. But it would be foolish to expect those problems to be creatively attacked before a working faculty is on the scene. The first efforts to establish a satisfactory curriculum in black studies will be experimental in many ways and as such subject to more rapid change than our established curricula.

ARE BLACK STUDIES LEGAL AND PROPER?

The question of legality of a black studies program requires examination. Like the closely related area studies program, the curriculum would seem to face no legal questions from federal or state law. However, it is in the realm of staffing and student access that the most serious questions arise. For example, can tests of color be applied for hiring faculty members in the black studies program? Posed in this sharp way, the answer to the question is probably no. The equal protection of the laws section of the United States Constitution and various state legal requirements about nondiscrimination in employment could very likely be interpreted to preclude the hiring of faculty simply because they are black. However, if the qualifications for hiring are put on a broader experiential basis than color alone, then the questions and answers may change. Already factors of ethnic background and experience play a role in hiring at the colleges and universities in the United States. While this is particularly obvious in the hiring of teachers in foreign languages and literature — note, for example, the number of people teaching Chinese language and literature who are Chinese — ethnic background has often been considered in other aspects of area studies and other programs from the Peace Corps to social work.

The question of hiring black faculty is probably not a legal question at all. Rather the critical focal point for the black studies program would seem to be, on the one hand, whether the particular experiences gained from a black ethnic background tend to make the faculty member a better scholar and teacher or, on the other hand, whether the ethnic emotional involvement will permit a useful scholarly detachment in the evaluation and presentation of data. Completely satisfactory answers to this dilemma are not likely to be found. A short-run solution to the dilemma may rest on the ability of black studies programs to attract black faculty with a passion for the truth as well as an emotional identification with the subject of blackness, and on the certainty that nonblack scholars will continue to view, comment upon, and analyze the black experience in various parts of the academic community. Enough flexibility and openness should exist for students majoring in black studies to encounter the views of nonblack scholars. Similarly, the educational experiences of the rest of the academic community would undoubtedly be enriched by the participation of black studies faculty in the general intellectual life of the college. It would be tragic if the black studies faculty were to be prevented from commentary on the general questions of man in society by their own preoccupation with black studies. Few would argue that the infusion of an increasing number of black faculty into the academic community is not desirable. The black studies program would speed the process and provide the black community with incentives and opportunities for greater partici- pation in the education of youth. The institutions of higher education cannot rely on narrow legal interpretation and conventional dogmas as trustworthy guidelines to hiring faculty in programs like black studies.

A second serious question about the legality of the black studies program is the question of student access to it. Can an academic institution worthy of the name deny access to any of its academic programs on the basis of color or ethnic background? The answer is no. Here the legal answer and the moral answer would seem to reinforce one another. If one of the purposes of the black studies program is to tell it as it really is, then the message should go out to students regard- less of color even though it is likely to have a particular additional value to the black student. The college cannot be a place where knowledge is developed and subjects taught in semi-secret. Just as any college contracting to the government for secret research would be open to serious charges of violation of the traditional ethics of scholar- ship, so would any academic program that excluded students solely on the basis of ethnic background raise serious questions of propriety and legality.

However, even in this connection a dilemma remains. As anyone who has participated in an area program in a Peace Corps training effort knows, the things that can be easily said about one's own culture and about another culture tend to be modified when there are members of another culture in attendance. It seems to become more difficult to tell it "as it really is" or at least as it "really is perceived" when the outsiders are in. This is a significant problem that will have to be faced by the black studies program. The fortunate thing about many of those who are advocating black studies is that they want to tell it as it really is to anyone who will listen. They have been shielding their feelings, perceptions, and analyses so long that it will probably be refreshing for them to speak honestly with non-black students as well as blacks. Nonetheless, they may feel that the first efforts to get their programs established will be so overrun by well-meaning whites anxious to gain new perspectives that black students will not have access to the courses.

In practice, the problem may not be so great, especially since courses about various ethnic communities will continue to be offered in the existing departments, with even the possibility of exchange of faculty on occasion. Nonetheless, the colleges must make every effort within the budgetary limitations imposed upon them to accommodate as many students as possible. No black student who enters the college should be denied an opportunity to take black studies courses; neither, of course, should he be forced to do so. In this connection, the attractiveness of the course offerings to whites as well as blacks may be important in the effort to sustain enrollments in a fledgling program, and thus help provide the necessary resources which are closely tied to the level of student demand for courses. So the question of student access seems to be not so much a question of legality as of the availability of faculty and other resources.

A sometime country lawyer once said: "The dogmas of the quiet past are inadequate to the stormy present. The occasion is piled high with difficulty, and we must rise to the occasion. As our case is new, so we must think anew and act anew. We must disenthrall ourselves, and then we shall save the country" (Abraham Lincoln). The time is now for higher education to show that it can disenthrall itself and become relevant to the problems of social change highlighted by the call for black studies. If a black studies program serves only to awaken whites to the desperate need to change themselves, it will have been worth the effort.

EUGENE D. GENOVESE
black studies: trouble ahead

No problem so agitates the campuses today as that posed by the growing pressure for black studies programs and departments. The agitation presents special dangers since it can be, and sometimes is, opportunistically manipulated by the nihilist factions of the radical white student movement. For the most part, black students have shown considerable restraint in dealing with dubious white allies and have given strong indication of being much more interested in reforming the universities than in burning them down. The black student movement, like some parts of the white radical student movement and very much unlike others, represents an authentic effort by young people to take a leading role in the liberation of an oppressed people and, as such, exhibits impressive seriousness and developing sophistication. The political forms that the agitation takes and the deep frustrations from which it stems nonetheless open the way to reckless elements among black, as well as white, student militants.

The universities must now choose between three courses: a principled but flexible response to legitimate black demands; a dogmatic, repressive adherence to traditional, liberal, and essentially racist policies; and a cowardly surrender to all black demands, no matter how destructive to the university as an institution of higher learning or to American and Afro-American society in general. This last option, which has been taken in a notable number of places, ironically reflects as much racism in its assumptions and implications as the second, and it takes little skill in prophecy to realize that its conclusion will be a bloodbath in which blacks are once again the chief victims. Yet, the debate over black studies proceeds without attention to the major features of the alternatives; it proceeds, in fact, in a manner that suggests the very paternalistic white racism against which so many blacks are today protesting.

The demand for black studies and for special black studies departments needs no elaborate explanation or defense. It rests on an awareness of the unique and dual nature of the black experience in the United States. Unlike European immigrants, blacks came here involuntarily, were enslaved and excluded from access to the mainstream of

American life, and as a result have had a special history with a profoundly national-cultural dimension. Unlike, say, Italo-Americans, Afro-Americans have within their history the elements of a distinct nationality at the same time that they have participated in and contributed immensely to a common American nationality. Despite the efforts of many black and some white scholars, this paradoxical experience has yet to be explored with the respect and intellectual rigor it deserves.

This essential justification for black studies, incidentally, raises serious questions about the demands by white radicals for "ethnic studies" and for special attention to people from the "third world," especially since the term "third world" is, from a Marxist and revolutionary point of view, a reactionary swindle. These demands, when sincere, have their origin in a proper concern for the fate of Mexican-Americans, Puerto Ricans, Asians, and other ethnic groups in a white-racist culture, but the study of the attendant problems does not, at least on the face of it, require anything like an approach similar to that of black studies. For the most part, the discrimination against these groups is largely a class question, requiring sober analysis of class structure in America; for the rest, much of the racism directed against these minorities can be traced directly to the by-products of the enslavement of blacks by whites and the ideology derived therefrom. In any case, the issues are clearly different, for the black question is simultaneously one of class and nationality (not merely minority ethnic status), and it is therefore a disservice to the cause of black liberation to construct a politically opportunist equation that can only blur the unique and central quality of the black experience in the United States.

The duality of the black experience haunts the present debate and leads us immediately into a consideration of the ideological and political features of the black studies programs. It is, at best, irrelevant to argue, as DeVere E. Pentony does in the April, 1969, issue of the *Atlantic*, that all professors of history and social science bring a particular ideology and politics to their classroom and that a black ideological bias is no worse than any other. There is no such thing as a black ideology or a black point of view. Rather there are various black-nationalist biases, from left-wing versions such as that of the Panthers to right-wing versions such as that of Ron Karenga and other "cultural nationalists." There are also authentic sections of the black community that retain conservative, liberal, or radical integrationist and anti-nationalist positions. Both integrationist and separatist tendencies can be militant or moderate, radical or conservative (in the sense generally applied to white politics in relation to social questions). The separatists are riding high today, and the integrationists are beating a retreat; but this has happened before and may be reversed tomorrow.

All these elements have a right to participate in the exploration of black historical and cultural themes. In one sense, the whole point of black studies programs in a liberal arts college or university ought to be to provide for the widest and most vigorous exchange among all these groups in an atmosphere of free discussion and mutual toleration. The demand for an exclusively black faculty and especially the reactionary demand for student control of autonomous departments must be understood as demands for the introduction of specific ideological and political criteria into the selection of faculty and the composition of programs. Far from being proposals to relate these programs to the black community, they are in fact factionally based proposals to relate them to one or another political tendency within the black community and to exclude others. The bloody, but by no means isolated, feud between black student factions on the UCLA campus ought to make that clear.

One of the new hallmarks of white racism is the notion of one black voice, one black experience, one black political community, one black ideology — of a black community without an authentic inner political life wracked by dissension and ideological struggle. In plain truth, what appears on the campuses as "what the blacks want" is almost invariably what the dominant faction in a particular black caucus wants. Like all people who fight for liberation, blacks are learning the value of organizational discipline and subordination to a firm and united line of action. Sometimes, the formulation of particular demands and actions has much less to do with their intrinsic merits or with the institution under fire than with the momentary balance in the struggle for power within the caucus itself. This discipline presents nothing unprincipled or sinister, but it does present difficult and painful problems, which must be evaluated independently by those charged with institutional and political responsibility in the white community.

The pseudo-revolutionary middle-class totalitarians who constitute one temporarily powerful wing of the left-wing student movement understand this dimension, even if few others seem to. Accordingly, they support demands for student control as an entering wedge for a general political purge of faculties, a purge they naïvely hope to dominate. These suburban putschists are most unlikely to succeed in their stated objectives of purging "reactionaries," for they are isolated, incoherent, and without adequate power. But they may very well help to re-establish the principle of the campus purge and thereby provide a moral and legal basis for a new wave of McCarthyism. The disgraceful treatment of Professors Staughton Lynd and Jesse Lemisch, among many who have been recently purged from universities by both liberal and right-wing pressure, has already set a tone of renewed repression, which some fanatical and unreasoning left-wing militants are unwittingly reinforcing. If black studies departments are permitted to become political bases and cadre-training schools for one or another political movement, the door will be open for the conversion of other departments to similar roles; that door is already being forced in some places.

Those blacks who speak in harsh nationalist accents in favor of all-black faculties, departmental autonomy, and student power open themselves to grave suspicions of bad faith. The most obvious objection, raised sharply by several outstanding black educators in the South, concerns the systematic raiding of black colleges by financially stronger white ones. The shortage of competent black specialists in black history, social science, and black culture is a matter of general knowledge and concern. Hence, the successful application of the all-black principle in most universities would spell the end of hopes to build one or more distinguished black universities to serve as a center for the training of a national Afro-American intelligentsia. One need not be partial to black nationalism in any of its varieties to respect the right of black people to self-determination, for this right flows directly from the duality of their unique experience in the United States. Even those who dislike or distrust black nationalism as such should be able to view the development of such centers of higher education as positive and healthy. If there is no place in the general American university for ideological homogeneity and conformity, there is a place in American society for universities based on adherence to a specific ideology, as the Catholic universities, for example, have demonstrated.

Responsible black scholars have been working hard for an end to raiding and to the scattering of the small number of black professors across the country. Among other obstacles, they face the effort of ostensibly nationalist black students who seek to justify their decision to attend predominantly white institutions, often of high prestige, by fighting for a larger black teaching staff. The outcome of these demands is the obscurantist nonsense that black studies can and should be taught by people without intellectual credentials since these credentials are "white" anyway. It is true that many black men are capable of teaching important college-level courses even though they do not have formal credentials. For example, the Afro-American tradition in music, embracing slave songs, spirituals, blues, jazz, and other forms, could probably be taught best by a considerable number of articulate and cultured, if sometimes self-taught, black musicians and free-lance critics who are largely unknown to the white community. But few good universities have ever refused to waive formalities in any field when genuine intellectual credentials of a nonacademic order could be provided. What has to be resisted firmly is the insanity that claims, as in one recent instance, that experience as a SNCC field organizer should be considered more important than a Ph.D. in the hiring of a professor of Afro-American history. This assertion represents a general contempt for all learning and a particular contempt for black studies as a field of study requiring disciplined, serious intellectual effort — an attitude that reflects the influence of white racism, even when brought forth by a black man.

The demand for all-black faculties rests on the insistence that only blacks can understand the black experience. This cant is nothing new: it forms the latest version of the battle cry of every reactionary nationalism and has clear antecedents, for example, in the nineteenth-century German Romantic movement. To be perfectly blunt, it now constitutes an ideologically fascist position and must be understood as such. The general reply to it — if one is necessary — is simply that the history of every people can only be written from within and without. But there is a specific reply too. However much the black presence has produced a unique and distinctly national Afro-American experience, it has also formed part of a broader, integrated national culture. It would be absurd to try to understand the history of, say, the South without carefully studying black history. Any Southern historian worth his salt must also be a historian of black America — and vice versa — and if so, it would be criminal to deny him an opportunity to teach his proper subject. Certainly, these remarks do not add up to an objection to a preference for black departmental directors and a numerical predominance of blacks on the faculty, if possible, for every people must write its own history and play the main role in the formation of its own intelligentsia and national culture. These measures would be justified simply on grounds of the need to establish relations of confidence with black students, for they involve no sacrifice of principle and do not compromise the integrity of the university. But preference and emphasis are one thing; monopoly and ideological exclusion are quite another.

We might mention here the problem of the alleged "psychological need" of black people to do this or that or to be this or that in order to reclaim their manhood, re-establish their ostensibly lost dignity, and God knows what else. There is a place for these questions in certain kinds of intellectual discussions and in certain political forums, but there is no place for these questions in the formation of university policy. In such a context they represent a benevolent paternalism that is neither more nor less than racist. Whites in general and university professors and administrators in particular are not required to show "sympathy," "compassion," "understanding," and other manifestations of liberal guilt feelings; they are required to take black demands seriously — to take them straight, on their merits. That is, they are required to treat political demands politically and to meet their responsibility to fight white racism while also meeting their responsibility to defend the integrity and dignity of the university community as a whole.

Only if the universities have a clear attitude toward themselves will they be able to fulfill their duty to the black community. Our universities, if they are to survive — and their survival is problematical — must redefine themselves as institutions of higher learning and firmly reject the role of cadre-training schools for government, business, or community organizations of any kind. Blame for the present crisis ought to be placed on those who, especially after World War II, opened the universities to the military, to big-business recruitment, to the "fight against Communism," to the CIA, and to numerous other rightist pressures. If Dow Chemical or ROTC belongs on a college campus, so does the Communist Party, the Black Panthers, the John Birch Society, the Campfire Girls, or the Mafia for that matter. Students have a clear political right to organize on campuses as Democrats, Republicans, Communists, Panthers, or whatever, provided their activities are appropriate to campus life, but the universities have no business making special institutional arrangements with this or that faction off campus and then putting down other factions as illicit. And government and business represent political intrusions quite as much as do political parties. The same is true for the anachronistic and absurd practice of having American universities controlled by boards of trustees instead of by their faculties in consultation with the students. In short, the black studies question, like the black revolt as a whole, has raised all the fundamental problems of class power in American life, and the solutions will have to run deep into the structure of the institutions themselves.

What the universities owe to black America is what they owe to white America: an atmosphere of freedom and dissent for the pursuit of higher learning. Black people have largely been excluded in the past, for the atmosphere has been racist, the history and culture of black people have been ignored or caricatured, and access to the universities themselves has been severely circumscribed. Black studies programs, shaped in a manner consistent with such traditional university values as ideological freedom and diversity, can help to correct this injustice. So can scholarships and financial assistance to black students and special facilities for those blacks who wish to live and work with some degree of ethnic homogeneity. But no university is required to surrender its basic standards of competence in the selection of faculty or the admission of students. If not enough black students are equipped to enter college today, it is because of atrocious conditions in lower education. The universities can take a few steps to correct this injustice, but the real fight must take place elsewhere in society and must be aimed at providing black communities with the financial resources, independence, and autonomy necessary to educate their people properly from the earliest appropriate ages. There are limits to what a particular institution like a university can do, and it dare not try to solve problems that can be solved only by the political institutions of society as a whole. And above all, no university need surrender its historical role and essential content in order to right the wrongs of the whole political and social system; it need only reform itself to contribute to a solution of the broader problems in a manner consistent with its character as a place of higher learning with limited functions, possibilities, and responsibilities.

Black studies programs have two legitimate tasks. First, they can, by their very nature, provide a setting within which black people can forge an intelligentsia equipped to provide leadership on various levels of political and cultural action. Black studies programs themselves can do only part of this job. For that reason many able and sophisticated sections of the Black Student Alliance organizations wisely call on their brothers and sisters to participate in these programs but also to specialize in medicine, engineering, sociology, economic analysis, or in fact any scientific or humanistic field. They know that only the emergence of a fully developed intelligentsia, with training in every field of knowledge, can ultimately meet the deepest needs of the black community. In this respect, notwithstanding strong elements of nihilism in their own organizations, their seriousness, maturity, discipline, and realism stand in striking contrast to the childish anti-intellectualism of those bourgeois whites who currently claim to speak for the radical student movement and who impose upon it their own version of generational revolt.

Second, black studies can help immeasurably to combat the racism of white students. The exclusion of whites from the faculty and student body of the black studies programs would therefore defeat half the purpose of the programs themselves. Undoubtedly, there are problems. To the extent that black students view these courses as places of refuge where they can rap with their brothers, they are certain to resent the white presence, not to mention a possible white numerical predominance among the student body. Black students who want an exclusively black setting are entitled to it — in a black university. They are not entitled to tear any institution apart to suit their present mood. The universities owe black people a chance to get a liberal or technical education, but that debt can only be paid in a way consistent with the proper role of the university in society. Beyond that, no university may safely go. If it tries, the result can only be the end of any worthwhile higher education. The inability of so many radical whites to grasp this obvious point is especially galling. It ought to be obvious that the elite schools will protect themselves from this kind of degradation, even if they continue to accept the degradation that accompanies complicity with the war machine and with big business. It is the others — the ones serving the working-class and lower-middle-class youth — that will perish or be transformed into extensions of low-grade high schools. Universities must resist the onslaught now being made against them by superficially radical bourgeois students who have exploited the struggles over black studies programs to advance their own tactical objectives. Fortunately, these elements do not speak for the radical student movement as a whole but represent only a tendency within it; the internal diversity of organizations like SDS, for example, far exceeds the level revealed in the press.

No matter how painful some of the battles are or will become, the advent of black studies programs represents a momentous step toward the establishment of relations of equality between white and black intellectuals. But, if these programs are to realize their potential in support of black liberation and in the fostering of genuinely free and critical scholarship, our universities must resolve honestly the questions of limits and legitimacy. Those who blindly ignore or cynically manipulate these questions, and the reforms they imply, corrupt the meaning of black studies and risk the destruction of institutions necessary to the preservation of freedom in American life.

ELLIOTT DUANE MOORMAN
the benefit of anger

An excellent case study in the workings of the collective American psyche might be found in the reaction of the American people in general, and of the academic community in particular, to the wave of college campus disorders precipitated, in many instances, by black student actions and demands. Most people have attempted to understand the disruptions in a safe, psychologically non-disturbing, "interpretable" way. In lieu of focusing attention on some of the fundamental features of the university and societal structure that have provided, in students' eyes, ample provocation for such disruption, observers and academicians have labeled youthful impetuosity and immaturity, "weak" administrators who do not squelch disruption with an iron fist, and a few left-wing rabble-rousers as the genuine culprits of the campus revolution. The most creative response that legislators were capable of providing was a negative one — no more guns on campus.

But unrest among black students on campuses across the country should be viewed as the legitimate and logical product of the functioning of the American higher educational system in its truest and most honored tradition. The role of the black student in the spectrum of higher education, indeed, in the larger context of society as well, lies in the creation and maintenance of an atmosphere of black anger and dissatisfaction.

If a higher education does nothing else, if it fails in all other respects, it should awaken the educated person to the realities of his environment. It should guide the student in the acquisition of the necessary cognitive and evaluative tools to make a clear determination about the world in

From *Saturday Review*, June 21, 1969. Copyright © 1969 by Saturday Review, Inc. Reprinted by permission.

which he lives, and to develop a system of values for coping with that world. Colleges and universities should provide a set of severely challenging and maturing experiences that will equip the student to function effectively in society. These institutions must then, of necessity, not be "safe" institutions. They should, in short, develop a man that is at once questioning and creative, critical and constructive.

It would follow, then, that any effective education of young black people must necessarily alert and sensitize them to some of the political and social realities of their environment. It must equip them with those tools to make clear determinations about the American societal structure, and develop a place in it for them vis-à-vis their white fellow students. If such education guides the student in the construction of a legitimate set of values, one in keeping with the Western theoretical ethic of freedom, equality, and opportunity, then the black student of necessity will be disappointed and dissatisfied when he applies his value criteria to the university and society at large. The institutions that serve young black America, if they succeed in their educational tasks, cannot be "safe" institutions; for sensitizing young black people to the deficiencies of their environment means making them dissatisfied, making them frustrated, indeed, making them angry. Competent college educators can do nothing less.

But the education of black Americans takes on yet another important dimension. Of the myriad of ethnic groups to enter the American ethnic "melting pot," none has historically suffered more of a near desertion by its best, most qualified leaders than the black community. For scores of years being a relatively successful black man in America necessitated a de-emphasis of all that you were and an often ludicrous yet desperate attempt to be, or at least appear, white. One worked hard at assuming white lingual and grooming patterns, studied the white value system, and kept silent on race issues. One either rejected or enjoyed clandestinely Negroid cultural preferences, which very often when they surfaced caused shame and embarrassment. The irony assumes tragic proportions when one considers the virtual devastation in young black children of any readily distinguishable and identifiable cultural heritage, a legacy jealously and legitimately guarded by the Italian-, Jewish-, and Irish-Americans.

Black America's young, with its leadership reservoir depleted and its culture and heritage devastated, have educational needs one dimension beyond those of the average American student. College must create a black leadership group that readily and permanently identifies with, and is culturally proud of, other black Americans in order to counteract the negative influences produced by centuries of Uncle Tom survival tactics that still plague the race. Hence the need for Afro-American studies, black student groups, and the black experience in general — at both black and white universities.

There is, then, a dual imperative for a college educating black people: the normal educational function of creating questioning, restless, dissatisfied students, and the added dimension of providing for heritage identification and enculturation. It cannot continue to churn out year after year acquiescent, quiet, satisfied members of the black bourgeosie, as many American colleges now do.

There is no question that this line of reasoning implies that the educational needs of black Americans are different from those of the white student community, but the needs of both can be served in a single institution. We must now, if we will really create a generation of intelligent, capable black leaders, stop anesthetizing ourselves with heartwarming talk about forgetting our differences and emphasizing our "common humanity." Where was our common humanity when the teachers of black people were slave traders, when the books were bullwhips, when the classrooms were cotton fields? We need to recognize the sociological, cultural, and historical differences that the collective American psyche has imposed on black and on white, and to serve the particular needs of each. And service of these particular needs does not necessarily imply creating a situation of confrontation and conflict. Creative, constructive dissent is endemic, indeed fundamental, to this country. And creative dissent can spring only from constructive anger.

It may be argued that bitterness will accomplish nothing, and gets the embittered nowhere. Campus disorder and disruption, if aimless and without goal, are worthless. What good is anger unless it's channeled? What good is frustration unless it transforms itself into action? I agree. Upon a close look at campus protest by blacks, it becomes clear that here is one of the most clearly goal-oriented movements in the country. Two important facts buttress this statement: first, black students have, in the vast majority of cases, labored not to disrupt university educational processes; the fiscal and administrative functions have been the targets for sit-in or takeover. Here at Princeton, black students protesting university financial involvement in companies operating in South Africa took possession of the financial and fiscal building; no classes were disrupted whatsoever. And second, almost all black students proceed from a set of concrete recommendations to make the school a better place for black students to work (which university officials' intransigence has forced students to label "demands"). Black students in general are not *simply* angry at the schools. They have proposed constructive alternatives, a statement that often cannot be made about the demonstrations of some other campus groups' protests.

I am therefore referring to a particular kind of anger — that which always precedes constructive social change; anger that realizes the void between the way things should be, indeed must be, and the way things are; anger that rejects mediocrity and settles for nothing less than a genuine approach to fulfilling an ideal. This type of anger has extensive precedent in American history. From the Boston Tea Party to the abolitionists' anger at slavery conditions, to the muckrakers' disgust at corruption in government, right down to the fiery strikes of labor unions seeking changes in working conditions, it has been an American political principle that fundamental social change can often only be brought about through a healthy anger at the conditions needing change and through a disruption of business as usual — a halt in the normal process of getting things done until conditions are changed.

Another argument may be that there is no special consideration given to the particular needs of white students; there are no "Anglo-American" courses or studies programs, no Anglo-American youth groups, no all-white dormitories. And I respond that the actual curriculum of most predominantly white universities *is* an Anglo-American studies program: the study of the culture and heritage of the American ideal as it has unfolded in the several disciplines — American politics, history, sociology, music, drama, the life sciences.

How many American colleges have American civilization programs? Literally hundreds. And the athletic teams, fraternities, special interest groups, and a host of other college activities become — either by accident or by intention — all-white Anglo-American groups that, in a very real sense, exist for the preservation and enculturation of the American heritage in the student. It may be called "good sportsmanship" or "fellowship" or "camaraderie"; it's essentially the preservation of some of the values of the American experience that have proved to be worthwhile. And all-white dormitories? They exist, again either by accident or by design, and in large numbers across America. Because such groups are so much a part of the college structure, they are not labeled "separatist" or "polarized"; yet, black student groups contribute no more to the polarization of attitudes than do these Anglo-American groups.

When black-initiated college disorder and disruption are viewed in this way, it becomes evident that such events clearly represent the healthy functioning of the highest ideals of the American university. And the anger that this functioning produces has historically proved to be one of this nation's greatest assets in terms of fostering constructive change. But, granting this thesis, where does that leave the black student? Does it predict that the university structure will come crashing down under the righteous indignation of its black students? Is the destruction of the university inevitable? The answer to this is, for the most part, dependent on the *response* of both those in university administrative positions and in governmental positions. Will academicians respond with complacent mediocrity? Will they respond (as in many cases they already have) with helmeted state troopers? Will they respond with the traditional historic banalities? Or will American educators respond with an honest and searching effort to identify the causes of campus unrest, and attempt to act upon these findings?

President Nixon might do well to appoint a national advisory commission on college and university disorders, seeking on a national level a profile of the antediluvian university attitudes and structures that have fostered such disorders, pledging at the outset some positive federal action — either legislative or administrative — based on its findings, so that what happened to the Kerner Commission Report (read and shelved away) will not occur.

At predominantly white institutions, it seems to me, a positive response is not difficult to frame. Rather than seek to crush black anger, the academic community should seek to keep the anger constructive. This can be done by taking a general attitude of cooperation and willingness to understand, and to make special attempts to accommodate student needs by providing the financial and technical assistance necessary to implement such changes as black studies, by increasing minority recruitment and admission, by hiring more black faculty, and by attempting to create an atmosphere of mutual trust and confidence. Massive police intervention can only serve to increase polarization and distrust and to convert constructive anger into vengeful and spiteful wrath.

At predominantly black institutions, the administrators would do well to view the gem they hold for what it can be: an institution uniquely equipped to create and develop a proud, aware generation of black leaders. A black college can, in the least dramatic sense, become a vehicle toward freedom, a vehicle toward meaningful knowledge — a vehicle toward black anger. Once the administrators view the black college for what it can be, then they must pattern their responses accordingly: an outpouring of all resources — financial, moral, and intellectual — toward meeting the *real* needs of black people today, not the illusory need of a one-way admission ticket to the comfortable black bourgeosie. This response becomes critical, since most black students are in all-black colleges.

The future? It is what the colleges themselves — faculty, administration, and students — wish to make of it, in terms of constructively responding to the needs and moral imperatives of each other. Negative responses may well mean destruction.

chapter four

The New Music:
A Return to the Tribal
or
Blowing Your Mind?

introduction

Questions about identity, love, the purpose of life, political protest, and hypocrisy all find their way into the music students play,
listen, and dance to. Such questions are posed in a variety of current styles: pop, jazz, rock, and acid-rock. New groups with basic
ingredients of guitars, drums, and voices continually appear on
the West and East Coast and perhaps die out as quickly as they
emerged. Some groups succeed, record companies boom, and the
youth culture is in full swing. Without a doubt the United States
is youth-oriented and there doesn't seem to be any prognosis for
change.

Perhaps we shouldn't look for change but rather for analysis
and understanding. All of the essays in this chapter attempt in a
variety of ways to discover the roots, the present mushrooming,

and the meaning of the new music. Albert Goldman's "The Emergence of Rock" does just that, beginning with an intriguing description of "The Electric Circus," a good way to involve his readers. He then goes back to the year 1954 and moves historically through complex developments up into the 1960's. Goldman's writing is skillful. He chooses unusual action verbs, bordering on onomatopoeia, and his description of "I'll Be There" — explaining and recreating both song and sound — is especially good. His final suggestion that rock is moving toward a new serious art form which would realize the "cherished dream of mass culture: to combine the low (crude) with the high" is similar to the opening statement of "The Sounds of New Music" by J. L. Simmons and Barry Winograd.

This second essay develops the idea that all the varieties in the new music have the common theme of a new emerging ethic and style of life, that the new music travels everywhere with the "happeners" and is a running commentary on their lives. The drugs and the "hang-loose" ethic as part of this new scene bring up major arguments against it: that the new music is tasteless and immoral. Simmons and Winograd, of course, refute such claims and invite the adult generation to listen more closely, again playing on the generation gap idea to persuade their readers.

In contrast, Gene Lees declares that there is not that much newness in rock, that there are definite links to its musical past, and that youth is being sold a plastic rebellion by big business. Yet all is not phony, he says, for the antiwar songs and Bob Dylan show concern for the drift of American society. Here is an essay which is less formal, more conversational in tone, and less analytical than most of the others in this collection. It brings up the critical question every writer must ask: who is my audience? Is Lee's writing an example of journalism? What, if any, are the differences between what some critics call journalism and good expository prose? According to Robert Christgau, "Journalism ought to survive with its limitations of time and place intact."

"Rock Lyrics are Poetry (Maybe)" is an interesting piece of personal opinion, full of the flavor of Christgau's own likes and dislikes. He never attempts to mask his arguments but instead persuades his readers through sheer volume of intimate knowledge about the current songs and individual groups or song writers.

He also attempts to persuade by sarcasm. He can be savage in his dislike for the poetry of Kahlil Gibran and, conversely, almost effusive in his assessment of who he considers the good song writers. Although Christgau could be clearer about what he finally decides to call rock "poetry," there is certainly a voice here and a definite tone throughout.

A more formal essay, H. F. Mooney's "Popular Music Since the 1920's: The Significance of Shifting Taste," is analytical and builds on contrasts and comparisons between the 1960's and earlier periods. Mooney studies trends and gives a historical perspective for the new music not found in the other essays here. Although Mooney presents a vast panorama of information to digest, he never lets his readers falter; he sums up a particular point or period in popular music and then continues to the next development. The essay is well-annotated, with bibliography and footnotes. The brilliance of organization in the first paragraph lets the reader know that he is in the hands of a skillful writer, a man who knows his subject and his craft.

ALBERT GOLDMAN
the emergence of rock

To experience the Age of Rock full-blast and to begin to grasp its weird complexities, one can't do much better than spend a Saturday night at The Electric Circus, the most elaborate discothèque in New York. Located on St. Marks Place, the main nexus of East Village otherness, The Electric Circus is up a flight of stairs from The DOM (one of the early landmarks of the rock scene which has since evolved into a "soul" club). One makes his way through a gaggle of very young hippies sprawled on the porch steps, and enters a long, narrow alcove where the faithful, the tourists, and those somewhere in between wait in line for admission in a mood of quiet expectancy, like people waiting to

From *New American Review* No. 3. Copyright © 1968 by Albert Goldman. Reprinted by permission of The Sterling Lord Agency.

get into one of the more exciting exhibits at the World's Fair. Once inside, the spectator moves along a corridor bathed in ultraviolent light in which every speck of white takes on a lurid glow, climbs a steep staircase, and passes through a dark antechamber. Here the young sit packed together on benches and, already initiated into the mysteries beyond, stare back at the newcomer with glazed, indifferent expressions as though they had been sitting there for days. Then, suddenly, there is a cleft in the wall, and the spectator follows the crowd pressing through it into a gigantic hall that suggests a huge bleached skull. Its dark hollows are pierced by beams of colored light that stain the walls with slowly pulsing patterns and pictures: glowing amoeba shapes, strips of home movies, and giant mandalas filled with fluid colors. The scream of a rock singer comes at one, the beat amplified to a deafening blast of sound. Housed within this electronic cave are hundreds of dancers, a number of them in exotic, flowing garments, their faces marked with phosphorescent insignia, hands clutching sticks of incense. Some of the dancers are gyrating frantically, as if trying to screw themselves down through the floor; others hold up their fists, ducking and bobbing like sparring partners; while others wrench their heads and thrust out their hands as if to ward off evil spirits. For all of its futuristic magic, the dance hall brings to mind those great painted caves such as Altamira in Spain where prehistoric man practiced his religious rites by dancing before the glowing images of his animal gods.

Magnetized by the crowd, impelled by the relentless pounding beat of the music, one is then drawn out on the floor. Here there is a feeling of total immersion: one is inside the mob, inside the skull, inside the music, which comes from all sides, buffeting the dancers like a powerful surf. Strangest of all, in the midst of this frantic activity, one soon feels supremely alone; and this aloneness produces a giddy sense of freedom, even of exultation. At last one is free to move and act and mime the secret motions of his mind. Everywhere about him are people focused deep within themselves, working to bring to the surfaces of their bodies their deep-seated erotic fantasies. Their faces are drugged, their heads thrown back, their limbs extended, their bodies dissolving into the arcs of the dance. The erotic intensity becomes so great that one wonders what sustains the frail partition of reserve that prevents the final spilling of this endlessly incited energy.

If one withdraws from the crowd and climbs to the gallery overlooking the dance floor, he soon succumbs to the other spell cast by this cave of dreams. Falling into a passive trance, his perceptions heightened perhaps by exhaustion or drugs (no liquor is served here), the spectator can enjoy simultaneously the pleasures of the theater, the movies, and the sidewalk cafe. At The Electric Circus the spectacle of the dancers alternates with the surrealistic acts of professional performers. An immaculate chef on stilts will stride to the center of the floor, where he looms high above the dancers. They gather around him like children, while he entertains them by juggling three apples. Then, taking out a knife, he slices the fruit and feeds it to his flock. High on a circular platform, a performer dressed to look like a little girl in her nightie struggles ineffectually with a Yo-Yo. A blinding white strobe light flashes across her body, chopping her absurd actions into the frames of an ancient flickering movie. Another girl comes sliding down a rope; someone dressed as a gorilla seizes her and carries her off with a lurching gait. Sitting in the dark gallery, one watches the crepitating spectacle below; the thumping music now sinks slowly through his mind like a narcotic; eventually he closes his eyes and surrenders to a longing for silence, darkness, and rest.

II

Like those fabled cities whose walls rose to the sounds of music, The Electric Circus and other such dance halls have been drawn into being and charged with their eclectic atmosphere by the magical power of the beat. The total-environment discothèque is principally an attempt to capture and concentrate, as in a giant orgone box, the multiple energies of rock, which have evolved during the past decade into a veritable witches' brew — part aphrodisiac, part narcotic, and part hallucinogen. There is no simple way of comprehending the extraordinarily rapid and complex development of the rock sound and culture. But perhaps the clearest way is to begin at the beginning and try to follow the principal trends of the music, along with their respective cultural ambiences and meanings, both in the Negro and in the white world.

Rock was born in a flashback, a celluloid loop doubled back inside a time machine. The date was 1954; the place was Cleveland, Ohio; the occasion, the first broadcast of Negro race records to an audience of white teen-agers. Alan Freed, a local disc jockey, made the experiment. Almost immediately, it became apparent that he had struck a nerve that was ready to vibrate. The records he played were known in the trade as "rhythm and blues." Ground out by tiny Negro record companies in the South, they were aimed at the black ghettos of the North. What they contained was a particularly potent strain of the same urban blues that had swept over the country in the late thirties during the vogue of the big bands. Indeed, if one can imagine an old Kansas City blues band crushed like a tin can so that nothing remains of it but top, bottom, and lots of rusty ragged edges, he will have a fair idea of how the early r&b combos sounded. Concentrating on essentials, these groups used a disproportionate number of instruments (electric rhythm and bass guitars, plus piano and drums) to hammer out the beat, while the solo performers, vocal or instrumental, worked way out in front, using a primitive style compounded of honks and cries and words bawled out like curses.

It was, therefore, an old and radically racial sound that Freed offered to his listeners in the Midwest, and later in New York: a sound that told of dirt and fear and pain and lust. But the white kids loved it; and soon, as if to signify that the music had been adopted by a new public, Freed changed its name to "rock 'n' roll," though even this new name came from an old blues, "My baby rocks me with a steady roll." The success of rock attracted white performers: the first r&b song recorded by a white singer was "Rock Around the Clock" by Bill Haley and the Comets. Haley initiated that process of white assimilation of Negro style that for many years has been a basic feature of the movement; but the tendency of early rock was to pull away from the heavy racial sound in favor of the lighter, swifter beat of hillbilly music, which was to be one of rock's more durable elements, and a subject matter (cars, Cokes, and heartaches) more suitable to white teen-agers. On this new wave of country blues, Chuck Berry and then Elvis Presley rode to fame. When Presley entered the army at the end of the decade, one expected the fad to recede and vanish. But the culture remained firmly rock-bound.

While rock was enjoying this first surge of popularity, Negro music was undergoing a series of changes among the most profound in its history. The music of the ghetto was being revived and recharged by powerful new performers bent on outdoing their white imitators, while its basic genres — blues and gospel — were coalescing to produce a new style of enormous strength and popularity.

The greatest of these singers — indeed, the greatest of all the basic rock performers — was Little Richard. Richard's records all sounded as if they were made in the Saturday night uproar of a turpentine logging camp. His raw strident voice was torn from his throat in a bawling, shouting torrent that battered and scattered the words until they sounded like raving. Behind this desperately naked voice worked a boogie-woogie rhythm section tightened to vise-like rigidity. The furious energy of the singing caught in the iron cage of the rhythm produced an almost unbearable tension. Instead of illustrating the words, which often spoke of pleasure ("I'm gonna ball tonight!"), the music conveyed the agonizing effort to break through to joy. (Or just to break through: Richard usually ended his chorus with the bloodcurdling scream of a man hurling himself over a precipice.) What Little Richard was saying musically — and the Negro ghetto with him — was not that he was having a good time, but that he had the right to one and would "cut" anyone who got in his way. His note was erotic defiance. As such, Little Richard represented a new type of Negro youth. Reckless and rebellious, he gave us the first taste of the voice that was later to holler, "Burn, baby, burn!"

Oddly enough, the other great performer who emerged in this period expressed a character of precisely the opposite sort. Ray Charles was the eternal Negro, a poor blind man crying out of his darkness, singing to assuage his pain. Yet as a musician he was far from being a traditionalist; in fact, in undertaking to mix gospel and blues he violated one of the strictest taboos of Negro music. Throughout modern times, gospel and blues had always been rigidly segregated expressions of the sacred and the profane. Blues worked cathartically, urging that everything painful be confronted, named, lamented, and exorcised in a lonely, impersonal, almost aloof style. Gospel had functioned in a completely opposite manner, one that overwhelmed unhappiness by a swelling evocation of the joys of life beyond the present world. Just as the blues was traditionally depressed, understated, ironic, and resigned, gospel was typically ebullient, extravagant, even at times orgiastic in its affirmation. The Negro community had preserved the solace of each of these traditions by maintaining a total separation between them. The singing of blues in church was forbidden, while the blues singer steadfastly confronted his troubles without ever looking heavenward.

That is, until Ray Charles and his followers stepped boldly over the boundary and ended the prohibition. One of the first effects of this revolution was an inversion of traditional modes. Not only did these singers perform minor blues in the style of plaintive dirges, such as one might hear in church; they also added blues lyrics to the hand-clapping, foot-stamping, tambourine-banging gospel shouts. On stage they adopted many of the mannerisms, practices, and rituals of the storefront Negro church. They testified, danced ecstatically, called for witnesses, appeared to be led from above, tore off their clothes, and fell and rose again like men in the grip of a religious revelation.

Charles's own manner was often that of the preacher: the voice deliberately crude, cracked, thickened with Southern Negro pronunciations; the style figured with cantorial embellishments. The effect was that of a man seized by emotion, spilling out his feelings with absolute candor. Typical of the original gospel-blues mix was "Yes, Indeed," one of Charles's most successful early numbers. The piece opens with soft church chords played on a harmonium; next, Charles gives out the text in his deep deacon's voice, a word or two — then the gospel beat, heavy and lurching, comes crashing in with a chorus of "Amen girls" hypnotically chanting after every phrase, "Yaas, indeed!" As the piece stomps through its traditional 16-bar course, the confidently rising intervals generate an aura of optimism that reaches its climax in a moment of pure "salvation." The horns riff joyously, the chord changes signal that we are coming home, and the lead voice sings: "Well, I know when it gets ya, you get a feelin' deep down in your soul, every time you hear that good old rock 'n' roll. Yaas, indeed." The lyrics tumble here to a dreadful anticlimax, just at the point where the music becomes most transcendent, for what would have been in the original a religious affirmation has been rubbed out and a pop music cliché scribbled in its place.

Once the barrier was down between gospel and blues, the distinctions between other Negro musical traditions also began to disappear. Singers, composers, instrumentalists, and arrangers began to take what they wanted from a racial ragbag of Delta blues, hillbilly strumming, gut-bucket jazz, boogie-woogie piano, pop lyricism, and store-front shouting. The result — less a new genre than a mélange of musical materials — was called "soul."

When one thinks of soul today, the image that presents itself is of a monotonously revolving kaleidoscope loaded with dozens of factory-stamped, smoky-colored bits of gospel, rock, blues, jazz, pop, folk, rock, pop, blues, and so on in endlessly shifting combinations of this week's, last month's, tomorrow's "sound." The agency most responsible for this commercialization of Negro music is Motown, the General Motors of rock. Its founder, owner, and manager is Berry Gordy, Jr., a one-time assembly-line worker, who since the early sixties has been turning out hit tunes produced by teams of composers, arrangers, and performers, all working closely to the specifications of the Motown formula.

The basic ingredient of the formula is the beat. Pushing beyond the traditional "and *two* and *four*" style of drumming, Berry's arrangers trained the drums to bark on every beat. Then they strengthened and enlarged the new beat by overamplification and by doubling it with tambourine, tom-tom, cymbals, bass, and, eventually, anything that would bounce. Today, Motown rocks with a driving, slogging rhythm that rumbles up through the floor of a discothèque like an earthquake.

The other active ingredient of the formula is the "shout," a short, arresting phrase that flashes the song's message. This is underscored and embellished with every resource provided by Negro tradition and the Hollywood sound stage. The most primitive types of plantation music — the sounds of Jew's harps, tambourines, pipes, and quills — have been unearthed to fill the formula's demand for a "funky" core. Around this core have been wrapped some fairly complicated arrangements, entailing the integration of strings, symphonic percussion sections, choirs, and soloists.

Motown's effort to concentrate all the sounds of Negro tradition into a super-soul has often produced the opposite of the intended effect — a typically commercial dilution of the Negro essence. But sometimes Detroit's stylists, especially the gifted team of Eddie and Bryant Holland and Lamont Dozier, have updated tradition so skillfully that they succeed in adding a genuinely contemporary voice to Negro music. Not content to paste pop lyrics over old church tunes, this team has approached gospel in a sophisticated spirit, seeking to exploit its ritual of salvation without sacrificing the love story indispensable to the pop ballad. In their best work they can telescope into three relentless minutes the events of a whole evening in a store-front church without dislodging the conventional facade of the ballad.

"I'll Be There," the most admired song of Motown's The Four Tops, opens on a characteristically exotic note: pipes and slap bass evoking a movie image of Genghis Khan and his men trotting across the steppes of Central Asia. Then this mirage is suddenly blown away and we are down to the bedrock of soul: the drums pounding, the tambourines jingling, and the anguished voice of Levi Stubbs exhorting his sweetheart in the manner of an evangelist preacher:

If you feel that you can't go on,
Because all of your hope is gone,
And your life is filled with much confusion,
Until happiness is just an illusion:

"Reach out!" cry the wraithlike voices that have been trailing and echoing Stubbs. "Reach out for *me!*" he adds, distending the word with a flourish of emotion. Then for one suspenseful moment, all the voices cease, and we gaze into a void in which there is nothing but the nakedly writhing beat. Suddenly the emptiness is filled with the solemn sound of the "shout," "I'll be there," sung in unison by leader and chorus and accompanied by the exotic pipes of the introduction, which now assume their proper place as a kind of stained-glass window behind the singers. The final touch of religious excitement was added during the recording session: when the break in the melody opened for the last time, Levi shouted to the girl, "Look over your shoulder!" For a Negro audience this phrase summons up one of the most intense moments at a gospel service: the sight of some believer pointing wildly toward a corner of the church where he has caught a glimpse of the Holy Spirit.

Motown does a dizzying business with its exploitation of classic Negro styles, and most of this business is done in the Negro ghettos (where nobody pays any attention to The Beatles). Generally, the success of the style is attributed to Negro pride, to the joy with which Negroes respond to the basic expressions of their culture. But the regressive, almost caricatured Negritude of soul, and even more importantly, the desperately naked avowal of suffering made in the more seriously expressive songs, suggest that this music celebrates blackness less for its beauty than for its strength as a revived resource against the white terror.

Soul's revival of gospel music has been accompanied by a return to archaic patterns of body movement which combine gestures of incantation and exorcism. In the currently popular boogaloo, for example, there is a complete pantomime of terror. The dancer's neck is twisted spasmodically as if by a lynch rope, his eyes roll up into his head, his hands shoot out past his face as if to avert blow, and his whole body tips as though he were about to collapse. The imagery of anxiety in such a performance accords perfectly with the character of the words and music which excite it, and all three qualify drastically the notion that rock is simply the revelry of orgy.

III

Not the least reason for the exaggeration of Negritude in soul music has been the emergence in recent years of rock groups composed of pale English boys. What The Beatles represented in their early unregenerate years was a Liverpudlian impression of Little Richard, Chuck Berry, and Bo Diddley, precisely the roughest, raunchiest Negro rhythm and blues men accessible through American records. When their manager, Brian Epstein, styled the boys' hair and dressed them in chic suits, he didn't comb any of the fuzz out of their sound. The result was that English dandyism was wedded to Negro eroticism, and every teenybopper in the Western world began to dream of possessing a mod moppet with soul. Other English groups have since become so adept at mimicking Negroes that the listener (white or black) can only identify the singer's race by the record liner. In fact, one may even prefer Stevie Winwood or Spencer Davis to the ordinary Detroit sound just because the English product seems more authentic, less bedecked with the gaudy trappings of Motown. This authenticity is, of course, only skin-deep; it is a mask that the singer sustains only because his narrow expressive gambit does not oblige him to flex his features with a full range of expression. For three minutes, the length of a "45" side, he can hold this pose; but it is just as unnatural for him as the spraddling stance is for the model who is out to make a "smashing" appearance in *Queen* or *Vogue*. It takes only one record like Aretha Franklin's recent virtuoso treatment of "I Can't Get No Satisfaction," written by Mick Jagger of The Rolling Stones, to remind us of the great gap that exists between those who have soul and those who merely pay it the compliment of imitation.

Once Negritude had been synthesized so that it could be manufactured anywhere in the world, rock began to cast about for fresh game. But this was less a matter of the normal development of popular music than of the cultural disorientation of the rock generation. On the face of it, there was no reason why the music that developed from white imitations of Negro styles should not have continued to evolve along the same path that swing had followed in the forties. Starting with a basic style derived largely from Negro sources, the swing bands added more and more non-Negro elements until they had created a new pop sound. At that time, as today, there had been a dialogue between black and white, with plenty of give and take. Miles Davis, for example, borrowed the arranger of the most refined white band (Gil Evans of the Claude Thornhill band) to act as midwife at the birth of the cool. But rock was not destined to play with counters that were only white and black.

The youth of the swing era thought they knew who they were; today's youth has no such illusion. But lacking any clear-cut sense of identity has only made them more keenly aware of everyone else's. Rock is, in one sense, a direct reflection of their hunger for the essence of every people or period that displays a striking or exotic style. The Rock Age has assimilated everything in sight, commencing with the whole of American music: urban and country blues, gospel, hillbilly, Western, "good-time" (the ricky-tick of the twenties), and Tin Pan Alley. It has reached across the oceans for the sounds and rhythms of Africa, the Middle East, and India. It has reached back in time for the baroque trumpet, the madrigal, and the Gregorian chant; and forward into the future for electronic music and the noise collages of *musique concrète*.

By virtue of its cultural alliances, the Beat has also become the pulse of pop culture. The creators of the new milieu vie with one another in proclaiming rock the inspirational force of the day. A discothèque like The Electric Circus is a votive temple to the electronic muse, crammed with offerings from all her devotees. The patterns on the walls derive from Pop and Op art; the circus acts are Dada and Camp; the costumes of the dancers are mod and hippie; the technology is the most successful realization to date of the ideal of "art and engineering"; the milieu as a whole is psychedelic, and the discothèque is itself a prime example of mixed-media or total-environment art. The only elements of rock culture that are not conspicuous there are the literary ones: the underground newspapers that report the news and gossip of this world; the put-on critiques of the New Journalism; and the social and political rhetoric of the folk-rock singers, the finger-pointers, like Bob Dylan, Janis Ian, and Joan Baez.

As for the audience for rock, they are apt to manifest the same eager feeling for cultural essences that is revealed by the musicians. They like to fashion modish simulacra of cherished periods like the twenties, thirties, or the Edwardian Age; they are strong on certain ethnic types, like the American Indian and the Slavic peasant; their holdings in the East are large and constantly increasing — and they all can do a pretty good take-off on W. C. Fields. They like to dress up in cast-off clothes purchased in thrift shops or old theatrical costume warehouses; on Saturday afternoons they make King's Road in Chelsea the scene of one of the most extraordinary pageants ever seen on the streets of a European city. To describe their dress as "masquerade" is not quite accurate because, like all true decadents, they prefer to the pure forms those piquant mixtures of unrelated things that show wit and fancy as opposed to mere mimicry. Yet their ideal costume is not obviously hybrid. It aims to achieve the integrity of familiar things. The first glance at it elicits the sense of *déjà vu*; the second, a frown of perplexity. "What country do you come from?" is a query often directed at The Beatles' costume designers, a Dutch group known as The Apple, as they walk about London in their enchanting peasant drag.

As this mode of dressing makes clear, the time has now passed when it was enough to seize a single style and make it one's own — as Bob Dylan first transformed himself into an Okie or Monti Rock III into a Harlem Negro. Today, the grand cultural ideal is encapsulated in the tiny word "mix." The goal is to blend various exotic essences into mysterious alchemical compounds.

Take for example The Beatles' "Strawberry Fields Forever," with its mixture of hippie argot, classic myth, and baroque music. Grave Elysian flutes lead the way as the singers chant, "Let me take you *down*"; then, swooning on the wave of an Hawaiian guitar, the voices drift into their subterranean lotus land. Gradually, the atmosphere grows heavy and murky; the tone of the singers is stoned; their speech is muddled and ambiguous ("No one, I think, is in my tree; I mean, it must be high or low; that is, you can't, you know, tune in, but it's all right; that is, I think it's not too bad"). As the music advances in trance-like time, the baroque bass line presses relentlessly downward, the drums beat a tattoo, and trumpets sound like autos jamming. The song swells into a massive affirmation of meaninglessness — a junkie anthem. After a final crescendo, the end is signaled by the conventional fade-out; but this is swiftly countermanded by an unexpected fade-in which brings delicate Indian sounds bubbling to the surface of the heavily doctored soundtrack. The effect is magical — The Beatles sink into the ground in London and pop to the surface again at Bombay.

The more farfetched and unlikely the ingredients, the better for the mix; and likewise, the more arts and media laid under contribution, the greater the impact. The ideal is strongly reminiscent of surrealism, of Max Ernst's formula of "the fortuitous meeting of distant realities."

It would be a mistake, however, to attribute any direct influence to such doctrines, no matter how prophetic they have proved to be. Life, not theory, and, more particularly, the electronic maelstrom that has shaped the sensibility of our youth best explain the syncretism of the present moment. Our youth are accustomed to being bombarded from every side by sounds and images that have been torn loose, distorted, and scrambled in a thousand ways. Nothing more is needed to suggest the frantic mix than the everyday act of twirling a radio or TV dial. It is not surprising that the archetypal image of so much Pop art is the fun house. Distorting mirrors, grotesque images, spooky vistas, traps, tricks, and shocks to every sense constitute in their aggregate a very brilliant metaphor for the contemporary experience. And, as if this were not enough, the youth have given their bizarre world one last crazy spin by turning on with anything they can get into their mouths or veins — narcotics, stimulants, hypnotics, hallucinogens.

Every contemporary medium has evolved some version of the mix, whether it be called collage, montage, assemblage, or *musique concrète*. The form most often associated with rock is the light show. Two seasons ago, Bob Goldstein installed his "Lightworks" in a roadhouse called L'Oursin at Southhampton, Long Island. To date the finest multimedia discothèque, Goldstein's club revealed a great deal about the potentialities of the mix. It was designed, like a giant Scopitone jukebox, to light up with a complete picture show every time a new record dropped on the turntable. The images that flashed upon its three towering screens (which were played contrapuntally, one against the other) were drawn from every source dear to the Pop sensibility. There were glass slides of New York's turn-of-the-century *haute monde*, film clips from Hollywood musicals of the thirties, twist films, old newsreels, poster patterns, and light paintings. The effect of this streaming phantasmagoria, which shuttled the spectator's mind back and forth along invisible tracks of association — from past to present, comic to sentimental, nostalgic to erotic — was that of a fantastic variety show, a Psychedelic Follies.

In such discothèques as L'Oursin, rock became a medium for producing a range of new sensations. Associating rock with images induces that sense of poring scrutiny, of lens-in-eye obsession, that is one of the most distinctive modes of contemporary sensibility. (Consider the excitement it generates in the central episode of *Blow-Up*.) Like the effect of LSD, that of rocking things is to spotlight them in a field of high concentration and merge them with the spectator in a union that is almost mystical. Few discothèque designers, to be sure, have Goldstein's taste and theatrical flair; most are content to break off bits and pieces of cultural imagery and embed them in the beat to produce a haphazard rock terrazzo. But the beguiling and tranquilizing effect of spending an evening in the contemplation of "Lightworks" assures us — far more than all the current theorizing — that the ideal of the synesthetic art work is perfectly valid and closer to realization today than at any time since its first statement in the writings of Wagner and Baudelaire.

IV

The concept of a psychedelic variety show is strikingly akin to the form evolved by The Beatles in the last two years. Young men of imagination who have grown up in the cultural greenhouse of show business, The Beatles have developed their own exotic blooms of parody and hallucination. Like all the members of their generation, but to a far greater degree than most, they have fashioned themselves out of borrowed materials. Year after year they have added other idioms to their vocabulary, and now speak a language that is as rich as any in the history of the popular arts. The terms of their recent work are sophistication and ambiguity. But looking back over their history, one finds a logical progression toward these higher qualities, for the art of which The Beatles are masters has always had a complex and somewhat factitious character.

The story of The Beatles is pop culture's redaction of the myth of innocence and experience. When the famous four set out on their careers, they knew nothing of art or life. At home only in the rough-and-tumble world of the Liverpool cellar club or the Hamburg *Lokal*, they were a shaggy and ignorant crew. They could not read music, they could barely play their instruments, and their idea of a joke was to come out on the bandstand wearing toilet seats around their necks. Since then their careers and lives have mounted upward and outward in dizzying gyres that have swept them around the whole world of twentieth-century life and culture and set them on terms of respect and familiarity with some of the most sophisticated minds in the contemporary arts. In the course of their jet-age development, they have already been twice transformed bodily and spiritually; now they stand poised on the verge of yet another metamorphosis as the result of their studies with Maharishi Mahesh Yogi, the apostle of transcendental meditation.

It was their manager Brian Epstein who transformed these coarse rockers into the adorable Eton boys known to fame, a change of costume that proved to be the shrewdest packaging job in the history of popular music. It would be a mistake, however, to claim, as LeRoi Jones has done, that The Beatles owe their early success entirely to the Epstein formula; for paradoxically, just as their imitations of Negro rock began to achieve universal popularity, the boys began to modify their sound in obedience to the promptings of their own souls. What emerged was a sort of ancestral reverberation, echoes of ancient English music reaching back to a time before the New World had been settled. In his recent book *Caliban Reborn*, Wilfrid Mellers, the distinguished British musicologist, provides an interesting analysis of the traditional English elements in The Beatles' music, identifying bits and pieces that once belonged to the musical vocabulary of Giles Farnaby and of Orlando Gibbons, the master of the sixteenth-century madrigalists. From this analysis, it would appear that The Beatles stand in somewhat the same relation to their culture as do the Negroes and hillbillies to ours: they, too, play by ear, and what they hear is still attuned partially to a kind of scale and tonality that has long since been forgotten by literate musicians. If Mellers is right, the tension between the "illiterate" and "literate" elements in the work of these quasi-folk artists may be what accounts for their unique effect, the resonance in their simple songs of something deep and agelessly innocent. One might add that The Beatles' feeling for baroque music is characteristically British: it is Handel that sounds the affirmative note in "Strawberry Fields Forever," as it is the Purcell of the trumpet voluntaries that wells up with such purity in "Penny Lane."

The appearance in 1966 of their album *Revolver* signaled an important transformation of The Beatles. First, the album soured the milky innocence of "I Want to Hold Your Hand" and "Michelle" with the sardonic tone of the city citizen, personified in the acrid sounds and sarcastic lyrics of "Taxman." The second change was formal: instead of singing in their one basic style, The Beatles became virtuosos and produced a pastiche of modes.

"Eleanor Rigby," one of the two most impressive songs, is couched in a nineteenth-century string idiom, suggestive alternately of a country fiddle and a Beethoven string quartet. Its old-fashioned style, urgent, chopping rhythm, and lovely plangent melody provide a setting rich in sentiment for the series of genre pictures sketched in the verses. There is Eleanor Rigby, a solitary spinster picking up the rice after a wedding; and Father McKenzie darning a sock in his room late at night. They are the lonely people who live outside the modern world. The very thought of their existence wrings from The Beatles a cry of bewildered innocence: "All the lonely people! Where *do* they all come from? Where *do* they all belong?"

"Tomorrow Never Knows" is composed in an antithetical mode and provides this generation's answer to the poignant sense of human futility expressed in "Eleanor Rigby." A futuristic chant intoned by a robot voice over a hubbub of jungle noises, squiggling strings, and sore boil guitar riffs — all this underscored by the pounding of a primitive drum — the song mechanically announces its message like an electronic oracle. The message is that of the hippies:

> Turn off your mind,
> Relax and float downstream;
> It is not dying.

Revolver also contains a number of other "answers": a pioneer effort to assimilate the sound of the Indian raga ("Love You To"); a street chanty, widely interpreted as a comical drug song ("Yellow Submarine"); "For No One," which evokes the Edwardian parlor musicale, with Auntie Ellen strumming the cottage piano and Uncle Wembley winding the French horn; "Good Day Sunshine," a perky tune sweetly reminiscent of straw-hat vaudeville; and "Here, There and Everywhere," an exquisite ballad. Altogether this album offers a remarkable range of material, comprising the nostalgic, the futuristic, the hortatory, the contemplative, the Oriental, and the American. It also demonstrates a great expansion of The Beatles' resources of instrumentation and recording techniques. For the first time, one really feels the presence of George Martin, the so-called "Fifth Beatle," a record producer and academy-trained musician of considerable sophistication who has supervised all The Beatles' recordings.

Revolver points the way to the variety mix, but it furnishes no general context for its excellent songs, and hence they gain nothing from being on one record. *Sgt. Pepper* remedies this deficiency by assembling its tunes inside the framework of an old-time band concert. Offering itself as a record of such an occasion, it harmonizes the stylistic eclecticism of its contents by presenting each song as an individual vaudeville turn.

At the same time the opportunity is created to step beyond the artificial glare of the footlights and deliver with chilling effect the final revelation of "A Day in the Life."

The effect of this last song is like that of awakening from turbulent but colorful dreams to stare at the patch of gray that signals dawn in the city. What we awake to in the song is the modern oscillation between anomie and anxiety punctuated periodically by the sound of a dynamo that has just been switched on. This sound is itself the ultimate symbol of The Beatles' world. It represents the state of being turned on, of getting high and escaping from our deadened selves; but at the same time, its alarming crescendo of speed and power suggests an acceleration to the point of explosion (an implication underscored by the Beethoven-like chords of a symphony orchestra, portending doom). The end of the song is a single tonic chord struck on the piano and then allowed to float away for half a minute, like a slowly dissolving puff of smoke.

"A Day in the Life" is a skillfully contrived microcosm of the contemporary world. Called by one critic "the Beatles' *Waste Land*," and by another "a little Antonioni movie," its brilliance lies in the exquisite adjustment of its tone, calibrated finely between apathy and terror. Reflecting meaning from every facet, the song not only evokes the chug chug of a mechanistic society and the numbed sensibilities of its anonymous inhabitants, but also sounds with conviction the note of apocalypse.

V

That a song of such intellectual sophistication and artistic resourcefulness should arise out of the same tradition that only a dozen years ago was spawning ditties like "Rock Around the Clock" seems almost unbelievable. But the very swiftness of the development indicates its real nature. Unlike other popular arts, rock has not been forced to spin its substance out of itself. Instead, it has acted like a magnet, drawing into its field a host of heterogeneous materials that has fallen quickly into patterns. No other cultural force in modern times has possessed its power of synthesis. Indeed, one of the common complaints of cultural critics has been that there were no coherent movements to animate and order the vast piles of cultural detritus under which we seemed destined to smother. Evidently, the only impulse at all equal to the task has been the primitive power of the beat.

Having assumed a role of cultural authority, rock has not, as was feared, dragged us down into the mire of cultural regression. The

Spenglerian anxieties have proven once again to be unfounded. Rather than either lowering or elevating us, rock has served to equalize cultural pressures and forces. It has cleared a channel from the lowest and most archaic to the highest and most recent, and through that conduit is now flowing a revitalizing current of energy and of ideas. The result has been the elevation of rock to the summit of popular culture and the accelerating expansion of its interests and resources.

Thus The Beatles have already journeyed so far from their starting point in American rock 'n' roll that their relation to the tradition has become problematic, perhaps irrelevant. In their steady drift toward the international avant-garde, however, The Beatles, and the other English groups like The Procol Harum that have followed in their wake, represent only one end of the lengthening rock spectrum. At the other end, stand the new musicians who have developed the sensuousness and violence of the original beat. Outstanding among these are the acid-rock groups of San Francisco and Los Angeles: groups with exotic names like The Grateful Dead, The Moby Grape, The Jefferson Airplane, Big Brother and the Holding Company, or Country Joe and the Fish. The California sound has sublimated the basic essence of rock and mixed it with the idiom of the hippies, the motorcycle gangs, and the surfers in a cultural fusion that is reminiscent of soul. Indeed, acid-rock is the closest approximation yet to an authentic white soul.

The finest of these West Coast groups is The Doors, four young Californians whose prior experience included college, jazz, and film-making school. The Doors think of themselves — as their name signifies — as the means or channel through which their audiences pass from ignorance to knowledge, from ordinary consciousness to ecstasy, from control and inhibition to revolt and freedom. They think of themselves as "erotic politicians" and as pioneers in a libidinal wilderness: "The world we suggest should be of a new wild West," proclaims Jim Morrison, the group's writer and singer. "A sensuous evil world, strange and haunting, the path of the sun. . . . We're all centered around the end of the zodiac, the Pacific."

Constrained in recording studios and falsified in their stage and TV appearances, The Doors need to be heard in their own milieu. They really do belong to the misty littoral of Southern California, facing the setting sun and leading a hippie tribe in their shamanistic rites. One can see Jim Morrison in the center of the circle, immense electric totems behind him, as he stands limply, his snaky body encased in black vinyl, his finely chiseled features framed in flowing Dionysian hair, his hands clutching, his mouth almost devouring the mike, as he chants with closed eyes the hallucinatory verses of "The End."

"The End" commences by evoking with solemn drones and shimmering metal the shadowy, consecrated atmosphere that surrounds the performance of an Indian temple dancer. But instead of sacred pantomime, we hear a voice — husky, pale, and weary — intoning words of farewell. Like all of The Doors' music, the theme hovers abstractly between sex, drugs, and death. What is ending: a love affair, an acid trip, the world? We cannot tell but it hardly matters. The emotion is produced by the ritual. First, the shaman or soul voyager launches himself with the aid of drugs and music into the spirit world; then he travels among its terrors, calling out his adventures to the awe-struck tribe. Sometimes his language is fragmentary and symbolic: he sings of an ancient snake, a gold mine, the summer rain. Sometimes the words are literal and dramatic, as in the climactic episode. "The killer awakes before dawn. He puts his boots on. He took a face from the ancient gallery. And he walks on down the hall. . . . And he came to a door and he looked inside." The Oedipal theme emerges with the cool violence of a Capote novel, " 'Father?' 'Yes, son?' 'I want to kill you. Mother? I want to —.' " The words explode into an incredible scream; the drums thunder and crash. But this is not the end. The tumult subsides, and the shaman croons like a seductive snake: "Come on baby, take a chance with us, and meet me at the back of the blue bus. Tonight, tomorrow night, blue bus, tonight, come on, yeah!" As he repeats the phrase with mounting urgency and indistinctness, the music — which has been coiling as if to strike — slips into a rocking raga and then races upward to an enormous crescendo. At the peak of the excitement, a sinister whine is heard (like The Beatles' dynamo) and then the sound erupts in crashing waves. Behind the uproar Morrison can be heard chanting hoarsely: "Kill! Kill! Kill! Fuck! Fuck! Fuck!" Then comes the end, not violently or cruelly but with a gradual subsidence into the dark and mysterious sounds of the beginning.

The mood of The Doors is revolutionary in that it represents a deliberate break with the mentality of the hippies — and for that matter, with that of the white rock generation. Instead of "flower power" and "love, love, love," The Doors project real and undisguised anger. The seriousness of their anger varies from the Lear-like rage of "The End" to the deadpan mockery of "She's a Twentieth Century Fox," one of many songs that score off the modern woman. But the important point about this anger is its calculated violation of a taboo. For in the overthrow of so many old prohibitions, there has grown up a new structure of forbidden things and denied emotions — and the first of these is anger. By venting their rage in the ceremony of the tribe, The Doors both express their own freedom and achieve their purpose as gurus, which is to confront their audience with the most basic unbearable truths. At the same time they achieve artistic effects that are finer than the adolescent moralism of Janis Ian or the monotonous, unmusical irony of Bob Dylan. They produce a purifying catharsis that leaves their audiences shaken but surer in themselves.

The Doors are no less revolutionary as musicians. Faced with the rigidifying conventions of hard rock, they have opened the door of free improvisation. The great moments at their recent concerts have been the extended treatments of tunes that were originally the constrictively patterned products of the rock formulary. By recovering the valuable skills that were lost to popular music through the abandonment of jazz, The Doors have begun to reestablish jazz on a rock foundation. But their development is completely independent of traditional jazz. The finest performing musicians on the scene today, their instrumental language owes more to Bach than bop and more than either to B movies. When The Doors jam, the effect is that of a mad organist tracing his fugue across an electric keyboard while beside him hovers a crazy chemist concocting psychedelics out of the sonorities of a steel guitar. Obviously, the boys have done a lot of their tripping in the vicinity of Hollywood.

Ultimately, what is most impressive about The Doors is the completeness of their commitment. Whether it be acid, sex, ritual, or rock, they are further into it than any other group. Perhaps this explains the air of dignity that accompanies all their actions. No matter how wild or strange this group behaves, one feels they are in the American grain — indigenous artists like Walt Whitman or Charlie Parker.

VI

By pushing toward higher levels of imaginative excellence, rock has begun to realize one of the most cherished dreams of mass culture: to cultivate from the vigorous but crude growth of the popular arts a new serious art that would combine the strength of native roots with the beauty flowering from the highest art. In America this hope had been baffled time and time again by the failure of any of our popular arts (with minor exceptions) to achieve, after generations of development, the stature implicit in their beginnings. Like thundering geysers from underground, the geniuses of jazz, for example, have hurled themselves at their lofty goals only to fall back, spent by their unaided efforts. And this hope would have remained futile had it not been for the simultaneous emergence of two necessary conditions: first, the widespread assimilation through the mass media of the themes and technical resources of the fine arts; second, the tendency of serious artists today to exploit the myths and devices of the popular culture.

The difficulty of such a convergence of high and low modern art is well attested by recent history. On two memorable occasions in recent decades, a self-taught genius of popular music has sought unsuccessfully to study with a contemporary master. In the twenties George Gershwin approached Maurice Ravel in Paris, only to be told that there was no way he could improve what he was already doing so perfectly. Again in the forties, in New York, Charlie Parker implored Edgard Varèse to take him on in any capacity (even as a cook) in exchange for lessons in composition. But again the artist demurred — not because he lacked appreciation of Parker's gifts but simply because he could not imagine what two such sundered arts might have to contribute to each other. Today the situation is radically different — so much so that if John Lennon were to sit down with John Cage to discuss music, one wonders who would come away the wiser.

J. L. SIMMONS
BARRY WINOGRAD
the sounds of new music

Popular music has troubled Americans ever since the turn of the century when ragtime and jazz first began to evolve and be played in the off-limits sections of southern and eastern cities. From its inception, it was colored with some of the ill-repute of the peoples from which it sprang: the emancipated Negroes, the migrant workers and tramps, the back country and hill folk. And ever since the 1920's when Dixieland, jazz, and folk music first began to make their way into the mainstream of American society, many people have worried over the vulgarizing and immoralizing influence of the wild new music. They were viewed as pied-pipings to moral decay and the young who flocked to listen were scorned. A girl's reputation could be ruined just by being seen at places where the music was played.

In a sense, Dixieland, Negro rhythm and blues, folk music, and rock and roll are considered the illegitimate off-spring of the American arts, and consequently they have been shunned and shamed as much as loved and supported. These kinds of music — although indigenous to certain aspects of American culture — have always been morally suspect and their successes have never lost a taint of notoriety. In their purest forms, they have mostly existed around the fringes, and the musicians who played them were almost entirely outsiders by birth or by choice. When they did reach the mainstream channels of the society, it was almost always in a watered down form in which the guttural chords and the frank and penetrating lyrics were cleaned up and little of their original vitality survived. Many of the conventional artists, who the man in the street might think of as great jazz musicians or folk singers, were seen as temporizing mediocrities by the originators and their followers. To this day, for instance, a symbol of true involvement in some scenes is the ownership of an old, original "Leadbelly" album, uncut and recorded by a company, it seems, no one ever heard of.

These various musical traditions — suspect in themselves — form the basis of the new music which now virtually dominates the sales charts of single records and albums. The new music is a synthesis which has evolved from these traditions and which holds promise of continuing change. This synthesis has produced a kind of music that is, in many ways, new in both content and style. As with other influences (such as literature and fashion), the culture becomes reshaped and the receptivity within the general populace for the new music is probably of a higher order than that given by previous generations to *their* own brand of new music. Aside from the fact that in a short time over half of our population will be under twenty-one, there exist other allies within society. Children of the fifties who grew up with Presley, Little Richard, *et al.*, are now the young marrieds of the sixties and the strands of musical bondage are strong enough to keep them tuned to pop music stations on the radio; to keep them somewhat up to date with the newest sounds.

Yet, even with these quiet colleagues on their side, the practitioners of the new sounds evoke a strangely antagonistic opposition. It is not a fight against the music itself that arouses many today, but actually a feeling of conflict with those things to which the new music has become attached, especially drugs.

"Forceful" is one word often used to describe the new music. Whether loud or soft, upbeat or slow, a flat-picked guitar or a plucked sitar, it is more direct and candid in its sensuality or protest or chagrin. Even the songs depicting the confusions of the modern scene are more bold and candid and less evasive than the songs of even the most recent past. The lyrics are more realistic and sophisticated in the sense that the veils of obvious romantic distance are gone. Simple-minded jingles, while still around, are now being replaced by what not infrequently amounts to good poetry. The impact of the new fashion (it is still too soon to call it a permanent facet of American music) goes even to those groups and individuals caught within the whirl of its sounds and sales. That is, few young people will say that the Beatles, the Stones, or Dylan of 1963 are the same today. The sound is moving, dynamic, constantly adjusting to new revelations about the way things are.

As a constant companion to the happeners, the new music and its themes are a running commentary on their own changing lives. It often verbalizes and clarifies their own vague feelings and sometimes it provides directions about what to do. People dance, read, make love, turn on, chat, and walk along the beach to the background of its sounds. Teenagers wash dishes and talk on the phone while listening to it and almost no one can escape overhearing the music on jukeboxes, TV commercials, neighbors' phonographs, or the transistor radios of strolling youths.

The new musicians are the poets and troubadours of what's happening, and their work, as it is disseminated, becomes itself an active social force which shapes and spreads the themes it is describing. As chroniclers, these artists therefore are acting also as innovators and propagandists. As propagandists, they still cloak their thoughts behind frequently murky lyrics; words that are vague to censors or parents, but "in" with the listeners. For example, anyone who is really happening knows about "Mr. Tambourine Man's" relationship to the drug scene on the first spin of the disc. And it takes little native intelligence to catch the essence of what The Fugs are saying when they clamor "Kill for Peace." The music has become a chronicle of events and messages, with the latter approaching the esprit of past eras' revolutionary ballads.

The words are different, and even though it's difficult to define the antagonists, the force of feeling and craving are all too clear.

There are many varieties of the new music and many aficionados would balk at even discussing them all together. Lumping them together aids us in discussing them, helps the student in comprehending their import for society, but it also diminishes what each style particularly offers. There are several distinguishable varieties of new jazz, a host of differing rock and roll sounds (variously called rock, folk rock, blue rock, jug rock, raga rock, and acid rock), a sprinkling of folk styles, and other sounds which do not exactly belong in any category and which give classification headaches to record store managers. But in most of the songs, the musical scholar can detect various admixtures of the influences mentioned earlier, and beneath the variety of style and phrasings runs the common theme of the new emerging ethos and style of life.

Taken as a whole, the new music embodies two messages. *"Come Swing With Me."* The crooning invitation to romance which was the mainstay of popular music during the thirties and forties and the essence of rock and roll in the fifties, has become more a direct invitation to dance the dance of life. This invitation — expressed in so many songs by the shout "c'mon" — is sometimes aimed specifically at a possible sex partner and is a thinly disguised proposition. But at least as often, it is a more diffuse exhortation for everyone to shuffle off their mantle of preoccupations and hangups and to come out where it's at. If you're uptight about things, well maybe you have good reasons, but when there's a whole world outside "a'grooving," why bother? Let's go where the action is. The invitation to the dance of life is, in the last analysis, extended to everyone and it is as cordial and indiscriminate as the morning sun.

The second underlying theme is more disturbing: *"Myself a Stranger and Afraid in a World I Never Made."* This poignant feeling of being a stranger moving through an alien environment comes through sometimes as a bitter indictment of the Establishment which sharply focuses upon nowhere men, universal soldiers, sounds of silence, or desolation rows. At other points, the tunes are about more personal distresses; a yesterday, a solitary man, the magic missing in a supposed magic town, or the larger question, "where do you or I go?" In still other instances, the songs express an uncertain yet determined reassurance that the new world is the rightful homeland of the modern spirit, you can walk a cat named dog, have a groovy kind of love, seek elusive butterflies, and catch reflections in a crystal wind.

When combined, these themes infuse a powerful sense of seduction in the happening way of life, into the spirit if not the substance of the hang-loose ethic. The music proclaims that you, sir, are not alone in your overall disenchantment with the state of most human relationships, that you are one of "the seekers" searching for meaningful values without an always hovering parent or dollar sign.

It has been common in the past few years to speak of the alienation modern youths feel when they consider their historical relationship to current meanings and older customs. What the new music trumpets, as it blares from record stores, stereos, and dance halls, is not as much the presentation of the subjective awareness of an alienated individual as it is that person's call to others like him. It is a call predicated on the belief that folks have enough in common now to transcend the sluggish, nerve-stilling impact of generational alienation and to proceed up and onward to some better world.

The music reveals this transition and is changing at this very moment. Perhaps this idea that things not only can change, but should become new and different, is part of the underground diffusion of the hang-loose ethic. The bitterness and rancor of earlier years is absent more often than not. When pity is presented in today's music, it is most frequently an expression of remorse about something that has happened to the total scene or an admonition to the majority that the path they are on leads nowhere but along the cliff of destruction. Now and again, the songs declaim the "other" world, but more and more often they proclaim the need to go out there "to bring them all on in."

But that is not all there is to the new music. Outside of the sales charts and the big names and mass distribution and communications business that have grown up around them are two other facets of the musical scene. The first is the army of local amateur and semi-professional young musicians who play the new music live at teenage night spots, college action spots, weekend dances, and shopping center moonlight sales. Their competence varies from embarrassing to as good and original as anything you can purchase at your town's "music city." A very few of these will get some measure of fame, the fleeting fame of one successful record and one big season in most cases. In almost every instance they simply make music for themselves and others and pick up a bit of money to help keep them in instruments, pot, and candy bars. A few reach such notoriety in their own locales that they are favored over most of the big national names in the new and emerging music. San Francisco's "Jefferson Airplane" has long been known in that area, and at this writing they are gaining momentum on national charts. This group, and a few others like them on the West Coast, such as "The Seeds" and the "Mothers of Invention" in Los Angeles, manage to pick up more than pure pocket money, but, consistent with the ethic, they are usually content without cross-country glory and all the hassles inevitably bound up with fame.

Secondly, there is a smaller, less known world of musicians and fans which exists outside the sales charts and TV shows, but which is an important part of the happenings among the avant-garde and the action capitals. It helps to set the tone and color the lives of the more far out groups in much the same way that literary magazines influence the more commercially successful literary world. Here new styles are experimented with, worked out, and improved upon. Tastes in this fringe world of music, in which each little "group" often has its own balladeer, may run months or sometimes years ahead of what one hears on popular radio. Bob Dylan, for example, was appreciated by thousands of people and scores of other musicians, some of them eminent, before the average American knew his name as part of the breakfast table chatter. Other artists manage to have long careers with only the support of such an informal and underground audience, and they never make it in the bigtime music world — a fact of life which really pleases many of them. The life of such artists is often checkered and gruelling and they live like vagabonds floating on a sometimes smooth, sometimes choppy sea of existence. But there are usually friends to give them a drink or a joint, friends to offer them a bed, and even a girl with whom they can share it. If they are rootless, they are also getting to do what they want (and that's something, isn't it?).

Since youths buy most of the records and put most of the money in jukeboxes, their tastes have come to dominate the popular music world, although, with constantly recurring payola scandals, their philosophy is often ignored and even abused. Whether moralizers like it or no, this market is big business and catering to it is a multi-million dollar enterprise. Only on Broadway and in nightclub circles do older tastes hold sway, a fact that helps explain the emergence of the hippies' very own ballroom discotheques.

The rhythmic cacophony of notes that explodes at San Francisco's Fillmore Auditorium is not unmatched in America — in terms of both the performers and the audience. Situated in an overwhelmingly Negro district in that city, the Friday and Saturday night concerts are attended by many from all races. Straight people go there, but they are obviously and splenderously in the minority and they tend to be happeners of a sort that simply groove on big sounds. Standing at the entrance is an enriching experience in that one human can see hundreds of others much like him, yet others who are often carved in a peculiarly individualistic way. This door standing exercise also reveals an extraordinary number of heads — marijuana, LSD, peyote, and so on — who have come specifically to experience. Indeed, the Fillmore is just that: an unforgettable journey into an arena not yet part of the American mainstream.

Proprietors of this establishment, and the owners of others in San Francisco and cities throughout the land, know how to cater to their select customers. Not only are the bands far better than those that usually play for high school or college dances, but the amplification is turned up to peak, enabling the listeners to immerse themselves in the music. Compounding this technical bombardment of sound are the musicians themselves who absolutely cover the microphones with their instruments and mouths. But music, even if it is good and loud, is not enough and it is the extra features that draw the Fillmore's exclusive clientele, that is, the drug happeners.

The first of the extra benefits, craved by even this unstructured union, is the accented darkness of the large ballroom. Punctuated by flashing rotating and changing lights, the walls and ceilings and floor provide ample physical and sensual delights for individuals who want to trip. One especially bright light, variously called a strobe or stroboscope, looks for all the world like burning magnesium foil, flips and turns and casts its powerful radiant glow over the entire crowd of happeners. If the eyes can be taken off this light and focused on others around the floor, they look strangely like actors from early motion pictures with a hurky-jerky appearance and a nonchalant unawareness of everything that is taking place around them.

The items provided for the benefit of these sensuous attenders goes on and on: a large block of seats just below and in front of the band platform provides space in which the individual can not only immerse himself in the music, but where he can really be drowned, if he so desires; a tableau above and behind the platform on which are cast movies without sound (such as a silent "King Kong") or liquid doodles in water color, thrown upon the wall by a distant projector; and the establishment keeps its cool, so to speak, by offering as refreshments such blase items as soda pop, near beer, gum, and candy. The Fillmore is a traveler's reality-fantasy revealing both the bond and the spirit of the happening world.

The lights that shine and spotlight, the lights that glow and reveal, are not the lights of an isolated instance in our culture. But neither is it in danger of being submerged amidst a mass produced glare of happening action spots around the nation. It is a demarcation line for most — a place in which people turn on to their own way of existence, and, for a growing number, it is a setting for realizing what could be termed America's redesigned style of life.

A survey of the record buying public's tastes indicates that except for a few distinct styles (such as hillbilly music, varieties of jug-band composition, and the Motown sound) the music of today goes from West to East, no longer traveling from New York's Tin Pan Alleys to the palm lined boulevards of Los Angeles or the hills of San Francisco. During the spring of 1966 for example, it was not uncommon to find big West Coast singers or groups virtually unknown in the East. It appears that the sounds, if not the musicians who make them, come from the shores of the Pacific, cascading across the continent to other scenes in other places. Ironic though it may be for the performers involved, it remains true that many of the current big figures in the new music found their first recognition amongst the record buying and concert attending public in the West. The majesty of these sounds draws musicians from all over the country in their effort to find a place in the sun; it also draws the attention of record manufacturers who realize the pace-setting nature of musical fashion that builds itself up under the flare of the California strobe.

The two main oppositions to the new music are that it is tasteless and that it is immoral. With its candor and irreverence, the music shocks many people, although some of the tamer tunes will set older toes to tapping. But to many people it is simply noise; humdrum tunes played badly, raucously and with little variation in style. Since they can find no musical merit to the sounds, and because they find the lyrics both "dirty" and "suggestive," they look about seeking the foundations of its popularity. The most common explanation is that the youth are sheep, following fads and being victimized by shady disc jockeys and managers. Others feel that the popularity is simply the result of the uneducated poor taste of youth and a reflection of the tendency towards outright barbarism, supposedly inherent in mass cultures. What we need, they claim, are more courses in musical appreciation, the presentation of "good" music on radio and television, and a self-servicing censorship body that would function for the record industry in much the same way as the movie industry's control board works to insure "cleaner" (and more insipid) films.

This view blends with the second charge that the music is vulgar in both a broad and narrow sense. Not only have the practitioners been branded on occasion with the stigma of sexual perversion, but some rightist groups have gone so far as to charge that the music is engineered and underwritten by the Communists as a means of subverting the morals of the country and as a hidden technique of brainwashing our populace. The evidence offered for such a conspiracy is that several people in the music world have been connected with such "Communist-front-groups" as the NAACP, the American Civil Liberties Union, SNCC, and naturally, the University of California.

In a more moderate vein, many parents and others are concerned that the music may be too suggestive, downright sexually arousing for young people listening and dancing to the sounds and lyrics. Many who are real believers in the new music would rather not defend themselves against such positions for, it is their feeling, the notes and words are accurate presentations of their attitudes and emotions. As for those who claim that the music replaces intimate sexual relations by providing mass scenes of rhythmic orgasms, they respond, "look again . . . and, while you're at it, look at your own generation's music and the inhibitions it covered up."

These are happening times and the music of these times, more openly and blatantly than most other aspects of the happenings, leads the way to where it's at. With its ties to almost all the current scenes, the new music offers a substantive look at bits and pieces of the hang-loose ethic. It does not pretend to speak for everyone and his brother, but it does speak *to* them if they would just sit down and listen. The fact that this music so well portrays the temper of the generational change we have been discussing, is, itself, an open invitation.

GENE LEES
rock: symptom of today's
sociological disturbances

The vast sentimental homecoming of weary, lonely men in the years after World War II produced a staggering number of marriages, an eyebrow-raising number of babies. Soon the shock wave of these events went racing down demographic charts into the future: experts in these matters predicted that in five more years we would need so many new kindergarten rooms, then so many new junior high schools, and finally millions of square feet of new college space.

That wave, that sudden arc in the population charts, finally is being felt in the adult world. Millions of those postwar babies reached voting age in 1966, millions more this year. Still more will come into that status every year for some time to come, and this fact is influencing every phase of American life from the design of automobiles (Ford's Mustang, Chevrolet's Camaro) to the way Bobby Kennedy combs his hair. But its heaviest impact thus far has been on entertainment.

Because they are not yet burdened with families and the concomitant responsibilities, young people have always been the primary consumers of entertainment. Not only are they free to move around in search of it, they have little else to do with their money but spend it on themselves, particularly in America's large and affluent middle class.

The men who manufacture entertainment have a shrewd awareness that millions on millions of dollars annually pass through the hands of adolescents, and, with more than fifty per cent of America's population now under the age of twenty-five, they tailor their product accordingly, give the kids what they want — or have been induced to want. In music, what they want is rock-and-roll, a term that has, as we shall see, lost all meaning as the form of the music has altered and evolved. Indeed, many young entertainers, such as the duo Simon and Garfunkel . . . eschew the term, though their work does in fact grow out of the rock "tradition."

The term rock-and-roll has a sexual connotation — rockin' and rollin' originally meant fornicating. But then, the word jazz, once a verb, meant the same thing. Both terms have long since lost their original meaning and become careless catchalls of musical categorization.

What rock-and-roll may be is more evasive of definition; but jazz too

From *High Fidelity*, November, 1967. Copyright © 1967 by *High Fidelity*. Reprinted by permission.

has consistently defied neat semantic pigeonholing. As a commercial phenomenon in American popular music, rock-and-roll (later called r & r, and currently rock) was first felt in the early 1950's, particularly with the arrival of Bill Haley and the Comets. It had begun to decline, the monster seemed to be growing pale, when a young man from Tennessee made his first records on a Nashville label called Sun. Later he moved to RCA Victor. His name was Elvis Presley, and the libidinous frenzy he touched off among young girls was the most feverish thing of its kind since the young Frank Sinatra left the Tommy Dorsey orchestra in 1943 to become a star.

Presley was a musical hybrid of Arthur Crudup and Hank Williams. A few musicians found real worth in him. Said jazz pianist Dick Katz, "He's an authentic white country blues singer, and a damn good one." Others demurred. Most adults, particularly critics, wished he would simply go away. He didn't. RCA Victor reports that Presley, a multi-millionaire, makes more money for them now than ever before in his long association with the label.

Presley has succeeded in cross-breeding the blues — a simple 12-bar form based on simple tonic-dominant chord relationships, the third, fifth, and seventh of the scale being flatted — with country-and-western music. That hybrid would not go away either.

Other figures, other styles, were to come and go — and a few to come and stay. The Everly Brothers had a significant impact on the development of rock; so did Little Richard, Fats Domino, and Chubby Checker. Dancing at the time of Presley's first fame was descended from the Lindy practiced by the young generation of the late 1930s and early 40s. With Chubby Checker came the Twist, and with the Twist body contact in dance was, for the nonce, ended. The parental generation found these dances "immoral." Ironically, the waltz in Johann Strauss's time was found "immoral" for the opposite reason: precisely because there was body contact, albeit polite and stiffly formal contact. Youth is invariably charged with immorality, though any man or woman of the world can tell you that seduction becomes conspicuously easier after thirty.

Herein lies another key to the significance of rock-and-roll — its restoration of dancing as a social pastime among the young. Irving Berlin's *Alexander's Ragtime Band* in 1911, with its jaunty four-four rhythm simple enough for even the most lead-footed to follow, actually launched the wave of social dancing that swept America, setting off the career of dancers Vernon and Irene Castle and giving rise to night-clubs as part of the American entertainment scene — they originally were places to go and dance — just as rock was later to spawn discothèques.

Through the Twenties, Thirties, and Forties, dancing continued to be a major form of socio-recreational-romantic activity for America's young. By the late Thirties, the music was an amalgam of jazz and popular music, played by big bands of as many as sixteen men. This era is remembered with nostalgic affection by a generation now in its forties as a golden age of American music. But if it was the age of George Gershwin and Jerome Kern, it was also the age of *The Hut Sut Song, A-Tisket A-Tasket, Three Little Fishes, Mairzy Doats, The Music Goes Round and Round*; and of Blue Barron, Sammy Kaye, Kay Kyser, and Shep Fields and His Rippling Rhythm. The few great bands were exceptions to the norm, oases of real musical fertility in a desert whose principal flora was corn. The kids today are quite right about the music their parents listened to: most of it was trash. The parents are quite right about what their young listen to: most of that is trash too.

By the end of the 1940s, the temporary and uneasy alliance of popular music and jazz was breaking up. Jazzmen, tired of the pop song format and the show biz limitations on their music, began to go their own way, taking a part of the pop music audience — the most perceptive part — with them. And pop music, deprived of the stimulus to excellence that jazzmen had brought to it, began to decline in quality: America was heading into a decade of *How Much Is That Doggy in the Window, Tennessee Waltz*, and similar exercises in trivia. The public, found itself with nothing to dance to — most pop music was too bland, too saccharine, and jazz had become undanceable. Since then, of course, jazz has run into serious aesthetic problems: finding itself unable to push its development any further in the direction of chromaticism, it went through a painfully synthetic and self-conscious experimentalism in the late 1950s and early 60s, and now finds itself with almost no audience at all — though lately there have been faint flushes of health on the patient's face, thanks in part to transfusions from other forms of music, including of all things rock. Rock, meantime, has begun borrowing from jazz. And both are borrowing from Indian music.

The dance music vacuum was filled in the mid-1950s by rock-and-roll, though today at least part of rock-and-roll is intended as listening, rather than dance, music. One of the best and most successful of the young English rock musicians, visiting New York after a long tour of the United States, told me: "I really detest those packaged rock shows.

We have to play all our worst material, and I simply have lost all tolerance for the teeny boppers. They're ridiculous. I think in future we'll try to do only college concerts. There we can play our good things, and they listen." The musician's age? Nineteen. An echo of jazz in the late Forties? Yes indeed. Will success spoil rock?

It seems to be inevitable that whatever one man learns to do, another will learn to do better, and this principle has been at work in rock for the last five years. Though rock musicians were at first crude and ignorant amateurs, a measure of professionalism has gradually come to the music. And even the young nonrock musicians are influenced by the style. Says Kenneth Ascher, a twenty-two-year-old graduate student of composition at Columbia University and, during his vacations, pianist (and sometimes arranger) for the still successful Woody Herman band: "Rock? I like it — even more now than before. I find the chord changes very free — freer than some jazz — and sometimes very interesting. Jazz now seems to be directionless, though of course some of it is wonderful. Some jazz people are going through an unnatural, forced evolution, rather than a natural one. It seems there's much less tension in rock groups, probably because of their corporate structure."

When Elvis Presley became famous, it is worth noting, Kenneth Ascher was ten.

Leonard Bernstein said during a CBS Television special on rock earlier this year that the popular music scene today is "unlike any scene I can think of in the history of all music. It's completely of, by, and for the kids, and by kids I mean anyone from eight years old to twenty-five. They write the songs, they sing them, own them, record them. They also buy the records, create the market, and they set the fashion in the music, in dress, in dance, in hair style, lingo, social attitudes."

Bernstein stresses the uniqueness of the present situation, but a musician of his erudition couldn't possibly have forgotten that at other periods in history most composers were composer-performers — and many of them were "kids." After all, Haydn had composed his first Mass by the time he was twenty. Mendelssohn had written his Octet for Strings by the time he was sixteen, Schubert was dead at thirty-one — and no one needs reminding of the incredible Young Mozart. And closer to our own day, Stan Getz recorded his first great solos when he was seventeen, Woody Herman headed his first band when he was little more than twenty. Duke Ellington had his first band before he was twenty. Artie Shaw, Gerry Mulligan, Ella Fitzgerald were professionals in their teens. Both Kern and Gershwin (whose first song was published when he was eighteen) had written Broadway shows before they were twenty-five. Cole Porter was a comparatively old man when he had his first Broadway hit — twenty-seven. As musicologist Henry Pleasants put it, "Music seems to be largely a young man's art. It has something to do with being in love."

Bernstein neglects to mention another point: how often styles in clothes have been linked to popular music in the past. The exaggerated wide-shouldered big-kneed style in men's clothes that followed World War II was derived from the "zoot suits" affected by jazz followers, and such idols as Cab Calloway. Bobby sox were a spin-off of Frank Sinatra's early popularity.

The young are ardent conformists. But the conformity is to what sociologists call their "peer groups." Any parent will tell you that children want to do and wear exactly what their friends do. The mod fashions of today are *de rigueur,* and conformity in dress has probably never been more rigidly enforced than it is among the more devoted pop music worshippers today. Robert Altschuler, press director of Columbia Records, observed at the recent Monterey pop music festival that a few youths showed up with short haircuts and comparatively conservative clothes. "The girls wouldn't look at them," he said.

In rebelling against conformity, the young invariably fall into this trap, a conformity that is perhaps the most rigid they will know in all the course of their lives. This makes them extraordinarily manipulatable in terms of commerce. Sociologists have been pointing out for years that America is gradually being converted into a consumer society. This generation of youth is the first in the country's history trained from birth to be consumers. Said a woman executive in a New York advertising agency, "If you could see how shrewdly and calculatedly the kids are led to buy things, almost by push-button control, it would make your blood run cold."

No industry manipulates youth with the cool surgical skill of the pop music business. But the function is not pure: partly the industry controls the kids' minds, partly it responds to them. Since the young are, and always have been, rebellious, the industry is shrewdly selling them rebellion — packaged, wrapped, plastic rebellion. The Monkees, a rock-and-roll group icily manufactured for television (an ad was put in a trade paper for actors who could sing: five hundred applied and four were picked) and a show vaguely imitating Beatles movies, recently recorded a song in which, according to current fad, they criticized adults, picturing them as mindlessly watching TV sets. But TV made the Monkees, most of the people who watch them are the young (the median age of viewers, according to a survey, is ten), and many adults say these days that they don't watch television — it's become too dull. Such is the hypocrisy of much of the rebellion preached in the world of rock.

Yet not all of it is phony. Among a certain intelligent and perceptive element among the young, the rebellion is deep and real. This is true among the performers and the fans alike. What is voiced in at least some of the music is a troubled concern for the drift of American society today — its materialism, its apparent selfishness, the rat race towards illusory accomplishment, the filth and stagnation of the nation's cities, the lethargy of Congress, the terrible moral questions posed by the war in Vietnam. It is significant that though there have been a few pro-war songs, the vast majority are anti-war. The young seem to feel that if they have to fight wars, they should have a voice in whether the wars are begun in the first place. It is difficult to refute this logic, particularly since, thanks to the proliferation of communications, they are on the whole the best-informed generation of the young in the country's history.

These concerns find their way into the music.

The switch to topicality in rock-and-roll resulted from the crossbreeding of "folk" music and rock, largely after the example of songwriter-singer Bob Dylan, about three years ago. Dylan's songs were rebellious, topical, astringent — not very good, in most cases, but at least rebellious, topical, astringent.

The second major influence on rock in the Sixties has been the Beatles, who also began hinting at meanings beyond the conventionally romantic. Later, drugs got into the picture. Many, probably most, of the rock groups began experimenting with marijuana, the favorite intoxicant of jazz musicians before them, and then LSD became mixed into it, particularly in San Francisco. Psychedelic rock was born.

By now the movement has grown so that it is as difficult to speak of rock in generalities as it was to sum up the pop music of the Thirties in a few phrases. The music varies enormously in quality. Where adults err is in thinking that all rock listeners accept the music blindly, uncritically. If the music is attacked, the young will of course rally to its defense, sometimes becoming a little ferocious. But if you get them talking quietly, you often find that they have well-developed critical faculties of their own.

Chris Curtis is a fifteen-year-old high school student at New York City's Trinity School. Trained on piano as a small boy, he acquired a guitar, taught himself to play it, organized a rock group of his own, and now plays semiprofessional dance jobs in the area.

"From the standpoint of my age," he says, "I would say that I like it 'cause it's loud. This is true. I know from the dances I used to go to. I'd walk in the door and the first thing that hit me was the volume. It would be really exciting — for about five minutes, anyway. If the band is bad, the music becomes annoying. Good or bad, by the end of a half hour, you usually have a headache.

"In jazz, there is a universal characteristic that I like. That is the very fact that it does vary. It has a greater scope of moods and a more unified, solid sound, generally, than rock.

"But rock, at least the good stuff, varies too, only on a lower level, musically, than jazz.

"The groups which, in my opinion, produce garbage are the Dave Clark Five, the Monkees, Sam the Sham and the Pharaohs, the Standells, Herman's Hermits, Question Mark and the Mysterians, and a lot more. They range from boring to terrible.

"Any adult who wants to find out what's good in the music, though, I'd advise them to listen to . . .

"The Beatles. I like them because they're original. They're truthful. They're funny, exciting, not too serious. Occasionally they write very beautiful songs. Their songs always have substance.

"The Byrds. They used to sing folk songs, but they're more into a mixture of country and jazz now. They're writing some good songs, and the unusual sound they project with the electric twelve-string guitar is interesting. Sometimes it sounds like different wind instruments.

"The Lovin' Spoonful. They're fun. Occasionally they write very good music.

"The Mamas and the Papas. I like their vocal blend. It's round and mellow. John Phillips, the leader, writes good songs.

"Simon and Garfunkel. The lyrics and music are always a perfect marriage. They're critical of the times, but a bit more positive than Dylan. The songs are ironic, but often hopeful.

"The Jefferson Airplane — the most exciting group. Their sound is sometimes empty and sloppy, but their vocal work makes up for it.

"Donovan. He's a contemporary folk singer. His songs contain beautiful imagery.

"There are some people I want to hear more of — The Mothers of Invention, Janis Ian, Buffalo Springfield.

"The new thing is the blues revival. Groups such as the Blues Project, Paul Butterfield, Spencer Davis, the Animals, are all in this bag. Unfortunately, the style of the new blues hardly varies between groups, so it can get pretty dull. This is what the teeny boppers are starting to go for, by the way."

Probably the most musical of all rock groups is the Mothers of Invention. Though they satirize musical styles of the past, they have a firm grasp on them, all the way from the voh-doh-dee-oh-doh of the 1920s through the ballad style of the '30s and '40s to the chromaticism of Miles Davis. They are the most greasy, seedy, crumby-looking group in the rock field — and the most skilled. Their approach to music and society is fierce, satirical, and often scatological. Their hero apparently is Lenny Bruce, the brilliant comic and social critic who died in 1966. Bruce is also a hero to a representative of the other end of the rock spectrum, Paul Simon of Simon and Garfunkel, whose music is as gentle as the Mothers' is harsh.

What distinguishes the Mothers (a notorious pun that every fan understands) is their cultural roots. Most rockers lack a knowledge of musical precedent, being prone to claim brilliant originality when they discover some harmonic or other device known to music for a century or even more. Sometimes, of course, they achieve genuine originality precisely through their lack of knowledge — which, if it does not breed skill, at least breeds a lack of inhibition.

For a long time, rock was fixed firmly in triadic harmony, and chromaticism was spurned. It is always convenient, of course, to denigrate what you cannot do: it relieves one of the responsibility of learning. It is noteworthy that the contempt for more complex harmony has diminished as the rockers slowly have begun to get the hang of it.

If, on the whole, the rockers have shown a lack of knowledge of past musical accomplishment, they are setting their sights higher today. Many are admirers of jazz. Their fans are often unaware of this, and this leads to some astonishingly grandiose claims for rock. Writes a student at the University of Toronto: "It is said so often, and it begins to sound monotonous to repeat it, but what the Beatles are producing is a genre new to the music field — a unique new art form . . . Within the simplifying format [of their "Sgt. Pepper" album] they have been able to make a wealth of comments on the banality, frivolity, and passivity of modern-day life."

The kids actually think this sort of thing is new. Few among them know Lorenz Hart's scathing (though by now dated) satire on the banality, frivolity, and passivity of life in the 1930s, *Too Good for the Average Man*. Fewer still know the grim anti-war lyrics Ira Gershwin wrote in the 1920s for *Strike Up the Band*. And practically none is aware of the impact William S. Gilbert's work had in the late nineteenth century; the Gilbert and Sullivan operettas caused a bit of trembling in the British ruling class and, in one instance, caused a crisis in diplomatic relations between England and Japan.

Says Graham Nash of the Hollies: "I think that pop musicians in today's generation are in a fantastic position — they could rule the world, man."

This illusion of power (John Lennon of the Beatles caused a scandal by saying the Beatles were more popular than Jesus, though he was probably quite right) is another of the curious characteristics of rock musicians and their followers — though even that is not entirely new; Peter Yarrow of Peter, Paul, and Mary said during the folk fad a few years ago that he thought the trio could swing a federal election. The rock musicians are impressed by the statistics of their sales and by the communications explosion — the television and phonograph industries through which they reach their audience. Yet the fact is that, thus far, no rock group, not even the entire rock movement put together, has made a government nervous, as Gilbert and Sullivan did.

Robert J. Wolfson, professor of economics at Syracuse University, said in a recent letter to the New York *Times:* "What is clearest about the under-30s is that they have suffered a grievous environmental deprivation which has stunted their social and intellectual growth and which may be very costly to all of us. They are probably the only generation of young people to have been cut off from their past, to have grown up ahistorical.

"Those of us who left adolescence in the early and mid-Forties and before had slightly older comrades who gave us the benefit of the accumulated experience of generations of socially conscious and active young people. But as a consequence of the political inactivity and non-commitment which prevailed among the nation's youth during the 1950s, this was not available to the kids who have grown up in the past eight years."

The arrogance of age lies in its belief that youth has nothing to say; the arrogance of youth lies in its belief that age couldn't understand anyway. If there is a generation gap, it is largely the fault of adults, too many (but by no means all) of whom are unwilling to listen. Certainly youth is talking, and largely in the musical form roughly called rock. They are expressing a yearning, a weariness with stupidity and brutality and greed, that may prove to be the healthiest thing to have happened to America since an earlier crowd of rebels told George III where to go.

So the music is loud? So was that of the Lionel Hampton and Woody Herman bands in the 1940s — ear-shatteringly loud. They wear funny clothes on the bandstand? So did Duke Ellington. So they talk about drugs in their songs? So did Cab Calloway.

Listen to this music. Listen selectively, of course, because like the popular music of the past, most of it is tripe. But the good is sometimes quite good indeed, and the hope it expresses may be the last one America is going to get.

ROBERT CHRISTGAU
rock lyrics are poetry (maybe)

Until it narrowed its programming, there was one hip radio station in New York, the station of the college kids and the bright suburban adolescents and the young professionals and the hippies — your station, if you're within range: WOR-FM. Not that there was much choice — AM radio in New York is antediluvian. But for a while, WOR-Stereo did seem to try. Its playlist was flexible and enormous and its deejays enjoyed much freedom. WOR was the home of the born-again Murray the K, with his "attitude music" and his tell-it-like-it-is (baby) cool, and coming up strong behind was the latetime (ten-to-two) jock, a spade named Rosko. Rosko emcees at the Village Theater, which is a story in itself, but not this one. This one is about Rosko and Kahlil

Gibran, now-deceased author of a dozen or so quasi-poetic, pseudo-religious texts, the most famous of which is *The Prophet*.[1]

Rosko quit WOR when the station decided to chase after the post-adolescent AM audience with a tight oldies playlist, but he had more in common with all the screaming-meemies than he probably suspected. Just like Cousin Brucie or B. M. R., he did not so much announce a show as preside over a ritual. Cultism is not confined to teenyboppers. All four jazz fans out there should remember Symphony Sid, who played virtually the same cuts night after night for literally years, announcing the same Stan Getz/Oscar Brown, Jr./Nina Simone/Willie Bobo/Miles Davis in the same throat-cancer growl. Rosko did Sid one better. He played the same stuff every night, Beatles/Stones/Dylan, plus hip hits and various cult heroes — Richie Havens, Vanilla Fudge, Jimi Hendrix, Big Brother, Judy Collins. Then, to ice the cake, he would climax his show with a reverent reading from Kahlil Gibran. "And he who has deserved to drink from the ocean of life deserves to drink from your little stream"; "The soul unfolds itself, like a lotus of countless petals"; "Vague and nebulous is the beginning of all things, but not their end, and I would fain have you remember me as a beginning," et cetera. In the background was poor Ravi Shankar, who hadn't been so ill-used since that nameless film poetaster discovered the quadruple-exposure raga. Rosko's fans loved it. They flooded the station with requests for printed versions, which Rosko answered with the sweet suggestion that they buy the book. A Gibran boomlet — you may even have been part of it.

I hope not. Admirers of books like *The Prophet* crave the enthrallment of poetry without the labor. For poetry — the Greek *poiein* means to contract or make — involves labor, in the creation and the understanding. Perhaps even too much so. Ever since the Industrial Revolution moved art out of the mainstream and produced the artistic rebel, whose avant-garde art comprises virtually all the good work in this century and much in the last, the arts have moved slowly and sadly beyond ordinary people. Artists have turned inward and concerned themselves with form. Not without superb results, either — whatever

[1] Already I can hear the screaming. You *like* Kahlil Gibran, right? So let's have it out. A critical essay — consider yourself forewarned — illumines nothing so much as the prejudices of its author. My tastes in music derive largely from Alan Freed and Thelonious Monk, but my tastes in poetry and philosophy were pounded into me by a phalanx of Ivy League professors. I think Kahlil Gibran is the worst kind of trash, much worse than Harold Robbins, say, because good people take him seriously.

disservices they are done in the classroom, Proust, Yeats, Pollock, Stravinsky, and all the others have produced work which is not only marvelous technically, but very real emotionally, to those who know the language. The problem is, not many do — art is still not very respectable, and it's a lot more trouble than it used to be. What's worse, many who take the trouble succeed imperfectly, and turn to mass art or kitsch.

I want to say right now that none of the categories I'm going to be using are worth much. All but a few artists resist categories; the good ones usually confound them altogether. So a term like "rock" is impossibly vague; it denotes, if anything, something historical rather than aesthetic. "Mass art" and "kitsch" are pretty vague as well. Let's say that mass art is intended only to divert, entertain, pacify — Mantovani, Jacqueline Susann, *Muscle Beach Party*, etc. Kitsch is a more snobbish concept, and a more sophisticated product. It usually has the look of slightly out-of-date avant-garde in order to give its audience the illusion of aesthetic pleasure, whatever that is. An important distinction, I think, is that many of the craftsmen who make kitsch believe thoroughly in what they are doing. That may be true of the creators of mass art, too, but their attitude is more businesslike — they don't worry about "art," only commercial appeal.

I think it is just because they didn't worry about art that many of the people who ground out the rock-and-roll of the fifties — not only the performers, but all the background people — were engaged (unconsciously, of course) in, making still another kind of art, folk art. If longevity is any criterion, then I say the Five Satins will be remembered longer than the Weavers, because consciousness tends to kill what is vital in folk art. Like any rule, this one is far from perfect. Paul Anka's songs were horrible even though he didn't worry about art; Pete Seeger did, and his stuff was good. Or take a better example. In 1944, James Agee wrote an essay called "Pseudo-Folk" that deplored contemporary jazz; Duke Ellington was marvelous in his way, Agee argued, but he was also effete, and gimme that Jelly Roll. Like everything Agee wrote, "Pseudo-Folk" was sensible and heartfelt. But as it was written a young alto-sax player named Charlie Parker was creating jazz that had all the vitality of folk art plus all the complexity and technical inventiveness of the "higher" arts. You never can tell.

The same kind of transformation may be occurring right now in what used to be called rock-and-roll. It is certainly fashionable to think so. But despite all the happy praise, no one really seems to understand what is going on. Here is Robert Shelton of the New York *Times:* "More than a few conservatives in and out of the academy will be quick to dismiss serious writing by pop stars as commercial gimmickry, box-office ploys and faddist ephemera. Time, I submit, will strain out the worthless and leave us with some valuable creative works, in music and in literature, by a wholesome group of new writers." Shelton's facts are okay, but there is something dreadfully wrong about his tone — wholesome indeed. Does time really "strain out the worthless," or is it merely that we judge what is present and what is past by two entirely different and entirely proper standards? Does Shelton want to imply that "commercial gimmickry, box-office ploys and faddist ephemera" are necessarily inconsistent with "valuable creative works"? The Beatles have long since pulverized that cliché. Another example comes from Leonard Bernstein, who told a nationwide TV audience, "Many of the lyrics, in their oblique allusions and wayout metaphors, are beginning to sound like real poems." In a way Bernstein was right. Many rock lyrics sound like poems, especially to those who don't read poetry, which is almost everyone. But then, so does Kahlil Gibran.

The songwriter who seems to sound most like a poet is Bob Dylan. Dylan is such an idiosyncratic genius that it is perilous to imitate him — his faults, at worst annoying and at best invigorating, ruin lesser talents. But imitation is irresistible. Who can withstand Paul Nelson of *Little Sandy Review*, who calls Dylan "the man who in every sense revolutionized modern poetry, American folk music, popular music, and the whole of modern-day thought"? Or Jack Newfield of the *Village Voice*, wandering on about "symbolic alienation ... new plateaus for poetic, content-conscious songwriters ... put poetry back into song ... reworks T. S. Eliot's classic line ... bastard child of Chaplin, Celine and Hart Crane," while serving up tidbits from Dylan's corpus, some of which don't look so tasty on a paper plate? However inoffensive "The ghost of electricity howls in the bones of her face" sounds on vinyl, it is silly without the music. Poems are read or said. Songs are sung.

Dylan gets away with it simply because there is so much there. The refrain of "My Back Pages," his renunciation of political protest — "I was so much older then, I'm younger than that now" — may be the finest line he has ever written. Its opening — "Crimson flames tied through my ears" — may be the worst. The song bulges with metaphors and epithets, some apt, some stuck in to fill out the meter. The tired trick of using a noun for a verb to spice things up reaches an all-time low with the word (?) "foundationed." Dylan's obsession with rhyme (which he has lately begun to parody: "Hear the one with the mustache say, jeeze/I can't find my knees") compels him to match "now" with "somehow" three times in six stanzas. Twice this is totally gratuitous. But the third time — "Good and bad, I define these terms, quite clear no doubt somehow — "somehow" becomes the final qualification in a series of qualifications, and works perfectly: a typical hit among misses.

"My Back Pages" is a bad poem. But it is a good song, supported by a memorable refrain. The music softens our demands, the importance of what is being said somehow over-balances the flaws, and Dylan's delivery — he sounds as if he's singing a hymn at a funeral — adds a portentous edge not present just in the words. Because it is a good song, "My Back Pages" can be done in other ways. The Byrds' version depends on intricate, up-tempo music that pushes the words into the background. However much they mean to David Crosby, the lyrics — except for that refrain — could be gibberish and the song would still succeed. Repeat: Dylan is a songwriter, not a poet. A few of his most perfect efforts — "Don't Think Twice," or "Just Like a Woman" — are tight enough to survive on the page. But they are exceptions.

Such a rash judgment assumes that modern poets know what they're doing. It respects the tradition that runs from Ezra Pound and William Carlos Williams down to Charles Olson, Robert Creeley, and perhaps a dozen others, the tradition that regards Allen Ginsberg as a good poet, perhaps, but a wildman. Dylan's work, with its iambics, its clackety-clack rhymes, and its scattergun images, makes Ginsberg's look like a model of decorous diction. An art advances through technical innovation. Modern American poetry assumes (and sometimes eliminates) metaphoric ability, concentrating on the use of line and rhythm to approximate (or refine) speech, the reduction of language to essentials, and "tone of voice." Dylan's only innovation is that he sings, a good way to control "tone of voice," but not enough to "revolutionize modern poetry." He may have started something just as good, but modern poetry is getting along fine, thank you.

It is fortunate that Dylan's most prominent disciple, Donovan, is not an imitator. His best stuff crosses Dylan's surrealist bent with the jazzy cleverness of thirties' songwriters like Cole Porter. Donovan makes demands on his listeners (tossing off an elliptical image like "To a leopard's you've been changin' " or devoting whole songs to his medieval fetish) and he delights in obscurity (everyone loves "Mellow Yellow" and "Sunshine Superman," but no one understands them — and don't tell me about bananas), but once again he is a songwriter, and in a much less equivocal way than Dylan. With a few tricks so well tried that they are legitimate *lingua franca*, at least for his special audience (that is us), he is working to deliver songwriting from superannuated sentimentalists like Johnny Mercer and shrewd camp followers like Tommy Boyce and Bobby Hart. In another way, Mick Jagger and Keith Richard are doing the same thing. They began by writing pungent pseudo-blues from their peculiar, ironic vantage — "Heart of Stone," "The Last Time," etc. Now, while sticking to old forms, they have allowed their sense of themselves to dominate their sense of blues tradition, producing a body of work that is as consistent and various as anything this side of Lennon-McCartney, but still song, not poetry. In the atmosphere that they and Donovan and especially Dylan have created, dozens of intelligent craftsmen — from folk-rockers like Marty Balin and John Sebastian to commercial talents like Neil Diamond and Mike Nesmith — are working down below to return popular songwriting to the honest stature it had in the thirties and beyond. The new songwriters are sentimental, not about the way the world is, but about their feelings toward it. This is a great step forward.

Dylan's influence has not always been so salutary. Lennon-McCartney and Jagger-Richard would have matured without him. But had there been no Dylan to successfully combine the vulgar and the felicitous, would we now be oppressed with the kind of vague, extravagant imagery and inane philosophizing that ruins so much good music and so impresses the Kahlil Gibran fans? I doubt it. Gary Brooker and Keith Read of Procol Harum, for an instance, obviously have a lot of talent. The opening of "Homburg" ("Your multilingual" — piano chord — "business friend") is my choice for line of the month, and the transformation of Bach in "A Whiter Shade of Pale" was brilliant and well executed. But is "A Whiter Shade of Pale" poetry? From the ads London placed in the trades, you might assume it was Shakespeare, newly unearthed. In fact there is a rumor that it was adapted from an Elizabethan poem. No matter. Full of obscure clichés ("skipped the light fandango"; "sixteen vestal virgins") with a clever (admittedly) title phrase and refrain, the overall archaic feel reinforced by literary reference ("the miller told his tale"), it sold because it did such a successful job of sounding like poetry, which, as we all know, is obscure, literary, and sort of archaic. Pure kitsch. Not much better is the self-indulgence of the Doors' Jim Morrison. "Twentieth Century-Fox," "Break on Through," "People Are Strange" and "Soul Kitchen," listed in ascending order of difficulty, all pretty much succeed. But Morrison does not stop there. He ruins "Light My Fire" with stuff like "our love becomes a funeral pyre" — Ugh! what does that mean? Nothing, but the good old romantic association of love and death is there, and that's all Morrison wanted — and noodles around in secondhand Freud in "The End." Morrison obviously regards "The End" as a masterwork, and his admirers agree. I wonder why. The music builds very nicely in an Oriental kind of way, but the dramatic situation is tedious stuff. I suppose it is redeemed by Morrison's histrionics and by the nebulousness that passes for depth among so many lovers of rock poetry.

The Doors and Procol Harum are good groups. Each has given me much pleasure. But I don't think "The End" and "A Whiter Shade of Pale" are just bad tries. I think they grow out of a bad idea, the idea that poetry — a concept not too well understood — can be incorporated into rock. This idea is old fashioned and literary in the worse sense. But young rock groups write "symbolic" lyrics that they like only because they wrote them, and they set them to music, and the cycle starts again. In a sense Morrison and Brooker-Reed are responsible for these kids in the same way Dylan is for them.

This phenomenon obviously has limitless depths (though in fairness it should be said that most groups — most of the ones you hear, anyway — avoid them), but I think its heights have been reached by a songwriter who has in abundance the one quality that Dylan, Morrison, and all their lessers lack. The songwriter is Paul Simon, and the quality is taste. Simon is so tasteful the media can't help but love him. Even Richard Goldstein has guessed that "chances are he's brought you closer to the feel and texture of modern poetry than anything since the big blackout." Goldstein does pin down the reason for Simon and Garfunkel's popularity, though: "They don't make waves."

Paul Simon's lyrics are the purest, highest, and most finely wrought kitsch of our time. The lyrics I've been putting down are not necessarily easy to write — bad poetry is often carefully worked, the difference being that it's easier to perceive flaccidly — but the labor that must go into one of Simon's songs is of another order of magnitude. Melodies, harmonies, arrangements are scrupulously fitted. Each song is perfect. And says nothing.

What saddens me is that Simon obviously seems to have a lot to say to the people who buy his records. But it's a shock. Like Kahlil Gibran all he's really doing is scratching them where they itch, providing some temporary relief but coming nowhere near the root of the problem. Simon's content isn't modern, it is merely fashionable, and his form never jars the sensibilities. He is the only songwriter I can imagine admitting he writes about that all-American subject, the Alienation of Modern Man, in just those words. His songs have the texture of modern poetry only if modern poetry can be said to end with early Auden — Edwin Arlington Robinson is more like it. Poets don't write like Robinson any more because his technical effects have outlived their usefulness, which was to make people see things in a new way. And even in such old-fashioned terms, what Simon does is conventional and uninspired. An example is "For Emily, Wherever I May Find Her," in which "poetic" words — organdy, crinoline, juniper (words that suggest why Simon is so partial to turn-of-the-century verse) and "beautiful" images (softer-than-the-rain, wandered-lonely-streets) are used to describe a dream girl. Simon is no dope; he knows this is all a little corny, but that's okay because Emily is an impossible girl. Only in order for the trick to come off there has to be an ironic edge. There isn't, and "For Emily" is nothing more than a sophisticated popular song of the traditional-fantasy type.

This kind of mindless craft reaches a peak in Simon's supposed masterpiece, "The Dangling Conversation," which uses all the devices you learn about in English class — alliteration, alternating concretion and abstraction, even the use of images from poetry itself, a favorite ploy of poets who don't know much of anything else — to mourn wistfully about the classic plight of self-conscious man, his Inability to Communicate. Tom Phillips of the New York *Times* has called this song "one of Paul Simon's subtlest lyrics ... a pitiless vision of self-consciousness and isolation." I don't hear the same song, I guess, because I think Simon's voice drips self-pity from every syllable (not only in this song, either). The Mantovani strings that reinforce the lyric capture its toughness perfectly. If Simon were just a little hipper, his couple would be discussing the failure of communication as they failed to communicate, rather than psychoanalysis or the state of the theatre. But he's not a little hipper.

Still, maybe he's getting there. A new album should be out shortly (there is one more track to record at this writing) and could be a surprise. Simon is going through changes. He has released almost nothing new since *Parsley, Sage, Rosemary and Thyme*, which contains "For Emily" and "Dangling Conversation." Last winter's "At the Zoo" is more concrete and less lugubrious than his other work, just a whimsical song about Central Park Zoo, and despite an occasional kernel of corn ("It's a light and tumble journey"), the metaphors work because

they are fun: "Zebras are reactionaries/Antelopes are missionaries."
"Fakin' It" is more serious, but the colloquial diction that dominates
the song — in the first, third, and fifth sections, there is no word that
isn't among the most common in the language: "The girl does what she
wants to do/She knows what she wants to do and I know I'm/Fakin' it/
I'm not really makin' it" — adds a casual feel; even when the verbiage
becomes more Simonesque, it is seasoned with a dash of the colloquial:
"A walk in the garden wears me down/Tangled in the fallen vines/
Pickin' up the punch lines." In addition, the song contains an extraordinarily subtle switch. "I own a tailor's face and hands/I am the
tailor's face and hands." No image-mongering there, just one little
changeover, from a clever metaphor to a painful identification.

In an oblique and probably unconscious way, I think "Fakin' It" is
true rock poetry, an extension of a very specific tradition. The pop that
preceded rock, and still exists today, was full of what semanticist S. I.
Hayakawa has listed as "wishful thinking, dreamy and ineffectual nostalgia, unrealistic fantasy, self-pity, and sentimental clichés masquerad-
ing as emotion." The blues, by contrast, were "unsentimental and realistic." Rock-and-roll combined the gutless lyrics of pop with the sexual
innuendo of blues music and delivery. What this meant in practice was
that it had no lyrics at all. Most rock fans just ignored what inane
content there was in favor of the sound and the big beat. So rock diction
became imbecilically colloquial, nonsense syllables proliferated, and
singers slurred because nobody cared. Be-bop-a-lula, you can really
start to groove it, caught Aunt Mary something and she ducked back
in the alley. In "Fakin' It," the basic-English diction, the eleven repetitions of the title, and that almost inaudible changeover not only avoid
Simon's usual pretensions; combined with the big-beat arrangement,
they create a mood that asks "Why should this mean anything?" Only
it does.

It is by creating a mood that asks "Why should this mean anything?"
that the so-called rock poets can really write poetry — poetry that not
only says something, but says it as only rock music can. For once
Marshall McLuhan's terminology tells us something: rock lyrics are a
cool medium. Go' ahead and mumble. Drown the voices in guitars. If
somebody really wants to know what you're saying, he'll take the trouble, and in that trouble lies your art. On a crude level this permits the
kind of one-to-one symbolism of pot songs like "Along Comes Mary"
and "That Acapulco Gold." "Fakin' It" does other things with the

same idea. But the only songwriters who seem really to have mastered it are John Phillips and Lennon-McCartney.

Phillips possesses a frightening talent. "San Francisco — Flowers in Your Hair," catering to every prurient longing implicit in teenage America's flirtation with the hippies without ever even mentioning the secret word, is a stunning piece of schlock. A song like "Once Was A Time I Thought" (as if to say to all those Swingle Singer fans, "You thought that was hard? We can do the whole number in fifty-eight seconds") is another example of the range of his ability. You have the feeling Phillips could write a successful musical, a Frank Sinatra hit, anything that sells, if he wanted to.

Perhaps you are one of those people who plays every new LP with the treble way up and the bass way down so you can ferret out all the secret symbolic meanings right away. Personally I think that spoils the fun, and I suspect any record that permits you to do that isn't fulfilling its first function, which pertains to music, or, more generally, noise. The Mamas and Papas' records are full of diversions — the contrapuntal arrangements, the idiot "yeahs," the orchestral improvisations, the rhyme schemes ("If you're entertaining any thought that you're gaining by causin' me all of this pain and makin' me blue, the joke's on you") and Phillips' trick of drawing out a few words with repetitions and pauses. Perhaps this isn't conscious. In songs like "California Dreamin'," "12:30" and many others, Phillips is obviously just a good lyricist (with a lot of tender respect for the fantasy world of pure pop that critics like Hayakawa derogate so easily). But his lyrics are rarely easy to understand. Maybe it's just me, but I wonder how many of you are aware that a minor track on the second album, "Strange Young Girls," is about LSD. No secret about it — there it is, right out in the open of the first stanza: "Strange young girls, colored with sadness/Eyes of innocence hiding their madness/Walking the Strip, sweet, soft, and placid/Off'ring their youth on the altar of acid." But you don't notice because there's so much else to listen to.

My favorite Phillips song is "Straight Shooter." By now, everyone knows "Straight Shooter" is about drugs. They printed it right in the *Times* and everything. But its genius is that it doesn't have to be — it works equally well as one of those undefined, meaningless love songs that have always been the staple of rock. Oh, there are a few little aberrations — baby is suspected of holding anything, not anyone, and the "half of it belongs to me" doesn't make sense. But this is rock-and-roll. It doesn't have to make sense. Even the "just get me high" has all sorts of respectable precedents, like the "I get highs" in "I Want to Hold Your Hand," which may be about spiritual high but is no drug song. In addition there is the irony of this bright, bouncy melody being all about some needle freak. It's a characteristic trick — Phillips likes to conceal the tone of a lyric in a paradoxical melody (the perfect example being the gentle-sounding "Got a Feelin' "). Every level of uncertainty makes the song more like the reality we actually perceive. Yet the whole effect occurs within a strict rock framework.

Phillips achieves rock feel with his arrangements. The lyrics themselves are closer to traditional pop — Rodgers and Hart's "My Heart Stood Still," on the second album, sounds less out of place than Bobby Freeman's "Do You Wanna Dance?" on the first. Lennon-McCartney do it with diction. Their early work is all pure rock — the songs are merely excuses for melody, beat and sound. Occasionally it shows a flash of the subtlety to come, as in the sexual insinuation of "Please Please Me" or the premise of "There's A Place" ("There, there's a place/Where I can go/When I feel low, when I feel blue/And it's my mind"). More often it is pure, meaningless sentiment, couched in the simplest possible terms. By the time of *A Hard Day's Night* the songs are more sophisticated musically, and a year later, in *Help!*, the boys are becoming pop songwriters. *Help!* itself is a perfect example. Words like "self-assured" and "insecure" are not out of rock diction, nor is the line: "My independence seems to vanish in the haze." This facet of their talent has culminated (for the moment) in songs like "Paperback Writer," "A Little Help from My Friends," and "When I'm Sixty-four," which show all the verbal facility of the best traditional pop and none of the sentimentality, and in deliberate exercises like "Michelle" and "Here, There and Everywhere," which show both.

Other songs like "Norwegian Wood," "Dr. Roberts," "Good Morning, Good Morning" are ambiguous despite an unerring justness of concrete detail; little conundrums, different from Dylanesque surrealism because they don't fit so neatly into a literary category (Edward Lear is their closest antecedent). Most of the songs since *Rubber Soul* are characterized by a similar obliqueness. Often the Beatles' "I" is much harder to pin down than the "I" in Donovan or Jagger-Richard, a difficulty that is reinforced by their filters, their ethereal harmonies, and their collective public identity. This concern with angle of attack is similar to that of poets like Creeley.

Lennon and McCartney are the only rock songwriters who combine high literacy (as high as Dylan's or Simon's) with an eye for concision and a truly contemporary sense of what fits. They seem less and less inclined to limit themselves to what I have defined as rock diction, and yet they continue to succeed — the simultaneous lushness and tightness of "Lucy in the Sky with Diamonds," for instance, is nothing short of extraordinary. They still get startling mileage out of the banal colloquial — think of the "oh boy" in "A Day in the Life," or the repeating qualifications in "Strawberry Fields Forever." But they have also written two songs which are purely colloquial — "She Said She Said," and "All You Need Is Love."

"She Said She Said" is at once one of the most difficult and banal of Beatle songs. It is a concrete version of what in "The Dangling Conversation" (despite all those details) remains abstract, a conversation between a hung-up, self-important girl who says she knows "what it's like to be dead" and her boy friend, who doesn't want to know. (If Simon had written it, the boy would have argued that he was the one who knew.) The song uses the same kind of words that can be found in "She Loves You" (the quintessential early Beatles song), yet says so much more. Its conceit, embodied in the title, is meaningless; its actuality is a kind of ironic density that no other songwriter (except Dylan at his best) approaches. One of its ironies is the suggestion that callow philosophizing is every bit as banal as the most primitive rock-and-roll.

"All You Need Is Love," deliberately written in basic English so it could be translated, makes the connection clearer by quoting from "She Loves You" while conveying the ironic message of the title. Is love all you need? What kind of love? Universal love? Love of country? Courtly love? "She Loves You" love? It's hard to tell. The song employs rock-and-roll — dominant music, big beat, repeated refrain, simple diction — and transforms it into something which, if not poetry, at least has a multifaceted poetic wholeness. I think it is rock poetry in the truest sense.

Maybe I am being too strict. Modern poetry is doing very well, thank you, on its own terms, but in terms of what it is doing for us, and even for the speech from which it derives, it looks a bit pallid. Never take the categories too seriously. It may be that the new songwriters (not poets, please) lapse artistically, indulge their little infatuations with language and ideas, and come up with a product that could be much better if handled with a little less energy and a little more caution. But energy is where it's at. And songs — even though they are only songs — may soon be more important than poems, no matter that they are easier too.

Once there were bards and the bards did something wondrous — they provided literature for the illiterate. The bards evolved into poets and the poetry which had been their means became their end. It didn't seem to matter much after a while, since everyone was literate anyway. But semiliteracy, which is where people go when they're not illiterate any more, is in some ways a worse blight.

The new songwriters think there should be bards again and they're right, but the bardic traditions are pretty faint. Too many of them are seduced by semiliteracy — mouthing other people's ideas in other people's words. But they are bards, and that is very good. Maybe soon it will be a lot better.

This essay was written (too fast, like most journalism) in the early fall of 1967 for *Cheetah*, now sadly departed. Though I haven't been able to resist a few stylish fixes, I have left it mostly as is. If the piece seems dated to me now, in the fall of 1968, then any revisions would no doubt seem dated by the time they appeared. Journalism ought to survive with its limitations of time and place intact.

Nevertheless I feel compelled to put things in some small perspective and right a few wrongs. I'm probably guilty of overkill on Paul Simon, who has since gone on to his just reward as the writer of a Number One filmscore, but when I wrote this he was still taken seriously by people who deserved better. And though I love "Mrs. Robinson" and consider *Bookends* S&G's finest album, I don't think Simon has lived up to the promise I discerned in "Fakin' It." As for John Phillips, I am now convinced the Mamas and the Papas are destined to become high camp, but that doesn't change what they were and sometimes still are for us, and I stand by my praise.

What I describe as the poetry of rock has to do with surprise, and it is still relevant: the effect of a lyric by John Kay of Steppenwolf, say, or even Gerry Goffin and Carole King, is frequently enhanced by indirection. But since last fall there have been only two completely successful examples of this tradition, the ultimate test being how broadly they sold: Lennon-McCartney's "Hello Good-bye" and Peter Townshend's "I Can See for Miles." I am beginning to think such specimens will become increasingly rare. The technique is based on one overriding assumption: that no one takes rock seriously. It can only survive as long as that assumption is viable, if not as a present truth then as a living memory. But even the memory seems to be dying. It may be that the most lasting verbal effect of what I can only call the rock ambience may be a new eloquence in popular songwriting, typified by a figure like Randy Newman, whose work has little to do with rock per se.

The key figure in all this is Bob Dylan, who as a vocalist and a writer has pointed out all sorts of new directions for song. I think I misunderstood what Dylan did for those of us who always knew he was a rotten "poet." It was his very badness that attracted us. His overwriting was the equivalent in folk music of the happy energy of the Beatles. He loved language enough to misuse it. Of course, if he hadn't had the genius to use it brilliantly as well, that would hardly have been a virtue. But he did, and so revitalized areas of language that had seemed exhausted. The songwriter who has learned most from this is Leonard Cohen, with his wry exultation in silly rhymes and inconsistent or overly consistent images. It may be, by the way, that poets have learned something from Dylan's freedom as well. In any case I know now that the work of poets like Robert Creeley was no longer really central when I wrote this. Anyone who would like to sample what has replaced it should refer to *Bean Spasms*, by Ted Berrigan and Ron Padgett.

H. F. MOONEY
popular music since the 1920s:
the significance of shifting taste

In the fall 1954 *American Quarterly*, this writer discussed the significance of shifting tastes in American popular music since 1890. In retrospect it appears that the major trends established over or during the previous seventy years continued into the 1960s. First, the long-range trend away from the blandness, urbanity or introspection of the 1920s and 1930s persisted. Second, the Negroid tone of popular music

From *American Quarterly*, Spring, 1968. Copyright © 1968 by Trustees of the University of Pennsylvania. Reprinted by permission.

as well as of jazz was increasingly prominent in "roots" jazz and in rock-and-roll dance music. Third, related to the Negroid tendency, a further plebeianization — to the point of crudeness — undermined older middle-class decorum. Fourth, along with this was a diminution of romantic love, amatory frustration and sentimental brooding or nostalgia. Fifth, the folk-protest vogue paralleled the aggressive "roots" movement in jazz and the general attack on what was called the "middle-class Establishment." Sixth, orchestration of popular songs rejected older standards almost as much as did jazz technique. Seventh, there was a reaction from the sort of music once produced copiously by the nostalgic or melancholy — and often quite sophisticated — urban Jew or Irishman so prominent for several decades among songwriters in New York. Into the vacuum created by what David Ewen calls the "death of Tin Pan Alley" after the 1930s exploded the rock-folks and soul shouts from a score of urban slums throughout the country. The public was predisposed to accept this vulgarization, the latest expression of eight decades of rebellious sensationalism in American popular music beginning with ragtime "coon songs." Thus, popular music after 1930 continued to express long-range tendencies evident by the 1920s or even before. Even so, however, the tastes of the mid-1960s were sufficiently different from those of the 1920s and 1930s to necessitate retrospection.

People in the 1920s and 1930s, as before then, were rebellious in certain ways — rebellious sexually and artistically; and economically as well in the 1930s. Their rebellion was evidenced in a greater infusion of jazz into popular music, and in the growing popularity of colored vocalists and instrumentalists; but it was limited by compromises with middle-class conventions. Most Negroes were little short of outcasts, too poor and too segregated from the mainstream of life to maximally influence taste. Colored musicians were discriminated against in commercial dance orchestras, in radio and, at least until the 1930s, in recording sessions.[1] The prevailing taste in popular music was shaped by a white middle class, self-consciously hedonistic, relatively prosperous at a time when — particularly during the depression of the 1930s — income was so narrowly distributed as to prevent many people from acquiring even necessities. By 1932, the sale of phonograph records had dropped to 6 per cent of the volume of 1927, a year which was itself somewhat below the sales of the postwar months of 1919–20.

---

[1] Neil Leonard, *Jazz and the White Americans* (Chicago, 1962), p. 146.

Small record companies which had catered to the Negro market in the 1920s were wiped out, and the larger companies curtailed or eliminated their "race" (i.e., Negro performers') catalogues as the marginal Negro market was, as usual, the first to dip in any recession.[2] Consequently, the influence of Negro jazz was further minimized. Middle-class Negroes who desired to "come up," as they put it, during the 1930s and the 1940s responded to the smoothly harmonized arrangements of a white Jimmy Dorsey's watered-down jazz. Duke Ellington himself was influenced by Guy Lombardo's "sweetest music this side of heaven," and brought something of the sound of the Roosevelt Hotel ballroom to Harlem. Commercial orchestras of the period around 1920–50 followed more or less the "safe bet" — the aesthetic aspirations of the middle-class market — as did, indeed, most of the big Negro bands. They presented a music which, despite solo variations, emphasized precise, lush, ensemble harmony.[3] The highest compliment most of the public could pay to big-band jazz between 1928 and 1950 was "symphonic" or "advanced." Orchestrations of bands like Boyd Raeburn's, Stan Kenton's, Claude Thornhill's or Elliot Lawrence's (out of which came some of the "cool" musicians of the 1950s) reflected the influence of Debussy, Ravel and the post-Impressionists.

Who were the middle class whose buying tastes thus helped create this trend? One hazards a reasonable guess that they were older than today's record buyers and on the whole higher on the socioeconomic scale. A sale of less than 20,000 records and a sheet music sale of 100,000 characterized a "hit" in the mid-1930s, as contrasted with a record sales of at least 500,000 and perhaps a million twenty years later.[4] Buyers would have belonged largely among the fortunate minority with steady income. In days when one was lucky to have a job even at less than one hundred dollars a month, expenditure of seventy-five cents

[2] Roland Gelatt, *The Fabulous Phonograph* (New York, 1955), pp. 191, 208, 246, 255; Leonard, p. 91.

[3] Chadwick Hansen, "Social Influences on Jazz Style," *American Quarterly*, XII (Winter 1960), 501–3; N. Ertegun, "A Style and a Memory," *Record Changer*, VI (July 1947), 7; Leonard, pp. 124 ff. For Ellington's absorption of Lombardo's style, listen to "Creole Rhapsody" (1931), reprocessed in RCA Camden Album CAL 459, *Duke Ellington at the Cotton Club*.

[4] Gelatt, p. 272; David Ewen, *Life and Death of Tin Pan Alley* (New York, 1964), p. 300; George Marek, "Oh, Dem Golden Records," and Jim Walsh "Crosby's . . . Disk Sales," *Variety*, CCV (Jan. 9, 1957), 237, 239. Frank Sinatra recalls that Bing Crosby's popularity in the 1930s was centered among post-adolescents and even older adults. "My Life and My Music," *Life*, LVIII (Apr. 23, 1965), 99.

or even thirty-five cents for a record or a piece of sheet music was limited. Very few, apparently, of the people who bought records desired truly Negro jazz—since, for one thing, even during past "prosperity" they had had so little opportunity to hear it. Radio networks, apprehensive over the reactions of sponsors and public, had exercised a ruthless veto over this "immoral" music. Although the censorship was aimed more at lyrics than orchestrations, it resulted in smoothing out roughness in both. The situation changed somewhat toward the end of the 1930s, when Benny Goodman, after having used the Negro Fletcher Henderson's arrangements for several years, took advantage of increasing liberalism to hire such colored artists as Teddy Wilson. But the times had not changed radically, Henderson was a middle-class Negro with remarkably sophisticated arrangements for that time; and even at that, Goodman carefully "polished" them so as to conform to the standards of European rendition.[5] Teddy Wilson's piano was urbane, light, deftly polished, as was that of the increasingly popular Count Basie. Soon Goodman hired the white Eddie Sauter to develop a rich, very "white" symphonic sound which caught public fancy so well that Sauter developed it further into the "progressive" sound of the highly acclaimed Sauter-Finnegan band of the early 1950s. Seen in retrospect, the very popular orchestral tendencies of the entire period between 1920 and 1950, from Paul Whiteman down to the progressive and "West Coast" movements which looked back at him with scorn, reflected the demand of the urban middle class for a highly refined, quasi-"classical" jazz.

Lyrics no less than orchestrations and vocal style reveal much about the music patrons of the 1930s. Songs like

> *I get along without you very well —*
>> *Of course I do*
>>> *— except perhaps in spring,*
>>>> *or when somebody laughs like you.*[6]

or

> *Thanks for the memory*
> *Candle-light and wine*

[5] Marshall Stearns, *The Story of Jazz* (New York, 1956), p. 144; Leonard, pp. 98–100, 122. Leonard's second chapter brilliantly analyzes the tastes of the older middle class and the reasons for its opposition to jazz.

[6] By Hoagy Carmichael. Copyright 1938, 1939 and renewed 1965, 1966 by Famous Music Corp. Lyrics reprinted by special permission of the copyright holder. A typical rendition was by Charlie Barnet's orchestra on Bluebird 10119.

> *Castles on the Rhine*
>   *The Parthenon, and moonlight on*
>   *The Hudson river line . . .*
> *Remember the night that we parted*
> *When I got as high as a steeple*
> *But we were intelligent people*
>   *— No tears, no fuss, Hooray for Us!* [7]

or (from George and Ira Gershwin's "But Not for Me"):

> *With love to lead the way*
>   *I've found more skies of gray*
>   *Than any Russian play could guarantee.* [8]

were subtle and understated, aimed at an audience of some maturity and education — of at least a smattering of and respect for art history and Maxim Gorky. They were very popular before the lifting of the depression by 1941 and the deepening of the market in the war and postwar years modified the prevailing taste.

The intense, lovelorn ballad, while it lasted, reflected taste and life in the 1920s and especially the 1930s, when the purchasers of records were older and more middle class — or middle-class aspiring — than those of the 1960s. As such they wanted more adult themes and an often timidly "respectable" jazz infused by a "sweet," "harmonious" (or sometimes even "advanced," dissonant), but always *European* tone. Teen-agers made up a relatively smaller segment of the population, and were not as affluent as later. Naturally, best-selling music dealt more fully with the problems of the post-adolescent consumer, as in "Mad About the Boy":

> *Lord knows I'm not a schoolgirl in the*
>   *flurry of her first affair . . .*
> *I'm hardly sentimental . . .*
> *I've got to pay my rental and I can't afford*
> *To waste much time.* [9]

[7] By Leo Robin and Ralph Rainger. Copyright 1937, renewed 1964, by Paramount Music Corp. Lyrics reprinted by special permission of the copyright holder. An original recording has been reprocessed on RCA Camden CA (S) 872e, *Memorable Vocal Performances With the Benny Goodman Orchestra.*

[8] Copyright 1930 by New World Music Corp. Used by permission.

[9] Copyright 1935, 1962, by Chappell, Inc. Lyrics quoted by special permission of the copyright holder. One of the top eighty or so best sellers in the United States in 1935. See Sigmund Spaeth, *History of Popular Music in America* (New York, 1948), p. 648.

Thoroughly middle-class sentiments! Also in deference to middle-class ideas of "taste," the best-selling records of the 1930s were frequently orchestrated like symphonic tone poems. Duke Ellington, and even a highly successful middle-of-the-road white band like Hal Kemp's, attempted to infuse Delius into ballad fox trots.[10] The popular tastemakers of the 1930s appear as somewhat cautious, compromising, middle-class young adults experimenting gingerly with jazz but tempering it with "highbrow" innovations or just sweetly pretty styling.

This ambivalent generation of 1920–50, which supported ambivalent orchestras like that of Glenn Miller, would have its cake and eat it too. A generation of transition, facing both ways, it compromised between the gentility of the Victorian parlor and the libidinism of the beatnik's pad. If the popular music of its time appealed strongly to young women, then the personality of the girl who bought the music is well expressed therein. The middle-class young woman of the 1920s and the 1930s who had broken her home ties to take a job and an apartment in the city lived in the hothouse of a pseudo-Freudian romanticism. The theme song of the day was, "Love, Your Magic Spell is Everywhere." And, said the pseudo-Freudian (perhaps sincerely, perhaps just to give the girl the latest "line"), "Love is not love, is not truly, healthily, wholly a giving and receiving, without Sexual Expression." So the girls in their little apartments, with their radios and record players, pulsed with desire unrecognized, unacknowledgeable or unfelt by the sheltered girls of the 1880s. Susceptible and vulnerable, increasingly without real religious convictions, they awaited the Great Experience and Fulfillment of Love (or Sex), listened in glaze-eyed anticipation to songs like "I Surrender, Dear." Singers, catering to the mood, moaned with frustration, "Blue Evening (After a Lonely Day)." There was the frustration of balked expectations; there was also the painful anxiety, the fear of losing love — ("How Long Will It Last?" "Why Can't This Night Go On Forever,

[10] See liner notes on RCA Camden Album 811, *Great Bands of Our Times*. The 1930s emerge as the most "intellectual" period in American popular music. The sales appeal of such songs as "Tender is the Night" and "Moon and Sixpence" was evidently to be enhanced by the titles of Fitzgerald's and Maugham's then new novels. In the late 1930s and early 1940s were concentrated many such adaptations of highbrow music as "Reverie," from Debussy; "Pavanne," from Ravel; "June on the Isle of May," from Tschaikowsky's *Andante Cantabile;* and Victor Herbert's "Yesterthoughts" and "Indian Summer." Tschaikowsky's *Piano Concerto No. 1 in B Flat* furnished "Tonite We Love," and his waltz theme from the *Pathetique* emerged as "The Night is Filled With Music," recorded like the others, as a slow, dreamy fox trot ballad with only the slightest pulsation of the bass fiddle and a light tapping of the cymbal or wire brushing of the drum to accent the rhythm.

Why Must the Morning Find You Gone?") ;[11] and finally, the denoue-
ment, the last bitter dregs of what had turned out to be mere sex without
love — the brushoff, the awakening, the sobbing; but still so often the
assertion that love had redeemed the whole sordid affair, as in Libby
Holman's number, "I'm Doing What I'm Doing for Love,"[12] and in
Grace Haye's 1930 recording of "My Lover."

> *And while I live, I'll want him madly;*
> *I'm not ashamed to admit it.*
> *All I could give I gave him gladly;*
> *And I'm not sorry I did it.*[13]

Such ballads reveal the interwar mood. In the 1920s and 1930s
middle-class girls were not prone to "play around" for the fleshy joy of
it. Despite an increasingly rebellious promiscuity, the code was still
tinged with the ideals of monogamous love — that is, sex could be
truly good and beautiful, truly redeemed, only if part of a romantic
love affair. If not chastity, if not marriage, there must be Love. And this
love must be, as in a marriage, monogamous, exclusive, rather than
"cheap," promiscuous. In the words of the song from Sigmund Rom-
berg's operetta *Desert Song* (1926): "One Alone." In short, something of Victorian sentiments remained. Love was not to be treated
casually. One might defy the Victorian double standard, but must up-
hold Victorian courtly fidelity. Such songs compromised in lyrics,
orchestration and vocal rendition between the sacred and the profane,
the "high class" and the low-down, the refined and the sensual. They
approached Sex obliquely — "Tonight is Mine," "One Night of Love."
The raw blues feeling underlying a ballad like Ruth Etting's "What
Wouldn't I Do for That Man?" was refined by a soft vocal, a limp
saxophone, violin and piano accompaniment.[14] Apparently girls who
wanted love, both sacred and profane, were attracted toward a music
appropriately ambivalent.

By 1960 the climate had changed. One reason for the shifting taste
was a change in the music business. By 1941, the virtual monopoly of

[11] An elegant 1932 recording of the latter is reprocessed on RCA Vintage LPV
504, *The Great Isham Jones.*

[12] Recorded on Brunswick 4459. An original pressing is in the Archives, Stanford
University Music Library.

[13] Copyright 1930 by Advanced Music Corp. Used by permission. Recorded on
Victor 22381.

[14] The original recording, along with others of the period and genre, is reprocessed in Columbia Album C3 L35, *The Original Sound of the Twenties.*

the ASCAP (American Society of Composers, Authors, and Publishers, organized in 1914), which had practically protected New York's ascendancy in the music market, was broken by legal judgment. The consequent opening of broadcasting and recording channels to non-ASCAP composers and publishers, many of them unknowns outside the conventional music establishment of Tin Pan Alley and catering to a wider public of newly affluent people — Negroes, workers who had migrated from rural areas, especially in the Southeast and Midwest to urban war jobs — marked the end of an era of increasingly urbane New York composers. These had been heavily Jewish. In 1930, for example, out of the forty-one hits listed in Sigmund Spaeth's *History of Popular Music in America,* seventeen were written by composers and/or lyricists with names *recognizably* Jewish.[15] Especially after 1945, however, the dispersal of composing and publishing throughout the nation tended to diminish their influence at a time when middle-class values had been weakened by war. Such New York Jews as Harold Arlen, George and Ira Gershwin, Jerome Kern, Vernon Duke (né Dukelsky), Herman Hupfeld and Vincent Youmans had produced a pensive music of finesse and polish, often using minor strains in the cantorial tradition. Their melodic concepts influenced "white" jazz instrumentalists — themselves frequently Jewish — flowing with increasing facility through plaintive but delicately restrained saxophones from Benny Kreuger in the early 1920s through Frank Trumbauer to Stan Getz; and through the arabesque clarinets of Benny Goodman and Artie Shaw. Until midcentury, immigrant and other minority groups, particularly in New York City, who as they rose became so influential in popular music, embraced standards still admired by many of the American middle class and by a more middle-class-aspiring lower class. The years 1920–50 were still much closer than our own to traditional WASP values. This is one reason why it was so difficult for Negro jazz to make greater headway. Aspiring Negro artists, jazz as well as nonjazz — Marian Anderson, Paul Robeson, Ellington, Henderson — themselves rejected much of the raw, gutty blues of an embarrassing past in favor of a concert style. The New York Jew and Negro, raised in the early years of the century — especially before Harlem became so largely a slum for ex-field hands from the South — were still awfully respectful of what some of their grandchildren would later call the "square" or "ofay" world of symphony, of refinement and gentility. Indeed, there is evi-

---

[15] Pp. 641–42.

dence that even the more contemptuous Negroes of the 1920s adopted the "sweet" tones of pseudo-"classical" middle-class music because they were determined to beat the white man on his own grounds as a performer.[16] Regardless of their motives and outlooks, songwriters and orchestrators, white and colored, adapted the Negro idiom to the gentility of their aspirations and/or to the tastes of the white middle class, who after all purchased so many leisure-time products, including music. It may have been true that both Negro and Jew had a certain common sense of alienation, a common bitterness or sadness, and a mutual empathy; but since they also both admired the culture of the Establishment whose doors they were forcing, their music, however, sad, alienated or bitter, had nevertheless passed through a "refining" process. Excellent examples of this are, again, Benny Goodman's music; and such performances as Duke Ellington's 1940 recording of Harold Arlen's "Stormy Weather," with Ivy Anderson's subdued (by 1960 standards) vocal.[17] But, encouraged by the breakdown of ASCAP's hegemony and by prosperous new markets among formerly depressed and minority groups, rival publishing and recording companies had arisen by 1950 in many other, frequently less sophisticated localities — the Negro slums of Chicago, Los Angeles, Philadelphia and Oakland and the rural-music center at Nashville, Tennessee, where Negroid and country music fused into Roy Orbison's "rockabilly" or "folk-rock." Many of the typical million-plus sellers in the 1950s and early 1960s were written, published and/recorded in such new centers. From Louisville, Kentucky, came "Slow Poke." From Nashville, Patti Page and "Tennessee Waltz"; Jimmy Dean's "Big Bad John"; Hank Williams' "Cold Cold Heart" and "Jumbalaya"; "Your Cheatin' Heart"; "Half as Much"; and the Everly Brothers' "Bird Dog." "Rose and a Baby Ruth" came from Chapel Hill, North Carolina; "This Old House" from Arcadia, California. Such early rock numbers as "Rock Around the Clock" and "A Whole Lot of Shakin' Goin' On," originated in Philadelphia,[18] later, from the Portland, Oregon, area came "Looie, Looie, Looie, Ya, Ya, Ya."

These titles amply suggest a trend. There were no references to the Russian drama, to Penthouse Serenades, to Park Avenue Fantasies, Stairways to the Stars or to the Parthenon. The nation was apparently too prosperous to glamorize wealth and highlife, and too juvenile, too

16 Hansen, pp. 496, 500.
17 Columbia 35556.
18 Ewen, pp. 328–29.

aggressively lowbrow or pseudo-lowbrow to admire "polished" or high-flown songs: many lower-class and minority-group high school students now *hated* the middle-class culture which they felt was being forced on them. Then too, cold war nationalism may have stimulated a marked taste for tunes with a folksy, grass-roots flavor. True, middle-brow holdouts for the old "culture" might in the early 1950s cling to Mantovani's "Shimmering Strings," but a decade later, even the worst "squares" had shifted to the Tijuana Brass, which in its own banal way leaned more to the Big Beat of the 1960s than toward the pseudo-"classic" modulations of the early 1940s. If any doubt remains about a change in mood between 1941 and 1966, the contrast between Herb Alpert and Gene Krupa's recordings of "Flamingo" tells the story.[19] During the period 1940–60, not only had many of the urban middle class become antibourgeois themselves, but also many buyers now came from newly prosperous segments of the population less influenced by WASP standards to begin with. Minority groups who shared in rising affluence and leisure were able in larger numbers to demand *their* kind of music. Negroes in particular, thronging from the rural South into Northern cities, intensified a demand for the gospel shouts and rough-edged blues which helped change the tone of urban popular music. Even the poorer among them, filled with a new sense of pride, were aware of grievances, bitter against whites, anxious to support Negro artists and Negro music. By 1960 they were at least prosperous enough, and sufficiently concentrated in cities, to nourish a demand for a self-consciously "black" music performed by black entertainers. Negroes had become purveyors of and consumers of a musical product which aggressively emphasized their "roots." An active and even violent black protest supported within and outside the Negro minority was reflected in the scorching heat, the volume, the drive, the guttiness, the slurred tones of "soul" or "roots" or "funky" jazz, as well as in rock-and-roll and in gospel shouts.[20]

Such music, which blacks in particular created, appealed to youth generally by 1960. Protest, rebellion, the muscular-visceral approach to music, the dance, to life itself, is of course typical of the adolescent and the very young adult at any time. By the later 1950s, youngsters

[19] Krupa's 1941 record is Okeh 6120. An original pressing is in the Rodgers and Hammerstein Archives of Recorded Sound of the New York City Public Library.

[20] Archie Shepp, tenor saxophonist with the late John Coltrane's 1963–66 group, tended to identify his music with the struggles of his black people, in particular with Black Nationalism, according to Martin Williams, "The Problematic Mr. Shepp," *Saturday Review*, XLIX (Nov. 12, 1966), 90.

were a relatively larger segment of the population than ever before in the twentieth century. They were also more prosperous than before as their parents' earnings and their own job opportunities increased. They were now catered to as consumers. Although relatively prosperous, they appeared to lack a sense of identification with the adult world. They were restlessly seeking status, pleasure, self-expression, sometimes an answer to the problems of the world. Such seeking brought them into conflict with the adult world. They were almost a minority group of their own. In 1959, Arnold Shaw found the major market for popular music to lie between the ages of nine or ten and seventeen or eighteen, among youngsters who were much less demanding of intricacy, restraint, nuance or polish than were a previous generation of older buyers.[21] These were the youth who "bopped" to the Big Beat of rock-and-roll, and who sang "Yakety Yak," a flippant take-off on parental discipline. Such lyrics as could be heard in the gregarious din of vocal groups of the late 1950s and early 1960s were often mindlessly extroverted expressions of the gang — "Yeah, yeah, yeah" — the lyrical equivalent of the teenagers' private street corner or drive-in banter. Nobody who bought "Rose and a Baby Ruth," one of the more tender and romantic songs of 1957, seemed to laugh at its bathos, so appropriate was it to a pre-adolescent taste — the same taste which brought out the little sensation seekers to gape at *Teen-Agers From Outer Space*. The somber, heavily orchestrated, introspective ballads of the young adults of the 1930s were passing out of the major trend.

So much for the obvious. The trend was away from suavity, however, not only in this music for children, but also to an extent in the jazz which had become a cult of many intellectuals. To a certain degree, jazz is always visceral; and to a certain degree, the popularity of visceral music among both adolescents and rebellious intellectuals is nothing new in the twentieth century — it has been, in fact, a long-range trend since the ragtime of the 1890s. But modifications in jazz as well as popular music after around 1954 appear significant, coming as they did at the height of the extremely irrationalist "white Negro" or "beatnik" movement among young writers. The anti-intellectual intellectuals followed Norman Mailer and Jack Kerouac, and then Norman Brown and Timothy Leary, into the outer reaches of thrill or even violence. By 1960, a searingly intense "hard bop" or "soul music" was crowding the chamber-music sound of the post-progressive cool or

---

[21] "Mr. Harper's After Hours," *Harper's*, CCXVIII (May, 1959), 82.

West Coast jazz. To be truly arty in the early 1960s, one had to be glandular.[22] Taste ran to a big, honking, stomping, earsplitting saxophone, heavier beat, shrieking revival shouts, recordings bursting with the din of screaming teen-age togetherness. The unobtrusive Maxine Sullivan and Connie Boswell of the 1930s; the Modernaires, Pied Pipers, Jo Stafford, Margaret Whiting, Mel Torme and June Christy of the "slick" 1940s; the husky-dreamy Julie London and Johnny Mathis, the Hilos and the Honey Dreamers and the Four Freshmen and other richly-chorded precision groups who held their popularity well into the 1950s despite a reversal in taste — all these were by 1960 paled by the church revival mood of the Clara Ward singers, Mahalia Jackson, Timi Yuro; or by the often inarticulate shouts of the transistor-set favorites — the Supremes, the Orlons. Popular music, often used as a psychedelic experience, became a "happening," a numbing bombardment of the auditory nerves. On whatever cultural level one might look, to Rojack of the *American Dream* or to James Bond, there must be rawness, constant stimulation. A primitive emotionalism (nonsentimental) must make no compromises with WASPishness in life, literature, music. The "well-adjusted," modal personality, the middle-class "average guy," was Out. Bing Crosby or Perry Como's accommodating, casual pleasantness was anathema: sweat and suffering made an artist popular in the early 1960s. He must, it would appear from the record jackets and liner notes, bear the stigma — or the stigmata, really, in the new religion of the Holy Barbarians — of Alienation from a crucificial Society — a Society composed of Crosbys and Comos with their casual tweeds and pipes and not-so-casual homes in Belair, their golf matches and stables of horses. Crosby and Como were passé in a period which sang, "Here's to the Losers." Perhaps the first indication of the change had been Johnny Ray's "Cry" in 1951. At any rate, music of the sort young people felt WASP over thirty would sing, compose or listen to, went into a decline. The liner blurbs, intended to sell records at first sight, spoke less of the home and family of the performer than of his "searchings," his bitterness, his inability or refusal to accommodate to the Establishment, his mental and/or physical handicaps or deviations, his daemonic immersion in environment-obliterating alcohol, sex or

[22] Thus, tenor saxophonist Stan Getz, once acclaimed in 1955 as "subtle" (liner notes of NorGran Album NGN 1032, *West Coast Jazz*) was acclaimed in liner notes of 1963 as "having a more mature emotionalism . . . a gutsy maleness" (Verve Album V/V6-8545, *Getz-Gilberto*). In the early 1960s it was indeed impossible to be *subtly* male — one must wear horsehide boots — or *subtly* feminine — one must wear barbaric globs of eye make-up and great varnished swirls and swatches of hair.

drugs. Such a recitation might in whole or in part apply to many of the folk heroes, or antiheroes (musical and nonmusical) of the 1960s — Ray Charles, Billie Holiday, Parker, Mailer and his Rojack, Brendan Behan, Bob Dylan, Thomas (did the identification of the folksinger's family name with the given name of the early-deceased alcoholic poet stimulate his popularity?). The stale remnants of the placid "boy-and-girl-next-door" singers of the 1930s could hardly compete with the lacerated, gorgeously uninhibited wailing of Ray Charles — blind, drug addicted, low class, black, and — needless to say, to the old middle class, thoroughly disreputable — with his "Get Your Buddy, and Go Get Stoned." A period in which the three leading playwrights were said to be militantly if obliquely homosexual in their work and, partly because of this, were extremely popular; a period, in short, of rising nonconformity, deviation and some sympathy for minorities, would find in Charles a welcome personification of the Outcast. The years of James Baldwin and LeRoi (*The Toilet*) Jones heard the violently surging saxophonic "sheets of sound" of John Coltrane, the explosive reed of Ornette Coleman. The suave colored singers of the 1940s and earlier 1950s who had accommodated to the white hotel-and-club world — Billy Eckstine, Sarah Vaughan, Lena Horne, Ella Fitzgerald (now much too poised and benignly self-possessed) were not much imitated among younger singers — a sure sign of obsolescence. Instead, Dinah Washington, Della Reese, Roy Hamilton, Brook Benton and Hank Ballard set the trend for the Chubby Checkers, Don Covays, Dee Dee Sharps and Sugar Pie Depintos who sang ever more intensely "black." All were Negro. In quantity as well as in vocal quality, singers were now substantially — and proudly — black. Into the 1950s most singers had been white, and on the whole, rather tepid crooners. By the mid-1960s Petula Clark, one of the few top white singers, sang "soul" like blacks, which meant a full-throated openly emotional delivery such as few white or black singers had demonstrated in the past. But by 1960 the old stiff-upper-lip Calvinist distrust of emotional expression had softened more than ever before. The grim lips relaxed and opened. Songs were shouted. The older ideal of the clean-cut crew-cut Nordic hero, silently self-controlled, was shrinking, along with the phase of conformity expressed in 1954's "Counting My Blessings." Music, like the film, documents a resurgent rebellion in the mid-1950s. James Dean, Elvis Presley, Sal Mineo — all were white, to be sure, but, like Mailer's "white Negro," dropouts from the WASP world who foreshadowed the popularity of Ray Charles's "Crying Time." Here was a *man* sobbing, and he was a glamorous youth hero on account of it. And unlike his less evocative predecessor, Johnny Ray, he was black.

By the 1960s, then, the bland "white" vocal was passé. And so was the polished "white" orchestration. The typical rock group of the late 1950s and early 1960s — amplified guitars, percussion, saxophone — was designed for rhythm and individual variations rather than for tone color. It dispensed with *fortissimo-pianissimo* modulations and played one way — loud. Never had such primitive jazz been exploited with such wide success among whites as well as Negroes. Even the more advanced jazz of the 1960s, which utilized the intricate techniques and rhythmic complexities of the bop revolution, also emphasized beat, solo variations and rhythmic experiment more than harmonics and modulation. Such a trend reflected the Negro's pride in his own roots, his "funky" contempt for white aesthetic standards; and also appeared to indicate that many whites as well, ashamed of or resentful of WASPishness, were seeking in music what some of them sought in LSD, a piling up of new sensation upon sensation to smash their Square prison.[23]

It would of course be naïve to call all this "new." Change, rebellion, the distortion or smashing of old forms, has long been a part of American culture. Change is the rule. Much of the change of 1960 was really a continuation of trends begun at least by the 1890s — the elevation of the once-degraded, the degradation of the once-elevated, the rebellion against older values. *Plus ça change, plus le même chose.* The intellectual and plebeian revolt against the middle class had by 1960 turned full blast against the generation of 1920–50, themselves once rebels of a sort now passé. The rejection of the big, white-stylized, highly arranged "swing" orchestra (once thought to be so untrammeled!) in favor of smaller, cruder groups; indeed, in favor of one singer and his guitar — the epitome of individualism — came when youth was attracted by the anarchism of Paul Goodman. Joan Baez's folksinging could be seen as a rebellion against the kind of society which had produced the Big Bands of the previous generation, where musicians had been straight jacketed into an Organization formula aimed at profits more than freedom,

---

[23] From liner notes by LeRoi Jones for Impulse Album A50, *Coltrane Live at Birdland* (1963): "The long tag of 'Afro-Blue,' with Elvin [Jones, drummer] thrashing and cursing beneath Trane's line, is unbelievable. Beautiful has nothing to do with it, but it is (I got up and danced while writing these notes, screaming at Elvin to cool it). . . . The crashing cymbals, bombarding tom-toms . . . [are] like the wild pulse of all living." Regarding another selection in the album, called "Alabama," he wrote: "If that real Alabama was the catalyst, more power to it, and may it be this beautiful, even in its destruction." Sorel had Arrived.

improvization, "soul." [24] If youth in the 1960s often tended to reject large organizations, the depersonalized, self-effacing vocalists who in the 1930s and 1940s had been merely components of the big orchestras were now scarcely heard among the folk and church-revival singers.

The immense popularity of the church-revival mood also suggested a return to or reformulation of "religion." Youth, never more millenarian than in the early 1960s, had rediscovered mysticism, the shared but intensely individual purification of the psyche through hallucinogenic "trips," which somehow suggested the transports of the old tent meeting. To those who, like Dr. Timothy Leary, searched for a transcendental "spiritual discovery," the soul singing of Sister Odetta could fill a need unsatisfied by delicate secular love ballads. Young people bored by what one critic called the "dessicated" cool jazz of the 1950s bought John Coltrane's best-selling album, *A Love Supreme* (Impulse A/AS 77), whose liner notes consisted of Coltrane's devotional poetry.[25]

The love music of the 1960s, sacred or profane, was not much like that of a previous generation. Of course, in all ages men sing of love, and so they did in the 1960s, sometimes with a lachrymose sentimentality which in itself catered to a different level of taste than did many of the brittle ballads of the 1930s. Nevertheless, sentimental love songs, lachrymose or otherwise, declined in popularity. Love lyrics were often so hopelessly submerged in and mangled by arrangements aimed primarily at rhythmic effect that observers could easily conclude that the love song as they remembered it had all but disappeared.[26] Certainly boys didn't worship girls in such 1942-style effusions as "You Are a Poem Set to Music." Nor did girls much attempt to promote this sort of veneration. If one heard fewer "pretty songs" one saw fewer girls in "pretty dresses," even on Sundays. A sexually more casual generation appeared to reject the tradition of chivalric *amour*. They might be aggressively sensuous and sensual, but casually so, and not with the great daintiness or delicacy which had once characterized days of a stronger double

[24] According to Miss Baez, her simple vocal-with-guitar rejected the "commercial." "The Folk Girls," *Time*, LXXIX (June 1, 1962), 40.

[25] A college student editor, Peter B. Riley, notes that the "tough" sound of such groups as the Butterfield Blues Band (called the "Marat/Sade of Blues") "seems to act on some people in the manner of an aural LSD." *Recorder* (Central Connecticut State College), Feb. 28, 1967, 3:2. Similarly, a review of another John Coltrane devotional album, *Meditations*, says "I *feel* this. . . . It opens up a part of myself that is tightly closed. Seldom recognized emotions well up and sear my consciousness." Don DeMichael in *Downbeat*, XXXIII (Dec. 1, 1966), 28.

[26] See for example, Tom Prideaux, "Whatever Happened to Love Songs?" *Life*, LXI (Sept. 16, 1966), 61–62.

standard and sense of sin. They were more direct and companionate in the minidress, car-coat-and-Levis era. God's death, or at least the weakening of Pauline concepts of deity, evidently meant you could junk much of your Platonism and let yourself go.

The noticeable dip in the popularity of the exclusive type of love song among many younger buyers cannot be traced to any one simple cause. A decline in traditional religion probably played a part. If God were not dead, He was, at least to the "hip" culture, a God created in man's image, a "swinger" to be found in "gay" bars and in jazz-happening services. As such, He did not demand chaste refinement in music. His demands of human nature were few, but He did demand of his flower children a communal love rather than middle-class monogamy. At any rate, many youths, whether "hip" or not, and particularly among the middle class, caught the spirit. They desired greater sexual freedom. They rejected the (to them) hypocritical compromises, the puritanical indirection, and often the exclusiveness as well, of many of the older ballads. For them, the egocentric, monogamous lyrics, the bourgeois-plushy orchestrations of even the passionate "Body and Soul" sort of thing was, as they would put it, "beside the point." The older love song, even the more sensual, no longer caught on. After all, among many students, particularly in the first half of the 1960s, sexual revolt was but part of a much wider rejection of middle-class mores and prejudices. It was part of a fervent attempt to regenerate man. Youthful energies flowed out toward social reconstruction — "We Shall Overcome" — or into the purification of or expansion of the individual psyche through hallucinogens — "Puff, the Magic Dragon," "The Trip." Such youth stressed the one-ness of mankind, the overcoming of the crippling guilt feelings imposed by an artificial Establishment. They opposed the middle-class mores of their parents, often attributing these to the egocentricity of Western civilization; and some turned to their version of a pantheistic Buddhism as a cure for the ills of the West. (Thus the "acid rock" emanating from San Francisco's Hashbury was infused with the raga of an oriental culture considered beatific by the hippies.) The more activistic youth in the 1960s, puritanical hedonists or hedonistic Puritans who equated sensual pleasure (widely diffused) and self-expression with cosmic betterment, saw in love not a misty-eyed, pallid, etherealized retreat from the world but a means of social regeneration. (At least so went the gospel of Lawrence Lipton's *Erotic Revolution*.) These outlooks hardly promoted the popularity of such old musical standards as "When Your Lover Has Gone." All compromise with artificial bourgeois social and sexual barriers must go — among these compromises, the romantic ballad of the past. If the middle-class record purchasers of the previous generation had stressed monogamy within or without marriage, the new, young communalists rejected songs which sentimentally glorified one girl. A new world could not be built upon middle-class hypocrisy, possessiveness, exclusiveness. This dislike of the middle class by the self-styled "neo-Marxists" contributed to the decline of the old-style love song.[27]

The youth culture we have been describing, though it did help shape a trend away from the old ballads, was only a minority of the market. However noisily influential, it is doubtful that its outlook totally determined popular trends. It just so happened that other, larger segments of the market were also not enthusiastic middle-class devotees of the old monogamous love ballad. Perhaps one of the most potent changers of taste was the horde of highly permissive and hedonistic lower classes entering the record market. These buyers, along with the less numerous upper-middle-class young rebels, weakened the hold of the romantic, oblique, sublimated "If I Loved You" approach toward love, taking it out of the sphere of the angels and pulling it down toward earth. (1955's "Earth Angel" was a step along the way.) Trends in music since around 1955 especially have appeared to bear out the assumptions of sociologists, and of Professor Hayakawa's invaluable work on jazz,[28] that the working class generally, and especially the colored lower class, lack the WASPish inhibitions which are apt to generate genteelly romantic, melancholy, frustrated songs. In short, they gratify themselves without

[27] Richard Goldstein's article on the "Flower Children" among the middle class, in the Denver *Post Contemporary* section, June 18, 1967, 12, 21, points up the generalized ideal of love. Such youth of course could have plenty of fun shocking the oldsters with their Four Letter Word Movement, all for a good cause. Two of the "frank" folksongs popular in the early 1960s were at least straightforward enough to ruffle the remaining hairs on a middle-class pate — especially if sung by girls of the rising generation: i.e., "Keep Her Good and Drunk and Goozy" and "Sally Let Your Bangs Hang Down," sung respectively by Gibson and Camp and by Dian and the Greenbrier Boys:

> *Now we know what Sally's got*
> *Makes a man think she's so hot*
> *Sally let your bangs hang down.*

(from Crestview Album CRS 7807, *The Original Hootenanny*). This was hardly Norman Burroughs, but neither was it Irving Berlin or Cole Porter.

[28] For example, "Popular Songs versus the Facts of Life," *ETC: A General Review of Semantics*, XII (Winter 1955), 83–95.

making a cosmic issue out of it. By 1955 a best-selling rock number, "Honey Love," reduced the description of desire to three little words — not "I Love You," but "I Want It." In contrast, fifteen years previously, Ray Eberle had softly vocalized, over Glenn Miller's Debussyesque background, this Lawrence-Shapiro ballad:

> *I recall a story of love in all its glory*
> *A night that left my heart romantic scars*
> *When I reached up to heaven ...*
> *And gathered you a handful of stars.*[29]

Boys and girls who take sexual freedom for granted would hardly be as captivated by such songs as would be the more frustrated. They would be just as interested in motorcycling and, the boys at least, in hot-rodding; finding in these activities something of the same muscular enthusiasm and visceral excitement involved in their sexual relations. Indeed, an infusion of prosperous, rather unsentimental lower-class leather boys into the record market — the kind who like to be out with their buddies Sunday afternoons — may have helped create the hot-rod music craze of the early 1960s.

Thus, lower-class youth unassimilated by middle-class culture joined with middle-class rebels against middle-class culture to alter the tone of American popular music. To the lower class, sex was nothing to moan over or sing pretty little sad poems about. To the crusading middle-class student rebels it was something which must be handled robustly, erotically, "honestly," rather than euphemized or sublimated out of all recognition as their parents had frequently done. Middle-class rebel and lower-class "swinger"; hippy and minority groups had a common distaste for pretty songs. The folk music of youth in the 1960s could hardly follow schoolmarmish rules of rhyme or the meter of Victorian poetry. Rejecting the formulae of the classroom, more and more lyrics were sung — or spoken — free style, like streetcorner or coffee-house conversation.

If monogamous romantic love was out in the music of the young and many of the would-be-young, *Agapé* was in. By 1964, the tone of Erich Fromm, Martin Buber and Paul Goodman pervaded even a Broadway hit musical, *Funny Girl*. Barbra Streisand (first name unconventionally spelled, last name obviously minority group; exotic-ugly non-Anglo

---

[29] Copyright 1939, 1940 by Leo Feist, Inc. Recorded on Bluebird 10893. Original pressings are in Rodgers and Hammerstein Archives, New York City Public Library; and Archives, Stanford University Music Library.

face; muscular voice throbbing with all the subtlety of a sledge hammer; personality problems[30] — how could she have failed?) sang "People Who Need People Are the Luckiest People in the World." Two years later, in similar Tennessee Williams spirit, Simon and Garfunkel (names which would have been anglicized by any sane public-relations man in 1930, but only by an insane one in 1966) popularized their ironic, "I Am a Rock, I Am an Island":

> *And a rock can feel no pain,*
> *And an island never cries.*[31]

The neo-proletarian Togetherness, like the rough-edged songs and singers, was appropriate to the jeans and horsehide boots of the young "neo-Marxists." This was still romanticism, of course, but it was not "bourgeois" prettiness. The point is that the "tastefully" orchestrated romantic love ballad had such severe competition that it was much less in evidence.[32] As middle-class youth conceived of the one-ness mankind and refurbished the vision of the noble savage, they gravitated toward the music of people considered inferior by their parents, by all who still aspired to older middle-class standards. Thus, the tastes of the young did not run heavily to "pretty" love ballads. With their fondness for the old films of James Dean and Marlon Brando and Humphrey ("gentle-tough guy") Bogart, they liked Roger Miller's "King of the Road."

This brings us back to a basic generalization. Despite eddies and cross currents always present in the streams of taste, the outstanding trend in American popular music in the 1950s and the earlier 1960s was a rejection of prettiness, overrefinement, academic orchestration and lyrics, smoothness, even subtlety. Although by 1965 a few of the lyrics written for the recently expanded college market, like "I Am a Rock," sensitively articulated the preoccupations of young adults, many lyrics, as well as most orchestrations, of the late 1950s and early 1960s were crude. Classicism, polish, formal discipline, carefully contrived arrangements, adherence to accepted rules in music, as in literature and art — these were likely to be anathematized even by many intellectuals for

[30] See Shana Alexander, "Barbra," *Life*, LVI (May 22, 1964), 52.

[31] Copyright © 1965, Charing Cross Music. Lyrics quoted with permission of the copyright holder.

[32] But not dead. Songs by Andy Williams, Jerry Vale, Al Martino and Tony Bennett (albeit more exuberantly and "cornilly" rendered than songs in the 1930s and 1940s) were still heard on TV and especially on jukeboxes in restaurants and bars catering to people around thirty or older.

coldness, lack of spontaneity or "hypocrisy." In short, there was an attack on middle-class standards, on that residue of puritanism which distrusted the "natural." It would be a mistake, however, to assert that since music contained much protest against all aspects of the Establishment, from war to "Ticky Tacky Houses" and conformity, a thoroughgoing iconoclasm was the order of the day. Even though the folk song might so often protest, it could also reaffirm for large audiences a traditional patriotism — "This Land Is Our Land," "Ballad of the Green Beret." Musical trends can hardly be made any more coherent or consistent than the society which produces them. Two hundred million Americans living in the same years could among them find room for Barry Sadler's "Green Beret" and Bob Dylan's "World War III Blues." And yet, there was a similarity between the performers. Both were leather-booted, wild-animal-type young men (one a disheveled gazelle, the other a wild boar). Both were typical of years in which some of the most popular vocal and instrumental groups were called the "Animals," the "Monkees," the "Critters." Both these men were as far removed as could be from the Regional Accounting Office, the classroom or "Cocktails for Two" in the sleek white-on-whiteness of an *art moderne* penthouse in Gotham.[33] They would, both of them, be classified at any employment agency as Non-U. To this extent they perhaps validate the one generalization we can make about the musical temper of the later 1950s and the earlier 1960s: It was one of those times when the perennial reaction of youth against the norms of older people is accelerated, heightened, intensified. Youth boldly threw in the faces of its elders its own musical description of love: "Gimme Gravy for My Mashed Potatoes." The very appearance of Cass of the Mamas and the Papas — lazy-fat, slovenly, serenely sensual, affronted the middle-class ideal of refined womanhood as a trimly neat, highly disciplined, meticulous housewife, teacher or stenographer.

Again, lest we interpret such a generalization to mean that all middle-class restraints, social and musical, were on the junk heap, Jeremy Larner reminds us that the popular songs of the early 1960s, if less than those of the 1930s, still paid some lip service to older values. Some sentimental lyrics continued to be written and sung even in rock-and-roll numbers, if only, as Mr. Larner explains, to sublimate the orgasm

---

[33] "Cocktails for Two" was introduced by Duke Ellington in a 1934 musical film. He played in full dress, and on a white piano. The song mentioned two hands slyly meeting beneath a serviette while an orchestra played "an exquisite *chansonette.*"

of the music. True, these lyrics were often not clearly articulated; engulfed in a pounding, shrieking sound, they were rarely audible. But they were there. The new generation of rebels still hedged a bit.[34] The Critters occasionally would sing soft, subtly blended arrangements of lovelorn ballads like "Mr. Die-ingly Sad"; and if you listened carefully enough to the young black voices of the Orlons shouting "The Rules of Love," you could hear the old plea for bourgeois fidelity.

[34] Jeremy Larner, "What Do They Get from Rock-'n'-Roll?" *Atlantic*, CCXIV (Aug. 1964), 48.

chapter five

Quests for Identity:
"You Take the High Road,
I'll Take the Low Road!"

introduction

Beginning this chapter with a passionate defense of marijuana and
an attack on the Federal Bureau of Narcotics may seem to indicate
an affirmative stand by the editor on the issue of drug use. Surely
Allen Ginsberg's essay reaches an extreme in the use of footnotes
for supporting evidence. His "First Manifesto to End the Bring-
down" is divided into two parts, the first being presumably written
under the influence of a marijuana "high." Ginsberg insists in both
sections of the essay that marijuana consciousness shifts attention
from stereotyped verbal symbols to *"more direct, slower, absorbing, occasionally microscopically minute, engagement with sensing
phenomena during the high."* He addresses his comments to the
inexperienced person and attempts, as he says, to relate in written
form a marijuana experience.

The question to ask is whether or not there is a difference in
Ginsberg's style in each section of the essay. If marijuana increases
one's sensibility, then it should follow that a marijuana experience with "sensing phenomena" should bring heightened results.
If this essay does not support the theory that marijuana increases
creativity, then what is the source of the creative process? Ginsberg's undeniable poetic and prophetic powers are gifts, neither
diluted nor enhanced by drugs. Is it possible then that a less gifted
person is simply deluding himself by thinking that marijuana or

other hallucinogenic drugs increase his sensitivity? The answer to the mystery of man's creativity — despite the current hypothesizing of psychoanalysts, biochemists, critics, and drug advocates — remains as elusive to us as it was to Plato.

In "Children of the Drug Age," the authors designate the brightest and most creative high school students as those who use drugs, finding in them "a way into an unconventional social framework" and perhaps "into an alienated subculture," while they categorize the rest of the students as non-users or those who experiment with drugs but remain attached to conventional values. William Simon, director of sociological programs at the Institute for Juvenile Research in Chicago, and John Gagnon, professor of sociology at Stony Brook, maintain that this group of brightest students, because they can't find meaningful social experiences in conventional patterns, search for experiences almost totally private. Drugs provide at least the illusion of intense, immediate, almost totally personal experience. The authors fear that such students will lose a sense of the "real capacity for experience" and will abandon the role of influence which could be theirs in society. However, Simon and Gagnon caution their adult audience against over-reaction to drug use. They suggest a redefinition of the legal status of drugs and a subsequent liberalization of access to marijuana but do not advocate making marijuana freely available to adolescents. They ask how the community responds to the issue of drug use and they suggest that the response must be serious and honest without surrendering youth to bigotry and ignorance. The essay does not rely on sociological jargon but presents a clear, well-organized analysis of drug use by adolescents.

Howard Becker, professor of sociology at Northwestern University disagrees with the concern over drug use as such and suggests that more attention should be given to drug incidents on campus, those occurrences which arouse public attention. The goal should be to reduce the number of drug incidents. The basis for his argument is that because marijuana produces no proven harmful effects, college administrators and students should form a "live and let live" bargain. Students should be educated to take precautions to avoid getting caught. Even though his idea sounds reasonable and is certainly original, the reader must test Becker's logic and evidence. The letters in response to Becker's article range from outright hostility to Becker as a sociologist to applause for his realism and correct assessment of the problem. Do these letters written by a variety of people, mainly professionals, respond to the major points of Becker's essay or do they take issue with minor personal antagonisms? Do they effectively argue for or against Becker's proposal? It should be possible to write a letter in response that becomes, in itself, a well-written argumentative essay.

In the same way that letters can take good argumentative form, Rollo May has succeeded in transforming a critical book review into an essay which reveals his argument against Timothy Leary's advocacy of "drugs as the source of a lifetime of joy." Instead of writing the usual pedestrian critical analysis of a book, Rollo May realizes that he must respond to Leary's *High Priest* and *The Politics of Ecstasy* as though he were responding to Leary himself and to Leary's vision or "new" religion. Of course, he includes the appropriate summary of plot or action with passages quoted from the text, but he questions Leary's philosophical statement: "When LSD has torn down the conventional cosmology, what content will Leary put in its place?" For May, drugs "like every other form of technology . . . only sharpen the necessity to forge human values through psychological and spiritual means." Rollo May becomes more than merely a book reviewer; he is a man with a vision of his own who challenges the author and the vision behind his book.

The hippie element in our society has been and is still influential in many ways. In "An Open Letter to a Hippie," Nicholas Charney as editor of *Psychology Today* raises a basic question about the hippie's future. Here is an example of a letter as an essay and a deliberate structuring of an editorial to elicit response from hippies or their defenders. Gretchen Horton's reply is almost gentle, as though she were trying to instruct a small child in comprehending something too vast for his limited reasoning ability. She counters most of Charney's points and argues that hippies or heads, as they prefer to be called now, have a totally different idea of success and don't wish to return to Charney's society anyway. Her letter is well-written, organized, personal, and yet instructive. Mr. Freeman's reply is more of an attack; he feels himself directly addressed by Mr. Charney and relates himself and his "breed of aware individuals" to generations of the past who were "joyful and yet cautious" about their world, too. He ends on a more revolutionary note, citing the population growth of people under twenty-five and prophesizing that a new society will arise from the debris of the old. Both letters show us that professionals are not the only ones who respond to issues in writing and that good letters are just as effective persuasive tools as formal essays.

The final selection in Chapter Five "Haight-Ashbury's Hippies and the Future Society" may appear dated in the description of Haight-Ashbury but its worth lies in its attempt to analyze the influence hippies have had or will have upon our society. Fred Davis, professor of sociology at the University of California Medical Center in San Francisco, proposes that hippies are showing us "a number of possible cultural solutions to central life problems posed by the emerging society of the future." He identifies three such problems: compulsive consumption, passive spectatorship, and the time-scale of experience. Davis's style, his frequent long sentences containing parenthetical phrases or sections set off by dashes, and his occasional formal word choices may confuse, but his essay is worth studying because it raises some thoughts about visions of the world to come.

ALLEN GINSBERG
first manifesto to end the bringdown

I THE FIRST HALF OF THE ESSAY WAS WRITTEN WHILE THE AUTHOR WAS SMOKING MARIJUANA.

7:38 P.M. Nov. 13, 1965
San Francisco, California, USA, Kosmos

How much to be revealed about marijuana especially in this time and nation for the *general* public! for the actual experience of the smoked herb has been completely clouded by a fog of dirty language by the diminishing crowds of fakers who have not had the experience and yet insist on being centers of propaganda about the experience. And the key, the paradoxical key to this bizarre impasse of awareness is precisely that the marijuana consciousness is one that, ever so gently, shifts the center of attention *from* habitual shallow purely verbal guidelines and repetitive secondhand ideological interpretations of experience to *more direct, slower, absorbing, occasionally microscopically minute, engagement with sensing phenomena during the high* moments or hours after one has smoked.

One who has the experience needs no explanations in the world of explanatory language, which is, after all, a limited charming part of the whole phenomenal show of life. A few people don't *like* the experience and report back to the language world that it's a drag and make propaganda against this particular area of nonverbal awareness. But the vast majority all over the world, who have smoked the several breaths necessary to feel the effect, adjust to the strangely familiar sensation of Time slow-down, and explore this new space thru natural curiosity, report that it's a useful area of mind-consciousness to be familiar with, a creative show of the silly side of an awful big army of senseless but habitual thought-formations risen out of the elements of a language world: a metaphysical herb less habituating than tobacco, whose smoke is no more disruptive than Insight — in short, for those who have made the only objective test, a vast majority of satisfied smokers.

This essay in explanation, conceived by a mature middle-aged gentleman, the holder at present of a Guggenheim Fellowship for creative writing, a traveler on many continents with experience of customs and modes of different cultures, is dedicated in the author's right mind (i.e., not high) to those who have *not* smoked marijuana, as an attempt to bridge the conceptual gap, or cultural gap as may be, to explain the misunderstanding that has too long existed between those who know what pot is by experience and those who don't know exactly what it is but have been influenced by sloppy, or secondhand, or unscientific, or (as in the case of drug-control bureaucracies) definitely self-interested language used to describe the marijuana high pejoratively. I offer the pleasant suggestion that a negative approach to the whole issue (as presently obtains in what are aptly called square circles in the USA) is not necessarily the best, and that it is time to shift to a more positive attitude toward this specific experience.[1] If one is not inclined to have the experience oneself, this is a free country and no one is obliged to have an experience merely because a great number of one's friends, family, or business acquaintances have had it and report themselves pleased. On the other hand, an equal respect and courtesy is required for the sensibilities of one's familiars for whom the experience has not been closed off by the door of Choice.

The main negative mythic images of the marijuana state that the general public is familiar with emanate from one particular source: the U.S. Treas. Dept. Narcotics Bureau.[2] If the tendency (a return to common sense) to leave the opiate problem with qualified M.D.'s prevails, the main function of this large Bureau will shift to the persecution of marijuana. Otherwise the Bureau will have no function except as a minor tax office for which it was originally purposed, under the aegis of Secty. of Treasury. Following Parkinson's Law that a bureaucracy will attempt to find work for itself, or following a simpler line of

---

[1] Editorial in The English Journal of Medicine *The Lancet*, November 9, 1963.

. . . At most of the recent references the question was raised whether the marijuana problem might be abolished by removing the substance from the list of dangerous drugs, where it was placed in 1951, and giving it the same social status as alcohol by legalising its import and consumption.

This suggestion is worth considering. Besides the undoubted attraction of reducing, for once, the number of crimes that a member of our society can commit, and of allowing the wider spread of something that can give pleasure, a greater revenue would certainly come to the State from taxation than from fines. Additional gains might be the reduction of interracial tension, as well as that between generations; for "pot" spread from South America to Britain via the United States and the West Indies. Here it has been taken up by the younger members of a society in which alcohol is the inheritance of the more elderly.

[2] Anslinger, Harry J. and Fulton Oursler: *The Murderers*, Farrar, Strauss & Cudahy, N. Y., 1961 (p. 38).

Much of the irrational juvenile violence and killing that has written a new chapter of shame and tragedy is traceable directly to this hemp intoxication . . .

As the Marijuana situation grew worse, I knew action had to be taken to get proper control legislation passed. By 1937, under my direction, the Bureau launched two important steps: First, a legislative plan to seek from Congress a new law that would place Marijuana and its distribution directly under federal control. Second, on radio and at major forums, such as that presented annually by the New York *Herald Tribune*, I told the story of this evil weed of the fields and river beds and roadsides. I wrote articles for magazines; our agents gave hundreds of lectures to parents, educators, social and civic leaders. In network broadcasts I reported on the growing list of crimes, including murder and rape. I described the nature of Marijuana and its close kinship to hashish. I continued to hammer at the facts.

I believe we did a thorough job, for the public was alerted, and the laws to protect them were passed, both national and at the state level.

thought, that the agents of this Bureau have a business interest in perpetuating the idea of a marijuana "menace" lest they lose their employment, it is not unreasonable to suppose that a great deal of the violence, hysteria & energy of the antimarijuana language propaganda emanating from this source has as its motive a rather obnoxious self-interest, all the more objectionable for its tone of moralist evangelism.[3] This hypocrisy is recognizable to anybody who has firsthand experience of the so-called narcotic; which, as the reader may have noticed, I have termed an herb, which it is — a leaf or blossom — in order to switch away from negative terminology and inaccurate language.

A marvelous project for a sociologist, and one which I am sure will be in preparation before my generation grows old, will be a close examination of the actual history and tactics of the Narcotics Bureau and its former chief Power, Harry J. Anslinger, in planting the seed of the marijuana "menace" in the public mind and carefully nurturing its growth in the course of a few decades until the unsuspecting public was forced to accept an outright lie.[4] I am not a thorough patient sociologist and this is not my task here, so I will limit myself to telling a few stories from personal experience, or relating stories that have been told me.

I must begin by explaining something that I have already said in public for many years: that I occasionally use marijuana in preference to alcohol, and have for several decades. I say occasionally and mean it quite literally; I have spent about as many hours high as I have spent in movie theaters — sometimes 3 hours a week, sometimes 12 or 20 or more, as at a film festival — with about the same degree of alteration of my normal awareness.

[3] H. J. Anslinger, Commissioner of Narcotics, Correspondence, *Jour. A.M.A.*, Jan. 16, 1943 (p. 212).

. . . information in our possession . . . that marihuana precipitates in certain persons psychoses and unstable and disorganized personality . . . may be an important contributory cause to crime . . . by relaxing inhibitions may permit anti-social tendencies . . .

Of course, the primary interest of the Bureau of Narcotics is in the enforcement aspect. From that point of view it is very unfortunate that Drs. Allentuck and Bowman should have stated so unqualifiedly that use of marihuana does not lead to physical, mental, or moral degeneration and that no permanent deleterious effects from its continued use were observed.

[4] "Traffic in Opium and Other Dangerous Drugs." Report by the Government of the United States of America for the Year Ended December 31st, 1938, by Hon. H. J. Anslinger, Commissioner of Narcotics (p. 7). "The Narcotics Section recognizes the great danger of marihuana due to its definite impairment of the mentality and the fact that its continuous use leads direct to the insane asylum."

To continue, I therefore do know the subjective possibilities of marijuana and herein take evidence of my own senses between my own
awareness of the mysterious ghastly universe of joy, pain, discovery,
birth and death, the emptiness and awesomeness of its forms and
consciousness described in the Prajna Paramita Sutra central to a
Buddhist or even Christian or Hindu view of Kosmos which I sometimes
experience while high, as for the last two paragraphs, and the cheap
abstract inexperienced version of exactly the same thing one may have
read in the newspapers, written by reporters (who smoke pot themselves
occasionally nowadays) taking the main part of their poorly written
squibs of misinformation from the texts and mouths of Chiefs of
Narcotics Bureaus, Municipal or Federal — or an occasional doctor
notorious for his ungracious stupidity and insulting manners.

One doctor, facing me across a microphone in a radio broadcasting
booth on a six o'clock chat show, pre-recorded, opened our conversation
reading aloud a paragraph of *Kaddish* (a poem I had written in
memory of my mother, and a tribute to her which made my own father
weep; a text widely read, set to music or anthologized in portions,
translations of which had met with some critical approval in various
languages — Spanish, French, Italian and German, by now some Bengali
or Hebrew; a text which I submitted as among my major "Poems" in
applying for monies from great foundations; a text applauded in
recitation before academies; a text recorded for a large commercial
business establishment's circulation; a text which I'd spent months
daily transcribing as a movie scenario — in short a straightforward
piece of communication integrating the subjective and objective, private
and public, and what is common between them) — disapproving and
confused — declared firmly that the dashes used as this — indicated
that the broken measures of phrase — moment-to-moment consciousness
during which syntax and meaning and direction of the — pauses for
thought — were a sign of marijuana intoxication and were incomprehensible. He could not follow the thought. He said, as I remember —
marijuana retains association and goes from one thought to another if
verbalized — that I was, in fact, quite mad.

Such a notion I thought quite mad on his part; my mother had been
that. They were both quite insistent in their obsessions, or opinions, and
sometimes harsh and premature in their judgments. This doctor and my
mother did not differ so much from myself; the announcer was sympathetic to both of us. After the show I got quite angry with the doctor
— it seemed quite a self-righteous remark; but I suppose I could not

match his Power by any other means at the moment and felt that Frankness and a show of emotion might shake his composure — alas, I yelled Fascist in his face, and had to be reprimanded by my companion Mr. Orlovsky for losing my temper with Dr. Baird. I have a most excellent reason in such cases and so calmed myself, but I did believe that he was a quack-mind of sorts and a sort of negative Judger with professional credentials. I had as friends many psychiatrists who treated me as interesting and no madder than themselves; and had in fact graduated from 8 months in a psychiatric institute to be told smilingly by a doctor that I was not schizophrenic but in fact a bearable neurotic, like many other people — but this was years earlier when I was a poet with a tie and an obsession with eternity. True, I had changed much in the intervening 13 years. I had pursued my thoughts to India and was now satisfied with my self and bodily existence, and a little more in harmony with desire for Life. I had begun singing mantras daily — Hindu practice of Japa and Kirtan — and I had smoked a lot of marijuana in those years; but I had not, despite my odd little biography in *Who's Who* maintained so much confusion over my identity as to forget to end a sentence, if I wished to, tying together simultaneously association and language and memory with correct punctuation and obvious thought for the reader (to make it obvious, I am doing it now): I had not so much changed and broken away from communication from my fellow selves on earth that anyone should judge me mad. His remark (on the radio) only made me feel slightly paranoid; and I suppose it is no cure to try to make the other fellow feel paranoid, so perhaps I misunderstood the doctor and must take a charitable position and assume that I am Mad (or Not-Mad) but that the doctors also misunderstood my syntax; and judged too abruptly before the Revelations possible thru pot had been deciphered. . . . In any case I had *not* been high on marijuana when *Kaddish* was composed. The original mms. were bought by NYU library and are clearly labeled as written primarily under the influence of amphetamines, more popularly known as Benzedrine or Dexadrine, familiar to many a truck driver, doctor student, housewife, and harried business executive and soldier in battle — a common experience not generally termed mad.

The mind does wander and that's another way around; to give by example a manifestation of the precise record of the effects of marijuana during composition on the subject itself, showing the area of reality traversed, so that the reader may see that it is a harmless gentle shift to a "more direct, slower, absorbing, occasionally microscopic minute, engagement with sensing phenomena" — in *this* case the phenomenon of transmuting to written language a model of the marijuana experience, which can be understood and related to in some mode by those who have not yet met the experience but who are willing to slow their thought and judgment and decipher the syntax clause by clause not necessarily as slowly as composed, so the affect will differ; and of course two bodies cannot, they say, occupy the same place in space. Yet in another light, they say we are one being of thought and to that common being — perceived in whatever mode one perceives — I address this syntax.[5]

Returning to the mundane world of order,[6] may I compare the mental phenomena of the preceding anecdote with the criminal view of it as presented by the Narcotics Dept. for years in cheap sex magazines and government reports — reports uninfluenced by the Narco. Dept. take a contrasting view[7] — base paranoia close to murder; frothing at the mouth of Egyptian dogs, sex orgies in cheap dives, debilitation and terror and physiological or mysterious psychic addiction. An essentially grotesque Image, a thought-hallucination magnified myriad thru mass-media, a byproduct of Fear — something quite fiendish — "Dope Fiend" the old language, a language abandoned in the early sixties where enough of the general public had sufficient personal experience to reject such palpable poppycock and the bureaucratic line shifted to defense of its own existence with the following reason:[8] necessary to control

[5] As stated in the text, which stands almost completely unrevised from first composition, the author smoked one marijuana cigarette at the beginning of the fourth paragraph.

[6] The author is still high to the end of Section I.

[7] The Phamacological Basis of Therapeutics, Goodman and Gillman, 1956 ed. (p. 20). "The federal narcotic regulations and a number of supplementary laws include drugs such as papaverine and marihuana which do not produce narcosis."

(pp. 170–177). "There are no lasting ill effects from the acute use of marihuana, and fatalities have not been known to occur.

"Careful and complete medical and neuropsychiatric examinations of habitués reveal no pathological conditions or disorders of cerebral functions attributable to the drug.

"Although habituation occurs, psychic dependence is not as prominent or compelling as in the case of morphine, alcohol, or perhaps even tobacco habituation."

[8] Hearings before the Committee on Ways and Means, U.S. House of Representatives, 75th Congress, 1st session April and May 1937: House Marijuana Hearings (p. 24).

Rep. John Dingall: "I am just wondering whether the marijuana addict graduates into a heroin, an opium, or a cocaine user?"

Anslinger: "No, sir. I have not heard of a case of that kind. I think it is an entirely different class. The marijuana addict does not go in that direction."

marijuana because smoking leads to search for thrills, kicks; this leads to next step the monster Heroin. And a terrible Fate.[9]

In sound good health I smoked legal ganja (as marijuana is termed in India where it is traditionally used in preference to alcohol) bought from government tax shops in Calcutta, in a circle of devotees, yogis, and hymn-singing pious Shaivite worshippers in the burning ground at Nimtallah Ghat in Calcutta, where it was the custom of these respected gentlemen to meet on Tues. and Saturday nights, smoke before an improvised altar of blossoms, sacramental milk-candy and perhaps a fire taken from the burning wooden bed on which lay a newly dead body, of some friend perhaps, likely a stranger if a corpse is a stranger, pass out the candy as God's gift to friend and stranger, and sing holy songs all night, with great strength and emotion, addressed to different images of the Divine Spirit. Ganja was there considered a beginning of saddhana[10] by some; others consider the Ascetic Yogi Shiva Himself to have smoked marijuana; on His birthday marijuana is mixed as a paste with almond milk by the grandmothers of pious families and imbibed as sacrament by this polytheistic nation, considered by some a holy society. The professors of English at Benares University brought me a bottle for the traditional night of Shivaratri, birthday of the Creator and Destroyer who is the patron god of this oldest continuously inhabited city on Earth. "Bom Bom Mahadev!" (Boom Boom Great God!) is the Mantra Yogis' cry as they raise the ganja pipe to their brows before inhaling.

All India is familiar with ganja, and so is all Africa, and so is all the Arab world; and so were Paris and London in smaller measure in high-minded but respectable 19th-century circles; and so on a larger scale is

[9] In historical context this excuse for repression of marijuana seemed to the author so irrational that it was unnecessary to analyze. Yet public confusion may warrant some precise analysis. A) There are no legitimate sociological/medical study documents warranting the Narcotics Department's assertion of causal relation between use of marijuana and graduation to opiates. B) There never had been any hint of such association before the two classes of drugs were forcibly juxtaposed in black market by said department; Anslinger testified to that in 1937 (see footnote #8). C) A greater number of opiate users started with bananas, cigarettes and alcohol than started with marijuana — no causal relationship is indicated in any case. D) The number of millions of respectable Americans who smoke marijuana have obviously not proceeded to opiates. E) In test sociological cases, i.e. societies such as Morocco and India where marijuana use is universal, there is very small use of opiates and no social association between the two classes of drugs. What juxtaposition there is in America has been created and encouraged by the propaganda and repression tactics of the Narcotics Bureau.

[10] Saddhana: Yogic Path or Discipline.

America even now. Young and old millions perhaps smoke marijuana and see no harm. And we have not measured the Latin-American world, Mexico particularly who gave the local herb its familiar name. In some respects we may then see its prohibition as an arbitrary cultural taboo.

There has been a tendency toward its suppression in the Arab world with the too hasty adoption of Western rationality and the enlarged activity of the American fanatic Mr. Anslinger as US representative to the UN World Health Organization Single Narcotics Commission — a position from which he circulates hysterical notices and warnings, manufactured in Washington's Treas. Dept., to the police forces of the cities of the world — so I was told by a police official in Tel Aviv, an old school chum who laughed about the latest release, a grim warning against the dangers of Khat, a traditional energizing leaf chewed by Bedouins of Arabia and businessmen and princes in Ethiopia, as well as a few traditional Yemenite Jews.

There seems to be a liaison between Anslinger and some policemen in Egypt, which has now formally outlawed its hashish or kif form of marijuana (even though masses of nondrinking faithful Muslims prefer a contemplative pipe of kif to the dangers of violent alcohol forbidden by the Koran). We find government bureaucrats and the well-to-do (as in India) taking knowing delight in alcohol as a more sophisticated and *daring* preference; and stories of mad dogs frothing at the mouth and asylums full of people driven mad by some unheard-of brand of hashish (would god it were imported to America like some fine brand of Scotch or pernod) circulated from the police information bureaus of Egypt — or perhaps some single cranky Egyptian Dr. Baird — thru the Treas. Dept. Narcotics Bureau and thence by interview and press release to the mass media of America and an inexperienced public (encouraged to drink intoxicating beer by millions of dollars' worth of advertisement). The Egyptian evidence has been quoted for years, most recently by the present head of the Narcotics Bureau, a Mr. Giordano, one of Mr. Anslinger's former intimates in the department.

Professor Lindesmith has already objected in public print to the Department's manipulation and attempted quashing of various medical-juridic reports; a Canadian documentary film on the drug subject has been blocked from being shown in this country thru activity of the Treas. Dept. — perhaps an import license was refused; the impartial LaGuardia Report was rudely attacked by Anslinger; a President's Judicial Advisory Council Policy Statement (1964) has characterized the activities of the Bureau as exceeding legal rightfulness in "criminalizing" by executive fiat and administrative dictum those addicted to addicting drugs who for decades have been prevented from going to a doctor for treatment unless it was under the aegis of Lexington jail and thru police channels. Memory of the British East India Hemp Commission report, the largest in history, done in the 1880s, which concluded that marijuana was *not* a problem, has been ignored,[11] memories of our own Panama Canal Military reports giving marijuana a clean bill of health have been unavailing in consideration of the Bureau,[12] doctors have complained of being harassed and framed by one or another police agency; sick junkies have died in jail; thousands of intelligent citizens

[11] Report of the Indian Hemp Drugs Commission, 1893–4, Ch. XIII (263–4, par. 552).

Summary of conclusions regarding effects. The Commission have now examined all the evidence before them regarding the effects attributed to hemp drugs. It will be well to summarize briefly the conclusions to which they come. It has been clearly established that the occasional use of hemp in moderate doses may be beneficial; but this use may be regarded as medicinal in character. It is rather to the popular and common use of the drugs that the Commission will now confine their attention. It is convenient to consider the effects separately as affecting the physical, mental, or moral nature. In regard to the physical effects, the Commission have come to the conclusion that the moderate use of hemp drugs is practically attended by no evil results at all. There may be exceptional cases in which, owing to idiosyncracies of constitution, the drugs in even moderate use may be injurious. There is probably nothing the use of which may not possibly be injurious in cases of exceptional intolerance . . .

In respect to the alleged mental effects of the drugs, the Commission have come to the conclusion that the moderate use of hemp drugs produces no injurious effects on the mind . . .

In regard to the moral effects of the drugs, the Commission are of opinion that their moderate use produces no moral injury whatever. There is no adequate ground for believing that it injuriously affects the character of the consumer . . . for all practical purposes it may be laid down that there is little or no connection between the use of hemp drugs and crime.

Viewing the subject generally, it may be added that the moderate use of these drugs is the rule, and that the excessive use is comparatively exceptional.

[12] Panama Canal Zone Governor's Committee, Apr.–Dec. 1925: (*The Military Surgeon,* Journal of the Association of Military Surgeons of the United States, November 1933, p. 274).

After an investigation extending from April 1 to December 1925, the Committee reached the following conclusions:

There is no evidence that marihuana as grown here is a "habit-forming" drug in the sense in which the term is applied to alcohol, opium, cocaine, etc., or that it has any appreciably deleterious influence on the individual using it.

Panama Canal Zone Governor's Committee, June 1931 (vide supra, p. 278):

Delinquencies due to marijuana smoking which results in trial by military court are negligible in number when compared with delinquencies resulting from the use of alcoholic drinks which also may be classed as stimulants and intoxicants.

have been put in jail for uncounted years for possession or sale of marijuana,[13] even if they grew it themselves and only smoked in private; youths have been entrapped into selling small or large quantities of the grass to police agents and consequently found themselves faced with all the venomous bullshit that an arbitrary law can create from the terror of arrest to the horror of years in jail; the author receives letters of complaint and appeals for help from many US cities, from acquaintances, fellow litterateurs, even scholarly investigators of the subject writing books about it, as well as from one energetic poet founding a fine project for an Artist's workshop (John Sinclair in Detroit, presently sentenced to 6 months for letting an agent buy marijuana for the second time) — one becomes awed by the enormity of the imposition.[14]

It is not a healthy activity for the State to be annoying so many of its citizens thusly; it creates a climate of topsy-turvy law and begets disrespect for the law and the society that tolerates execution of such barbarous law,[15] and a climate of fear and hatred for the administrators of the law. Such a law is a threat to the existence of the State itself, for it sickens and debilitates its most adventurous and sensitive citizens. Such a law, in fact, can drive people mad.

It is no wonder then that most people who have smoked marijuana in America often experience a state of anxiety, of threat, of paranoia in fact, which may lead to trembling or hysteria, at the microscopic awareness that they are breaking a Law, that thousands of Investigators all over the country are trained and paid to smoke them out and jail them, that thousands of their community are in jail, that inevitably a few friends are "busted" with all the hypocrisy and expense and anxiety of that trial and perhaps punishment — jail and victimage by the bureau-

[13] 12,229 convictions for marijuana in 1963 and 1964 reported from California alone, according to Prof. Lindesmith. The whole scene is so shrouded in bureaucratic mystery that there are no national figures available *anywhere*.

[14] By March 1966 Dr. Timothy Leary faced a minimum of 5 years in jail and A.P. reported that the celebrated novelist Ken Kesey was a refugee in Mexico threatened with extradition by the FBI to face marijuana charges in California.

[15] Proceedings White House Conference on Narcotic and Drug Abuse, September 27–28, 1962, State Department Auditorium, Washington, D.C. (p. 286).

It is the opinion of the Panel that the hazards of Marijuana per se have been exaggerated and that long criminal sentences imposed on an occasional user or possessor of the drug are in poor social perspective. Although Marijuana has long held the reputation of inciting individuals to commit sexual offenses and other antisocial acts, the evidence is inadequate to substantiate this. Tolerance and physical dependence do not develop and withdrawal does not produce an abstinence syndrome.

cracy that made, propagandized, administers, and profits from such a monstrous law.

From my own experience and the experience of others I have concluded that most of the horrific affects and disorders described as characteristic of marijuana "intoxication" by the US Federal Treasury Department's Bureau of Narcotics are, quite the reverse, precisely traceable back to the effects on consciousness not of the narcotic but of the law and the threatening activities of the US Bureau of Narcotics itself. Thus, as the Buddha said to a lady who offered him a curse; the gift is returned to the giver when it is not accepted.

I myself experience this form of paranoia when I smoke marijuana, and for that reason smoke it in America more rarely than I did in countries where it is legal. I noticed a pronounced difference of affect in my case. The anxiety was directly traceable to fear of being apprehended and treated as a deviant criminal and put thru the hassle of social disapproval, ignominious Kafkian tremblings in vast court buildings coming to be Judged, the helplessness of being overwhelmed by force or threat of deadly force and put in brick and iron cell.

This apprehension deepened when on returning this year from Europe I was stopped, stripped, and searched at Customs. The dust of my pockets was examined with magnifying glass for traces of weed. I had publicly spoken in defense of marijuana and attacked the conduct of the Bureau, and now my name was down on a letter dossier at which I secretly peeked, on the Customs search-room desk. I quote the first sentence, referring to myself and Orlovsky: "These persons are reported to be smuggling (or importing) narcotics. . . ."

On a later occasion, when I was advised by several friends and near-acquaintances that Federal Narcotics personnel in NYC had asked them to "set me up" for my arrest, I became incensed enough to write a letter of complaint to my Congressman. He replied that he thought I was being humorless about the reason for my being on a list for Customs investigation, since it was natural (I had talked about the dread subject so much in public) ; anyway, not Kafkian as I characterized it. As for my complaint about being set up — that, with my letter, was forwarded to the Treasury Dept. in Washington for consideration and reply.[16] I

16 Reply received December 22, 1965: "I would advise you that I have been in touch with the Bureau of Narcotics and am of the opinion that nothing has been done in your case that is illegal or inconsistent with law enforcement practices designed to enforce the narcotics laws." In this case it was police request to arrested friends that they carry marijuana to *my* apartment and to that of the novelist William S. Burroughs.

had schemed writing some essay such as this in addition to a letter of reminder to my Representative, for it would be to my safety to publish.

I had had the earlier experience after a nationwide TV discussion show, during which the moderator, John Crosby, the anthropologist Ashley Montagu, and celebrated fellow-writer Norman Mailer all concluded — perhaps for the first time over a nationally publicized medium of communication in the last three decades — that as far as we knew there was nothing wrong with marijuana — of learning that the Treasury Department, true to its obsession, had forced its opinion back on the medium thru a 7-minute video-taped Refutation (including an incredible rehash of the Egyptian mad dogs), and placed it on the air against the wishes of Mr. Crosby on the insistence of his network, which had received a communication from the Narco. Bureau, possibly thru intervention of FCC. Years later I read an account of the incident by Mr. Crosby in his syndicated column, formally complaining about the affair.[17]

At that time, looking forward to the occasion of this essay, a difficult one, I made a preliminary epistle on the subject to Anslinger himself, a ten-page composition saying I thought he was a dangerous fraud, responsible for untold death and suffering, and that some day soon, those who had experience of the matter would band together with reasoning and documentation — such as one may find in this book — to come out in the open to explain the actual horror of the US Treas. Dept. Fed. Narcotic Bureau to an already suspecting public.

Allen Ginsberg
2 A.M. Nov. 14, 1965

II

Rather than alter the preceding composition — let it remain, for the reader who has not smoked marijuana, a manifestation of marijuana-high thought structure in a mode which intersects our mutual consciousness, namely language — the author wishes to add here a few thoughts.

The author has spent half a year in Morocco, smoking kif often: old gentlemen and peaceful youths sit amiably, in cafes or under shade trees in outdoor gardens drinking mint tea, passing the tiny kif pipe, and looking quietly at the sea. This is the true picture of the use of kif in North Africa, exactly the opposite of the lurid stereotype of mad-dog human beings deliberately spread by our Treasury Department police

[17] New York *Herald Tribune*, November 22, 1963.

branch. And I set this model of tranquil sensibility beside the tableau of aggravated New York executives sipping whiskey before a 1966 TV set's imagery of drunken American violence covering the world from the highways to Berkeley all the way to the dirt roads of Vietnam.

No one has yet remarked that the suppression of Negro rights, culture, and sensibility in America has been complicated by the marijuana laws. African sects have used pot for divine worship (much as I have described its sacred use in India). And to the extent that jazz has been an adaption of an African religious form to American context (and will have been in no small measure the salvation of America, if America survives the decades of coming change), marijuana has been closely associated with the development of this indigenous American form of chant and prayer. Use of marijuana has always been widespread among the Negro population in this country, and suppression of its use, with constant friction and bludgeoning of the Law, has been one of the major unconscious, or unmentionable, methods of suppression of Negro rights. The mortal sufferings of our most celebrated heroic Negro musicians, from Billie Holiday thru Thelonious Monk, at the hands of police over the drug issue are well known. Such sadistic persecutions have outraged the heart of America for decades. I mean the cultural and spiritual Heart — US Music.

Although most scientific authors who present their reputable evidence for the harmlessness of marijuana make no claim for its surprising *usefulness*, I do make that claim:

Marijuana is a useful catalyst for specific optical and aural aesthetic perceptions. I apprehended the structure of certain pieces of jazz and classical music in a new manner under the influence of marijuana, and these apprehensions have remained valid in years of normal consciousness. I first discovered how to see Klee's *Magic Squares* as the painter intended them (as optically 3-dimensional space structures) while high on marijuana. I perceived ("dug") for the first time Cezanne's "petit sensation" of space achieved on a 2-dimensional canvas (by means of advancing and receding colors, organization of triangles, cubes, etc., as the painter describes in his letters) while looking at *The Bathers* high on marijuana. And I saw anew many of nature's panoramas and landscapes that I'd stared at blindly without even noticing before; thru the use of marijuana, awe and detail were made conscious. These perceptions are permanent — any deep aesthetic experience leaves a trace, and an idea of what to look for that can be checked back later. I developed a taste for Crivelli's symmetry; and saw Rembrandt's *Polish Rider* as a sublime Youth on a Deathly horse for the first time — saw myself in the rider's face, one might say — while walking around the Frick Museum high on pot. These are not "hallucinations"; these are deepened perceptions that one might have catalyzed not by pot but by some *other* natural event (as natural as pot) that changes the mind, such as an intense love, a death in the family, a sudden clear dusk after rain, or the sight of the neon spectral reality of Times Square one sometimes has after leaving a strange movie. So it's all *natural*.

At this point it should be announced that most of the major (best and most famous too) poets, painters, musicians, cinéasts, sculptors, actors, singers and publishers in America and England have been smoking marijuana for years and years. I have gotten high with the majority of the dozens of contributors to the Don Allen *Anthology of New American Poetry 1945–1960*; and in years subsequent to its publication have sat down to coffee and a marijuana cigarette with not a few of the more academic poets of the rival Hall-Pack-Simpson anthology. No art opening in Paris, London, New York, or Wichita at which one may not sniff the incense-fumes of marijuana issuing from the ladies' room. Up and down Madison Avenue it is charming old inside knowledge; in the clacketing vast city rooms of newspapers on both coasts, copyboys and reporters smoke somewhat less marijuana than they take tranquillizers or benzedrine, but pot begins to rival liquor as a non-medical delight in conversation. Already 8 years ago I smoked marijuana with a couple of narcotic department plainclothesmen who were trustworthy enough to invite to a literary reception. A full-page paid advertisement in The *New York Times*, quoting authoritative medical evidence of the harmlessness of marijuana, and signed by a thousand of its most famous smokers, would once and for all break the cultural ice and end once and for all the tyranny of the Treasury Department Narcotics Bureau. For it would only manifest in public what everybody sane in the centers of communication in America knows anyway, an enormous open secret — that it is time to end Prohibition again. And with it put an end to the gangsterism, police mania, hypocrisy, anxiety, and national stupidity generated by administrative abuse of the Marijuana Tax Act of 1937.

It should be understood once and for all that in this area we have been undergoing police-state conditions in America, with characteristic mass brainwashing of the public, persecutions and deaths in jails, elaborate systems of plainclothes police and police spies and stool-pigeons, abuse of constitutional guarantees of privacy of home and person (even *mode of consciousness*) from improper search and seizure.

The police prohibition of marijuana (accompanied with the even more obnoxious persecution of sick heroin addicts who all along should have been seeing the doctor) has directly created vast black markets, crime syndicates, crime waves in the cities, and a breakdown of law and order in the State itself. For the courts of large cities are clogged with so-called narcotic crimes and behind schedule, and new laws (such as the recent NY Rockefeller Stop and Frisk and No-Knock) spring up against the citizen to cope with the massive unpopularity of prohibition.

Not only do I propose end of prohibition of marijuana, and total shift of treatment of actually addictive drugs to the hands of the medical profession, but I propose a total dismantling of the whole cancerous bureaucracy that has perpetrated this historic fuck-up on the United States. And not only is it necessary that the Bureau of Narcotics be dismantled and consigned to the wax-museum of history, where it belongs, but it is also about time that a full-scale Congressional Investigation, utilizing all the resources of the embattled medical, legal and sociological authorities, who for years have been complaining in vain, should be undertaken to fix the precise responsibility for this vast swindle on the administrative, business and mass-media shoulders where it belongs. What were the motive and method in perpetrating this insane hoax on public consciousness? Have any laws of malfeasance in public office been violated?

Not only an investigation of how it all happened, but some positive remuneration is required for those poor citizens, many of them defenseless against beatings, sickness, and anxiety for years — a minority directly and physically persecuted by the police of every city and state and by agents of the nation; a minority often railroaded to jail by uncomprehending judges for months, for years, for decades; a minority battling idiotic laws, and even then without adequate legal representation for the slim trickery available to the rich to evade such laws. Pension must be made obviously for the cornered junkies. But for the inoffensive charming smokers of marijuana who have undergone disgraceful jailings, money is due as compensation. This goes back decades for thousands and thousands of people who, I would guess, are among the most sensitive citizens of the nation; and their social place and special honor of character should be rewarded by a society which urgently needs this kind of sensibility where it can be seen in public.

I have long felt that there were certain political implications to the suppression of marijuana, beyond the obvious revelation (which Burroughs points out in *Naked Lunch*) of the cancerous nature of the marijuana-suppression bureaucracy. When the citizens of this country see that such an old-time, taken-for-granted, flagwaving, reactionary truism of police, press, and law as the "reefer menace" is in fact a creepy hoax, a scarecrow, a national hallucination emanating from the perverted brain of one single man (perhaps) such as Anslinger, what will they begin to think of the whole of taken-for-granted public REALITY?

What of other issues filled with the same threatening hysteria? The spectre of Communism? Respect for the police and courts? Respect for the Treasury Department? If marijuana is a hoax, what is Money? What is the War in Vietnam? What are the Mass Media?

As I declared at the beginning of this essay, marijuana consciousness shifts attention from stereotyped verbal symbols to "more direct, slower, absorbing, occasionally microscopically minute, engagement with sensing phenomena during the high . . ." Already millions of people have got high and looked at the images of their Presidents and governors and Representatives on television and seen that all were betraying signs of false character. Or heard the impersonal robot tones of radio newscasters announcing mass deaths in Asia.

It is no wonder that for years the great centers of puritanism of consciousness, blackout and persecution of the subtle vibrations of personal consciousness catalyzed by marijuana have been precisely Moscow and Washington, the centers of the human power war. Fanatical rigid mentality pursuing abstract ideological obsessions make decisions in the right-wing mind of America, pursuing a hateful war against a mirror-image of the same "sectarian, dogmatic" ideological mentality in the Communist camp. It is part of the same pattern that both centers of power have the most rigid laws against marijuana. And that marijuana and versions of African ritual music (rock and roll) are slowly catalyzing anti-ideological consciousness of the new generations on both sides of the Iron-Time curtain.

I believe that future generations will have to rely on new faculties of awareness, rather than new versions of old idea-systems, to cope with the increasing godlike complexity of our planetary civilization, with its overpopulation, its threat of atomic annihilation, its centralized network of abstract word-image communications, its power to leave the earth. A new consciousness, or new awareness, will evolve to meet a changed ecological environment. It has already begun evolving in younger generations from Prague to Calcutta; part of the process of re-examination of certain heretofore discarded "primitive" devices of communication with Self and Selves. Negro worship rituals have invaded the West via New Orleans and Liverpool, in altered but still recognizably functional form. The consciousness-expanding drugs (psychedelics) occupy attention in the highest intellectual circles of the West, as well as among a great mass of youth. The odd perceptions of Zen, Tibetan Yoga, Mantra Yoga, and indigenous American shamanism affect the consciousness of a universal generation, children who can recognize each other by hairstyle, tone of voice, attitude to nature and attitude to Civilization. The airwaves are filled with songs of hitherto unheard-of frankness and beauty.

These then are some of the political or social implications of the legalization of marijuana as a catalyst to self-awareness. The generalizations I have made may also apply to the deeper affects and deeper social changes that may be catalyzed thru the already massive use of psychedelic drugs.

And it is significant that, as Marijuana was once monopolized by a small rabid bureaucracy in the Treasury Department, the psychedelic drugs have this year in America been officially monopolized by the Pure Food and Drug Administration — within months a large amateur police force has mushroomed. I've heard it rumored that the precise group of citizens *least* equipped for "responsibility" in this area — the *least* "mature" pressure-group in the States — already acts in an advisory capacity on licensing. This group is the Chemical Warfare Division of the Pentagon.

WILLIAM SIMON
JOHN H. GAGNON
children of the drug age

The use of marijuana has leaped from the peripheral zones of the society to its very center. Just a few years ago marijuana was limited to the ghetto scene, jazz circles, and the highly alienated young in flight from families, schools, and conventional communities. Today, one finds an increasing incidence of marijuana use among young — and not so

From *Saturday Review*, September 21, 1968. Copyright © 1968 by Saturday Review, Inc. Reprinted by permission.

young — adults otherwise pursuing ordinary careers, among high school students who remain relatively conformist in most other regards, and even among the culturally underprivileged fraternities and sororities on a number of college campuses. More importantly, there is good reason to assume that it will not emerge and fade like some passing fad, but rather that it will both persist and spread. Marijuana use is very likely to become a continuing fact of life for American society.

These new patterns of marijuana use, for all their apparently unpredictable and perhaps revolutionary character, must be seen in terms of their continuity with general trends in contemporary American culture. One of these trends — one that is almost something of a cliché in "pop" sociology — is the fact that we have become, as a nation, a population of pill-takers. Both the actual miracle and the myth of modern medicine have made the use of drugs highly legitimate, as something to be taken casually and not only during moments of acute and certified distress. Our children, in being casual about drugs — particularly casual in their acceptance of them and their promises — far from being in revolt against an older generation, may in fact be acknowledging how influential a model that generation was.

A second factor is that marijuana as an idea and possibility has become a widely available cultural fact; this article, in itself, is a part of this. For our generation and older generations, exposure to marijuana even as a concept was highly limited. To gain a knowledge of marijuana beyond a few jokes about jazz musicians, one had to journey to the margins of conventional society, and to experience the drug, one had to carry hard-earned credentials. Now, seemingly all at once, it has become a proper topic for the mass media. Major magazines discuss the problem at great length. TV comedians and film-makers have at it. It is a commonplace in the imagery and lyrics of youth culture, upon which so much of adult culture seems to draw.

The irony is that, in something of a re-creation of the absurdities as well as costly stupidities of the prohibition era, "pot" has become an object of information and entertainment exchanges all over the society at the same time that its possession or sale remains a felony offense at both the state and federal level. Once out of the cultural pockets of secret knowledge — the ghettos that no one ever saw or the jazz musicians that no one ever knew personally — marijuana use becomes almost universally available *as an idea*. This development may or may not be deplored. However, the question raised by those for whom censorship is an answer remains moot, for marijuana has become a general cultural institution. The fact is that the cat is out of the bag or, as one might say, the pot is out of the cat.

The very nature of marijuana itself facilitates the development of this trend. Unlike other both "hard" and "soft" drugs, marijuana requires no sophisticated technology nor complex organizational structure for either production or distribution. Unless the policing of marijuana sales becomes more efficient or repressive than anyone presently contemplates, it will probably remain a relatively low-cost drug and will continue to be available from numerous, relatively unorganized sources.

These factors combine to give us predisposition to use, knowledge of the idea of use, and growing access to opportunities for use of marijuana. Little appears on the social horizon to suggest that the presence of these mutually reinforcing factors will not produce patterns of increased marijuana use in our society. However, it is important to understand that the effect of changing patterns of marijuana use upon the society and — more immediately — upon the quality of life in this society remains somewhat open-ended. Only the most hysterical or self-interested talk in terms of necessary or predictable outcomes, and these outcomes invariably involve decay and disaster for both the individual users and the society. Our sense of possible general and social effects is very much like our sense of the effects of immediate use: Marijuana tends to produce the kinds of feelings in the user that the user has been trained to expect. In line with this, we suspect that much of what will follow by way of impact upon the society will depend upon how the society chooses to respond. And what one comes to fear is the possibility of a continued societal reaction of employing old rigidities and old assumptions in dealing with new patterns of use by new populations.

A crucial population to consider is that of high-school users and potential users. They are crucial in several senses. First, the young are often in the forefront of social innovation, and in this case, so much of the current public imagery of concern about marijuana use focuses upon the teen-ager. Second, they are important because much of the meaning of the marijuana experience is derived from the language of contemporary youth culture. Perhaps because it is a relatively new phenomenon in the human experience to have youthful adults — youthful well into what used to be called middle age — we have to turn to the presently young for images of self. As part of this, adult culture seems increasingly to feed off youth culture. This is suggested by several elements of both men's and women's current fashions. The language of youth culture is found in the current idioms of adult language. How many of us are "doing our thing"? How many of us casually describe ourselves or others in terms of this or that "bag"? Third, and most important, we should give particularly serious consideration to the young because they require our protection; indeed, following Erik Erikson, one might say that the very meaning of adolescence in our society is to be defined by the protected status we extend to the young while they manage the uncertainties of both changing senses of self and changing social expectations.

Along the same line, our concern for teen-age drug use requires special consideration because for this population the drug experience and the attending attachment to drug-using subcultures is more likely to be an *ego-forming* experience. Drug use has a greater potential for becoming an organizing pivot during adolescence than during any subsequent stage in the life cycle. In talking to the youthful marijuana user, for example, one cannot help but be struck with how strongly the imagery of that experience influences ideas of the good and the desirable, how quickly it becomes the standard of happiness, how effectively it impoverishes the rewards and rewarding experiences that the larger society appears to offer. On this latter point, one might consider that the ease with which such rewards or rewarding experiences have been supplanted indicates the degree to which they are the unrealistic and unrealizable illusions of an older generation.

What, then, can be said of high-school-age marijuana users? In very specific terms, the answer must be: not very much. There are no real estimates of the number of young people that one is talking about. Much of the blame for this lack of knowledge must fall upon uneasy parents and timid school administrations who have "protected" their children from responsible inquiry and in doing so have also protected our ignorance. There is little one can say on this except that the weight of observations and impressions is that the rate of increase in teen-age drug use has been substantial and that most indicators point to further increases. At this point, one must begin, if unable to specify numbers, to tentatively specify some of the characteristics of the populations involved.

Clearly, if marijuana use among teen-agers in the urban ghettos has increased in recent years — and it may have — this is not the source of renewed societal concern. Marijuana use has long been prevalent in the urban ghettos; it was just that no one really cared. It was only when Holden Caulfield came face to face with Claude Brown — only when marijuana became desegregated and upwardly mobile — that there was an increase in societal attentiveness. The new population of teen-age users, from all indications, appears to be from social backgrounds that are substantially middle class or higher. The appearance of marijuana among working-class or lower-middle-class youth, who — for the moment — lack both social and intellectual connections to marijuana, seems to be slower in coming. This tendency for marijuana use to appear among middle-class and upper-middle-class youth was reflected in a recent survey reported by Louis Harris. One in six parents with substantial incomes and some degree of higher education reported knowing at least one teen-ager who used marijuana. The parents also reported holding values increasingly less hostile to such use.

One of the characteristics of marijuana use — as is true for many other drugs — is that the idea of use creates availability and rarely the reverse. Early experiments with marijuana rarely produce desirable effects. Indeed, as Howard Becker has observed, for marijuana to produce markedly pleasurable effects often requires a great deal by way of social learning and social support. Relatively few users at any age level come to marijuana in isolation or practice its use in isolation; to become and remain a major phenomenon marijuana use requires a sustaining culture. The crucial question becomes: Who or what are the carriers of marijuana culture? And once one abandons the simple-minded imagery of the dirty old man standing outside the high school or the profit-crazed crime syndicate, the "infectious carriers" turn out to be aspects of public culture that are fully legitimate and social relationships that involve persons very much like the potential marijuana user.

As we have already indicated, much of the imagery surrounding "pot" use is transmitted increasingly through the mass media, especially that part of the commercial media that serves the youth market. Lyrics of popular songs refer to the drug itself or the drug experience in barely coded terms, often coded just enough to establish an illusion of membership among the listeners. Elements of the music are described as having an additional message *if* the hearer is properly turned on. More crucial is the fact that the media — frequently in articles and programs designed to "inform" and "warn" an adult audience, as well as to excite its fantasies — provide an ideology and a definition of self that makes marijuana use legitimate; it is somehow tied to a "new spirit," a new honesty, a new quest for substantial values and experiences, a children's crusade organized around the reinvention of Rousseau, Thoreau, and Lawrence. In this way the mass media provide not only a basis for legitimating the use of pot, but also a structure of rationalizations after the fact of use. One cannot help but be struck by the uniformity of explanations for the use of marijuana given by the young — a uniformity of response not only in the expected environments like Haight-Ashbury or the East Village, but in the suburbs of major cities across the land and in relatively small college towns.

However, the general availability of marijuana as a cultural possibility is not automatically translated into active use; what is required is an effective, intermediate link, and this most often turns out to be peers or near peers. One significant point of entry for marijuana use in particular high schools is the intersection between the college experience and high school experience. Our best current estimate is that between 10 and 15 per cent of college students have ever used pot, about a third of these using it fairly regularly. Marijuana is frequently introduced to high school culture by high school students with close siblings at college, older girls who have begun to date college boys, or youngsters who are drawn to intellectual, political, or artistic activities that are shared with college students. This latter group is of course increased if there is a college campus close at hand or a relatively handy location where such commitments can be acted out — Haight-Ashbury in San Francisco, the East Village in New York, Old Town in Chicago, Plum Street in Detroit, and the like. And with the current affluence of America's middle class and the utilization of "youth fares" offered by major airlines, even a relatively provincial city can claim several who have made the pilgrimage to one or more of these communities.

It should be noted that while high school students who are involved with the intellectual, political, or artistic activities common to college students may be predisposed to drug use, they are also likely to be more intellectually and even more emotionally mature than most of their immediate peers. This kind of teen-ager will tend to be among the least likely to conform to the naïve image of the adolescent that elicits the adult world's response to the teen-ager. They are even less likely to conform to the self-consciously dishonest image that elicits the response of the American high school. For them the way to marijuana will be encouraged partly by the refusal of significant adults to respond to their discovery of the world with candor and an equal sense of commitment. This group, it should be acknowledged, may also contain many whose "vulnerability" to drug use was increased by psychological stresses of a more individual genesis.

The probable pattern of use of marijuana among high school students is not a simple one. To say that X per cent of high school students may be using it does not mean X per cent in all or even most high schools have been "turned on to pot." The proportion of high school students who are users is at the moment probably very small and the proportion of high schools even smaller. While the mass media may make the idea of marijuana almost universally available, not all high schools possess appropriate actualizing mechanisms. Thus it is likely that the vast majority of high schools in the country have yet to directly encounter the marijuana issue. In a much smaller group of high schools — those in major metropolitan areas and smaller college towns — use may be limited to a very small and self-isolating minority. In another relatively small group of schools, use may have become fairly widespread, with students who use marijuana remaining fairly conventional, not particularly "hip" or "cool."

This gives us three distinct types of high school populations: those without experience and for whom marijuana exists only as a culturally available idea, those who have begun experimenting with marijuana but who remain attached to conventional values and social relationships, and those for whom use is associated with entry into an unconventional social framework and perhaps ultimately into an alienated subculture. This latter group deserves particular attention not only because they may well contain many of our brightest children, but because the long-term costs to them may be the highest.

All of the students — users and non-users — for whom the marijuana issue is salient will have one thing in common: they will all be interested witnesses to the larger society's response, and for many of them it can only be a demoralizing spectacle. Initially, they are confronted with a mass of claims and counter-claims; the "scare" rhetoric by those who would advocate more repressive actions is matched by the counter-arguments of those advocating more permissive policies, who deny a cause for alarm and, in many instances, claim a potential for joyful and mind-expanding experience. For those without immediate reference to experience — either their own or that of close peers — this debate can only increase a sense of distrust, if not cynicism. For those with experience for reference, the arguments of the permissives — even if they promise more than marijuana can deliver — turn out to be confirmed more often than not. For many other drugs, including alcohol, much of the negative imagery surrounding their use, which in many cases serves to inhibit use, is actually confirmed by the experience of the teen-age experimenter or someone in his immediate environment.

Alcohol does tend to make you sick, produces wild, acting-out behavior, and leaves you feeling "hung-over." There is a growing negative imagery surrounding LSD use beyond what remains for the present solely a claim that it damages chromosomal structure. There is the experience of the "bad trip" and "freaking out" for uneven and unpredictable lengths of time. Use of the amphetamines is now associated with experience that suggests its addictive qualities, its damaging effects upon the body, and the unpleasant depression that follows use which has become known as "crashing." But if marijuana use is damaging to the young, it is clearly not damaging in the ways that many of its hysterical critics allege that it is.

One dangerous by-product of using excessive scare tactics is that it produces the "wolf-wolf-wolf" or boomerang effect. The discrediting of the illegitimate claims made for the dangers of marijuana use tends to rub off on legitimate claims for the dangerous effects of other drugs. Among the young who are involved with drugs, a credibility gap exists that is far greater than that associated with government pronouncements on the Vietnam conflict. Moreover, this credibility gap extends not only to research undertaken by government agencies, but also to academic research that is supported by governmental agencies. Exaggerated and disprovable claims for the effects of marijuana may actually encourage experimentation with more immediately dangerous drugs by discrediting all warnings.

If one of the functions of largely unsubstantiated claims about the dangerous character of marijuana use is educational — educating against use — it has obviously failed and failed almost totally. However, it has another apparent function: that of maintaining and justifying the present repressive legal sanctions against use, possession, and sale. On this level, the campaign has been far more successful, but successful because its appeal has not been to users or potential users, but to anxiety-ridden adults whose observations are often filtered through the hysteria of some part of the mass media, as well as their own uneasiness, confusion, distrust, and even envy of the presently young. This helps to sustain a structure of law enforcement that is at best erratic in its application. One consequence of this is to produce a dangerous sense of invulnerability on the part of many users: they know it happens but not very often. One young user equated the risk of arrest with "that of being hit by something falling from a window." Moreover — since the pattern of enforcement is either accidental, capricious, or hostile — when the sanctions imposed are severe, they are defined as unreasonably punitive (and beyond hypocrisy when joined with the language of reform and correction), and when the sanctions imposed are minimal they are viewed as an admission that the society does not believe its own pronouncements about the dangers of drugs.

In general, then, the entire population of high school youth, particularly those who are middle-class in background, is part of a potential audience highly critical of what is often defined as the older generation's hypocrisy or denial of reality. This kind of reaction, of course, obtains in areas well beyond drugs — two that come to mind immediately are politics and sex. It is even possible that we have trained the young in this kind of ideological response; increasingly one notes adult commentators, journalists, educators, and liberal religionists who appear all too eager to confess the guilt of the adult world on this count — often confessing long before the accusation is made. But nonetheless, we must bear in mind that the response of the society to marijuana use is another situation in which the young may learn an attitude toward the society. Even for the young person with little or no likelihood of marijuana use, the response of the organized community is instructive about the community's capacity to be rational, honest, or humane.

There will also be, as we have already observed, a growing number of young persons using marijuana who are, in the terms of their generation, otherwise fairly conventional. They will be the equivalents in many respects of their peers who are experimenting with drinking during this same period. To date, there is no evidence that suggests that the pot user will necessarily come to worse ends than those who to varying degree experiment with alcohol. From what little we currently know about the effects of marijuana, it is possible that the marijuana users may well fare better. They are less likely to become hostile and aggressive, wildly uninhibited, and they would have to work very hard to equal the impressive record of the young who drink and drive.

Again, the greatest risk this group runs may not have anything to do with the effects of the drug as such, but with the quality of societal response to marijuana use. For many of the youthful users of pot — young people for whom use itself and the frequency of use may vary considerably — a dreadful cost factor may suddenly emerge as a result of the vagaries of law enforcement. The possibilities of being found "in possession" (or being caught "holding") are both many and few. These possibilities include a momentary loss of "cool," being investigated for something other than marijuana use, and the like. But once the possibly casual user is caught, he or she ceases to be a casual user and becomes a socially defined user and often a legally liable user. As a result, school careers are often interrupted as suspension or expulsion becomes the response of nervous school administrators. This is something that typically does not follow with equal severity when a liquor violation is reported. It is almost as if such school administrators act to ward off an incipient epidemic, instead of realizing that such arrests are a late symptom of the drug's arrival and diffusion.

Financially costly, emotionally disturbing, and socially stigmatizing contact with the courts is also common. In both the schools and the courts a language is used to describe the seriousness of the offense that bears little resemblance to what the individual "offender" or his witnessing peers feel about themselves or what they are doing. Thus, an experience that in itself carries little direct potential for alienating the young person from conventional or orderly process of development, may all at once — in an unpredictable way — become profoundly and even traumatically disordering and alienating.

The present legal status of marijuana also increases the risks of social dislocation by pushing the youthful users into contacts with highly alienated subcultures that are sources not only for marijuana but also for hard and soft drugs whose effects are either unknown or known to be dangerous. In a sense, by trying in dubious ways to protect the young from the "ravages" of marijuana we may actually have increased their possible exposure to still other, more dangerous drugs, and we do this at a time when we have also been successful at minimizing our own credibility.

Possibly the smallest, but at the same time most visible group of high-school-age marijuana users are those for whom drug use has become an important subcultural value, young people for whom pot use has taken on both ego-forming and ideological aspects. These are boys and girls for whom drug use is not an occasional adventure into the forbidden or a kick, but an important part of the context of values and the reordering of relationships that impinge directly upon the emerging sense of self-identity of the young person. Disproportionately, this group will include many of the brightest and potentially the most creative of our young people. 'They tend to come from home environments culturally rich, sophisticated, and socially concerned. They are often young people with the kind of endowment that enables them to ask the hard questions of a society that the society either evades or responds to with the most fatuous of answers. It is extremely important that we understand something of these young people, because they are often the cadres who, more than merely responding to "youth culture," generate new forms of "youth culture."

The main focus of this essay has been on marijuana. This leads to something of a distortion. While drugs — marijuana as well as the others — appear to play an important part in the current experience of the young, they may well be more symptom than cause. Indeed, it is somehow comforting to adult observers to worry about the young in terms of something as alien to them as "the menace of drugs." It is almost as if some totally remote and strange factor emerged to threaten our young people. We, the adult world, need not be implicated or if implicated, it is only because we have been remiss in developing the proper defense against this menace. While this is not the appropriate place to raise the question of the general condition of the society and its ability to cope with its major problems, it is necessary to indicate that such an examination is the minimal context within which the problem of the young and drugs must ultimately be considered.

Here we suffer from many things, but not from a communication gap. If anything, the adult world has said both too much and too little, and the young have really been listening. The young did not, out of some innocent wisdom, suddenly invent the idea that the contemporary American education industry on all levels has failed its clients — both its pupils and the society at large; there is an abundance of data to that very effect and a large number of adult critics have been saying so for a long time. If there is a difference, it is that while many adults know it, many of the young know it and have to experience it at the same time. (On a personal level, a dilemma of one of the authors, who is in the process of completing a study of the college experience, is to try to persuade a teen-age son to continue his education while the data suggest a great deal of the experience may be meaningless and some aspects of it even destructive. How does one do this without appeals to the purely personal and the purely opportunistic?)

The young did not invent the horrors of segregated society or the ghetto; they did not even invent the description of those horrors. Similarly with the cynicism that surrounds the wedding of statement of national purpose with what we are presently doing in Vietnam. Even the very language of alienation, which many of the young have learned so well, has derived from the more articulate anguish of an adult world. If many of the young have learned to distrust the police, it has to do with more than the drug question. How many of us trust the police when it comes to civil disturbances, civil rights, or peace demonstrations? And if many of the young feel that little can be done and that purely personal solutions should properly be pursued, how many of us — particularly those of us who try to link the character of the recent Presidential primaries and public opinion polls with the ultimate choice of candidates and programs — are about to offer them a viable and effective alternative? We seem to have none for ourselves.

And insofar as much of what is new in the current pattern of drug use is that its users come from homes of affluence and not deprivation, it is important to resume a consideration of the pathologies of affluence that we, as a nation, began to consider out loud before we were shamed into silence by the specter of poverty that still haunts the society. The fact that the poor suffer does not lessen or make less painful the wounds of affluence. In many ways, we have made the world costly for the children of the middle class by essentially making most achievements relatively inexpensive. Earlier generations could strive for achievement (something we have transformed into some kind of universal truth) even if the experiences or rewards of achievement were kindly left unspecified because the consequences of failure were so terrifyingly real; it was perhaps enough merely not to have failed. One aspect of achievement was a capacity for pleasure, for accumulating a capacity for what appeared to be personal experiences. These, too, we left hazy and unspecified. We accumulated this capacity for pleasure very much like a check that no one wanted to cash; we rarely, if ever, wanted to scan the landscape on the far side of achievement.

A generation is now emerging that tests our imagery of failure and finds it even more mythic than our imagery of achievement. It is possible that the affluence that exists for a large section of our society has allowed a Deweyian commitment to survive its brutalization and banalization at the hands of professional educators. What the young in some cases want, and what appears to adults as unreasonable, is that the prize be located at the top of the Cracker Jack box, not at the bottom. When they find that the prize is not a meaningful social experience, they are prepared to seek out experiences whose dimensions are almost totally personal and private. The attraction of drugs and subcultural activities within which the "drug experience" plays an important role is precisely that they allow the illusion of intense and immediate experience that is almost totally and safely referential to the self and not to the world. Unfortunately that sense of self remains pathetically thin and unsubstantial for there is little that is intrinsic to this private world. It is not that they "drop out," but that they haven't as yet been "turned on" by the world. Even with the drug experience, with its supportive and learned rhetoric of intense experience, they continue to ask: what is there to do? It is not that they are frantic or full of inner turmoil, but that they are bored.

For this last group of youthful marijuana users, the real danger is not that they will fill our prisons or psychiatric facilities, not that they will become addicted to more dangerous drugs, and not that they will do harm to anyone but themselves. A small number of them will, with a tragic lack of necessity, do some of these, but the real danger is that they will lose a sense of their real capacity for experience and that they will abandon, and in many cases have already abandoned, claims for an influential role in the collective enterprise of the society. Their future will become a progressive drift toward a totally privatized existence. In a sense, while they appear to be in revolt against suburban values — an appearance reinforced by their easy appropriation of the language of adult commentators — when at all specified, their values appear to be precisely the values of suburban life, the values of suburban life stripped of ritualistic references to larger social purposes.

In essence, they merely want to be left alone to "do their thing," with as little unenjoyed or alienating labor as possible. While many of them strongly identified with the hero of *The Graduate*, few of them could describe what it could possibly be that he wanted that was different from what his parents had or were, except perhaps the desire to remain the child of affluent parents. There is in this development a profound feeling of loss, but one is equally uncertain about realistic alternatives. For these young people marijuana use ranges from a temporary easing of the pains of boredom to a protected illusion of their own existence and importance, as a way of protecting themselves from the illusion they have learned from us — that something significant ought to happen.

Throughout this essay we have leaned in the direction of a necessary redefinition of the legal status of marijuana, a redefinition in the direction of liberalization of access. *In no way, however, do we think that marijuana should be freely available to adolescents.* Adolescents should no more be encouraged to use marijuana than they should be encouraged to use alcohol. But, by the same token, we don't feel that experimentation with marijuana is in itself an immediate indication of impending personal or social disaster. Indeed, many of the young people we have talked to who previously were pot smokers are now turning on to alcohol. Possibly they sense that it is even easier to get, involves less of a hassle with parents and community, and that — if properly defined by group values — can provide them with the same important illusions that marijuana previously provided.

How, then, does a community respond to this issue? Clearly, law reform, if ultimately possible, appears nowhere on the immediate horizon. More important, the underlying crisis of our young people would not be substantially altered by that occurrence. One could not help but be struck by how many of the youthful supporters of Senator McCarthy abandoned pot along with their beards in the situation of what appeared to be a direct encounter with social life. One was also struck by the number who continued to "turn on" with marijuana, but how much less important it became. One was further struck by how many were unmoved by the entire campaign because of a deep-seated pessimism about the possibilities of genuine participation in social affairs and how confirmed they must now feel in their dark view. This begins to suggest something of the style of solutions: that we begin to take both young people and ourselves more seriously — in terms both of our commitment to social life and of our capacities for personal pleasure.

As we have said, it is not that the young do not listen; they appear to listen all too well. Nor is it that they don't talk; they talk too much. The problem is that adults rarely listen and that our talk, when it occurs, often doesn't make sense. At least not to the young. It is perhaps understandable that this is the way things happen in the midst of the complexities of family life. The failure of this kind of effective communication is equally evident in the schools of the country. This too can be explained. The question remains: Where do we go from here? It might begin with the admission to ourselves and to the young that they are not necessarily what we expected them to be; indeed, no more like we expected them to be than the present social world is what many of us expected it to be. That we are prepared to begin talking in terms that allow the young to recognize themselves as well as recognize our expectations, and the reasons for those expectations. That our talk be honest — honest about them, about ourselves, and about our communities. And, of crucial significance, that we will not surrender them to the forces of hysteria, bigotry, ignorance, and dishonesty in our communities.

HOWARD S. BECKER
ending campus drug incidents

The use of drugs — primarily marijuana and LSD — has become an increasingly important and time-consuming problem on college campuses. Much of the thinking and writing (that done by adults, anyway) focuses on the drug use itself, asking why so many students take drugs and what can be done to prevent them, or lessen the impact of their use of drugs.

But instead of asking why students use drugs, let us ask how a campus comes to have a drug incident — thus suggesting that we *ought* to be concerned with a problem somewhat different from the one we conventionally are.

I propose this, first, because it is very likely impossible, given our resources and our will, to stop students from using drugs. No college administration has the personnel to root out drug use by itself. (It may try, however, to achieve the same end by opening the college to undercover agents of off-campus police forces, or it may — as in the recent action at Stony Brook, Long Island — find off-campus forces invading the campus openly, without asking permission first.)

In addition, we need more knowledge before we can get any firm answer to the question of why students use drugs — and any program designed to eradicate drug use not founded on this knowledge will surely fail. Third, it seems to me that the processes involved in a campus drug incident do not require intensive study, and that we may find a way out of our current difficulties by attacking the problem at this level.

Finally, available evidence and the experience of campus physicians indicate that drugs are a minor health hazard. LSD apparently presents some difficulties, but marijuana (the most widely-used psychedelic) has no demonstrable bad effects. Campus psychiatrists know that alcohol presents them with far worse problems. In short, students who think there is no good reason for attempting to restrict student drug use are right.

I thus mean to distinguish campus drug incidents from campus drug use. Students may use drugs without incidents occurring. An incident occurs when students use drugs, the college administration is confronted with the fact publicly, and it takes some punitive action in consequence. The press, radio, and TV are frequently involved.

What do students and administrators do that produces the typical campus incident? Students contribute to the growing number of incidents in two ways. First, more and more of them use drugs. My guess is that marijuana use is now viewed by many college students in the same way that chastity is said to be viewed by college women. Once students did not recognize any legitimate argument in favor of drug use; they knew that it was, quite simply, "wrong," just as the "nice" college girls knew that "nice girls don't." But college girls now see chastity as a matter for individual decision; they can envision many circumstances in which premarital intercourse is morally acceptable. So each girl must make up her mind for herself; she no longer believes that an absolute moral rule governs such decisions. Similarly with drugs. Students who once thought all drug use immoral now believe that the consequences of use are so negligible that it is a matter for each student to decide.

Further, the greater availability of scientific information convinces students, approaching it as they do in a rational and "scientific" manner, that they have nothing to fear. This, of course, occurs most frequently with respect to marijuana, where the scientific evidence most clearly favors that interpretation.

But increased student drug use alone is not sufficient to create a campus drug incident. For that to happen, students must also be caught, which they are doing more and more frequently. Students get caught in a variety of ways. A number of incidents have been triggered by students who sold marijuana to policemen. Sometimes students smoke the drug so openly as to make detection almost inevitable — the very openness of the act, in fact, makes the police or other officials feel that they are being taunted and thus increases the students' chances of arrest. Sometimes students create a campus incident by giving drugs to other people without their knowledge, possibly as a prank. These people may respond very badly, and official action is provoked by the medical opinion that drug use is thus very dangerous.

What students do to provoke a drug incident, then, is to get caught. And they get caught for two reasons: ignorance and ideology. They are either ignorant of the devices and precautions that might protect them against arrest, or they are willing to risk it on ideological grounds. Most of the college students who use drugs today have no desire to get caught. On the contrary, they fear arrest and its effect on their lives. They do not want to be kicked out of school, or have police records, or be branded as dope fiends. But they have learned to use drugs in an atmosphere where strict security measures do not seem essential to avoid arrest, and where no one has told them what those measures are.

Drug users of past generations knew that they had to fear the police. These experienced users were cautious about whom they bought drugs from and whom they sold them to, about where they used drugs and whom they allowed to know, about where they kept their supplies and about the people before whom they would dare to appear "high." These precautions were part of the culture that drug users learned at the same time they learned to use drugs, and the necessity for such precautions and their character were passed on from one user to another. It appears now that a large number of college students have gained access to drugs without acquiring this aspect of the drug-using culture. They know how to get high, but they don't know how to get high without getting caught.

Other students, a smaller number, get caught for ideological reasons. Some believe they have a constitutional right to get high on drugs. (Indeed, constitutional issues have been raised in many cases, some of which will probably find their way to the Supreme Court: These students may be right.) They want to use drugs, feel that they are legally entitled to do so, and wish to provoke a legal confrontation on the question. Or they simply do not wish to bother about being secretive. They may adopt an ideology of psychological freedom, believing that the psychic energy they expend in secretive maneuvers could be spent better in other ways. They recognize that they are taking a chance, but consider the chance worth the price. Either of these ideologies leads students to be quite open about their drug use, perhaps using drugs in public places, or announcing publicly that they use drugs.

In short, whether out of ideology or ignorance, students use drugs with increasing openness and lack of caution. This leads to situations in which they are very likely to get caught and become the objects of publicity. And at this point college administrations complete the process of creating a campus drug incident.

College administrations, as a rule, respond to the pressures of publicity by taking some kind of action. They will very likely not have a reasoned approach to the problem. Confronted with letters and calls from angry and worried parents, with strong pressure from boards of trustees (and, in the case of public institutions, from state legislatures), with continuing newspaper questioning, they act hastily. They may expel the student. They may pass new harsh regulations, or make new interpretations of the broad discretionary powers they already have.

These responses assume that the number of drug users is small; that, once weeded out, they will not be replaced by new users; and that the problem can be dealt with within the confines of the campus proper. But none of these assumptions are correct. The number of users is large and growing; they cannot be weeded out, only driven underground. Since students can always purchase drugs "in town," in nearby cities, or on other campuses, no college can contain the activity on its own. So harsh action by university authorities simply brings even more cases to light and increases the unfavorable publicity — at least until students get the message and become more cautious.

The same considerations apply to the increased surveillance that students are subjected to. Many of the actions students are now caught for might have gone unnoticed, flagrant as they are, if campus officials had not alerted campus police, dormitory counselors, student-health personnel, and others to bring relevant evidence to the attention of the authorities. Some of this increased attention followed F.D.A. Commissioner James L. Goddard's appeal for such cooperation with federal and local law-enforcement officials; some was probably a simple response to massive national publicity. All increases in surveillance, of course, multiply the number of cases that come to public attention as campus drug incidents and thus increase the difficulties the surveillance was supposed to solve.

Administrators take strong actions because they fear there may be some danger to the students involved — and because of the pressure of publicity.

Many deans of students worry about the dangers of drug use. After all, we cannot expect that they will have expert knowledge of drugs. Nor is the most appropriate time for such an educational effort likely to be in the midst of a great public-relations crisis.

In any case, knowledge alone will not solve the problem. Many college administrators know perfectly well that marijuana is a harmless drug. Nevertheless, their public-relations problem persists. We can see how the maintenance of a favorable image lies at the heart of the administrators' concern by comparing the amount of activity against marijuana and LSD use to that against the use of amphetamines, quite wide-spread on many campuses for years (students use Benzedrine as an aid for staying up and studying at exam time). I do not recall any administration's taking severe action on the use of amphetamines, though I believe that physicians agree that amphetamines are potentially a great deal more dangerous than marijuana. And we can note the same kind of differential response to students' use of alcohol.

Suppose we take as our goal the reduction of the number of campus drug incidents. This might be accomplished by trying to do away with student drug use. But students want to use drugs and can easily do so; few college administrations will decide to use the totalitarian methods that would be required. One might institute a daily search of all student rooms and perhaps, in addition, inaugurate a campus "stop-and-frisk" law. But they are not going to do these things, so student drug use will continue.

We might also educate administrators to take a calmer view of the problem. This, no doubt, would do some good, but even the most knowledgeable administration would not be able to avoid the difficulties of a public-relations crisis.

We might, finally, educate students to take precautions to avoid detection. If an educational program of this kind, perhaps sponsored by the student government, were started on a campus, and if students took their lessons seriously, many fewer might engage in those actions likely to provoke arrest or detection. There would be fewer incidents to make publicity about, fewer incidents for the administration to respond to. The administration no doubt would still be aware that students were using drugs on campus, but it would not be confronted publicly with that use and would not be required to respond.

If students could be so educated, some kind of implicit bargain might be struck between university administrators and student drug users, a bargain not unlike the one that seems to characterize homosexuality on most college campuses. All campuses of any size have a homosexual underground that probably includes both students and faculty members, yet we hear very little about homosexual incidents on campus. Administrations seldom seem to get upset about this problem, seldom take strong punitive measures, and almost never make a big public outcry about it. I suspect that this is because they have, in effect, come to terms with the homosexual community on their campus. They regard it as an evil, no doubt, but not as an evil that can be easily done away with. They worry about the physical and psychological harm the community's existence may cause members and non-members. But they know they must live with it, and they do. They take action only when some provocative incident occurs, such as when a student blackmails a faculty member, when minors are involved, or when the matter comes to police attention (as it seldom does). In effect, the homosexual community and the university administration have made a bargain that goes something like this: The homosexuals agree to keep things out of the newspapers and the administration agrees not to look for trouble. An ethic of "live and let live" prevails.

This strikes me as the most likely solution to the problem of campus drug use. Administrators must take a calmer view of drug use, and students must become more cautious. The main obstacles to such a bargain will be nervous administrators afraid to take such a step, and ideological students who wish a confrontation on the issue.

But college administrators have learned to live with sex and drink. They may yet be able to learn to live with drugs as well.

feedback from our readers

ENDING CAMPUS DRUG INCIDENTS

Howard Becker's solution [April] to the student drug problem — that students be taught to use drugs covertly — reminds me of an argument I once heard for Murder, Inc. If you want someone killed, hire a stranger to do it. Then the act will seem irrational rather than motivated, and fewer people will worry about it. Or, better still, make murder legal; then, rest assured, the murder rate will drop dramatically.

Becker's argument is empty. In the first place, there is very clear evidence that most of the "mind-expanding" drugs either do definite damage to the brain, or cause people to do things that are injurious to others, things they probably would not ordinarily do. The statement, "Many college administrators know perfectly well that marijuana is a harmless drug," is based on flimsy factual data. Some 20 years ago a group of physicians in New York wrote a report, based largely on clinical, not experimental, studies, which concluded that the stuff was harmless. There has been next to no research since then; in point of fact, the methods used in that "research" paper (the "La Guardia Report") are so full of holes I have sometimes assigned students to read it as a good example of what to avoid when doing research.

It is quite true that alcohol is injurious; but it has been around a long time, and we know pretty well what it will do to you, and an elaborate social ritual has grown up around it to curtail its use and prevent people from using it beyond certain limits. No one is really sure just what marijuana, LSD, and so forth, do to people, and there is no way of setting limits. Until further research on animals and humans is forthcoming, therefore, I unhesitatingly endorse total and complete abstinence from these kinds of drugs as the only safe course for any sane person.

Which brings up an interesting point: Why take the stuff in the first place? Why the necessity for the underground? The few drug addicts I have tested, and the larger number whose records I have seen, all wish to escape reality, to return to an emotional level about that of a 3-year-old child (indeed, some are stuck at that level, and use the drug to stay there). My question is, why do we have a nation of teenage infants? And, for that matter, professors of sociology?

STANLEY A. RUDIN
Chief, Behavioral Research Laboratory
Rollman Psychiatric Institute, Cincinnati, Ohio

We feel that some comment on Becker's ingenious solution to drug problems is called for. Educating students in deviousness, and asking administrators to ignore the problem in hopes that it would somehow go away, are solutions of such originality that we are sure we should all respond by saying, "Now, why didn't I think of that!" Regardless of the degree of sophistication of this "new approach," we seriously question the accuracy of Becker's global "scientific" assertions about the harmlessness of marijuana.

We would tend to agree with Becker's implicit assumption that the laws relating to the use of marijuana leave a great deal to be desired. However, Becker implies that the only danger in marijuana use is a legal one. He states that "available evidence and the experience of campus physicians indicate drugs are a minor health hazard,... marijuana has no demonstrable bad effects." This is so contrary to our own experience as campus psychiatrists that we must question whether Becker is at all aware of the "available evidence" or "the experience of campus physicians."

At the University of North Carolina Student Health Service, we have seen a significant number of individuals who have had serious and often disabling accentuation of existing problems because of their use of marijuana. To a lesser extent, we have also seen individuals who have had serious psychiatric difficulties precipitated by the use of marijuana. (See Keeler, "Adverse Reactions to Marijuana," *American Journal of Psychiatry*, November, 1967)

Surveys conducted in areas where marijuana is prevalent, and the relatively few experimental studies of the drug, have indicated a fair frequency of adverse reactions. These studies, however, have been questioned on several bases. Probably the most critical is that a predisposition to difficulty must have existed in the user for trouble to occur. However, unless one takes the monolithic approach that a drug that does not produce psychopathology in everyone is utterly safe, this does not serve to exonerate marijuana.

The allegation (repeated several times in the article and apparently the basis for his entire argument) that use of marijuana is completely harmless is *not* supported by available evidence. The risks in terms of the frequency of adverse reactions may be small, but may be of sufficiently serious nature that some individuals may elect not to run such a risk, particularly if the potential benefits are also small. For the individual who does have a serious, incapacitating reaction related to marijuana use, the problem is no longer "a minor health hazard." It is little solace to him or to the physician responsible for his treatment that some individuals also react adversely to alcohol or, for that matter, to penicillin. The comparisons to potential dangers of other drugs (amphetamines and alcohol) that Becker makes not only beg the question, but are a retreat to authority, personal opinion, and argument by analogy. In addition, he falsely ascribes to medical authority a lot more unanimity and a lot more certainty than is justified by the small amount of available evidence. His cavalier contribution toward understanding and dealing with a complex medical and sociological problem is scientifically irresponsible to a degree incompatible with Becker's esteemed scholarly position and reputation.

We're afraid our agreement with Becker's article is limited to the proposition that education is important: Education about the possible effects of marijuana is of great importance for students who may use it, for administrators who may react to it, and for sociologists who may write about it.

Clifford B. Reifler, M.D.
Assistant Professor of Psychiatry and
Senior Psychologist to the Health Service
Martin H. Keeler, M.D.
Associate Professor of Psychiatry
The University of North Carolina, Chapel Hill, N.C.

...there is far from unanimous support by informed people of Becker's statement that marijuana is nonaddictive. It does tend to be psychically addictive, and this kind of addiction is the worst. But even apart from this, marijuana use tends to lead to the dangerous and highly addictive heroin, because the users want something with a stronger kick.

To the extent that Becker's article may influence the thinking of young people and of those responsible for their welfare, it will have extremely unhappy social effects.

DWIGHT E. ALLEN, Bradenton, Fla.

Howard Becker's advice regarding the campus drug-use problem is refreshing in its practicality and realism. Certainly it is the *incidents* involving marijuana use that are a problem, and their reduction in frequency — not only on campuses but elsewhere — would be a boon to all concerned. I wish more professors had the courage to publicly declaim the impracticality of rooting out the growing use of marijuana.

There are some flaws, however, in Becker's position. First, the use of drugs is probably growing as fast among faculty as among students. The article treats drug use entirely as a student problem. Are we to believe that graduate students who blow grass suddenly stop when they get their Ph.Ds and join the faculty?

Second, Becker concedes that marijuana use is not intrinsically wrong. The wrongness comes from rocking the academic boat by getting caught. The decision to smoke marijuana, like the decision regarding chastity or homosexuality, "is a decision for each student to decide." (I would add, for each faculty member as well.) If this is true, then there is an important and unavoidable issue. Why should public policy toward essentially harmless personal behavior, as expressed in law and consequent police harassment, be allowed to continue? Why do all of us, through our political structures, go on making decisions for other people — decisions that are inherently personal? These issues need to be confronted and the students willing to confront them should be applauded. Yet Becker admonishes them not to cause "public-relations crises" for administrators.

BROOKS K. TRUITT
Social Service Administrator
Department of Social Welfare, Los Angeles, Calif.

ROLLO MAY
book review of high priest *and*
the politics of ecstasy *by timothy leary*

It is hardly surprising that these days large numbers of people — especially those in the younger generation beset with malaise and apathy — should have become fascinated with hallucinogenic drugs. Our technology rolls ahead while human values languish, until the products of the technology are themselves transformed into substitutes for missing human values. When the prospect of discovering God is combined with the joy of escape that drugs promise, you have a power whose attraction is great indeed.

There are several reasons for taking hallucinogenic drugs. The first, sheer escape, is effectively defined by William Burroughs on the last page of "Junky" (written under a pseudonym): "Kick is momentary freedom from the claims of aging, cautious, frightened flesh." Another reason is adventure — the lure of the excitement, usually pleasant and often ecstatic, of the trip. Still another is rebellion, which is stressed by Timothy Leary when he exalts "dropping out" as a laudable goal. A fourth is experimental: drugs are a part of modern consciousness, and it behooves us, as it did William James in exploring the fringe experiences of his own day, to find out what they can and cannot do. My own motivation for taking LSD falls, I trust, into this last category.

But we shall never understand the drugs unless we can avoid the Scylla and Charybdis of two ever-present dangers. One is reacting with establishment hysteria, as if confronted by some dire threat, whenever the topic is raised. The other is the equally unrealistic, uncritical advocacy of the drugs as the source of a lifetime of joy in a single weekend — a danger not avoided by Timothy Leary in his two books, "The Politics of Ecstasy" and "High Priest."

"The Politics of Ecstasy" is a collection of essays, by Leary and his associates, on hallucinogens, their effects, and their supposed future. "High Priest," more interesting, is the record of Leary's trips from the time he first ate the sacred mushrooms in the Mexican village of Cuernavaca and experienced the "classic visionary voyage" ("I came back a changed man. . . . You are never the same after you've had the veil drawn."). The autobiographical account goes on through his experi-

From The *New York Times Book Review*, January 26, 1969. Copyright © by The New York Times Company. Reprinted by permission.

mentation at Harvard, his affirmation of LSD, his work with inmates in a state prison, the famous turning-on of the divinity students on Good Friday, his dismissal from Harvard, down to the beginnings of the movement with which he is now involved.

Jaunty, sharp, ecstatic and often fascinating, "High Priest" presents graphic vignettes of Leary's experience taking the drugs with Allen Ginsberg, the inveterate spirit of nonviolence; Alan Watts, who comes on as Leary's strongest supporter; William Burroughs, who turned against the drugs; Richard Alpert, his colleague at Harvard and at his psychedelic retreat at Millbrook, N.Y.; Arthur Koestler, who also had a bad trip; down to Dr. Dana Farnsworth of Harvard, who seems to be the only one toward whom Leary feels any rancor.

But most of all it is a rich portrayal of Leary himself. We see Leary — intelligent, likable, gullible — trying to be both father and mother to his children and ending up responsible and irresponsible at the same time. We observe Leary the Irish rebel, near expulsion in high school, busted out of West Point as a martyr — in his own words, "an arrogant disdainer of fear-directed bourgeois conformity."

It becomes clear from Leary's accounts of the drug experience that a consistent effect of these hallucinogens is the breaking down of the person's confined sense of space and time. The waters of the Pacific do not stay in their ocean bed but are always about to heave up into the California hills; and eons of time are experienced in what turns out to be a few seconds. The source of the enriched fantasy-life of the person — the "visions" — is not so clear; it seems to come from an activation of the person's own buried experience to which, in a normal state, he does not have access. And while the subject experiences increased emotional depth and a loosening of associations, there is no evidence that LSD increases the creativity of creative people, though it may shake rigid persons into becoming more aware of their creative potential.

Leary is aware that this very breaking down of time and space can, in persons who have tendencies toward disintegration, cause psychosis. He chronicles the bad trips as well as the good; there is the long struggle with a friend when he looked rat-faced, "seething with futile rage. Again the rat-face and fangs, and his face even seemed gray and furry."

Leary's famous interview in Playboy, reprinted in "The Politics of Ecstasy" is an illustration of his ability to accommodate himself to the circumstances of an interview. "There is no question," he states baldly, "that LSD is the most powerful aphrodisiac ever discovered by man."

He goes on about the "several hundred orgasms" which can be experienced by women in a properly conducted trip. My understanding of the research is that LSD has exactly the opposite effect: it temporarily turns off the sexual functions. R. E. L. Masters, an authority on both psychedelics and sex, was prompted to write about Leary's article that "such claims about LSD effects are not only false, they are dangerous. . . . That occasional rare cases might support some of [Leary's] claims, I don't doubt; but he suggests that he is describing the rule, not the exception, and that is altogether false."

The whole of "High Priest" invites us to consider the relationship between the drugs and Leary's new "religion." On taking LSD on his return to Mexico, Leary writes, "I was in heaven. Illumination. Every object in the room was a radiant structure of atomic-god-particles. . . . Matter did not exist. . . . And the incredible shattering discovery: consciousness controlled it all . . . all was consciousness. . . . An endless variety of ecstatic experiences spiraled out around me. I had taken the God-step. . . . I called to Pat and Parsons. Hey, isn't this incredible? We are here, we've made it. . . . Isn't it beautiful?"

But Parsons jumped up and began to talk about God like a fundamentalist minister, and Leary "could see that he would ruin everything by acting so nutty." He coaxed Parsons to sit down with him and Pat, the three making a triangle of the Holy Trinity. Then: "Horror! My flesh is decomposing, merging with a million strange bodies . . . a moss-mattress fibered organic connection with the steamy, odorous, saggy corpulence of an alien race." Later: "I was liberated. Free to do anything I chose. Stay in the garden. Stay in Tepoztlán. Go back and wander through the planet as anyone I chose to be. . . . I was a visitor to this modern artificial stage set, this cardboard fake prop studio backdrops. . . . We're in heaven." We have, he writes, the sacrament, and the ritual. Now we must find the religion to go with them.

But no religion ever starts that way. Religions are born out of new truths in man and his cosmology, which give a new view of ultimate reality, illuminate man's relationship to it, and carry ethical imperatives. Then sacraments and rituals are born. When LSD has torn down the conventional cosmology, what content will Leary put in its place? Here he always runs into the stone wall of solipsism; he can only repeat ad infinitum, "You are God," everything "is in your consciousness." The almost tragic reduction of this is shown in that horrendous drive to Mexico City with which the book ends, in which Leary ponders that if the fence separating the superhighway from the precipice is "only in my own mind I can accelerate the car, leap the fence, and be free!" Only an upsurge of love of life leads him to change his mind after he has begun the acceleration to suicide.

It is beside the point to argue that Indians use peyote in their religious services. The peyote does not have genuine power except as part of a larger cosmology. Like the body and blood of Christ in the Christian sacrament, the symbols of the religion encompass and express a reality, and whether the "wine" has alcohol in it or not is irrelevant. Leary's religion is as complete a self-enclosing system as one can imagine. The drugs — which are the most exquisite product of our machine-electric age — are applied from the outside, a chemical force which one "takes" and then reacts to. Great as this experience may seem to be, it does not make heaven or hell or any fundamental truth. It only clears away the debris, the false faiths, the conventional hypocrisy. What the person substitutes depends upon the struggle of his own consciousness with a reality which he does not create but participates in.

The drugs do accomplish some things — and the blind opposition to them in Washington serves only to drive control of them into the hands of the Mafia. But like every other form of technology, they only sharpen the necessity to forge human values through psychological and spiritual means. Hence young people to whom Leary mistakenly entrusts his work, have largely exhausted "the drug routine," and moved on to something more complete.

NICHOLAS CHARNEY
an open letter to a hippie

This has been your fleeting hour in the glaring and even searing spotlight of publicity. Your manners, mind, mores, and even your right to dissent have been constantly scrutinized, occasionally applauded, and more often condemned. Public discussion about you has revolved mainly around three questions: Are hippies right or wrong? Are hippies a dangerous and drug-drenched subculture? Are hippies living up to their responsibilities when other young men are dying for their country?

Yet with all the controversy, people seldom discuss your needs, your problems, your potential — your future. They seldom give you credit for exposing cracks in society's structure. They seldom look at you.

The fact is, the cracks are there. Our democracy is turning away from the individual and our government is not entirely candid. Big business is impersonal and wasteful. Mass education is inefficient and boring. Some of our laws are archaic and unfair. Foreign policy is obscure. The list goes on and on.

You should be given credit for recognizing ills in our society and for acting according to your convictions. You should not be regarded as a threat to society, nor are you intentionally harming anyone around you.

I want to give you all this, and I also want to make a proposal for your consideration.

Leave your hair long and grow a beard. Nobody cares. Go ahead and live your hippie life, but do it in such a way that you do not close doors behind you and in front of you that you can never open again. Society, rightly or wrongly — but necessarily — has its formal requirements and sometimes it's worth playing society's little game according to the rules.

For example, in tomorrow's world it will be next to impossible to find a challenging job and a fulfilling life without significant formal education. Competition will be fierce, and society will run with the statistics every time. So do anything you want, take a few years off, but work it in such a way that you can always go back to school. Make it so that if you drop out you can drop back in. I know many people who needed time out to find themselves, but they were bright enough to arrange it so they could come back.

Certainly, there is something very appealing about having little responsibility, about living like a totally sensual being, about doing what you want, feeling what you want, and even not having much to live on. I think in your case, as a hippie, this is really looking for *people contact*. There are others your age who must drop out and fulfill their urge to travel. They are looking for new *world contacts*, as the pioneers did.

Chances are that you are intelligent, or you wouldn't be so actively passive now. But unless you are careful, you may lose the opportunity to use that intelligence in a creative and constructive way.

Most likely, your good feeling about what you are doing now will be short-lived. What if you become sated with your particular search within two or three years, and what if you haven't handled things properly? You may remain a hippie whether you like it or not. The choice may no longer be yours.

Right now, the hippie is a conversational fad for most people, but society is going to move on and pay attention to something else and to someone else. The public is fickle and your parents may give up. Right now you are like the eleven-year-old piano prodigy. Everyone is interested in him for a couple of years but he really doesn't play very well and suddenly there is neither applause nor criticism. No one even remembers his name.

If you will believe that education will give you your own future and the bone-deep understanding that may benefit society, and if you can be sensible in a state of insensibility (and in a sometimes senseless world) you will keep the door open. There have always been ills in society, and civilization has advanced through the centuries because of active, critical involvement in searching and sometimes finding cures.

As a hippie, you have helped society a little bit because you have made the rest of us reexamine ourselves and the problems of society a little bit more. But what a horrible price you will have paid if you drop out of the future. There is challenge in being a hippie, but there is also challenge in being a man — and that challenge is a far greater one. Where will you be, if you don't keep the door open? Where will you be if you can't return to society?

hippies and heads

SIRS:

Your editorial in the February issue presents adequately the views and position of the "hip liberal." However, your attempt to communicate with the hippies must ultimately fail, for you have forgotten one prerequisite for communication: an understanding of the people with whom you desire to speak. You forgot that hippies are different...

"The Hippie" was created by mass media, and today connotes an amoral or unmoral, drug-taking, do-nothing young punk, who thinks he can withdraw from society, but who will nevertheless accept unemployment checks from that same society. You have the vision and wisdom to see that such a state of withdrawal cannot last forever. But the scene has already changed. Last August the hippies in the Haight-Ashbury conducted an extensive funeral, complete with the coffin, for "The Hippie." This was open rejection of your advice and your tourists' money. Since that time (and before), communes have been springing up all over. The hippies have moved out and away from the cities; their Bible is the Sierra Club's *Wilderness Survival Handbook*. They are doing things that you were not free to do.

A hippie never called himself, or his friends, hippie. The real hippies of a year or so ago now use the term "head" to describe those people who have been through the drug experience, and who can and will gladly verbalize the experience for you, on an intellectual level. Thus, a head is much, much more than the *San Francisco Chronicle's* young hippie . . .

A head . . . knows he *is* society, that he is part of it. He knows he must contribute to the society, but much more important, he *wants* to contribute. The heads do not merely negate; they are an incredibly busy and active lot, already hard at work, changing society by communicating with the people they touch, and by BEING what they believe . . .

You fear for the hippie who cannot return to you. After acid, he CAN'T . . .

This single substance is the pivotal point — it makes the difference between this generation and any other generation of the long, long past. The age-old devices of "taking time out to find yourself" and "sowing wild oats" are simply no longer valid. Acid has opened new doors — places and things that no other generation has been able to see . . .

Acid and grass are merely opening-up devices. It makes possible for many what used to be the opportunity for a very, very elite group. There are undoubtedly other means to understanding and knowledge. Religion (Eastern), education, therapy, etc. For the masses, the family formerly served this purpose of giving structure and security and experience of love. But the families have fallen apart (because they aren't necessary to survive), the cars are all in the garages. The jobs are meaningless and the competition is fierce — and so the young have naturally asked "what for?" Why compete to get ahead and succeed and achieve that "happiness" which they can see is not really happy at all? Most important, they say, "For *me*??"

In hopes of avoiding your putting me into the "bag" of a proselytizing, irresponsible advocate of LSD, let me say that most heads are *no longer* using acid. The most common thing to hear, these months, from those who used to "trip" as often as possible, is that *"acid has done its thing.*" They took acid, they learned, some had their "minds blown," some few fell apart, literally (though much fewer than the media would have you believe). But they don't take it anymore because they don't need it. They have been freed; they have seen. It is now possible for them to be totally whole and totally aware. They don't need the drugs. Many only smoke marijuana to be sociable. They turn on naturally.

Can you open up enough to allow me to advise you? Can you really listen? Consider the possibility that society's requirements as they now stand *are not worth filling.* A happy hippie, doing his thing (even stringing stupid little beads together), already has *no* desire to get that degree from Berkeley. He does not feel that competition is the testing-ground, and that only the good and careful and strong will succeed. He has a new and totally different idea of success. He's going in a different direction. Don't be afraid of him. He will not hurt you ...

Try to open up completely ... It is frightening to be so open, but only at first. Then you can gradually see what the Beatles meant when they asked "How does it feel to be one of the beautiful people?" You'll want to chuckle and laugh and say "Great" ...

Many heads have come up with a few answers about how they, on a personal, individual basis, wish to live; at the least, they know how they don't want to live. They have been given a vision of sorts, and many heads fear that the kids will "fuck it up" by trying too much too soon. Many, many turned-on people do not bother with things like psychology. They have dismissed the "reasons why" for more active pursuits: they are so damn busy doing their beautiful things that they don't have time, or interest, to think about why some are ugly. They demonstrate beauty, as opposed to explaining ugliness.

Their main purpose is to change the world, starting, of course, with themselves.

GRETCHEN HORTON
Sausalito, California

SIRS:

I enjoyed your editorial, appreciative of the fact that it was directed at me. Have you not, however, heard of the happening celebrated by the people of the Haight-Ashbury, in which they proclaimed the death of "hippy" and the birth of free man? It might be wise to pay more attention to the activities of those involved than to the pablum served up by the daily press.

You say that we are the product of public attention. This is not quite so. We are the children of the Atom bomb and of the insoluble

Korean "conflict." As we grew up, McCarthyism was spreading like an open sore. While we watched television, our president was killed before our eyes, and now we watch the CIA try to cover up. And let's not forget Vietnam. Though it would be a relief, I am afraid these causes will not vanish. Nor will we ...

We are a generation that is little different from past generations. In Greece, we would have worshipped Dionysus. In Britain we would have been Romantic poets and Bernard Shaws. We are a perennial breed of aware individuals, joyful and yet cautious about our world ...

What, then, has happened to all the "dead" hippies? First off, many have yet to enter the death throes, but they will, for once an idea dies, its devotees move on to greener pastures. Many who joined the bandwagon as middle class novitiates have blossomed into cultural revolutionaries. In this case, those who once spent their time stoned on LSD have branched out into new areas of spiritual revelation and direct action.

There is one major difference between our generation and its precursors. Numbers. The amount of people smoking grass (this seems to be the lowest common denominator) is staggering. And in a few years there will be a voting majority of people under 25. Soon after, we will adopt control of all major processes. The problem is not returning to Society, but rather, constructing another, better one from the debris of the old.

MARK FREEMAN
San Francisco State College

FRED DAVIS
haight-ashbury's hippies and the future society

And thus in love we have declared the purpose of our hearts plainly, without flatterie, expecting love, and the same sincerity from you, without grumbling, or quarreling, being Creatures of your own image and mould, intending no other matter herein, but to observe the Law of righteous action, endeavoring to shut out of the Creation, the cursed thing, called Particular Propriety, which is the cause of all wars, bloud-shed, theft, and enslaving Laws, that hold the people under miserie.

Signed for and in behalf of all the poor oppressed people of England, and the whole world.

GERRARD WINSTANLEY AND OTHERS
June 1, 1649

This quotation is from the leader of the Diggers, a millenarian sect of communistic persuasion that arose in England at the time of Oliver Cromwell. Today in San Francisco's hippie community, the Haight-Ashbury district, a group of hippies naming themselves after this sect distributes free food to fellow hippies (and all other takers, for that matter) who congregate at about four o'clock every afternoon in the district's Panhandle, an eight-block strip of urban green, shaded by towering eucalyptus trees, that leads into Golden Gate Park to the west. On the corner of a nearby street, the "Hashbury" Diggers operate their Free Store where all — be they hip, straight, hostile, curious, or merely in need — can avail themselves (free of charge, no questions asked) of such used clothing, household articles, books, and second-hand furniture as find their way into the place on any particular day. The Diggers also maintained a large flat in the district where newly arrived or freshly dispossessed hippies could stay without charge for a night, a week, or however long they wished — until some months ago, when the flat was condemned by the San Francisco Health Department. Currently, the Diggers are rehabilitating a condemned skid-row hotel for the same purpose.

Not all of Haight-Ashbury's 7500 hippies are Diggers, although no formal qualifications bar them; nor, in one sense, are the several dozen

From *Trans-action*, December, 1967. Copyright © 1967 by *Trans-action* magazine, St. Louis, Missouri. Reprinted by permission.

Diggers hippies. What distinguishes the Diggers — an amorphous, shifting, and sometimes contentious amalgam of ex-political radicals, psychedelic mystics, Ghandians, and Brechtian avant-garde thespians — from the area's "ordinary" hippies is their ideological brio, articulateness, good works, and flair for the dramatic event. (Some are even rumored to be over 30.) In the eyes of many Hashbury hippies, therefore, the Diggers symbolize what is best, what is most persuasive and purposive, about the surrounding, more variegated hippie subculture — just as, for certain radical social critics of the American scene, the hippies are expressing, albeit elliptically, what is best about a seemingly ever-broader segment of American youth: it's openness to new experience, puncturing of cant, rejection of bureaucratic regimentation, aversion to violence, and identification with the exploited and disadvantaged. That this is not the whole story barely needs saying. Along with the poetry and flowers, the melancholy smile at passing and ecstatic clasp at greeting, there is also the panicky incoherence of the bad LSD trip, the malnutrition, a startling rise in V.D. and hepatitis, a seemingly phobic reaction to elementary practices of hygiene and sanitation, and — perhaps most disturbing in the long run — a casualness about the comings and goings of human relationships that must verge on the grossly irresponsible.

But, then, social movements — particularly of this expressive-religious variety — are rarely of a piece, and it would be unfortunate if social scientists, rather than inquiring into the genesis, meaning, and future of the hippie movement, too soon joined ranks (as many are likely to, in any case) with solid burghers in an orgy of research into the "pathology" of it all: the ubiquitous drug use (mainly marihuana and LSD, often amphetamines, rarely heroin or other opiates), the easy attitudes toward sex ("If two people are attracted to each other, what better way of showing it than to make love?"), and the mocking hostility toward the middle-class values of pleasure-deferral, material success, and — ultimately — the whole mass-media-glamorized round of chic, deodorized, appliance-glutted suburban existence.

THE HIP SCENE IS THE MESSAGE

Clearly, despite whatever real or imagined "pathology" middle-class spokesmen are ready to assign to the hippies, it is the middle-class scheme of life that young hippies are reacting against, even though in their ranks are to be found some youth of working-class origin who have never enjoyed the affluence that their peers now so heartily decry.

To adulterate somewhat the slogan of Marshall McLuhan, one of the few non-orientalized intellectuals whom hippies bother to read at all, *the hip scene is the message,* not the elements whence it derives or the meanings that can be assigned to it verbally. (Interestingly, this fusion of disparate classes does not appear to include any significant number of the Negro youths who reside with their families in the integrated Haight-Ashbury district or in the adjoining Negro ghetto, the Fillmore district. By and large, Negroes view with bewilderment and ridicule the white hippies who flaunt, to the extent of begging on the streets, their rejection of what the Negroes have had scant opportunity to attain. What more revealing symbol of the Negro riots in our nation's cities than the carting off of looted TV sets, refrigerators, and washing machines? After all, aren't these things what America is all about?)

But granting that the hippie scene is a reaction to middle-class values, can the understanding of any social movement — particularly one that just in the process of its formation is so fecund of new art forms, new styles of dress and demeanor, and (most of all) new ethical bases for human relationships — ever be wholly reduced to its reactive aspect? As Ralph Ellison has eloquently observed in his critique of the standard sociological explanation of the American Negro's situation, a people's distinctive way of life is never solely a reaction to the dominant social forces that have oppressed, excluded, or alienated them from the larger society. The cumulative process of reaction and counterreaction, in its historical unfolding, creates its own ground for the emergence of new symbols, meanings, purposes, and social discoveries, none of which are ever wholly contained in embryo, as it were, in the conditions that elicited the reaction. It is, therefore, less with an eye toward explaining "how it came to be" than toward explaining what it may betoken of life in the future society that I now want to examine certain facets of the Hashbury hippie subculture. (Of course, very similar youth movements, subcultures, and settlements are found nowadays in many parts of the affluent Western world — Berkeley's Telegraph Avenue teenyboppers; Los Angeles' Sunset Strippers; New York's East Village hippies; London's mods; Amsterdam's Provos; and the summer *Wandervögel* from all over Europe who chalk the pavement of Copenhagen's main shopping street, the Strøget, and sun themselves on the steps of Stockholm's Philharmonic Hall. What is culturally significant about the Haight-Ashbury hippies is, I would hazard, in general significant about these others as well, with — to be sure — certain qualifications. Indeed, a certain marvelous irony attaches itself to the fact that perhaps the only genuine cross-national culture found in the world today builds on the rag-tag of beards, bare feet, bedrolls, and beads, not on the cultural-exchange programs of governments and universities, or tourism, or — least of all — ladies' clubs' invocations for sympathetic understanding of one's foreign neighbors.)

What I wish to suggest here is that there is, as Max Weber would have put it, an *elective affinity* between prominent styles and themes in the hippie subculture and certain incipient problems of identity, work, and leisure that loom ominously as Western industrial society moves into an epoch of accelerated cybernation, staggering material abundance, and historically-unprecedented mass opportunities for creative leisure and enrichment of the human personality. This is not to say that the latter are the *hidden causes* or tangible *motivating forces* of the former. Rather, the point is that the hippies, in their collective, yet radical, break with the constraints of our present society, are — whether they know it or not (some clearly do intuit a connection) — already rehearsing *in vivo* a number of possible cultural solutions to central life problems posed by the emerging society of the future. While other students of contemporary youth culture could no doubt cite many additional emerging problems to which the hippie subculture is, willy-nilly, addressing itself (marriage and family organization, the character of friendship and personal loyalties, the forms of political participation), space and the kind of observations I have been able to make require that I confine myself to three: the problems of *compulsive consumption*, of *passive spectatorship*, and of the *time-scale of experience*.

COMPULSIVE CONSUMPTION

What working attitude is man to adopt toward the potential glut of consumer goods that the new technology will make available to virtually all members of the future society? Until now, modern capitalist society's traditional response to short-term conditions of overproduction has been to generate — through government manipulation of fiscal devices — greater purchasing power for discretionary consumption. At the same time, the aim has been to cultivate the acquisitive impulse — largely through mass advertising, annual styling changes, and planned obsolescence — so that, in the economist's terminology, a high level of aggregate demand could be sustained. Fortunately, given the great backlog of old material wants and the technologically-based creation of new wants, these means have, for the most part, worked comparatively well — both for advancing (albeit unequally) the mass standard of living and ensuring a reasonably high rate of return to capital.

But, as Walter Weisskopf, Robert Heilbroner, and other economists have wondered, will these means prove adequate for an automated future society in which the mere production of goods and services might easily outstrip man's desire for them, or his capacity to consume them in satisfying ways? Massive problems of air pollution, traffic congestion, and waste disposal aside, is there no psychological limit to the number of automobiles, TV sets, freezers, and dishwashers that even a zealous consumer can aspire to, much less make psychic room for in his life space? The specter that haunts post-industrial man is that of a near worker-less economy in which most men are constrained, through a variety of economic and political sanctions, to frantically purchase and assiduously use up the cornucopia of consumer goods that a robot-staffed factory system (but one still harnessed to capitalism's rationale of pecuniary profit) regurgitates upon the populace. As far back as the late 1940s sociologists like David Riesman were already pointing to the many moral paradoxes of work, leisure, and interpersonal relations posed by a then only nascent society of capitalist mass abundance. How much more perplexing the paradoxes if, using current technological trends, we extrapolate to the year 2000?

Hippies, originating mainly in the middle classes, have been nurtured at the boards of consumer abundance. Spared their parents' vivid memories of economic depression and material want, however, they now, with what to their elders seems like insulting abandon, declare unshamefacedly that the very quest for "the good things of life" and all that this entails — the latest model, the third car, the monthly credit payments, the right house in the right neighborhood — are a "bad bag." In phrases redolent of nearly all utopian thought of the past, they proclaim that happiness and a meaningful life are not to be found in things, but in the cultivation of the self and by an intensive exploration of inner sensibilities with like-minded others.

Extreme as this antimaterialistic stance may seem, and despite its probable tempering should hippie communities develop as a stable feature on the American landscape, it nonetheless points a way to a solution of the problem of material glut; to wit, the simple demonstration of the ability to live on less, thereby calming the acquisitive frenzy that would have to be sustained, and even accelerated, if the present scheme of capitalist production and distribution were to remain unchanged. Besides such establishments as the Diggers' Free Store, gleanings of this attitude are even evident in the street panhandling that so many hippies engage in. Unlike the street beggars of old, there is little that is obsequious or deferential about their manner. On the contrary, their approach is one of easy, sometimes condescending casualness, as if to say, "You've got more than enough to spare, I need it, so let's not make a degrading charity scene out of my asking you." The story is told in the Haight-Ashbury of the patronizing tourist who, upon being approached for a dime by a hippie girl in her late teens, took the occasion to deliver a small speech on how delighted he would be to give it to her — provided she first told him what she needed it for. Without blinking an eye she replied, "It's my menstrual period and that's how much a sanitary napkin costs."

PASSIVE SPECTATORSHIP

As social historians are forever reminding us, modern man has — since the beginnings of the industrial revolution — become increasingly a spectator and less a participant. Less and less does he, for example, create or play music, engage in sports, dance or sing; instead he watches professionally-trained others, vastly more accomplished than himself, perform their acts while he, perhaps, indulges in Mitty-like fantasies of hidden graces and talents. Although this bald statement of the spectator thesis has been challenged in recent years by certain social researchers — statistics are cited of the growing numbers taking guitar lessons, buying fishing equipment, and painting on Sunday — there can be little doubt that "doing" kinds of expressive pursuits, particularly of the collective type, no longer bear the same *integral* relationship to daily life that they once did, or still do in primitive societies. The mere change in how they come to be perceived, from what one does in the ordinary course of life to one's "hobbies," is in itself of profound historical significance. Along with this, the virtuoso standards that once were the exclusive property of small aristocratic elites, rather than being undermined by the oft-cited revolutions in mass communications and mass education, have so diffused through the class structure as to even cause the gifted amateur *at play* to apologize for his efforts with some such remark as, "I only play at it." In short, the cult of professionalism, in the arts as elsewhere, has been institutionalized so intensively in Western society that the ordinary man's sense of expressive adequacy and competence has progressively atrophied. This is especially true of the college-educated, urban middle classes, which — newly exposed to the lofty aesthetic standards of high culture — stand in reverent, if passive, awe of them.

Again, the problem of excessive spectatorship has not proved particularly acute until now, inasmuch as most men have had other time-consuming demands to fill their lives with, chiefly work and family life, leavened by occasional vacations and mass-produced amusements. But what of the future when, according to such social prognosticators as Robert Theobald and Donald Michael, all (except a relatively small cadre of professionals and managers) will be faced with a surfeit of leisure time? Will the mere extension of passive spectatorship and the professional's monopoly of expressive pursuits be a satisfactory solution?

Here, too, hippies are opening up new avenues of collective response to life issues posed by a changing socio-technological environment. They are doing so by rejecting those virtuoso standards that stifle participation in high culture; by substituting an extravagantly eclectic (and, according to traditional aestheticians, reckless) admixture of materials, styles, and motifs from a great diversity of past and present human cultures; and, most of all, by insisting that every man can find immediate expressive fulfillment provided he lets the socially-suppressed spirit within him ascend into vibrant consciousness. The manifesto is: All men are artists, and who cares that some are better at it than others; we can all have fun! Hence, the deceptively crude antisophistication of hippie art forms, which are, perhaps, only an apparent reversion to primitivism. One has only to encounter the lurid *art nouveau* contortions of the hippie posters and their Beardsleyan exoticism, or the mad mélange of hippie street costume — Greek-sandaled feet peeking beneath harem pantaloons encased in a fringed American Indian suede jacket, topped by pastel floral decorations about the face— or the sitar-whining cacophony of the folk-rock band, to know immediately that one is in the presence of *expressiveness* for its own sake.

In more mundane ways, too, the same readiness to let go, to participate, to create and perform without script or forethought is everywhere evident in the Hashbury. Two youths seat themselves on the sidewalk or in a store entranceway; bent beer can in hand, one begins scratching a bongo-like rhythm on the pavement while the other tattoos a bell-like accompaniment by striking a stick on an empty bottle. Soon they are joined, one by one, by a tambourinist, a harmonica player, a penny-whistler or recorder player, and, of course, the ubiquitous guitarist. A small crowd collects and, at the fringes, some blanket-bedecked boys and girls begin twirling about in movements vaguely resembling a Hindu dance. The wailing, rhythmic beating and dancing, alternately rising to peaks of intensity and subsiding, may last for as little as five minutes or as long as an hour, players and dancers joining in and dropping out as whim moves them. At some point — almost any — a mood takes hold that "the happening is over"; participants and onlookers disperse as casually as they had collected.

Analogous scenes of "participation unbound" are to be observed almost every night of the week (twice on Sunday) at the hippies' Parnassus, the Fillmore Auditorium, where a succession of name folk-rock bands, each more deafening than the one before, follow one another in hour-long sessions. Here, amidst the electric guitars, the electric organs, and the constantly metamorphizing show of lights, one can see the gainly and the graceless, the sylph bodies and rude stompers, the crooked and straight — all, of whatever condition or talent, *dance* as the flickering of a strobe light reduces their figures in silhouette to egalitarian spastic bursts. The recognition dawns that this, at last, is dancing of utterly free form, devoid of fixed sequence or step, open to all and calling for no Friday after-school classes at Miss Martha's or expensive lessons from Arthur Murray. The sole requisite is to tune in, take heart, and let go. What follows must be "beautiful" (a favorite hippie word) because it is *you* who are doing and feeling, not another to whom you have surrendered the muse.

As with folk-rock dancing, so (theoretically, at least) with music, poetry, painting, pottery, and the other arts and crafts: expression over performance, impulse over product. Whether the "straight world" will in time heed this message of the hippies is, to be sure, problematical. Also, given the lavish financial rewards and prestige heaped upon more talented hippie artists by a youth-dominated entertainment market, it is conceivable that high standards of professional performance will develop here as well (listen to the more recent Beatles' recordings), thus engendering perhaps as great a participative gulf between artist and audience as already exists in the established arts. Despite the vagaries of forecasting, however, the hippies — as of now, at least — are responding to the incipient plenitude of leisure in ways far removed from the baleful visions of a Huxley or an Orwell.

THE TIME-SCALE OF EXPERIENCE

In every society, certain activities are required to complete various tasks and to achieve various goals. These activities form a sequence — they may be of short duration and simple linkage (boiling an egg); long duration and complex linkage (preparing for a profession); or a variety of intermediate combinations (planting and harvesting a crop). And the activity sequences needed to complete valued tasks and to achieve valued goals in a society largely determine how the people in that society will subjectively experience *time*.

The distinctive temporal bent of industrial society has been toward the second of these arrangements, long duration and complex linkage. As regards the subjective experience of time, this has meant what the anthropologist Florence Kluckhohn has termed a strong "future orientation" on the part of Western man, a quality of sensibility that radically distinguishes him from his peasant and tribal forebears. The major activities that fill the better part of his life acquire their meaning less from the pleasure they may or may not give at the moment than from their perceived relevance to some imagined future state of being or affairs, be it salvation, career achievement, material success, or the realization of a more perfect social order. Deprived of the pursuit of these temporally distant, compexly modulated goals, we would feel that life, as the man in the street puts it, is without meaning.

This subjective conception of time and experience is, of course, admirably suited to the needs of post-18th century industrial society, needs that include a stable labor force; work discipline; slow and regular accumulation of capital with which to plan and launch new investments and to expand; and long, arduous years of training to provide certain people with the high levels of skill necessary in so many professions and technical fields. If Western man had proved unable to defer present gratifications for future rewards (that is, if he had not been a future-oriented being), nothing resembling our present civilization, as Freud noted, could have come to pass.

Yet, paradoxically, it is the advanced technology of computers and servo-mechanisms, not to overlook nuclear warfare, that industrial civilization has carried us to that is raising grave doubts concerning this temporal ordering of affairs, this optimistic, pleasure-deferring, and magically rationalistic faith in converting present effort to future payoff. Why prepare, if there will be so few satisfying jobs to prepare for?

Why defer, if there will be a superabundance of inexpensively-produced goods to choose from? Why plan, if all plans can disintegrate into nuclear dust?

Premature or exaggerated as these questions may seem, they are being asked, especially by young people. And merely to ask them is to prompt a radical shift in time-perspective — from what *will be* to what *is,* from future promise to present fulfillment, from the mundane discounting of present feeling and mood to a sharpened awareness of their contours and their possibilities for instant alteration. Broadly, it is to invest present experience with a new cognitive status and importance: a lust to extract from the living moment its full sensory and emotional potential. For if the present is no longer to be held hostage to the future, what other course than to ravish it at the very instant of its apprehension?

There is much about the hippie subculture that already betokens this alteration of time-perspective and concomitant reconstitution of the experienced self. Hippie argot — some of it new, much of it borrowed with slight connotative changes from the Negro, jazz, homosexual, and addict subcultures — is markedly skewed toward words and phrases in the active present tense: "happening," "where it's at," "turn on," "freak out," "grooving," "mind-blowing," "be-in," "cop out," "split," "drop acid" (take LSD), "put on," "uptight" (anxious and tense), "trip out" (experience the far-out effects of a hallucinogenic drug). The very concept of a happening signifies immediacy: Events are to be actively engaged in, improvised upon, and dramatically exploited for their own sake, with little thought about their origins, duration, or consequences. Thus, almost anything — from a massive be-in in Golden Gate Park to ingesting LSD to a casual street conversation to sitting solitarily under a tree — is approached with a heightened awareness of its happening potential. Similarly, the vogue among Hashbury hippies for astrology, tarot cards, I Ching, and other forms of thaumaturgic prophecy (a hippie conversation is as likely to begin with "What's your birthday?" as "What's your name?") seems to be an attempt to denude the future of its temporal integrity — its unknowability and slow unfoldingness — by fusing it indiscriminately with present dispositions and sensations. The hippie's structureless round-of-day ("hanging loose"), his disdain for appointments, schedules, and straight society's compulsive parcel-ing out of minutes and hours, are all implicated in his intense reverence for the possibilities of the present and uninterest in the future. Few wear watches, and as a colleague who has made a close participant-observer study of one group of hippies remarked. "None of them ever seems to know what time it is."

It is, perhaps, from this vantage point that the widespread use of drugs by hippies acquires its cultural significance, above and beyond the fact that drugs are easily available in the subculture or that their use (especially LSD) has come to symbolize a distinctive badge of membership in that culture. Denied by our Protestant-Judaic heritage the psychological means for experiencing the moment intensively, for parlaying sensation and exoticizing mundane consciousness, the hippie uses drugs where untutored imagination fails. Drugs impart to the present — or so it is alleged by the hippie psychedelic religionists — an aura of aliveness, a sense of union with fellow man and nature, which — we have been taught — can be apprehended, if not in the afterlife that few modern men still believe in, then only after the deepest reflection and self-knowledge induced by protracted experience.

A topic of lively debate among hippie intellectuals is whether drugs represent but a transitory phase of the hippie subculture to be discarded once other, more self-generating, means are discovered by its members for extracting consummatory meaning from present time, or whether drugs are the *sine qua non* of the subculture. Whatever the case, the hippies' experiment with ways to recast our notions of time and experience is deserving of close attention.

THE HIPPIES' FUTURE

As of this writing, it is by no means certain that Haight-Ashbury's "new community," as hippie spokesmen like to call it, can survive much beyond early 1968. Although the "great summer invasion" of émigré hippies fell far short of the 100,000 to 500,000 forecast, the influx of youth from California's and the nation's metropolitan suburbs was, despite considerable turnover, large enough to place a severe strain on the new community's meager resources. "Crash pads" for the night were simply not available in sufficient quantity; the one daily meal of soup or stew served free by the Diggers could hardly appease youthful appetites; and even the lure of free love, which to young minds might be construed as a substitute for food, tarnished for many — boys outnumbered girls by at least three to one, if not more. Besides, summer is San Francisco's most inclement season, the city being shrouded in a chilling, wind-blown fog much of the time. The result was hundreds of youths leading a hand-to-mouth existence, wandering aimlessly on the streets, panhandling, munching stale doughnuts, sleeping in parks and autos and contracting virulent upper-respiratory infections. In this milieu cases of drug abuse, notably involving Methedrine and other "body-wrecking" amphetamines, have showed an alarming increase, beginning about mid-summer and continuing up to the present. And, while the city fathers were not at first nearly so repressive as many had feared, they barely lifted a finger to ameliorate the situation in the Haight-Ashbury. Recently, however, with the upcoming city elections for Mayor and members of the Board of Supervisors, they have given evidence of taking a "firmer" attitude toward the hippies: Drug arrests are on the increase, many more minors in the area are being stopped for questioning and referral to juvenile authorities, and a leading Haight Street hippie cultural establishment, the Straight Theatre, has been denied a dance permit.

It has not, therefore, been solely the impact of sheer numbers that has subjected the new community to a difficult struggle for survival. A variety of forces, internal and external, appear to have conjoined to crush it. To begin with, there is the hippies' notorious, near-anarchic aversion to sustained and organized effort toward reaching some goal. Every man "does his own thing for as long as he likes" until another thing comes along to distract or delight him, whereupon the hippie ethos enjoins him to drop the first thing. (Shades of the early, utopian Karl Marx: ". . . in the communist society it [will be] possible for me to do this today and that tomorrow, to hunt in the morning, to fish in the afternoon, to raise cattle in the evening, to be a critic after dinner, just as I feel at the moment; without ever being a hunter, fisherman, herdsman, or critic." From *The German Ideology*.) Even with such groups as the Diggers, projects are abandoned almost as soon as they are begun. One of the more prominent examples: An ongoing pastoral idyll of summer cultural happenings, proclaimed with great fanfare in May by a group calling itself the Council for the Summer of Love, was abandoned in June when the Council's leader decided one morning to leave town. Add to this the stalling and ordinance-juggling of a city bureaucracy reluctant to grant hippies permits and licenses for their pet enterprises, and very little manages to get off the ground. With only a few notable exceptions, therefore, like the Haight-Ashbury Free Medical Clinic, which — though closed temporarily — managed through its volunteer staff to look after the medical needs of thousands of hippies during the summer, the new community badly failed to provide for the hordes of youth drawn by its paeans of freedom, love, and the new life.

Perhaps there is some ultimate wisdom to "doing one's own thing"; it was, however, hardly a practical way to receive a flock of kinsmen.

Exacerbating the "uptightness" of the hippies is a swelling stream of encounters with the police and courts, ranging from panhandling misdemeanors to harboring runaway minors ("contributing to the delinquency of a minor") to, what is most unnerving for hip inhabitants, a growing pattern of sudden mass arrests for marihuana use and possession in which as many as 25 youths may be hauled off in a single raid on a flat. (Some hippies console themselves with the thought that if enough middle-class youths get "busted for grass," such a hue and cry will be generated in respectable quarters that the marihuana laws will soon be repealed or greatly liberalized.) And, as if the internal problems of the new community were not enough, apocalyptic rumors sprung up, in the wake of the Newark and Detroit riots, that "the Haight is going to be burned to the ground" along with the adjoining Fillmore Negro ghetto. There followed a series of ugly street incidents between blacks and whites — assaults, sexual attacks, window smashings — which palpably heightened racial tensions and fed the credibility of the rumors.

Finally, the area's traffic-choked main thoroughfare, Haight Street, acquired in the space of a few months so carnival and Dantesque an atmosphere as to defy description. Hippies, tourists, drug peddlers, Hell's Angels, drunks, speed freaks (people high on Methedrine), panhandlers, pamphleteers, street musicians, crackpot evangelists, photographers, TV camera crews, reporters (domestic and foreign), researchers, ambulatory schizophrenics, and hawkers of the underground press (at least four such papers are produced in the Haight-Ashbury alone) jostled, put-on, and taunted one another through a din worthy of the Tower of Babel. The street-milling was incessant, and all heads remained cocked for "something to happen" to crystallize the disarray. By early summer, so repugnant had this atmosphere become for the "old" hippies (those residing there before — the origins of Hashbury's new community barely go back two years) that many departed; those who remained did so in the rapidly fading hope that the area might revert to its normal state of abnormality following the expected post-Labor Day exodus of college and high-school hippies. And, while the exodus of summer hippies has indeed been considerable, the consensus among knowledgeable observers of the area is that it has not regained its former, less frenetic, and less disorganized ambience. The transformations wrought by the summer influx — the growing shift to Methedrine as *the* drug of choice, the more general drift toward a wholly drug-oriented subculture, the appearance of hoodlum and thrill-seeking elements, the sleazy tourist shops, the racial tensions — persist, only on a lesser scale.

But though Haight-Ashbury's hippie community may be destined to soon pass from the scene, the roots upon which it feeds run deep in our culture. These are not only of the long-term socio-historic kind I have touched on here, but of a distinctly contemporary character as well, the pain and moral duplicity of our Vietnam involvement being a prominent wellspring of hippie alienation. As the pressures mount on middle-class youth for ever greater scholastic achievement (soon a graduate degree may be mandatory for middle-class status, as a high-school diploma was in the 1940s), as the years of adolescent dependence are further prolonged, and as the accelerated pace of technological change aggravates the normal social tendency to intergenerational conflict, an increasing number of young people can be expected to drop out, or opt out, and drift into the hippie subculture. It is difficult to foresee how long they will remain there and what the consequences for later stages of their careers will be, inasmuch as insufficient time has passed for even a single age cohort of hippies to make the transition from early to middle adulthood. However, even among those youths who "remain in" conventional society in some formal sense, a very large number can be expected to hover so close to the margins of hippie subculture as to have their attitudes and outlooks substantially modified. Indeed, it is probably through some such muted, gradual, and indirect process of social conversion that the hippie subculture will make a lasting impact on American society, if it is to have any at all.

At the same time, the hippie rebellion gives partial, as yet ambiguous, evidence of a massiveness, a universality, and a density of existential texture, all of which promise to transcend the narrowly-segregated confines of age, occupation, and residence that characterized most bohemias of the past (Greenwich Village, Bloomsbury, the Left Bank). Some hippie visionaries already compare the movement to Christianity sweeping the Roman Empire. We cannot predict how far the movement can go toward enveloping the larger society, and whether as it develops it will — as have nearly all successful social movements — significantly compromise the visions that animate it with the practices of the reigning institutional system. Much depends on the state of future social discontent, particularly within the middle classes, and on the viable politica options governments have for assuaging this discontent. Judging, however, from the social upheavals and mass violence of recent decades, such options are, perhaps inevitably, scarce indeed. Just possibly, then, by opting out and making their own kind of cultural waves, the hippies are telling us more than we can now imagine about our future selves.

further reading suggested by the author:

It's Happening by J. L. Simmons and Barry Winograd (Santa Barbara, Calif.: Marc-Laird Publications, 1966).

Looking Forward: The Abundant Society by Walter A. Weisskopf, Raghavan N. Iyer, and others (Santa Barbara, Calif.: Center for the Study of Democratic Institutions, 1966).

The Next Generation by Donald N. Michael (New York: Vintage Books — Random House, 1965).

The Future as History by Robert L. Heilbroner (New York: Grove Press, 1961).

Alpha and Omega:
Man's Stumble
Toward Meaning

introduction

In a discussion of the need for God or religion in modern life, it is impossible not to touch upon the concepts of identity, self-awareness, and commitment discussed in Chapter One. The first essay in Chapter Six, Michael Novak's "God in the Colleges: The Dehumanization of the University," first appeared in *Harpers*, October 1961, was revised, and has since appeared in such publications as *The New Student Left*. His analysis of student agnosticism on American campuses as a kind of bland tolerance which commits a person to nothing relates to issues raised in all the essays in Chapters One, Two, and Three. Rollo May's free man, the "hangloose" ethic, Roszak's "technocracy," student activism, and the proper role of the university and of its faculty are all relevant to Novak's assessment of the problems facing modern man, especially the modern college student. His question and answer technique involves the reader and works effectively to persuade him that "religion can thrive only in a personal universe;

religious faith, hope, and love are personal responses to a personal God." Novak proclaims that "God, if there is a God, is not dead" but will return to the colleges when man does.

The Bishop of Woolwich, John A. T. Robinson, takes issue with the words "need" and "a" from the title of his essay "Do We Need A God?", a chapter in his book *But That I Can't Believe!* The Bishop changes the question to "Can we finally get away from the reality for which the word God has stood?" and he answers with an unreserved no. He defines God as a level of reality which cannot be denied but which, of course, takes various forms for different people. The believer may not "need" it and may not represent it as "a" person, but he cannot deny that level of reality. The Bishop also discusses the idea of self-awareness and one's desire to truly know a person — the "I Thou" relationship. His definition essay, short and well constructed, relates not only to the ideas in Chapter One but also to the question of drugs as a new religion and to the problem of communal living suggested by today's hippies and discussed in Chapter Five.

Proposing an intriguing counter-argument to Roszak's condemnation of technology in Chapter Two, Myron Bloy, Jr. suggests that "we are not only freed by technology from many of the material, social, psychological, and spiritual restraints which so pinched and enslaved most men in the past, we are also made much more aware of the presence and plight of our fellowman than heretofore." Although Mr. Bloy takes a religious point of view rather than the humanist-psychotherapist position of Rollo May, he makes the same case for freedom and responsibility as May and extends it with the idea that moral maturity depends on awareness and on making a "normative commitment" to fellow man. He alludes to early works of such writers as Daniel Bell and Kenneth Keniston and then analyzes the student movement up through 1967 in order to point to such youthful involvement as a model for commitment. He calls for change in the church, for a commitment on· the part of men of faith in our technological culture.

A lack of commitment is one of the characteristics found in the experience of contemporary people suffering from a crisis of religious consciousness. Thomas O'Dea, a major sociologist of religion, begins his lengthy essay with a formal explanation of what he intends to investigate in his study of this crisis. Description as a technique for introducing the reader to the variety and range of personal crises is especially effective because of the more formal, analytical nature of the bulk of O'Dea's essay. Although the reader may initially find the essay formidable, he will discover that O'Dea's insights are profound, his content well researched, and his conclusions about the relevancy of religion most cogent. Like the writers in Chapter One, O'Dea also analyzes man's search for self: "Without an orientation to being, modern man cannot put himself together into a whole. Having lost transcendence, he finds himself without practical leverage in effectively changing his world. Without God or his memory in Enlightenment philosophy, he no longer knows what it means to be man, and hence, cannot utilize his enormous capacities to humanize the conditions of his life." Lacking such orientation modern man finds himself questioning his ability to act as a moral person.

Finally, Allen Wheelis illustrates this problem in his meditation "The Moralist" taken from his book *The Illusionless Man*. The traditional meditation was a highly structured, closed schema. The brilliance of Wheelis's reworking of this form lies in the openness that he maintains by paradoxically employing a structure that traditionally conveys powerful premises of an ordered universe but in its twentieth-century reworking says with equal power that all these premises are in profound doubt. Like the formal argumentative essay, Wheelis's meditation starts with a presentation of the problem: If there is no God, what is the nature of our morality? With his "Let us think," perhaps a parody of "Let us pray," he shifts into a consideration of the rationale contemporary man may find as a basis for his moral stance or his immoral behavior. Wheelis places himself in the middle of two extremes: the missionary physician and Jeff, his amoral friend. He considers the arguments of both sides in a question and answer format, similar to the dialogue Joe has with his other self in Saul Bellow's *Dangling Man*. Wheelis puts aside rational thought, however, when he seems unable to counter Jeff's argument except with the suggestion that a leap of faith may be all that contemporary man can summon in the face of such frustration. He shifts to the description of the car accident and the killing of the dog, which leaves him wondering just how to return to the real world. Here is the despair of the intensely educated, sophisticated modern man's desire and yet utter inability to make the leap of faith.

MICHAEL NOVAK

god in the colleges: the dehumanization of the university

The professor looked into the faces of the freshmen in Philosophy i. "How many of you," he asked, "believe in the existence of God?"

He walked up and down a little. The class was intellectually alive and usually argued. No hands went up.

"Good. I'll give you Anselm's proof for the existence of God." In a few minutes of lecturing, the professor presented Anselm's proof. "Now," he paused. "How many of you see anything wrong in this proof?"

No hands went up.

"Well, then, some of you now believe in God. How many?"

Still no hands went up. When the professor told about it later, he shrugged. "What can you do when thinking doesn't seem to make any difference?"

The experience of this professor is not a solitary one. The fact that the life of personal conviction is separated from the life of academic intelligence is frequently remarked in university life. The phenomenon is not even confined to this country, for it is well known in England. In *Lucky Jim*, Kingsley Amis makes fun of the non-commitment and the sham which he finds in middle-class education; Wilfrid Sheed's American-English novel, *A Middle Class Education*, extends the observations well beyond the classroom. In our day it is precisely this that education in England and America has become: middle-class. John K. Galbraith's *The Affluent Society* brought the emergence of the new and numerous educated class to our attention; it is there for anyone to see.

The present essay pretends to no special statistical wisdom; its material has been gathered from a long-time interest in religion and the university, from reading, from conversations at Harvard and other colleges. Undoubtedly, the essay has fuller relevance for the liberal arts college; I have hardly broached the problem of religion in the scientific and technological schools. Also, in the smaller colleges and the huge state colleges, the focus may be somewhat different.

How does God fare in a middle-class education? What happens to religion in a middle-class education?

First of all, we must remember that since medieval times the West has been becoming a middle-class civilization. The rise of the bourgeoisie has been concomitant with the rise of technology. And underneath the social and economic changes that made Europe capitalist and then industrialist, there was a change in world view. Even though the bourgeois classes might cling to the conventions and forms of an older tradition and an older faith, the impersonality of business and the objectivity of scientific method were molding their weekday spirits and their habitual attitudes. The very bourgeoisie that nourished the technological and scientific revolution nourished within itself an intellectual avant-garde that strove to point out to it how very empty its forms had become. The avant-garde was usually increasingly irreligious: from Voltaire and Hume, Comte and Zola, to Shaw and Russell, it has come to take its battle *vis-à-vis* religion as won. For its point has been that our culture is now at base irreligious, that the bourgeois businessman who pretends differently is either hypocritical or blind. Catholicism was long content with the status quo, and Protestantism for a long time praised the thrifty and the rugged and the strong. Thus the war on poverty which Marxism declared and which the democracies have taken up is (though it need not have been) a secular war, and the ideals which international civilization now pursues are secular ideals: the abolition of poverty and disease, of ignorance and indignity, of colonialism and tyranny. Giving itself to science and technology, our culture makes religion not central but optional, and the avant-garde has been trying to point out — and to form — change.

Secondly, it is necessary to see that while Europe was torn nearly to its death by the ideological and physical contortions of recent revolutions and wars, America and England have tried earnestly to go on as before, as if nothing has happened. The war washed away the intellectual foundations of Europe's past, and intellectuals like Camus, Sartre, Marcel, Barth, and Guardini have fought desperately for intellectual starting points — whether they deny or affirm the possibility of religious faith. But in America and England, philosophy and art showed little such desperation; men tried to pick up where they had left off, a little more tired, a little more angry, worried about the bomb, but not fundamentally changed. Moreover, education in England and America has become financially cushioned as never before. The government, corporations, and unions all give grants for specialized research or simply for the maintenance of students and professors. A distinctly comfortable and entrenched kind of existence is growing up. The small, modestly optimistic world view which Europe shared before the wars is still almost possible. The radicalism of the American 1930's has been fragmented by prosperity and by disillusion with ideology.

Although the colleges pride themselves on the awakening of young minds, on the asking of the Big Questions of life (who and what is man, whence has he come, where is he going, what is love, what is passion, what is reason, is there a God), it is soon clear to college students that the Big Questions don't count — in academic standing, or in later life, or in research grants.

In the first place, the standing assumption is that ultimate questions are in principle unanswerable, and hence not worth asking seriously. This assumption may not discourage freshmen, but over a four-year period it is pretty well driven home. In the second place, nobody is much interested in students' answers to such questions, or deems them worth putting in competition with anybody else's. Even among the professors it is assumed that ultimate questions are nonintellectual, personal, and, if matters of supreme importance and self-commitment, nevertheless not matters for passionate academic dispute. The university, on principle, concentrates on statistics, historical facts, historical intellectual positions, logic modeled on the discourse of the physical sciences, and ample documentation. Even the literature courses, under the impact of the New Criticism, have the students noting the occurrences of words, running down allusions, and abstracting from the conditions of history. The Anglo-American university has committed itself to all that is "objective," countable, precise, publicly verifiable. Though this commitment suits the middle-class temper capitally, it stifles religion almost to death.

A TINY TASTE OF RELIGION

Not only religion is stifled. More fundamentally, it is possible — it is even common — for a student to go to class after class of sociology, economics, psychology, literature, philosophy, and the rest, and hardly become aware that he is dealing with issues of life and death, of love and solitude, of inner growth and pain. He may never fully grasp the fact that education is not so much information and technique as self-confrontation and change in his own conscious life. He may sit through lectures and write examinations — and the professors may let him do through and deciding about any new aspect of his own life in any course. The dilemma of education has always been to combine merely merely that — collecting verbal "answers," without really thinking mental skills with personal experiencing and growth. The educational currents in American colleges tend to oscillate from one pole to the other; and at present the attention in college to the formal and the public easily leaves the inner life of the student untouched.

It is true that in a place like Harvard, or among more serious students everywhere, the young collegian may experience beneficial crises of growth. He gets a taste of rebellion against his origins; he may become, for a while, "avant-garde." The folks at home find him restive, critical, hostile, in his approach to a world he had hitherto peacefully shared. He has learned to despise the organization man and the many patterns of conformity in mass culture; he has learned a certain contempt for suburbia and its values. Yet he likes the comforts of home. Worst of all, in college he has not really had to rebel (except perhaps against not having Latin on his diploma). The college gave him rebellious, critical books, but also gave him a cool grove to read them in. No commitment, no crusading is asked of him. The college merely wants him to "have the facts," to show mental control of the concepts. Yet he, so everyone tells him, is not at all like the collegians of the thirties, or even of the forties. He is cautious, quiet, studious. And no wonder. So is the institution in which he is studying. The higher-powered institutions are committed to testable information and techniques; the patterns of conformity in lower-powered institutions do not far transcend the interests of the society that fosters them.

"say nothing"

Middle-class Christianity — the bourgeois Christianity which Nietzsche, Kierkegaard, Péguy, Bloy, and others so hated — was always prudent, small-visioned, secure. It dared little, with its gaudy-colored plaster statues, or its devices to protect the little world of the entrepreneur. In the person of many university professors, middle-class secular humanism is not much more daring. It thinks of itself as humble in its agnosticism, and eschews the "mystic flights" of metaphysicians, theologians, and dreamers; it is cautious and remote in dealing with heightened and passionate experiences that are the stuff of much great literature and philosophy. It limits itself to this world and its concerns, concerns which fortunately turn out to be largely subject to precise formulation, and hence have a limited but comforting certainty. (It has a particularly comfortable ambiance if it works within the physical sciences, or mathematics, or the statistics of sociology and economics.) If we cannot control the great uncertain questions in the universe, nevertheless we can make a universe of little certainties we can control.

The agnosticism — atheism would be too strong a word — of the classroom is not militant. It is only, in principle, unconcerned. It is bourgeois Christianity all over again, to so great an extent that, in college, in spite of differences in belief, the behavior of agnostic and of religious man is pretty much the same.

The agnosticism of the classroom does not have to be militant. Once upon a time it was fighting for its life; now it is an accepted part of the college scene, in fact the predominating part. The old battles between positive science and religion which delighted, or angered, our grandfathers — about chance and design, monkeys and Adam — seldom resound now in academic halls. The distinction between empirical and theological activity seems pretty well recognized; each side preserves a certain calm and only occasionally do tempers flare. Perhaps psychologists more than others are given to writing off religion as illusion; anthropologists, in turn, are habituated to data on revelations and recurrent religious themes, and are correspondingly casual about the traditions of Judaism and Christianity. One school of analysis in philosophy, of which Russell and Ayer among others are examples, believes that nothing that cannot be reduced to sense experience can have meaning, and most religious questions of course lie outside this restricted zone. Some partisans of another movement, linguistic analysis, following the later Wittgenstein, do not require the discourse of faith and theology to conform to other kinds of discourse, but study it in its own right; but religion does not lie in words.

Professional disciplines aside, a bland tolerance seems to be everybody's ideal. Say nothing that will offend. Say nothing that involves personal commitment. Stay close to the public facts. "You've got to teach these youngsters to forget the shoulds and musts they came here with," one new teaching fellow was recently admonished by his program director. "The students have to learn to be objective." And of course such a critique is excellent, since some shoulds and musts are what a man dies for. But there seems to be correspondingly little concern about which ones he will acquire and keep.

Professor Raphael Demos of Harvard was once quoted as saying, with perhaps his touch of irony, "*Veritas* means we are committed to nothing." It may be that the American consensus has forced a "commitment to nothing" upon our universities; we are a pluralist people, and it seems very difficult to discover a way to teach about those differences on ultimate questions that make us so. The colleges make a "commitment to noncommitment," have a "faith in non-faith." They demand perpetual re-examination and have nowhere to rest.

Thus the new middle-class tolerance of the colleges neither destroys nor transforms the religion of the incoming freshmen. Of one hundred students who marked themselves "atheistic or agnostic" on the poll of the Harvard *Crimson* in 1965, only ten felt "obliged ... to enlighten others to abandon their faith." The new tolerance merely established, officially and in principle, that personal conviction be separated from teaching and learning. If a student wishes to commit himself to answers to ultimate questions (by commitment to some personal synthesis, or to traditional religion or ethics, or anything), he may do so — is even encouraged to do so — but not publicly, nor officially, not in his daily work. He will do well to keep his answers to himself. In term papers and on tests they will not be welcome; there he is obliged to prove rather that he knows facts and correlations, and can run, seeking, as well as anyone else. No one in *official* university life seems to care about his convictions.

There is good reason for the university's position. One of its tasks is to turn out professional men. Think of the difficulty there would be in correcting exams and term papers if each student were engaged in a highly personal way in working out a position important to himself. What if the student found that something of importance to him was of minor importance to the course — or outside its confines? The dilemma of professionalism versus full human experience is a pressing one and cannot be solved by making light of it.

TRIALS BY WEAK FIRE

How relevant is this dilemma to the actual church affiliations of college students? A Catholic report published in *America* (April 8, 1961) quotes Bishop Robert E. Lucey as saying: "The dangers to faith and morals are at least as great in a downtown office as on a secular campus." The national survey of *Time* magazine (1952) is cited to the same effect. "No appreciable number of defections," say Newman Club chaplains at the University of Illinois and the University of Iowa; those which do occur "result rather from weak religious background prior to college than from campus living and experiences." The Harvard *Crimson* poll I referred to earlier records a high rate of defections (40 per cent among

Protestants, 25 per cent among Catholics, 12 per cent among Jews) among the 310 students who answered. But in almost every case the defection had its roots in precollege days, especially in high school experience.

Although it is not clear what constitutes religious "strength," it is clear that if the student's faith goes through a personal trial-by-fire, that is his affair. There are few courses in critical theology, few in modern Biblical theory, few in the theory and practice of organized religion, to help him explicitly and formally to mature his theological intelligence. In the view of some religious men, this is a good thing; religion, after all, is not something that can be formally taught. It is a living commitment to be enkindled from person to person, a life to be lived rather than lessons to be learned. Besides, formal theological studies imply a living content of religious experience; but it is precisely this living content which in our day most men no longer possess. If religion is to enter the university, it must enter first at the most elementary level: in experience, in awareness, in slow and gradual exploration. The traditional words are not relevant to the present religious development of most men. Our times are sub-, not only post-, religious. The institutionalized forms of religion did not originate in modern life, and modern science and technology have grown up outside them; the two worlds of religion and modernity are strangers to each other. Were there to be merely formal courses in theology at the university, genuine religious life would fare hardly better than at present. As the New Criticism is to art, so is critical theology to religious awareness. Theology, like the New Criticism, has a role to play, but it is neither necessary nor sufficient for religious life.

If we admit that theologians would also contribute to the professionalism and formalism already thriving in the modern university, who might do better? The answer, I suggest, must be that the greatest contribution to the religious life of the university could come from teachers and scholars — formally religious or not — who could lead the student to the profound human experiences lying below the surface of the academic curriculum.

These experiences are often "prereligious"; they are barely starting points for full religious life. But they are the only foundations on which anything living can be built. I mean man's experience of his fragility, of his transitoriness, of his tininess; his consciousness of his uniqueness on the earth, of his endless and restless questioning; his personal choices whose motives and consequences he cannot fully know; his vast ability to be proud and to fail, to be isolated and to love, to be — and yet not to be — the master of his own destiny.

These experiences, and others like them, underlie the statistics of economics and of sociology, the laws and hypotheses of psychology, philosophy, and other disciplines; they are at the source of great poems and novels and histories now often taught as if they were technical puzzles.

Large and unsettling personal questions arise from these experiences. And it is by their answers, explicit or implicit, that men finally differ from one another: how they react to achievement, to pride, to love, to suffering, to feelings of life and energy, to death. Implicit in the actions of every man is his own particular bias and approach to economics, to social and political affairs, to all matters with which he deals. What are the biases and beliefs that make a student unique and color all his judgments even in his professional concerns? Instead of concentrating on this question, and hence helping the student toward self-discovery, the university takes the easier path: it tries to maintain an area of "objectivity" and "fact." But the truly crucial element in human knowing (I repeat: even in professional knowing) lies in the recesses of our personal judgment. Our critical sciences, unlike our creative arts, have favored the "objective" over the "subjective." Our universities favor the one pole over the necessary two: notional-verbal competence over the self-knowledge and self-commitment that also affect professional careers, and make up personal life.

UNTESTED PRETENSE

If university teachers could right the balance, would religion begin to thrive? Those who have made faith central to their lives — who believe in the reality and relevance of God, and the interaction (in dark faith) of God and men — hold that it would. And if theology, as such, came to the campuses and became there embattled and truly controversial, this would be welcome; for the very fact that fundamental questions were posed would transform the experience of university life.

No one can know what the full consequences of such a transformation might be, but surely it would mean that university people would be far more closely engaged with the world outside than they are today. Religious men in colleges could follow the example of the clergymen who took part in the Freedom Rides, went to jail, went on a hunger strike in the name of justice and brotherly concern. Religion has played a large role in the commitment of the young Negroes to struggle for their rights. It must suggest other ways of acting when situations in our society call for justice and compassion and protest. Religious men must be "active." They are obliged to consider the forms a just society should take, and ways to achieve them. Again, in the silence, self-control, and patience required by the tactics of passive resistance, they find an excellent school in the "passive" strength of religion. The intellectual resources from which such a transformation might grow are now latent on our campuses. And they are quite carefully neglected.

Meanwhile, the student on the secular campus works out his religion for himself. Often his previous religious background will have been uncritical, informal, and unsophisticated; he may be the first member of his family pursuing a university education. His grasp of religious concepts like faith, hope, love may well be far less precise and intellectually defensible than it ought to be; his university career will offer him very little formal help in clarifying and criticizing them. It is possible that college life may be for him, then, a period of searing but private examination. For a time at least he may stop going to church or synagogue, and believe himself atheist or agnostic. But the chances are — in most schools and among most students — that no such honest and fruitful personal critiques will occur, at least none of any lasting depth. Where they do seem to occur, experienced religious men are pleased. "It's a more thoughtful kind of religion," seems to be the consensus of chaplains near Harvard. "It's better than merely going to church out of habit. They may be missing church services and undergoing changes now; but they'll be back when they return to their local communities and all the better for it."

But will they be? The fact seems to be that even among the more searching students, religion follows the pattern of their other personal convictions. The pattern of conformity they are taught in college, by which they systematically separate their inner convictions from the "objective" work of the classroom, will simply be continued in their business affairs, legal practice, or work of whatever kind in later life. A civilization pervaded by the laws and spirit of technology — on which profit and life itself are based — is a civilization prone to expediency and nonmoral, nonpersonal considerations. The vice of academicians is to become intellectual technologists; this vice prevails. The consequent bourgeois life of the American university becomes with hardly a hitch the middle-class life of the organization man and the suburbanite. The pretense of nonconformity and intellectual liberty on campus is seldom tested by real and fundamental disagreement; for such disagreement is usually "subjective" and not amenable to the kind of debate the university tacitly approves. "Liberals" and "conservatives" in politics, for example, seldom touch the basic issues separating them; they both try to argue in terms of "facts"; but why they are committed, each in his separate way, to different ideals, and what precisely these ideals are and whence they are derived — this kind of discussion does not suit the pragmatic and "objective" temper of present intellectual life. It is too intangible, dialectical, personal, however lethal, in its effect upon action.

"GOD IS NOT DEAD"

One might have hoped that the religiously committed private schools in America might have made by now some major contribution to American intellectual life. In part, they have been too concerned with putting up buildings, with more or less ghetto-like defensiveness, and with hesitating between secular standards and their own long-ago tradition. In part, general American intellectual life rules out of professional discussion the very commitment which the religious schools primarily exist to foster. In any case, the potential strength of the religious school now goes almost for nought.

One might have hoped that religious men within the secular colleges might by their understanding and their leadership have restored to American universities a chance for a living and critical experience of religion. It is true that the Danforth Foundation, the National Council for Religion in Higher Education, and other groups are trying to favor the presence in our universities of talented religious men. But the strident tones of Fathers Feeney and Halton, and of William F. Buckley, Jr.'s essays and talks have sometimes soured the air. And for decades there have been too few men, at once intellectual and religious and wise on the campuses. Vast empty spaces seem to surround the Niebuhrs and the Tillichs. The churches are filled with worshippers but intelligence has fled from the ranks of religion. Who or what can bring it back?

What, then, is the place of God in our colleges? The basic human experiences that remind man that he is not a machine, and not merely a temporary cog in a technological civilization, are not fostered within the university. God is as irrelevant in the universities as in business organizations; but so are love, death, personal destiny. Religion can thrive only in a personal universe; religious faith, hope, and love are personal responses to a personal God. But how can the immense ques-

tion of a personal God even be posed and made relevant when fundamental questions about the meaning and limits of personal experience
are evaded?

"God is dead ... What are these churches if they are not the tombs
and sepulchers of God?" Nietzsche asked. But much of Western humanism is dead too. Men do not wander under the silent stars, listen to the
wind, learn to know themselves, question, "Where am I going? Why am
I here?" They leave aside the mysteries of contingency and transitoriness, for the certainties of research, production, consumption. So that it
is nearly possible to say: "Man is dead ... What are these buildings,
these tunnels, these roads, if they are not the tombs and sepulchers of
man?"

God, if there is a God, is not dead. He will come back to the colleges,
when man comes back.

JOHN A. T. ROBINSON, Bishop of Woolwich
do we need a god?

An American magazine is reputed to have sent a telegram to Einstein:
"DO YOU BELIEVE IN GOD STOP PREPAID FIFTY WORDS." Asked, "Do we
need a God?" I am inclined to reply on a postcard: "If the question is
put like that, no."

First, however, let me say that it is a good question. For it reflects
well enough what people actually ask. But I should want to go on to
insist that it's a bad question, if one is looking for a simple answer that
gets to the truth of the matter. For the question of God as ordinarily
put is hardly any longer about the real issue. No wonder people are
confused.

It has been said that "the creed of the English is that there is no God
and that it is wise to pray to him from time to time." Ostensibly, however, the creed of the English is emphatically that there *is* a God (the

From *But That I Can't Believe* by John A. T. Robinson, Bishop of Woolwich. An
NAL book. Copyright © 1967 by John A. T. Robinson, Bishop of Woolwich.
Reprinted by permission.

latest opinion poll gave 84 percent for, with only 2 percent definitely against) and that it is wise to pray to him from time to time (43 percent, incredibly, said "regularly"); but their other answers show that in terms of that God they are practical atheists.

The polls merely reflect the fact that somehow the traditional question has ceased to be the relevant one. Reverse the percentages and one would get an equally plausible picture. People say yes because there's something they don't wish to be put in the position of denying, when the truer answer might be no. Conversely I, who find the reality of God inescapable, would doubtless be recorded among the 16 percent doubtfuls or unbelievers if asked for a straight yes or no to the question "Do we need a God?"

The reason I would jib is summed up in the two little words "need" and "a." To explain will help to clear the ground for what I believe to be the real question.

First, do we *need* a God? The whole history of the past two hundred years has been a questioning of the need to bring God into one department of life after another. When in the eighteenth century Newton wrote about physics and Kant about ethics, both believed that God was necessary in order to round off their systems — for Newton, to intervene and regulate the planets' motions; for Kant, to ensure that virtue was in the end matched with happiness. God was a necessary hypothesis, even in a rationalistic age.

The revolution of the nineteenth century is represented by the famous remark of the mathematician Laplace, when asked by Napoleon where God fitted into his system: "Sir, I have no need of that hypothesis." In other words, scientific explanation can be complete without having to introduce God. And today we all accept this. It is simply bad science to resort to God to fill the gaps. And for religious people to resist this process, to suppose that room can be found for God only by keeping open a space in the circle of explanation or control, is merely to ally faith with ignorance.

But it is not simply in the field of intellectual explanation that God has ceased to be needed. Marx and Freud in their different spheres have revealed the extent to which the figure of God has been used as a compensation or projection. Religion has been a prop or a sop. Men have run to God, expecting him to intervene or to correct the balance (here or hereafter) in a way that has merely revealed their emotional immaturity.

One of the effects of secularization has been to compel man to take responsibility for his destiny in matters which before could be left "in the lap of the gods." For good or for ill, he has "come of age." One of the most influential of Christian voices today, that of Dietrich Bonhoeffer, hanged by the Nazis in 1945, warned against resisting this in the name of God, and against exploiting needs in the last recesses of the soul which only "God" could answer. For this once again is to ally faith with man's weakness and ignorance rather than with his maturity.

For these reasons I would refuse to test the truth or falsity of the reality of God by whether or not it can be shown that we *need* him.

I would have equal reservations about the expression *a* God. For *a* God is almost by definition no God — a puppet, an idol created by the finite imagination of man.

From time immemorial men have projected their deepest spiritual convictions and values on the heavens and have visualized beings who embodied them in some supernatural realm above or beyond this one. This is a process we recognize readily enough, say, of the gods of ancient Greece and Rome. No one seriously believes these gods "existed," on the top of Olympus or anywhere else. The realities of Greek and Roman religion, however, remain — insights into the deepest things of life from which we can still learn, as we can from the art or philosophy of the same cultures. The projection, the description, of these insights as beings inhabiting another, separate world of their own is now recognized as a human creation, a personification in terms of superhuman characters of the profoundest realities of religious experience. We can acknowledge this without questioning the realities they sought to represent.

In the same way, the conception of God as *a* Being, a Person — like ourselves but supremely above or beyond ourselves — will, I believe, equally come to be seen as a human projection. (Most people already recognize this in the case of the Devil.) It is a way of making real and vivid to the imagination, by personification, the conviction that reality at its deepest is to be interpreted not simply at the level of its impersonal, mathematical regularities, but in personal categories such as love and trust, freedom, responsibility, and purpose. *The real question of God is not whether a Being exists whom we visualize as embodying this in his Person. It is whether this conviction about the ultimate meaning of things is true.*

It is quite possible that we may *not* need a God, any more than a Devil. For most people till now such a supernatural person has in fact been an indispensable focus for the imagination, both in prayer and in communicating the reality to others. But then most people till now, at any rate in the West, have lived in a universe divided mentally into two realms, a natural and a supernatural.

But though it may have helped — and many would regard it as unexpendable — I am convinced that this projection of God as a Being in another realm has equally succeeded in making him marginal to vast numbers of people today. They cannot recognize the reality of God in experience because the image which should be making it vivid locates him in an area in which they no longer "live." He is banished to the edges of life — to the uncanny (the significance now of the supernatural), to what men still cannot understand or control (so-styled acts of God), or to what is revealingly called the afterlife. People turn to him at the end of their tether; but in the ordinary course of affairs he comes in, if at all, only after the vital connections have been made. In fact, once again, almost by definition he has ceased to be God. Consequently it has become insignificant whether 84 percent of the English say they believe in him or 16 percent.

Having thus tried to clear the ground, I come to what I believe is the real question — not "Do we need a God?" but "Can we finally get away from the reality for which the word God has stood?"

God stands, as the medieval Scholastic philosophers insisted, for the *ens realissimum*, the most real thing in the world. The word relates to what is most deeply true and real, to what is of ultimate concern and significance.

Now there are obviously various levels at which we can view reality. Human beings, for instance, can be interpreted perfectly validly from the point of view of the physicist or the chemist, in terms of the same patterns of vibration and molecular composition as any other matter. But this tells us little distinctively about them as men and women.

The sociologist or psychologist can add information that takes us a good deal further into what makes human beings what they are. But the relation in which the analyst or social scientist stands toward his subject is still an impersonal one.

We get down, as we say, to "the real person" only when this I-It approach yields to an I-Thou relationship in which he ceases to be an object of inquiry and is met as a subject in and for his own sake, in friendship, love, and trust. It is only at this level that we can truly know a person (as distinct from knowing about him) and the real depths and heights of human existence are disclosed.

In the same way, the universe discloses its true nature at different levels. At one level the world can be understood and controlled in terms of its mathematical regularities. Indeed, at this level it is possible in theory to give a complete explanation. Certainly, as I insisted at the beginning, the believer has no interest in finding a place for God in the gaps of such explanation — any more than the truth of the I-Thou relationship with persons depends on holes in the scientist's analysis.

But no pattern of mathematical regularities, however complete, can provide values or quality or meaning. Unless there are realities in the universe deeper than these, to which the mind and spirit of man responds, then all features of life which distinguish human beings from the animals — civilization, art, ethics, science itself — rest on no more than subjective attitudes of the kind: "I like mustard; I don't." But the artist, the reformer, or the scientist speaks characteristically of a claim upon him to which he must be faithful. And this presents itself with the same givenness as the quantitative aspects of the universe — as a reality once sensed from which he cannot get away without selling out.

The level of reality for which men have required the word God is one that presupposes and underlies all these others. It is evidenced in the response to the sacred, the holy, the absolutely unconditional: "Here stand I: I can do no other." It comes with the same sense of inescapable, compelling objectivity — of something profoundly disturbing yet profoundly gracious, ultimate yet intimate.

It comes in many forms — in the "Thus saith the Lord" heard by Isaiah or Jeremiah; in Wordsworth's "sense sublime of something far more deeply interfused"; in the haunting Alleluias of Stravinsky's *Symphony of Psalms*; in the testimony of mystics and prophets, saints and ordinary men and women the world over.

This is the reality which the believer finds it impossible to deny. He may not "need" it — though he discovers his life fulfilled in it. He may not represent it as "a" Person — though the nearest analogy in his experience is the kind of claim that meets him in personal relationships. But, however dimly perceived or obeyed, it is for him, as supremely it was for Jesus, the reality in whose grace and power the whole of his life is lived.

MYRON B. BLOY, JR.
technological culture: a theological response

Technology, considered both as the cumulative weight of an increasing proliferation of radical innovations in what might be called the "economics" of man's existence and also as an "objective spirit" or certain life-style, is the major force which is shaping the emerging culture. What are the most potent aspects of its power for cultural change? On the positive side, I would argue that technology, far from enslaving man as some writers (especially Jacques Ellul) aver, releases us into new dimensions of freedom from ancient restraints. Furthermore, far from depersonalizing man as others have argued, technology commits us to a much more profound awareness of other persons than has heretofore been generally possible.

For the two-thirds of the world where grinding poverty, incessant work, debilitating disease, life-long hunger, and early death are still the essential conditions of existence, technology is the primary instrument of freedom. I would not mention this obvious fact if so many Western critics didn't cavalierly denigrate it; our cultural critiques should never become so effete that this fact is overlooked. For us, however, technology is opening up subtler forms of freedom. Consider first three examples of how technological innovations affect our traditional value system. The so-called "prudential ethic" which has used the triple threat of infection, conception, and detection to enforce extra-marital chastity has been all but knocked out by three new technologies — penicillin, Enovid, and the automobile and motel. Man's traditional habit of finding his self-identity through his work in the productive enterprise is being challenged by the astounding productive capacities of cybernation — the meshing of automation and cybernetic devices into a single productive process. And the family, heretofore the almost exclusive value-forming power for children, has been seriously eroded by rapid, easily accessible transportation and television which brings the whole raw world into the family living-room.

Furthermore, the spirit of technology, given philosophical form as

From *Motive*, March–April, 1967. Copyright © 1967 by *Motive*. Reprinted by permission.

pragmatism, has undermined every metaphysically fixed value system: as William James has said of the pragmatist,

> He turns away from abstraction and insufficiency, from verbal solutions, from bad *a priori* reasons, from fixed principles, closed systems, and pretended absolutes and origins. He turns towards concreteness and adequacy, towards facts, towards action, and towards power. That means the empiricist temper regnant and the rationalist temper sincerely given up. It means the open air and the possibilities of nature, as against dogma, artificiality, and the pretense of finality in truth.[1]

Those of us with a vested interest in the traditional culture are bound to be dismayed by these developments, but, in fact, each one of the changes I have described does enlarge man's freedom over heretofore implacably contingent factors of his existence. The prudential sex ethic, based on nothing but fear, made moral morons of us all; now we can make decisions about sexual behavior on the basis of a positive understanding of sexuality. Similarly, by breaking the stranglehold that the necessity of productivity has always had on man's self-identity, cybernation is giving us the opportunity to evolve richer, more satisfying models of self-identity for ourselves. And the family, which has traditionally exacted an often tyrannous value-conformity in exchange for the security it provides the child, is now in a position to become a supportive setting in which the young have the freedom to explore value systems other than those of their parents. Finally, there is no gainsaying the sense of exhilaration and release in James' description of man freed from the ideological straightjackets of the traditional culture.

We are not only freed by technology from many of the material, social, psychological, and spiritual restraints which so pinched and enslaved most men in the past, we are also made much more aware of the presence and plight of our fellowman than heretofore. Consider, for example, James Reston's description of how television and the airplane counted in the Selma freedom movement: "We are told by our philosophers and sociologists that our machines are enslaving and debasing us, but in this historic battle over voting rights these machines are proving powerful instruments for equality and justice." Television forced on our awareness the plight of fellow human beings, in fact made them our neighbors, and mass transportation allowed us to go to their assistance. Because we are so inescapably aware of the sufferings of so many more

[1] From *Pragmatism: A New Name for Some Old Ways of Thinking*, by William James. P. 51. Longmans, Green & Co. Copyright 1907 by William James.

neighbors, we often draw the false conclusion that suffering itself abounds as never before and technology is often (ironically enough) blamed; actually our burgeoning awareness of every man as neighbor is possibly the first step in the solution of suffering which before now was hardly known outside its immediate context.

But modern electronic developments may be fostering the "age of man's encounter with man" in more subtle and compelling ways than those just described. For example, Marshall McLuhan has argued that students increasingly are restive under the traditional episodic, piece-meal curriculum. This "linear" approach to learning was designed to add up, after four years spent abstracted from society, to something meaningful. Television has formed their perceptive modes from an early age to in-depth expectations and deep involvement in human interactions. Literate man tends to be so horrified by the shoddy content of most television programming that he fails to see how television, whether its content is "good" or "bad," defines for those who live with it from an early age the scale of "reality" for all their future encounters with the world. Man as a discrete individual, participating in the world from a rational, detached point-of-view, is giving way to "re-tribalized" man, who lives almost completely *with* others, in almost total involvement, and for whom the point-of-view has little meaning. This new man fills out the shape of his life only insofar as he is involved dynamically with others.

Now, freedom and awareness are precisely necessary conditions for the growth of man towards his moral maturity. The freer we are the more responsibility we can take for our behavior, and the more aware we are of the presence and plight of the other person the more oppor-tunity we have to exercise that responsibility. When man is enslaved by superstitions and brutalities of nature and lives in ignorance of the real plight of his fellow men, the possibilities of growth towards moral maturity are severely limited. But if the freedom and awareness which technology have fostered are necessary conditions for growth towards a culture of moral maturity, they are certainly not sufficient causes for such growth. Freedom *from* restraints of one kind or another only achieves its inherent meaning when it becomes freedom *for* fulfilling in action a normative commitment to the neighbor. An awareness of the presence and plight of our fellow men only becomes creative when spurred by that normative commitment; it occasions more sensitive decisions in their behalf. Without some strong guiding norm freedom collapses into chaos and awareness into the anxiety of "information overload." The ironic dilemma we face is that the same spirit of technology which has increased our freedom and awareness has also decreased our ability to make normative commitments and thus destroys for many of us our ability to exercise that freedom and awareness.

Daniel Bell uses the phrase "eclipse of distance" to describe the dissolution of normative commitments; he says,

> The underlying social reality, the stylistic unity of the culture of the past hundred years lies, I would argue, in a structural form of expression that I have called the "eclipse of distance," of psychic, social and esthetic distance. Modern culture began as an effort to annihilate the contemplative mode of experience by emphasizing *immediacy, impact, simultaneity,* and *sensation.* It is today at the point of breaking up all fixed points of reference in formal genres.[2]

This is not the place to enter into an analysis of how man experiences normless existence, but the following two images are suggestive. The prophet Amos, after cataloguing many of the terrible things — such as darkness at noon, sackcloth and baldness, the mourning for an only son — which will befall the people because they have departed from the Lord's purposes for them, sums up their doom in this haunting description of normless existence:

> "Behold, the days are coming," says the Lord God,
>   "when I will send a famine on the land;
> not a famine of bread, nor a thirst for water,
>   but of hearing the words of the Lord.
> They shall wander from sea to sea,
>   and from north to east;
> they shall run to and fro, to seek the word of the Lord,
>   but they shall not find it.
> In that day the fair virgins and the young men shall
>   faint for thirst." (Amos 8:11-13)

And Arthur Miller, seeming almost to paraphrase Amos' word of doom for our ears, summarizes his *Death of a Salesman* in "the image of private man in a world full of strangers, a world that is not home nor even an open battleground but only galaxies of high promise over a fear of falling."

Contemporary man, trapped in the frustrating situation of having

[2] Daniel Bell, "The Disjunction of Culture and Social Structure: Some Notes on the Meaning of Social Reality." in *Daedalus,* 94:220, Winter 1965. Collected in Austin, ed., *The Revolutionary Imperative* (MSM Books, 1966), and in Holton, ed., *Science and Culture* (Houghton Mifflin, 1965).

achieved at last the capacity to create his own destiny but unable to discover normative commitments commensurate with that capacity, often reacts convulsively in one of the two ways. On the one hand, he plunges into intense technological activism: if the activity towards some contingent end is intense enough it can create the illusion of purpose, it can cover up the normative anarchy which exists just beneath the surface. On the other hand, he may grasp at a reactionary idealism like those represented by the John Birch Society or Moral Re-Armament. The Birchers, unable to tolerate their new freedom and increasingly present neighbor, construct a paranoid model of reality which reduces their freedom to some form of counter-plot against the communists in behalf of a Jeffersonian political paradise, and they deny the demanding presence of the neighbor by reducing him to either a spy or patriot. The MRA pattern is similar, except it is in the sphere of metaphysics and morals instead of politics.

Religion is often a more passive form of this same regression: there are, it is argued, certain immutable "moral and spiritual values" to which we must "return," but these values are purposely left honorific and lifeless so that they cover the abyss of normlessness without having to submit to the test of action. The escapist route of higher education is often "the discipline": one can spend a lifetime paying homage to its cabalistic intricacies and defending it against its detractors without ever seriously facing the question of the purpose of learning.

A further irony of our time is that the struggle for cultural purpose seems to be polarized around these two escapist positions: the idealist is called reactionary dreamer by the operationalist, and the operationalist is called a superficial manipulator by the idealist, and both are right.

What we need in order to achieve our cultural maturity is a sense of purpose passionate enough to overcome the anti-normative tendencies of our time and use our new freedom and awareness in behalf of man. This purpose must be weighty enough to escape both moralistic reductionism and calculated operationalism, and is best conveyed by the following story about St. Francis. It seems that Francis, with several of his friends, was walking down a road on a wintry afternoon; he was wearing a heavy cloak against the weather. Presently they approached a nearly naked beggar shivering with cold, and Francis promptly gave him his cloak. Some of his friends remonstrated with Francis, saying that if he caught cold and were incapacitated through lack of his cloak their movement would be without a leader, while the others congratulated him on the "goodness" of his act. Francis angrily silenced their squabble and told them that this man, like every man, was a brother and that therefore the cloak was his by right if he needed it: it could not be kept from him by self-interest, however enlightened, nor could its giving be called "good" since it was already the beggar's by right. I take it that our new freedom and reality fulfill their "natural" ends when they are pressed into the service of such a vision of reality.

The passionate vision of a Francis, held expectantly within each present situation, has the power to use our new freedom and awareness for the shaping of our culture to human and humane form. But where do we find such power? Is there a cultural sub-community, like the roaming bands of prophets in early biblical times, where this power is operative? I think such a way of life is evolving among the college and university students who, together with a few faculty, clergymen, and ghetto-dwellers, make up the so-called "freedom movement."

It is hard to realize that just two years ago, in *The Uncommitted* — a book on the American "youth culture" — Kenneth Keniston could argue that college students were marked by a lack of rebelliousness, by social powerlessness, and by privatized values. Erik Erikson was making the same sort of judgment when he described life for the college students as a "psycho-social moratorium." Slick journals were mildly deploring the passivity and the lack of good old-fashioned grit and gumption in the American college student. After quoting statistics which indicated that college seniors entering the work world were primarily concerned with pension plans and job security, editorials urged them to accept instead the risks of economic and professional life which have been the time-honored lot of the successful American entrepreneur.

But now the teach-ins are taking the place of panty-raids, voter registration campaigns in the deep South and northern ghettoes are replacing the spring bacchanals on the Florida beaches, tutorial programs are succeeding religious clubs, and — after graduation — the Peace Corps and politics are taking the place of company apprenticeship programs, editorialists are telling students to "stick to their books" and to remember that time-serving apprenticeships are a necessary prelude to success in life. What, in fact, has happened, and why?

The passive, powerless, privatized "youth culture" which Keniston described had its more immediate roots in World War II: veterans returning to college had taken all the risks they wanted, and now they were ready for college as a recompense for those harsh years. Although higher education was already participating much more than it had in the research and development needs of the nation, the prevailing undergraduate assumption was that college represented a socially detached enclave, replete with its own romantic mythologies, designed to prepare persons in due and leisurely course for following a personal career trajectory. Society at large was simply the shadowy, yet stable and secure, background against which this trajectory was to be traced.

As the Cold War deepened, this model of higher education was clung to by students with something like desperation. University administrations, by and largely, happily sanctioned the youth culture because it tacitly supported their *in loco parentis* power, and more or less confined their problem areas to the campus and to issues of private morality. Faculty were not inclined to disturb the youth culture because student passivity allowed them the time and energy to indulge more fully in the exciting, status-making research and development possibilities which the government was opening up for them.

The revolt against the youth culture was occasioned by the Negro struggle for civil rights in the South and has so far moved through three stages corresponding to three different levels of insight. The intense moral pressure caused by the southern civil rights struggle, led in many areas by the Student Non-Violent Coordinating Committee which was composed largely of Negro students, was enough to lead a few northern, white students into the struggle themselves. In the course of this participation, they began to discover that American culture and society, far from being the stable, secure world assumed by the youth culture, was wracked with such cruel and systematic injustice that commitment to revolutionary change was the only reasonable stance to take.

Furthermore, they discovered — through participation in direct action projects such as freedom rides and sit-ins — that their action could count for something in the world of political and social affairs. When these students returned to the campus, their achievement of moral commitment (of "the point beyond which there is no turning back," which is a crucial discovery for the maturity of each man) and of a real share in social power had a contagious quality for many other students who hadn't hitherto realized what a spiritual deprivation the youth culture was.

The second stage emerged when students began to realize that dramatic, random forays into the South was not a serious enough response to the problem, and that they had to regularize and localize (in the North) their activities. The Northern Student Movement was born out of this realization. Turning their own talents to use, they organized far-reaching tutorial programs for children in the social and racial ghettoes near their campuses. Some students moved into the ghettoes. They helped organize the disestablished to fight against local establishments, and they kept up a drum-fire of pressure to participate in the struggle on their uninvolved fellow-students. In this stage of development, students in the movement lived a kind of intellectual and spiritual schizophrenia, passively accepting and fulfilling the demands of a remote and static academic establishment while passionately involved in the struggle to change the character of an unjust society.

But when the students began to learn that intellectual and spiritual understanding, as well as simple political activism, would be necessary to bring about the social change they envisaged, it was inevitable that the academic establishments themselves should come under their fire, since these establishments were, by and large, unequipped to respond to the students' urgent needs. The Free Speech Movement at Berkeley was, for many students, the beginning of this discovery, and although most adults could echo President Eisenhower and see it only as "disgraceful riots," we must look beneath the turmoil to see what was really at stake. Mario Savio spoke for morally and socially sensitive students everywhere when he said, during that famous sit-in in Sproul Hall,

> Many students here at the university, many people in society are wandering aimlessly about. Strangers in their own lives, there is no place for them. They are people who have not learned to compromise, who for example have come to the university to learn to question, to grow, to learn — all the standard things that sound like cliches because no one takes them seriously. And they find at one point or other that for them to become part of society, to become lawyers, ministers, businessmen, people in government, that very often they must compromise those principles which were most dear to them. They must suppress the most creative impulses that they have; this is a prior condition for being part of the system. The university is well structured, well tooled, to turn out people with all the sharp edges worn off, the well-rounded person. The university is well equipped to produce that sort of person, and this means that the best among the people who enter for four years wander aimlessly much of the time questioning why they are on campus at all, doubting whether there is any point in what they are doing, and looking toward a very bleak existence afterward in a game in which all of the rules have been made up, which one cannot really mend.[3]

3 Mario Savio, "An End to History," edited from a tape of his talks in Sproul Hall and mimeographed by the Free Speech Movement for general distribution. Collected in Cohen and Hale, eds., *The New Student Left* (Beacon Press, 1966) and in Jacobs and Landau, eds., *The New Radicals* (Vintage, 1966).

Although it is easy to criticize the naivete of Savio's rhetoric, it is impossible to avoid the essential rightness of his analysis.

These students, finally driven by their moral passion to a new intellectual concern (How do societies and cultures work and how can they be changed?) and a spiritual quest (What is man's real life and what is the meaning of history?) are challenging the educational establishments in two ways. First, as in Berkeley, they are bringing direct pressure for specific reforms: student rallies support good teachers who have been fired because they failed to measure up to research-oriented tenure criteria; philosophy departments which, in their preoccupation with esoteric linguistic and mathematical games, are unequipped and uninterested in helping students to assimilate intellectually their new social and moral experience, are under attack in student editorial columns, teach-ins pressure curricula committees to respond more relevantly to students' real questions. Secondly, the so-called "free university" movement is becoming an embarrassing challenge to the academic establishments. These independent, student-led "communities of learning" are springing up near every large academic center because, as the "Proposal for a Free University in Boston" points out, "Students returning from civil rights activity and community organizing projects found little of relevance in academia to the problems central to their concerns." The new free university in Boston aims, in the words of its prospectus, to involve the following groups:

> students and organizers seeking both the theoretical and empirical bases for ideology; people in community organizations who want to learn organizing skills, participate in political discussion, and gain or regain some aspects of general education; suburban opponents of the war who will want information as well as tools and perspectives for organizing in middle-class neighborhoods; professionals who are trying to redefine their roles in terms of social objectives; teachers and students dissatisfied with the content of their previous educational experience, as well as by the university's approach to learning and to the social relevance of intellectual activity; artists, writers, and actors who seek to explore new dimensions in their work, or to relate their work to the movement.

Thus, the students' exhilarating discovery of moral commitment and social power, occasioned by the civil rights movement in the South and solidified and deepened in the ghettoes of the North, has opened their eyes to some of the inadequacies of higher education and led them to attempt reforms.

Now let us consider the life-style of the participants in the movement: it is from this life-style that we have most to learn, I believe, since it is born out of the Franciscan vision of the neighbor as brother and the perspective of historical realism. One way of seeing this life-style is through the eyes of its critics. On the one hand, operationally oriented change-agents like Saul Alinsky and many liberal politicians, who might be expected to be allies of the students, are very critical of them for not being pragmatic enough in their approach to social problems. I remember one Alinsky man saying to an S.D.S. member, "What we want to know about you people is whether or not you're for real: You act like a bunch of poets!" But the students feel that Alinsky and the politicians, by playing the game in terms and for the stakes essentially established by the *status quo*, don't raise the necessarily radical questions about the character of our society. They have read Silone's *Bread and Wine*, and they identify with Pietro Spina. On the other hand, they are criticized by academics, idealists and conservatives generally for compromising principle for political ends and for participating in political action when they ought to be sticking to their books. But the students argue that no serious involvement in social change is possible without being changed oneself, and that education without direct, concrete involvement in cultural issues is not education at all. In short, because they remain open to both the depths and the surface of events they are scored by idealists and operationalists from opposite directions.

But, to turn to a direct description of them, I believe that their suffering — their intellectual, moral, and spiritual suffering — is what is most authenticating about their prophetic identity. I have spent long evenings with student radicals while they struggled to discover an "ideology." Most of them have studied Marxism but now feel that although Marx's analysis of society is useful, his anthropology of the individual is faulty. Existentialist philosophers, on the other hand, are usually far too simple-minded about political and economic realities to be accepted. As a matter of fact, it is doubtful, for all their desperate effort to find a secure ideological niche from which to see themselves and their history, that they will ever arrive in this promised land. Their honesty and openness to the myriad intellectual and emotional claims of experience will deny them the neat ideologies they search for. But they find it equally difficult to be operationalists. Nothing is more frustrating to a political wheeler-dealer than to participate in an S.D.S. organizational meeting because questions of substance, of goals and essential meaning, are always in order and continually break down the smooth logic of cause and effect that is ostensibly being put together. The "really real" for them is to be discovered only by accepting the full weight, both the insistent depth and the empirical surface, of the here and now in their drive to keep faith with their vision of every neighbor as a brother. Only this precarious and passionate commitment, they feel, lets them into the action of life and allows them to be the shapers, not just the victims, of history.

By now my not-so-hidden theological agenda should be obvious. Our new freedom and awareness and concomitant inability to assume an easy normative focus for the emergent culture really adds up to "the world come of age" which Bonhoeffer described. God is, in effect, kicking us in the pants and telling us that it is time to grow up. We are given the tools needed to shape a new culture and allowed to use them effectively only in the service of a prophetic commitment. We are even provided, in the student movement, one significant model of how that commitment can be assumed. Of course, there is no assurance that society will accept this challenge rather than hide in increasingly frenzied operationalism or increasingly brittle idealisms until we are overwhelmed by chaos, but these are our only two options.

The church, as that community whose formal function is to bear witness in its life to the intentions of God for mankind and to support and celebrate God's action wherever it is discovered, does not fulfill its role effectively in our present situation. The church might learn a good deal from the student movement about what it means to be men of faith in our technological culture. Tillich in fact argues that the mature form of historical realism, which he calls "self-transcending realism," can only be held through faith. He says,

> Self-transcending realism is based on the consciousness of the "here and now." The ultimate power of being, the ground of reality, appears in a special moment, in a concrete situation, revealing the infinite depth and the eternal significance of the present. But this is possible only in terms of a paradox, *i.e.*, by faith, for, in itself, the present is neither infinite nor eternal. The more it is seen in the light of the ultimate power, the more it appears as questionable and void of lasting significance. So the power of a thing is, at the same time, affirmed and negated when it becomes transparent for the ground of its power, the ultimately real. It is as in a thunderstorm at night, when the lightning throws a blinding clarity over all things, leaving them in complete darkness the next moment. When reality is seen in this way with the eye of self-transcending realism, it has become something new. Its ground has become visible in an "ecstatic" experience, called "faith."

It is no longer merely self-subsistent as it seemed to be before; it has become transparent.[4]

Is not the commitment to the neighbor as brother, revealed freshly through the "eye of self-transcending realism," precisely the commitment that the church is called to live out of?

But, if the church has much to learn about its own calling from the student movement, the movement stands in need of a reawakened church. Students reject the church because they see that its "faith" is often really an escape from rather than a commitment to, history. As Tillich points out, "The man of today, who feels separated by a gulf from the theistic believer, often knows more about the 'ultimate' than the self-assured Christian who thinks that through his faith he has God in his possession."[5] The problem of the Movement, however, is that it has no way to perceive that its apparently anomalous stance between operationalism and idealism, its inability to find a secure resting place in some Platonic form of Truth, is precisely its calling. The students do not have conscious access to the Judeo-Christian tradition in which their commitment is recognized as *the* calling of man. Their intellectual and spiritual suffering is often self-destructive because the tradition of *celebrating* their commitment has been rendered unavailable to them by the keepers of that tradition, *i.e.*, by the church. Thus the church, by recovering its own ability to live and celebrate the life of prophetic commitment as the authentic life of man, would also stand as an encouraging sign of the authenticity of every manifestation of that commitment which emerges in society. This is precisely the calling of the church in our technological culture.

[4] Paul Tillich, "Realism and Faith," in *The Protestant Era*, University of Chicago Press, 1948, p. 78.
[5] *Ibid.*, p. 82.

THOMAS F. O'DEA
the crisis of the contemporary
religious consciousness

During times of religious crises, existence tends to be experienced in terms of manifold contradictions. People have neither the poetic capacity to integrate an organized outlook nor the psychological ability to achieve a sense of meaningful participation in their society. In recent decades, this condition has come to characterize the outlook of strategic strata in Western countries. It represents a severe crisis of Western religious consciousness. There is much in the present situation that is not new; unbelief, ambivalence, and the temptation of nihilism have characterized religious crises in the past. The inherently close but fundamentally incompatible relationship between faith and doubt is a permanent and perennial characteristic of the religious experience. Yet the conditions of Western man today present this perennial and abiding element of crisis in a new setting — a dynamic and secularized society embodying a scientific world view. This new setting alters radically both the meaning of the perennial crisis and the modes of handling it available to men. At the same time, the combination of perennial and novel elements creates a genuinely new human situation and justifies speaking in terms of the crisis of contemporary religious consciousness. Still, this crisis is experienced differently by people from different social backgrounds, cultural traditions, and religious faiths. But whatever be the differential incidence and different degrees of involvement in the crisis among the various groups in America and the West, the democratization of higher education brings the crisis and involvement in it to ever increasing numbers.

For a sociologist to attempt an analysis of this crisis is to undertake a task that transcends the conceptual tools of his profession, however useful they may prove in certain respects. Behind any analysis of this kind lie an individual experience, a particular perspective, a personal vision. The overview of any writer on this topic will reflect both his professional and his personal biography, his own individual confrontation of and mode of adjustment to the basic elements of the crisis. In the present case, it reflects not only two decades spent in the scholarly study of man's historical and social existence, particularly in relation

From *Daedalus*, Journal of the American Academy of Arts and Sciences, Boston, Massachusetts. Volume 96, Number 1. Reprinted by permission.

to his cultural productions and his religious concerns, but also a life lived in a time of war and revolution, of chaotic violence and routinized extermination, of rising expectations and increasing anxieties, of promise and unprecedented threat to man's future. Intellectual and sociological analysis alone can delineate the elements of crisis; this will be attempted with soberness and objectivity. But the configuration they assume will reveal the significance that the analyst sees in them or attributes to them, a significance that expresses not only objective reality but the author's relation to the world. What is attempted here will be a reasonable and open-minded exposition of one sociologist's view of the contemporary religious crisis, eschewing both the smug flattening out of disturbing implications that some social scientists mistake for objectivity and the overdramatic wallowing in catastrophe of certain of their intellectual critics.

Five aspects of the contemporary religious crisis, each of which deserves more attention than can be given it within the scope of this article, will be investigated: (1) the range and variety of crisis experiences; (2) the perennial elements of the religious crisis; (3) the urgency of the contemporary situation; (4) the available modes for confronting the crisis; and finally (5) the problem of relevance for organized religion today.

I. THE RANGE AND VARIETY OF CRISIS EXPERIENCES

Let us begin by describing in ideal, typical, and somewhat foreshortened and stereotyped terms several kinds of people recognizably suffering in one way or another from the implications of the religious crisis.

We start with a bright Italian-American student on the campus of a Catholic college. Reared in a traditional Catholic home, he attended a parochial elementary and high school and is now in his junior year of college. He is a major in the humanities or the social sciences and has read widely, especially in serious modern thought and literature. He strongly identifies with Catholic intellectuals critical of the tenor of American Catholic life, with progressive theologians, and with the so-called "liberal" party at Vatican II. He champions ecumenism and liturgical revival within his church and is generally sympathetic to new departures in religious thought and action. He considers the problem for people like himself to be that of developing a contemporary and relevant Catholicism that remains, at the same time, true to itself as the bearer of an authentic hierophany. He sees the religion of his parents and, even more, that of his grandparents as "folk" Catholicism, once a protective cocoon for a living religious tradition and experience but now thoroughly dysfunctional for people like himself. He thinks that his fellow students who take refuge in conservative politics or in a combination of conservative politics with a preconciliar Catholicism are practicing an ostrich-like obscurantism, forgivable in aging priests but lamentable, if not reprehensible, in his contemporaries. To him, many of his older clerical teachers and pastors, and possibly his bishop, vary from well-meaning but ineffectual religious conservatives to religious neanderthalers. Beneath this posture — as genuine and authentic as possible for him — there lurk both anguish and dread. He experiences genuine crises of meaning and the real threat of meaninglessness.

We leave the Catholic college and go to a nearby secular campus. Here we see a young man, Jewish by descent, who was brought up in a socially mobile family in which religious teaching, religious atmosphere, or religious concern was at a minimum. He has taken courses in history and the social sciences. In college he has discovered that he is a Jew, not in the sense that he had somehow always known it, but in a new way. He has discovered that there exists a religious, an intellectual, and a legal tradition in which the term *Jew* takes on new meaning for him. He puts on a yarmulke, perhaps even begins to grow a beard, learns Hebrew — or rediscovers the value of some he reluctantly learned in childhood — becomes meticulous concerning dietary regulations and the proper observance of the Sabbath. His secular friends, also of Jewish background, ridicule him somewhat good-naturedly for his "Jew-cap" and his interest in "pilpul," but they nevertheless sense something significant in his behavior. Moreover, they feel that his behavior relates them to him through some unvoiced bond. He is not always sure what he believes about the God of Abraham, Isaac, and Jacob, but his mentors assure him that with faithful observance in terms of what have been called "action symbols" the rest will somehow take care of itself. Beneath this posture — as genuine and authentic as possible for him — there lurk uncertainty and nervousness, which sometimes issue in inner desperation, sometimes in outer aggressiveness.

In a nearby school of theology we observe a young American Protestant from a small town in the Middle West. He is a candidate for the degree of Bachelor of Divinity. Although he studies the traditional subjects prescribed for such a course, he is intensely interested in protest movements, especially those which he thinks involve an ethical challenge. He is aware of the current theological situation in American Protestantism, and he is confused by it. The "obsolescence" of the

Social Gospel, the "contributions" of neo-orthodoxy, the "challenge" of the new Death-of-God theology affect him, but often leave him groping for a sense of direction. He is not sure what he believes, but he has maintained the notion that through the Christian idiom in some way, and within the context of the churches somehow, he can and will find the path to the experience that will relate him significantly to life. He participates in protests against the war in Viet-Nam and joins the marches for civil rights. In these activities he may meet the two young men sketched above; if he does, he will experience a momentary but exhilarating epiphany of ecumenicity and solidarity. Through it all, he looks for a more profound epiphany — a showing forth of the divine for which he still uses the sacred name of Christ. He is not certain he believes in God or what belief in God really means; nor is he clear about what Christ means to him. Still, he hopes for the authenticity of his goal and is convinced of the genuineness of his search. Beneath this posture — as genuine and authentic as possible for him — lurk self-diffusion and anxiety, which at times throw him into fits of depression and at others provide him with the energy for heroic action.

There are many other types of young people seeking significance in action, in politics, in psychedelic drugs, in sexual experimentation. All of them are touched in some way by the contemporary crisis that has so deeply affected the relevance and significance of traditional and institutionalized religion today. But let us look for a moment at the older generation.

In a sizable city in a southwestern state there is a banker — head of a medium-sized commercial bank — who belongs to a family long prominent in the region. The population has grown greatly in the last two decades, and his position in the community has become less visible, less secure. Moreover, in the nation as a whole, changes in corporate business, in the tax structure, and in the role of government in economic life have created a new world in which he does not feel at home. Politics have changed, and the international situation reveals a world in which he feels strange and more than a little afraid. Changes in the relationship of the races have instituted a world he never made, one that he finds difficult to understand. His daughter returns from college — and not an eastern college either — with ideas on all these topics and even on the relationship of the sexes that bring home to him the frightening quality of his newly recognized status as stranger, as outsider. He is sure of one thing, one stable element in his life — his membership in the United Presbyterian Church. He has been its con stant supporter, although irregular in attendance. His Presbyterianism has always been part of his selfhood, alongside his bankership, his Republicanism, and his family lineage. He has also been attracted to conservative politics, in which he has sought some defense — at least symbolic — of a better day. One morning a couple of years ago, he picked up his morning paper to find that the Stated Clerk, the highest elected officer of his denomination, had been arrested on a civil rights picket line. The world he was holding together so precariously threatened then and there to come apart. Fortunately for him, he found a local schismatic Presbyterian church that combined fundamentalist religion with radical-right politics. He now finds his refuge in this group. With this man we can speak less of a posture than of a condition, but it is a condition that draws near to the edge of the void that can threaten human consciousness when one is out of step with a world one cannot understand.

In an eastern city there is a Roman Catholic pastor who has served a local church for thirty years, first as curate and then as parish priest. He is an Irish American. Graduating from the diocesan seminary of his day, he learned little sophisticated theology, and soon after ordination found himself so involved in the practical tasks of his pastoral assignment that he had little time for theology at all. Throughout the years he found his parish to be a bastion of traditional belief surrounded by what seemed like a sea of indifference, unbelief, and even aggressively anti-religious sentiment. He lived through the local repercussions of the Spanish Civil War. He and his parishioners saw that war as the struggle of the forces of unbelief against a Catholic nation and culture. His non-Catholic neighbors who had other associations with Spanish history than those of the Irish-Catholic memory saw different values at stake in the Iberian struggle. He experienced the 1930's as an increasingly "red decade," and during the forties saw his country an ally of militantly atheistic and anti-religious Soviet Russia. He was aware of the reality of danger to his faith and to the world in which his own variety of that faith had been at home. In the early 1950's he rejoiced temporarily in the exorcism of the threat by the late Senator Joseph McCarthy. The calm of the fifties under a conservative president was a relief to him. He received some ambivalent satisfaction in 1960 with the election of a member of his church to the highest office in the land and the end of the last shred of the stigma of his second-class citizenship, but he was quite aware that the outlook of the new President was perilously close to the secular liberalism that had threatened him all his life. Then came Vatican II, which reversed the basic religious tone in which he had been reared and which had been reinforced in his adult experience on almost every crucial issue. It looked to him as though the Catholic Church was indeed being Protestantized. He continued to obey his superiors, grateful when they put the brakes on this *aggiornamento*, as they frequently did. He is really not sure what to make of it all. Questions from his parishioners — a new phenomenon in his parish — irritate him, especially those on birth control. He fears the apostasy of the young. He still believes — believes in the Nicene Creed, believes that he offers Christ to the Father in his morning Mass. But it becomes harder and harder to relate these beliefs to the world about him — even to the church about him. Sometimes, like T. S. Eliot's magus, he "would be glad of another death." To him, the world seems to be approaching chaos — what the ancient Hindu writers called the "confusion of castes." He, also, seeks some succor in right-wing politics, but his troubles are deeper, and his surcease must be sought elsewhere. He manages to maintain the traditional posture, but within he is a baffled and defeated man.

This list could be prolonged with profit. We could consider the Mormon youth who, uneasy in the religion of his forebears, is searching for a new stance by rebelling against the symbols of the older provincial orthodoxy or by embracing them with an over-determined rigidity and a heightened defensiveness. Or the southern youth at the northern university who embraces a new liberalism in hopes of finding both an outlet for the moral conviction imbibed from a Christianity in which he can no longer believe, and a way of entering and participating in the larger, unprovincial, intellectual world. Yet for him, beneath this genuine and useful posture, lurk real guilt for his revolt against his fathers and his deviance from regional loyalties, and resentment of any condescension involved in his acceptance by his new northern friends. We might also consider those young people who seek meaning in new secular ideologies that offer themselves as the psychological, functional equivalents of religion. Or we might continue to examine the older and more established who seek in professional identifications and activities sufficient self-definition and expression to keep the inroads of the current crisis at a distance.

All of these represent people who are trying to live in and cope with change — change in society, change in thinking and styles of life, change in education, in community structure, in the churches. The younger ones are looking for a self-definition with which to face life;

the older ones are clinging to an old identity rooted in circumstances and beliefs, habits and values now being rendered irrelevant. Other elements beside the religious crisis are involved in these personal predicaments. Personal crises are always to be found in times of social change; but in this time of exceptionally rapid social change they are more numerous and more significant. Moreover, beneath the contemporary identity crises hides the void created beneath the institutionalized assumptions by the religious crisis itself. These little stereotyped biographies, those described and those suggested, are idiosyncratic and selective refractions of the spiritual history of today. They are as real a part of the present crisis as the explicit anxieties of the intellectuals who attempt to formulate and meet the problems involved on the explicit conceptual level.

These representative biographical types — representative, of course, in the Emersonian rather than the statistical sense — not only mirror the spiritual condition of our time; they also reflect the history of America. Immigration and assimilation, westward expansion, industrialization and urbanization, the communications revolution, and the increasing democratization of education on all levels have all affected the American milieu. Each American religion seems at present to occupy its own half-way house in which defense of its traditions and its vested interests is found in short-term adjustment to a severe situation for which no final solutions are envisaged. The biographies of all Americans reflect the profound uneasiness of the religious communities.

Moreover, the different religious traditions place different emphases upon the role of ideas in religious life. Consequently, intellectual issues affect some groups more directly than they do others. Because Catholicism continues the Patristic and medieval synthesis of religion and culture and emphasizes the central significance of intellectual assent in the act of faith, it is most vulnerable to the pressure of intellectual skepticism and conflicting ideologies. Protestantism, though deeply affected by the challenge of intellectual research, study, and theorizing in philosophy and Bible study, has faced modernity with less defensiveness, though hardly with fewer debilitating consequences. Moreover, the residual effects of Protestantism's earlier unofficial establishment in America has made it, on the whole, far less defensive before the challenges of modern life. In American Judaism, the substrate of ethnic identity and the abiding centrality of the family have enabled many to accept any ideological, philosophical, or religious position and to remain in some sense Jews. Thus, within these three traditions, the identity crisis and the religious crisis are likely to be differently related and to assume different forms. For those of secularist background — an old and honored tradition in the history of America, the progressive impetus of traditional conceptions appears to share in the general crisis and to offer little to the on-coming generation in its search for identity and meaning.

II. THE RELIGIOUS CRISIS: ITS PERENNIAL ELEMENTS

The primal crisis of religious consciousness is revealed, albeit covertly, in religious myth, the earliest and most holistic form of religious expression. Myth, to use the terminology of Theodor Gaster, translates reality into ideal terms, and preserves the momentary experience by giving it duration. Myth, moreover, is the affirmation by man that he is at home in his world — that he belongs, a being among the many beings, in the orderly and meaningful world of his experience. Yet myth is the obvious product of consciousness and imagination — the creation of a being who has already eaten of the Tree of Knowledge and has, thereby, disrupted a psychic, primal harmony with reflection, questioning, and doubt. Myth reveals itself to the modern scholar as a meaningful assertion made in the face of a potential threat of meaninglessness. It can be inferred, in a manner analogous to that by which Freud posited the existence of unconscious motivation, that there existed for mythic man a potential crisis of consciousness; this became the setting for myth-creation and for an assertion, through myth and ritual, of "faith" in a world of meaning. In the face of possible doubt, myth declares man's relationship to and significance in the world of his experience.

But man not only related himself to the world of his experience; he also attempted to exert control over elements of his surroundings. According to L. S. B. Leakey, some two million years ago *Homo habilis* made and made use of tools. As man slowly extended his control over nature, he increased and multiplied, and according to the modest standards of his time proceeded to subdue the earth. Alongside this growing mastery and intricately related to its later stages, mythic apprehension and expression made way for logical conceptualization and rational discourse. Men broke through the enchanted garden of the mythic world.

Earlier man had made a peculiar kind of relation to his total situation: He apprehended it and responded to it as "sacred" through ritual and myth. Man's success in developing his control over nature and his consequent development of new forms of social existence introduced and enlarged areas of experience from which the sacred quality was removed. In thought, as in action, manipulation produced a world more and more shorn of its emotional and projective character. The fruits of these developments are to be seen in the agriculture and engineering, the administrative and legal structures of the ancient empires, and the growing sophistication technologically and strategically of the conduct of war. They assume a new quality, however, in the peculiar religious experience of the Hebrews. By positing the existence of a transcendent God, the Hebrews demythologized the earth, thereby emancipating man from the magic circle of older religious world-views. Whatever may seem the mythological character of the Bible to modern man, Biblical religion stands in stark contrast with myth in its genuine form. Moreover, the rationalizing implications of men's thought and effort reached their manifest expression in Greek philosophy. Socrates showed men how to overcome myth, demonstrating that they could achieve a new freedom through the positive power of self-knowledge. His contribution was joined to those of the Hebrew Bible by the Fathers of the Christian church. In a great creative adjustment, they brought into being the religious core of the cultural epoch of European civilization.

Yet Biblical religion and Hellenic rationality could not do away with the primal crisis involving the simultaneity and incompatibility of faith and doubt that lay at the core of religion in its mythic form. Three instances sufficiently demonstrate the way in which this basic crisis comes to the surface of man's consciousness in the Hebrew and Hellenic contexts. Within the Hebrew Bible is an odd book whose inclusion in the canon has long perplexed the pious and puzzled the scholarly. The ruminations of Qoheleth — known as Ecclesiastes, the Greek transformation of his name — present an example of religious crisis. They show that the emancipation from myth together with its positive religious achievements uncovered and revealed more fully the crisis elements primordially lurking at the core of man's religious experience. Uprooted from the closed community of his forebears, Qoheleth lived in the wider world that trade and war had created. Under the conditions of Jewish life in the early Hellenistic period, he spoke to men as individuals facing intimately the problem of meaning.

Qoheleth's religion reflects his confrontation of the threat of meaninglessness and cosmic aloneness that lay concealed behind the mythic assertion of earlier religions and the belief and hope in a relation to a transcendent God of his Hebrew forefathers. He sees a world characterized by movement without genuine change, effort without authentic profit. Events are predetermined, but their reasonable comprehension remains forever impossible. All values are negated by their opposites, just as life eventually is by death. The facts of life contradict the optimistic Hebraic idea that retribution from God inevitably overtakes evil and that goodness is repaid in prosperity. Neither character nor works affect one's fate. Before the incomprehensible frustrations and enigmas of human life, Qoheleth cries, "A vapor of vapors! All is vapor!" But he does not despair completely. Rather, he seeks to find happiness in a kind of anemic vitalism, by enjoying the day-to-day experience of living itself and avoiding the restlessness and unhappiness inevitably involved in straining after religious peace and certitude. What Qoheleth sees and recommends to others is the little life of modest ambitions in a disenchanted world.

The mythic assertion concerns itself with the problem of meaning, to which the problem of evil is central. Biblical religion attempts to handle the problem of evil even more optimistically than had many older mythic views. "Right will protect the blameless life, but sin overturns the wicked" (Prov. XII:6). Qoheleth's disenchantment challenges this view, but it is questioned most seriously and most poignantly in the Book of Job. In this great inconclusive classic of theodicy, a righteous man is overwhelmed by disaster and subjected to the taunts of his conventionally righteous associates. The Book of Job fails to answer the question of how the facts of existence can be reconciled with the reality of divine justice or the existence of a benevolent Providence. Job expresses faith as his solution. Although based upon despair and resignation, his is a faith nevertheless capable of asserting unshakable trust and genuine hope. Through Job's suffering there is brought into existence the religion of the "twice born." Unlike Qoheleth's mild, this-worldly resignation and his acceptance of a naïve natural enjoyment of life, Job finds the stance of faith as the mode of conquering meaninglessness and aloneness.

Nihilism remains a constant potential of religious thought and feeling. With the broadening of human experience and the rationalization of thought, nihilism threatens increasingly to come to the surface. Its most impressive surfacing may be seen at the beginning of the Christian era in the religion of the Gnostics.

The Gnostics, various as they were, saw a world from which men were fundamentally estranged, a world produced by an evil or, at best, a neutral and inferior creator. Men must find emancipation from this world through esoteric knowledge of a hidden god and his ways. Man's was not a disharmony of body and soul because of sin, but an ontological dualism rendering him an acosmic being, radically alien in and alienated from the world. Gnosticism represents a desperate faith driven to find an answer to its severe disarticulation with existence in an escape to a god who is himself alien to the world of human experience in the most fundamental way.

Doubt was not unfamiliar to Jeremiah and the Prophets, nor to deeply religious men of all ages who plumbed the depths and discovered the religious crisis for themselves. But doubt was confronted and resolved by incorporating it into a larger affirmation of faith. God may chastise men, he may even appear to desert them, but he was ultimately just; God was God.

The Christian church accepted the conviction of classical antiquity from Plato to the Stoics that the world was a *cosmos*, a knowable order, and that there existed a fundamental harmony between this order and man's nature. It brought together this conviction with its Hebraic antecedents. God was thought to reveal to mankind knowledge of himself and of the path to salvation. The harmony of microcosm and macrocosm transcended the world; man's ultimate place was determined by his eternal relationship to God. Peter Lombard (1100/1164?) in his *Four Books of Sentences*, which from the thirteenth to the sixteenth century was the most important single work in European religious education, said that man can achieve knowledge of the invisible things of God "through creatures visible and invisible. For he was aided by two means, namely by nature which was rational and by works performed by God that truth might be manifested to man." Christianity succeeded in burying for centuries the possibilities of radical nihilism to which Gnostic religion had given expression. But doubt came to plague Christianity as its late medieval resort to inquisitorial and authoritarian repression sadly testifies. The elements of crisis continued to lurk beneath the surface throughout the ages of faith themselves.

First to be doubted was the second of Peter Lombard's propositions — that God had performed works that truth might be made manifest to man. The first proposition — that nature was rational and that rational man was, therefore, at home in the world — stood up longer. Religious doubt in early modern times did not, by and large, transgress the cosmological and human limits of earlier Christian views. Progress replaced Providence; perfectibility through grace gave way to perfectibility through effort. The city of man belonged in the world of nature. History was no longer a religious drama but a natural process.

But pessimism — and behind it the threat of meaninglessness, of spiritual nothingness — continued to lurk beneath the surface of an optimistic revolt against other-worldly religion. Even Descartes, who saw in science the instrument to make man the "master and possessor of nature," and who dared to turn doubt into a method, toyed with the Gnostic hypothesis that an evil genius might have created the world. By joining subjective and objective in an ontological argument for God's existence, he found his personal and intellectual solution and, concomitantly, the necessary basis for his world-view. In Hume's philosophy, secularized optimism was itself seriously challenged. Human reason was not self-sufficient, but rested upon premises beyond proof. Kant answered Hume, but in a way that undermined once and for all a comfortable acceptance of such premises as self-evident. Earlier, Pascal had faced, as a Christian, the implications of man's aloneness in the new world that science and philosophy were making known. He saw a silent universe that did not answer man's cry or longing, but remained alien and indifferent to his aspirations. Before the incomprehensible immensity of that world Pascal was frightened. He came to see man's aspirations rooted in reasons beyond reason and made his wager on a hidden God who was still the God of Christianity. Yet he retained the classic pride in man's capacities — a thinking reed superior thereby to a universe that might at any moment crush him.

Science has revealed to man a world with which he has no inner resonance; it has trained him to a stance toward the world which makes lack of mystic response "natural," "proper," and "objective." Moreover, the scientific study of man himself has revealed a historical and ontological relativity concerning all human accomplishments and productions — whether in thought or in life. Cultures and societies stand revealed as "compromise formations" formed from competing interests, points of view, and cognitive perspectives upon the world of experience. Entities of limited durability, they are destined to pass away. Indeed, individual identity itself is seen to be problematic, highly dependent upon circumstances; most cherished spiritual achievements rest upon a potential void. Social science has rediscovered in a new idiom the older mythic insight into the relation of primal order to primal chaos. But is modern man able to make an act of faith and an assertion of resonance comparable with that made in myth and in Jewish and Christian religion? While these developments characterized the emerging modern consciousness, Christianity tended to become either a culture religion raising no fundamentally disturbing questions or to remain in a spiritual ghetto in militant opposition to developing modernity. Kierkegaard experienced this alienation, this estrangement from the world of being; he sought escape in an act of faith more desperate than the wager of Pascal. Nietzsche saw nihilism, "this weirdest of all guests," standing before the door of his century and the world standing before man as a "gate to deserts stretching mute and chill." Projecting himself in his parable of the madman, he proclaimed, "God is dead. God remains dead. And we have killed him."

Modern developments bring the perennial latent crisis to actuality and in a setting shorn of traditional compensations. Modern men appear to make two fundamental responses within the general tradition. Following Job (and Pascal and Kierkegaard), they attempt to posit an act of faith; or like Qoheleth, they seek in mundane experience — not just daily trivia but this-worldly experience seen in the this-worldly frame of reference of the Enlightenment, often seasoned with Christian elements — satisfactions of an ante-penultimate character. Thus is revealed the neo-Christianity and the neo-Stoicism of today. Both accept the deeper substrate — the reasons beyond reason of Pascal — in one form or another. Man has aspirations, he displays an effort after the ethical, but he is not part of a cosmos with whose immanent logos he can feel any sustained and dependable kinship. He is a stranger creating meaning out of his own estrangement. His reflective acts reveal his naked aloneness in a nature that is purposeless. He clings to values that lack all ontological support. Existence is seen, by some, as absurd; man, once the capstone of creation, is but a futile passion. Men struggle with their absurdity and, in accepting it, attempt to transcend it.

The cosmic backdrop of medieval Christianity or of Enlightenment unbelief has dropped away and with it the resonance between subjective orientation and objective setting upon which all cultures have ultimately rested. The lurking primal crisis of the religious consciousness is unveiled for modern man. He may either accept it with faith or with stoic resignation, or attempt to avoid it in the busyness of less than ultimate pursuits. Writing in the nineteenth century, John Henry Newman told how Napoleon responded to his excommunication by asking, "Does the Pope think that the muskets will fall from the hands of my soldiers?" Newman commented that a few years later the muskets literally did fall from the hands of the Emperor's troops on the plains of Russia. Men who consider themselves in some sense "religious" have smiled at this story. Yet how many modern men could make such a statement as

Newman's in today's world? This was the point of view of the prophets, of the evangelists, of the Fathers, of the Reformers. Its practical disappearance marks the end of an epoch and heralds a form of the religious crisis unique in the history of Western man. Nietzsche's guest stands in our midst.

III. THE RELIGIOUS CRISIS: ITS CONTEMPORARY URGENCY

Genuine religious experience issuing in authentic faith and wholeness of spirit and combining with contemporary relevance has become increasingly rare and difficult. Consequently, this age lacks relevant religious exemplars. Today, as in past ages, most men adhere to religions by a more or less uncritical acceptance of what is established. But conventional religion has always depended ultimately upon the existence of the profound and authentic religious experience of its *megalopsychoi* — the great souled ones. Without that, even conventional religion falters. It draws its strength from the past, which it does little to preserve at the deeper psychological level. In this situation, institutional religion displays two kinds of irrelevance. Either it has maintained some significant personal meaning for its adherents, but has lost a relationship to man's larger history; or it struggles to attain historical relevance and exhibits little personal significance for ordinary men. Seen in itself this represents a severe and advanced form of religious crisis, but when viewed in the total setting of modern man a new urgency and even desperation is brought to light.

Men have achieved the technical capacity to alter the conditions of human life to an extent that was undreamed of even twenty years ago, but these very men in the advanced industrial countries are unable to go beyond piecemeal and contradictory programs in shaping these conditions. Ivan Karamazov commented that without God, everything is possible. Modern man has experienced to his sorrow what this can mean. But it is also true that without God nothing is possible; man can now also experience what this means. In the development of technology a great bureaucratic structure has been elaborated. All men, except the "culturally deprived," fit into this structure; they have become parts of a great social machine. The social relationships and institutions formed to enable men to control the world of nature have become a second nature controlling them. Modern man finds himself consuming in order to work, reversing the ancient causal formula; in a hundred ways he adapts himself to the social leviathan he has brought into being. Mastery over nature has become objectified into a social structure that controls all men. The capacities of technology for humanizing life have not been realized. As the irrationality of such a situation becomes more evident, the possibility of a rational understanding of the human situation and of programs based upon this understanding recedes beyond the grasp of the immense intellectual establishment. In fact, this establishment has become increasingly integrated into the great machine as the provider of the trained personnel which it more and more requires. Among the peoples of the world not simply discord but potential chaos threatens continually. In the West, the problem-solving mentality, the product of science and pragmatic effort, finds itself capable of solving any problem, but without the reservoir of world-view and value-orientation that would define and attribute priority to needs and aspirations of contemporary men. The problem-solving mentality reigns supreme, but it does not rule. Rather, it adapts itself to the initiative of circumstances and the caprice of events. The use of reason in the broad service of life retreats before the mind of modern man to join the powers and principalities of myth and the God of the Bible. Without an orientation to being, modern man cannot put himself together into a whole. Having lost transcendence, he finds himself without practical leverage in effectively changing his world. Without God or his memory in Enlightenment philosophy, he no longer knows what it means to be man, and hence, cannot utilize his enormous capacities to humanize the conditions of his life. The irrational, affluent societies of the advanced industrial countries begin more and more to resemble the society projected in the imagination of Auguste Comte — a technocracy dominated by the organizers of industry and knowledge. Today, however, the military must be added. In the present Comtean condition, the three religious traditions play the role of the "religion of humanity," often shedding even their partial and truncated transcendence for a common "civic religion." In a world that cries out for authentic transcendence and genuine community, the trumpets of conventional religiosity give forth the sounds of uncertainty. Enlightenment philosophers naïvely hoped that by crushing the "infamy" of supernatural religion and liberating men from the tyranny of a supernatural city of God, men would be free to construct a humane, this-worldly city of man. These hopes threaten to become as remote as Jeremiah's and Newman's Yahwistic notions of a divine and providential lord of history. In this situation, certain people, the more stubborn, the more sensitive, or the more disturbed, attempt to assert a measure of freedom and transcendence in sheer refusal — combating the absurd with the absurd. Their efforts, confused and confusing, assume a bewildering variety of forms.

Since the establishment of Charlemagne's Empire, Christianity has provided the noetic integrator and the spiritual sustenance that made possible the rise of Europe as a sociological and historical reality. It provided convictions in terms of which man could act and judge action, develop discourse, and project self-realization. Today man lives on the echoes and memories of that situation. In the face of current opportunity and contemporary urgency, most people are unable to believe with the depth and fervor that would provide direction to their thinking and motivation for their actions in meeting the demands of modernity. Nor are they able to disbelieve with the genuineness, conviction, and vigor that would produce the creative negation that might eventuate in a new and positive human orientation. In the past, the recalcitrance of nature, human and nonhuman, separated ideal and real. Today, inability to form the ideal with reason and conviction leaves man controlled by circumstances, despite the enormous capacities of his technological rationality.

IV. MODES OF ADJUSTMENT TO THE RELIGIOUS CRISIS

Some men avoid the contemporary religious crisis by relying upon an enlightened and sophisticated common sense. Accepting older values as humanly self-evident although without ontological foundation, they leave questioning to those whom they consider esoteric and impractical. Scientific research, human understanding, human rights, abolition of hunger, the "Great Society" are all ideals derived from the older situation. Although they still seem adequate, it is sometimes noticed that these old war cries no longer stir the troops, especially the young recruits, as they once did. Other men stay within the safe confines of academic disciplines and professional pursuits. They do not question fundamentally the implications of their methodology, their results, or their functions. Within particular institutions petty authoritarianism may be practiced to keep out dangerous thoughts likely to infect the young and untried. Such behavior is by no means peculiar to religious institutions. The resulting fragmentation of intellectual and spiritual life passively abets the developing crisis situation.

How, in fact, is the crisis to be met? Concern for the religious quality of contemporary life or belated urges to return to the classics in education appear almost the gestures of a bored and defeated complacency. Obviously, spirituality today needs its authentically relevant exemplars, and reason its humanly relevant embodiment. This history of religious crises suggests certain solutions.

It would be possible to institutionalize religion in the old way with some functional equivalent of a church presiding over society, yet reasonably accommodated to its needs. Here the model in history is the medieval church; in philosophy, Plato's *Republic* and *Laws*. New generations would be brought up within a culturally sanctioned "right reason"; a genuine, if strait-jacketed, transcendence would offer satisfaction to men's religious needs. Yet the church discovered it needed inquisitions, and Plato foresaw the need of a Night council. This solution did not prove viable in more appropriate historical conditions; it had to break up or eventuate in tyranny. Post-Tridentine Catholicism attempted to institutionalize a version of this solution within its own ranks. That, too, proved of ambiguous value and has been abandoned by Vatican II. The solution of such an institutionalization of religion is virtually closed for it would entail serious spiritual regression.

The present situation of pluralism of religions in a secular society could be prolonged and primacy given to secular values. While superior to the first solution, this half-way house offers no final escape from the current predicament. The present religious communions continue to transmit the spiritual heritage with varying degrees of profundity and success. The present religious dialogue continues to place before men the reality of the religious challenge. But the old heaven and the old earth have irretrievably passed away. The language of religion remains ambiguous and confusing: Sometimes it points the way to deeper spiritual realities; other times it beguiles its listeners with obsolescent memories.

Attention might be shifted from religious confrontation to the attempt to utilize the findings and methods of the social sciences in constructing secular communities and developing secure ego-formation among children. The conscious development of family life, friendship, and local community might attack the problem more successfully. Yet such a program requires value-consensus on both a small and a large scale. In quest of value-consensus, men would encounter all the problems of the current religious crisis head on. Matthew Arnold could appeal to love and urge men to be true to one another. A few years ago Archibald MacLeish could propose love as the final solution in his dramatic reworking of the Book of Job. But it appears a remnant of the Western religious tradition that by itself does not promise to generate either its own motivation or justification.

A possible solution could also be found in the new nationalisms. Yet the Communism of the Chinese, the nationalism of the Arabs, Africans, and Asians, the Zionism of Israel, and the sense of mission of America and France are also half-way houses of ambiguous value. While any rational philosophy will recognize the just demands of the secular community and its proper claims for individual support, it must provide for individual consciousness and effort. Nationalistic reasons beyond reason contain dangerous possibilities as history has so unmistakably demonstrated.

The current attempt to find meaning in the ultimate admission of absurdity could provide still another solution. Here many follow the injunction of Joseph Conrad — in the destructive element, immerse — and seek significance in the sheer experiential quality of experience. The possibilities are great, ranging from the ascetic, crypto-Christian action-mysticism of T. E. Lawrence to the newer, less confined "holiness" of Saint Genet. In these terms, all escapes from the limited world of contemporary consciousness, all plunges into the unconscious are seen as possibly productive of spiritual worth. Sexual experience, available to the poorest of the underprivileged as Ernst Toller once observed, becomes a favorite area for experimentation, though by no means the exclusive one. New drugs promise new possibilities. Extreme experiences lived at a heightened intensity substitute for and replace the religious experience. It is difficult to see at present the ultimate significance of this important current development. It alone does not appear capable of effecting spiritual and cultural metamorphoses.

V. RELIGION AND RELEVANCY TODAY

To rediscover the relevance of his heritage, man must achieve authentic transcendence and genuine community. Institutionalized religion must contribute to this goal to the best of its capacity. To be relevant today, religion must translate into a contemporary idiom the "foolishness of the cross." By synthesizing joy and tradgedy in a new way, man could become at home in his world, even while remaining forever a sojourner and a pilgrim in the midst of his fondest, this-worldly achievement and values. Religion must nourish and sustain an interiority that makes external relationship and accomplishment possible. But this interiority must never lose itself in its products; it must be able to find its own way among the many ways it creates in the world. To be relevant today, religion must support those human aspirations that cry for fulfillment in terms of the modern technological capacity. It must become relevant to the effort toward a more abundant life for man. It must teach not only the appropriateness of justice, wisdom, fortitude, and courage, but it must also bear witness to a faith, hope, and charity rendered relevant to the new world man has made and the new man whose promise it contains. Institutionalized religion and institutionalized learning must strive to beget honesty and transmit seriousness in facing problems, eschewing fixated ideologies and petty interests. Then, spirit and reason will find their own embodiment, for one may still hope that the spirit bloweth where it listeth. Let men learn, in the words of Dag Hammarskjöld, to become recipients, out of humility, and to be grateful for being allowed to listen, observe, and understand.

ALLEN WHEELIS
the moralist: a meditation

Almost a hundred years since Nietzsche announced the death of God, since Ivan Karamazov declared that everything is permitted; and ever more clearly we see a universe without transcendence, animated by nothing beyond the likes of us — strange beings probably on the planets of other stars, but no God — nothing up there beyond the spiral nebula, no guiding principle, nothing to give the law, to stand apart from the human adventure and judge. Not that God has averted his face, it was a face in our dreams; not that the universe is indifferent, it does not perceive. Only we judge; and, having renounced ascription to heaven, our judgments lack the authority of reaching us across great distances. As they have but the authority of ourselves, we know how fallible, arbitrary, even shabby, they must be.

Yet a morality of sorts survives. Once we thought that, without threat or promise of ulterior punishment and reward, man would run amuck. He may still, and if with our new ways we should destroy the world a

From *The Illusionless Man* by Allen Wheelis. Copyright © 1966 by W. W. Norton and Company, Inc. Reprinted by permission of the publisher.

strong case might then be made — were anyone left to make it — that restraint was lost with the discovery of permissiveness, that morality did not survive God. But we've got a chance apparently, and meanwhile decency is not lost; we hold ourselves in check, many of us, act more like men than beasts. Why?

"I could not bear to break my word or to kill," wrote Nietzsche. "I should languish, and eventually I should die as a result — that would be my fate." Why? He has already diagnosed such sentiment as the morality of slaves, germinating from the submissiveness into which they are beaten. Could he make no use of his insight? And whether he could or not, cannot we? If we agree with his findings can we not surmount the neurotic guilt imposed by a bourgeois morality, seize the freedom we have at last been able to formulate? "I became a traitor," writes Sartre, "and have remained one. Though I throw myself heart and soul into what I undertake, though I give myself up unreservedly to work, to anger, to friendship, I'll repudiate myself in a moment, I know I will, I want to. . . ." Yet in the very next breath he is saying, "I fulfill my commitments like anyone else. . . ." Why? Would he have us think it simply suits his inclination to do so — constantly, for a lifetime? Beyond belief! Why then, on what basis, does he deny the vagrant appetite which would violate commitments?

We're all Nietzsche, we're all Sartre, unbelievers, spinning wildly for a moment on our cinder through a silent universe, unnoticed, talking our heads off, nothing to cling to but ourselves — so what, then, is the nature of our surviving morality? What validity, if any, has it? And what basis, if any at all, have we for strictures against those who ignore it, who enter upon a license we deny ourselves?

Let us think.

When morals can no longer be validated above they must be validated below. By life — of which it may be said, at the very least, there isn't anything else. What serves life, enlarges and enriches it, is good; what destroys or diminishes it is bad. Is this the source and meaning of morals?

But what life is meant? Cannot be all life. We go out of our way to save skylarks and otters, condors and the saber-tooth tiger, but as indulgence not sacrifice. When it's we or they we chose ourselves, waste no tears over cancer cells or tubercle bacilli, bugs on our windshield, or sheep in the slaughter house. So who is "we"? All mankind? But men tear at men: where else but here do we need a guide? Do I, as a German in 1934, acquiesce to the Third Reich, fight it from underground, or flee? Do I, as an American in 1966, support my country's stand in Vietnam, oppose it, or do nothing? And what about deprivation of the rights of Negroes? Do I shrug, fight, or send ten dollars to CORE? To stand above such conflict, holding hands with God, loving all men, is to dodge the question, walk out on the examination as if having wandered into the wrong classroom: "I didn't approve," said the German, "but what could I do? Anyway, I really didn't know what was going on."

Whose welfare is to be served by morals? Men of good will? But who is to point them out? I want to fight with the good guys, but many of the (to me) bad guys are themselves convinced of rightness, and though we Americans know that, while the Germans usually and the Russians always are bad guys, and the French and Italians take turns, *we* are always the good guys — are we not growing less sure?

We may remind ourselves that morals serve principles, not men, but that's no help; for principles, if they have not the authority of God, have the authority only of men, and men differ. The principles of *which* men? Moreover, even with agreement on principles there is conflict in application; armies destroy each other in the name of freedom.

Whose life, then, shall be served? In psychological terms the issue is identification: how wide, how narrow is the range of empathy? how far does it reach into alien land? what determines its expansion and contraction? But morality is imperative, not descriptive; psychology restates but does not solve. The question remains: What is to be the field, the extent, of identifications? All one's friends? All white people? All Americans?

There is a point of view which holds that the test of right conduct can be, interchangeably, one's own good or the good of society, for the reason that in the long run they tend to coincide. Don't anguish over these alternatives, this view would say. Seeming opposition masks a hidden unity. Forget this soul-searching; be practical; come down from the metaphysical mists or you'll lose your way and end a martyr and absurd. The good life is simple: Follow your own interests with intelligence — with due regard for the rights of others — and be assured you serve the good of all. What's good for General Motors is good for the United States.

This is a view that deals with moral conflict by first denying its existence, then rationalizing self-interest. It's the ethics of money, of success, of generous social views and community responsibility, of contributions to CARE and Boys' Town and (increasingly with age and the hardening of arteries) to the Cancer Society and the Heart Association; it guards the sleep of men in mansions, in king-size beds, behind oak doors; is tailor-made for the likes of men. It is an ethic to justify a way of life already being lived, not one to question that way. Maybe what serves one and serves all do tend in the long run to coincide; but in the short run — which is where we live, where all our lives are spent — they clash and men die, and we must choose to intervene or to look away. A point of view that overlooks this choice, deaf to the din of this battle, is fine perhaps for the philosophic viewing-boxes of civilization where the strategy of progress is plotted in millennia but is no help to me. I'm on the field, I see what happens, and I know it's possible to do other than I'm doing.

My way of life looks good when viewed alone, questionable alongside the Christian way. Like the rich man of whom St. Matthew speaks, I am of good will and generous acts, have kept all the Commandments, so what lack I yet? " '. . . go and sell that thou hast, and give to the poor . . . and come and follow me.' But when the young man heard that saying, he went away sorrowful: for he had great possessions." I am he and have been going away sorrowful all my life, haunted by an admonition which allows me comfort or virtue, but not both. My possessions are not so great, but we are, each of us, rich in having a life to give or withhold. The ideal of sacrifice is clear as day: it asserts conflict between my good and the good of all and calls for the giving up of my life for others. If you don't see any such need or conflict, it would add, just pick up a newspaper, and it will hit you in the face.

A young physician was killed recently in Africa. He could have treated the sick in St. Louis or New York; but, as these places already have some medical care even for the poorest, he took his skill where the need was greatest, which happened to be a dangerous place. He was unarmed, represented no government, taught no religion, sought no publicity; he was treating the sick. He was half my age, his profession is mine; but I have elected to practice this skill in San Francisco. Am I entitled to regard myself and him as morally equal? How about it? Congo, Zanzibar, California, what's the difference? People get sick everywhere, rich men and poor, civilized and savage. Somebody has to treat the neurotics of this jeweled promontory, and if I choose this task and this place am I not, as much as he, in the service of mankind? He was more adventurous, perhaps, had a different style, liked to travel; but we are brothers, we treat the sick — he and I and the Park Avenue surgeon.

Is this not credible? I could make a stronger case, I'm not really trying because I don't believe it. My way of life and the way of my young colleague are at variance. My way, whether admitted or not, exemplifies the position that the good is what is *both* good for others and good for me; the way of my colleague, now rotting in Africa, that the good is what is good for others even if bad for me, even if it cost my life. We shall not add to the dignity of language if we use it to obscure this difference.

But for what motive might I elect to serve others at such cost to myself? If it were God's will and I wanted to please him or feared his anger, there would be a reason. Christ promised the rich man treasure in heaven, but not me; Christ and his Father and heaven have disappeared and no getting them back. Nobody promises me anything, and this life right now — the sacrifice of which is under consideration — is all there is.

So what else? What could motivate sacrifice? What honor beckon? What fear spur? . . . Nothing. Continuing on the old path I have nothing to fear. No one criticizes, no one shames; honors fall upon me. Could I perhaps do it without reason, without motive, simply from wanting to? Sure. And if my aunt had wheels she'd be an omnibus. It happens I *don't* want to; if I did I would do it. It is easier, more comfortable, and much safer to stay here and do what I've been doing. That, obviously, is what I want, and I'll not exchange a way of ease for a way of sacrifice unless I come to feel I ought, am bound to, must. And what could bring me to that?

If nothing impels me to sacrifice, perhaps nothing restrains me from license. Consider my friend Jeff — becoming more and more self-centered as he grows older, yet so charming, urbane, intelligent that he is loved all the more. His psychiatric research is a thing of the past, his clinical dedication but an elegant posture, and right now . . . ten o'clock in the evening . . . he is probably having dinner at Trader Vic's with an old wine and a young female, savoring the former, enticing the latter, plying her with profundities and wit, then to the Fairmont for another drink and some dancing, and on to his flat high on Telegraph Hill where he will roll her in bed with an orgiastic view of the ships and the bay and both bridges. Is this the way to live? . . . It's not for me, I think, however much I envy it. Instinctively I feel it's wrong.

Yet this reaction must be disallowed. Instinct affirms the past and calls for reënactment, gives voice to what I am, knows not of what I should be, speaks my prejudices, finds reasons, enunciates my stops where self-seeking is halted by guilt. It tells me what's fit and proper, but tells another, with the same certainty, "niggers gotta be kep' in their place." It would be a miracle and incredible if my stops — acquired as they were from all the random genetic and experiential dice-throwing that goes into the making of character — had authority transcending my circumstances. I can't believe it. My stops rationalize the position I'm in, cannot judge it. Like an automatic pilot they keep me going in the same direction, at the same speed and altitude; they correct deviations but do not validate my destination. The aircraft is steady, on course due west, weather clear as can be expected; engines okay, not like new but reliable still for quite a while. Everything is in order, I am the captain and have time now to walk around, observe the airship, look at maps, and to realize that the course, however steady, was a random fall. No one waits. Strange that a machine so delicate and complicated, proceeding on so costly a flight, should have no dispatcher, no mission. But that's the way things are. I happen to be going this way, and that's all. I could change, and may ask, equally, Why should I? and, Why should I not? Is there then no way to judge ends? no escape from arbitrariness?

The trouble, perhaps, is that we can reason about ends only by viewing them as means to more distant ends, while morality, by its nature, is final. An honest man whose honesty derives from his reasoning that honesty is more profitable than deception presents us with strategy, not morals. We can be reasonable, it seems, only in the pursuit of something set by unreason, by passion, prejudice, chance; intelligence without limits, like mathematics without content, is sterile.

Now here's a paradox: no problem more urgent than morals, yet when, trying to deal with it, we seize complete freedom for the exercise of our problem-solving faculty, that faculty suddenly is impotent. Like a lever free of its fulcrum, it moves nothing. The old fulcra were the Ten Commandments, the Gospel of Christ, the Natural Order — all with capital letters. In the past we would discredit one absolute only to replace it with another; now we have thrown out the whole kit and caboodle and find that intelligence, lacking a fixed point, has no force at all.

But why must morals be embodied in a final end? Perhaps we must accept now that they are instrumental, the end being life itself. Perhaps the life process, which is all we have, must now become the fixed point, the ulterior consideration on the basis of which reasoning about morals will become possible. What serves life is good, . . . but this is a circle. Whose life? Mine or my neighbor's?

But wait. Might not biology in some more basic sense still be the fulcrum? A kind of cellular intuition perhaps, a tropism for avoiding extremes? Might not the very moderateness of my moral position, midway between my narcissistic friend and the selfless missionary, reflect this basic strategy of conserving life?

I think not. Intellect without limits, though it may not create, can still criticize, and in this capacity can shoot holes through such an armor for the status quo. My position is moderate because I call it moderate, and for no other reason. I select two moral positions that are on either side of me, equidistant, and designate them as extremes; then, using them as referents, I take my bearings and find to my gratified surprise that I'm in the middle. That's how I come to be situated between Jeff and the missionary. But I could just as well have designated the missionary and Dag Hammerskjöld as the extremes, whereupon I would be far out in self-interest. Or, equally, I could have chosen Jeff and an embezzler, perhaps that cool young man who took a million from an Oakland bank last month and disappeared into South America. No, . . . that's too risky: rather, Jeff and one of the robber barons who steal legally. In relation to them I would be far out in the direction of guilt, inhibition, and impoverished life.

The acceptance of moderation as the criterion of virtue yields no answer. For how possibly, if we ascribe no special merit to where we happen at the moment to be, can the moderate be known? We can know that where one is is the starting point of any journey, and moderation may be considered an attribute of process rather than location: any movement far or fast being radical, any movement slow or slight being moderate. But this is no help; for in which direction, I must then ask — at that cautious pace which defines moderation — should I proceed?

So what's wrong with narcissism? It's unfair to take without giving, to live for one's self when everything of value comes from others. But fairness is not the source of a moral rule but the rule itself, which is what is being questioned. What is the authority of fairness? Not the fairness that may be imposed, which may be dangerous to ignore, but the rule of fairness that one may or may not impose on one's own life. The rich man's son, for example, enjoying all the goods and services of the world — why should he be fair? If he doesn't produce something, it might be argued, all that he has may be taken away by revolution.

But not in his time, he may suppose, and he may be right. What then? Perhaps the welfare of his own son or grandson might hinge on his present fairness? Yes, but why should this move him? Here again: good for whom?

In a world of peril we huddle together, and from the proximity and coöperation of that huddle derives the identification of one's self with others, our tendency, in many circumstances, to think "we" not "I." Identifications may be narrow or wide, the extreme of narrowness being the opportunist whose boundaries of concern go no further than his skin, the extreme of breadth being the mystic who identifies not only with all life but with stones and stars, all that happens and all that is. At neither of these extremes can morality, which concerns the conflict of rights, exist. The opportunist, lacking identification with others, does not experience their rights as binding on him, hence deals with others in terms only of the opportunities and dangers they present. The mystic avoids the issue by so elevating and limiting his experience as to deal only with the unity behind, or below, the conflict: "Killing merely is one form of our wandering sadness . . ." wrote Rilke, embracing the universe. Most of us fall, between these extremes, in the land of morality. We identify ourselves, with an intensity inversely proportional to the psychological distance, with some considerable number of others — family, community, race, nation, religion, species — acknowledge their rights, and struggle with the conflict between theirs and ours. Differences in the character, the extent, and the intensity of identifications dictate our differing moral positions. Therefore, since identifications are ultimately to escape peril, morality may be seen as the distillate of security operations.

Now there's a view of things to take the grandeur out of sacrifice. Victor and victim, the selfish and the serving, honest man and cheat — in motivation they're all the same. Christ and Pontius Pilate pursue in their differing ways the same goal. The missionary facing death to save a child, the psychopath with his *"Semper fidelis* to you, Bud! I've got mine, now you get yours," the driver who looks away from the accident, saying "I don't want to get involved," Rilke accepting everything, even the murder of innocents — all bear witness in the name of right and wrong only to the limitless variety of ways in which security, as mediated by identifications, may be conceived and pursued. But no reason to sneer. Having lost transcendent authorization, why not relocate morals, openly, on the ground of security?

. . . for whom? The old question is but transposed. A sharp and intelligent concern for the security of all will hardly dictate the same conduct as an equally sharp and intelligent concern for the security of one's self; the two are at odds, and morality can no more be validated by the conflict over which it presides than a court by its litigants. Believing as I do that a general war is the greatest collective peril, I might — were my motive the security of all — follow the path of Leo Szilard, create an organization for disarmament, write and lecture and campaign. This would mean the giving up of a comfortable, lucrative, and stable profession, and the taking on of a demanding, costly, and unstable life of planes and hotels and conference rooms, of failure too, most likely, and ridicule; yet such is as possible for me as it was for Szilard. If, however, the security of most concern to me is my own or my family's, I may simply go on as I am — perhaps giving a hundred dollars, instead of ten, to the World Federalists.

On second thought, I might give nothing, might simply drop the appeal in the wastebasket along with all the others. What's a hundred dollars, or ten, but a sop to my guilt for doing nothing? And why, if I freely elect my personal security as the referent of morals, should I feel guilty? Can't I do something about that?

My actual security, as it happens, has increased over the years, while those automatic promptings of conscience upon which depends the subjective sense of security have lagged, reflect still an earlier, more threatened, state. As an adolescent and young adult I was without place or purchase in society, alone, unskilled, always close to failure, rejection; and was prompted by such peril to far-reaching identifications, became what is called idealistic, strongly inclined to service, even sacrifice. Such insecurity, leading to such identifications, creating my particular moral principles, becoming automatically operative in conscience, controlling conduct with guilt . . . such is the chain of events which arrives now at the signing of checks for causes. But among the elements of the security I have gained — profession, property, reputation — is a skill particularly well suited to give some leverage with guilt. Not much, it's hard to change, but perhaps not impossible. If morality is indeed the distillate of security operations, and if I now elect — frankly, deliberately — to regard my individual security as the standard, and if that security is indeed much greater now than when my morality first crystalized — then what, if anything, could or should deter me from diminishing the extent and intensity of my identifications? of coming to live more for myself? of moving more in the direction of my friend Jeff?

Perhaps that man is social by nature. That even the most isolated of us lives in relatedness and interdependence. Alone in a locked room, despising men, one can't read a book or eat an apple without becoming indebted to countless of the despised; the room itself was hammered together by them. Man is the animal who remembers the past, preserves it, adds to it, passes it on. To be a man, by definition, means to share in this relatedness, to give to it as well as take from it; and maybe the only source of morality for godless men is the free choice to be a man rather than a beast. For to elect diminished relatedness and participation, less responsibility, narrowed identifications, is to move toward the jungle.

Yet this, too, begs the question. For these alternatives offer no choice, but rationalize an antecedent choice. "Man or beast" means "man or sub-man," which means "good or bad"; and to elect in this context to be a man means only to wish to be good, and that's admirable indeed but establishes no basis for morals. Evil, however we conceive it, pursues its course in the lives of countless men who want to be good.

So why, we must ask, must relatedness, however characteristic of man, be identified with good? Cows and coyotes huddle together too. Even if we should accept that man is social in essence and even if we accept that his biological and historical development has tended ever toward more relatedness, larger groupings, wider and stronger identifications — even then we have no ground for morals; for we are talking only of what is, or was, or will be, not of what should be. Teilhard de Chardin, extending into evolutionary time man's capacity for interrelatedness, foresaw the development of a universal mind, one all-embracing "envelope of thinking substance" covering the world. Let us grant this as a possibility but ask what reason have we for believing it good. Why should Teilhard's man of the future, lacking unique mind, be viewed as superman rather than sub-man? Why, given a choice, should we not elect Nietzsche's superman? Why not Jeff?

I have wider and stronger social identifications than Jeff, am more concerned with the welfare of others. Am I thereby superior? Not, I am sure, to his view. Even were he to grant that the difference between us is so marked and so significant that, if I be man, he must be non-man, even then . . . "Don't press me," he would say, smiling with characteristic affection and lightness, but in his thoughts he would say, "Very well, if you insist: of the two of us, *I* am the superman. Because more free, less guilty, more able to live. I don't think so much as you, nor probe morals, but I enjoy life more; and since from the vantage of the Horsehead Nebula in Orion neither you nor I nor anything we think matters a damn, pleasure is the only referent of value, and by that criterion I'm more advanced than you." And how is this gainsaid?

Not by force of logic. By leap of heart, if at all.

I am in the fast lane, in a drizzle of rain at dusk; ahead of me, at a safe distance, a gray Mercedes convertible; beyond the convertible a trailer truck. The brake lights of the truck go on; the Mercedes slows; then the truck speeds on; the brake lights go off on the Mercedes. I put my foot back on the accelerator — then suddenly the convertible is broadside; my foot hits the brake; the blurred horizon spins . . . fast . . . faster . . . raindrops coming toward my eyes, remembering wife, child . . . oh, darling! I'm so sorry! . . . expecting the crash . . . a wild tearing roar of tires, a fountain of gravel rising by the window, the car coming then to a stop, without impact, upright, on an embankment. The Mercedes is not ten feet away, miraculously undamaged, facing the wrong way in the slow lane, a young woman with brown hair stumbling out. I catch her by the shoulders, pull her off the roadway, hold her, trembling, as she twists back as if searching, making then an inarticulate sound of distress and pointing: in the fast lane is a dog, hindquarters crushed (by the truck probably, and that's why she tried to stop), struggling up on its forelegs, head straining upward, yelping feebly. I look up at four lanes of oncoming traffic — almost dark, faint streaks of rain slanting through the headlights — cars in the fast lane swerving outward to miss the dog, cars in the slow lane swerving inward to miss the Mercedes. The woman moves toward the road. "No," I say, "don't!" She twists toward me for a moment, her face frozen in horror and accusation, jerks away, runs for the road; hits me in the mouth as I catch her and pull her back, scratches at my eyes, screaming, "Coward! Coward! Let me go!" I pin her arms and we stand struggling in the rain, locked together, swaying, while the dog yelps; a car skids, a truck hits the dog, then a car with a thud, then another, and the dog is dead; the sirens then and flashing red lights and a police officer explaining that it's the fault of the dog's owner, who is liable, and who will be located from the tag on the dog's collar.

I could never have made it, I tell myself later, driving on alone. But what if it had been a child? I would have tried. . . . Would I? I have an image of my own child, lying there, of my running out to her, of being hit in the third lane just a moment before I would have been able to scoop her up. But I might just make it, not altogether hopeless; I would try; it would be unthinkable not to try.

But there *is* a child, I think, just not so close as that dog. So the woman is right, and I am a coward. And it seems to me that some-where, at some forgotten corner, I made a wrong turn — away from the real world that had seemed to betray me, to look inward, to burrow ever more deeply within, coming to live with shadows, the real world lost to me now, no sureness in it, not even knowing where the fast lane is.